LEARNING TO TEACH SCIENCE IN THE SECONDARY SCHOOL

Learning to Teach Science in the Secondary School, n̶ indispensable guide to the process and practice of teaching and learning new edition has been fully updated in the light of changes to professional knowledge and practice – including the introduction of Masters level credits on PGCE courses – and revisions to the National Curriculum.

Written by experienced practitioners, this popular textbook comprehensively covers the opportunities and challenges of teaching science in the secondary school. It provides guidance on:

- the knowledge and skills you need, and understanding the science department at your school
- the development of the science curriculum in two brand new units on the curriculum 11–14 and 14–19 NEW!
- the nature of science and how science works, biology, chemistry, physics and astronomy, and earth science
- planning for progression, using schemes of work to support planning NEW! and evaluating lessons
- language in science NEW!, practical work, using ICT NEW!, science for citizenship, sex and health education, and learning outside the classroom
- Assessment for Learning and external assessment and examinations.

Every unit includes a clear introduction, learning objectives, further reading, lists of useful resources and specially designed tasks – including those to support Masters level work – as well as cross-referencing to essential advice in the core text *Learning to Teach in the Secondary School*, fifth edition.

Learning to Teach Science in the Secondary School is designed to support student teachers through the transition from graduate scientist to practising science teacher, while achieving the highest level of personal and professional development.

Jenny Frost was formerly Senior Lecturer in Science Education at the Institute of Education, University of London, UK.

LEARNING TO TEACH SUBJECTS IN THE SECONDARY SCHOOL SERIES

Series Editors: Susan Capel, Marilyn Leask and Tony Turner

Designed for all students learning to teach in secondary schools, and particularly those on school-based initial teacher training courses, the books in this series complement *Learning to Teach in the Secondary School* and its companion, *Starting to Teach in the Secondary School*. Each book in the series applies underpinning theory and addresses practical issues to support students in school and in the training institution in learning how to teach a particular subject.

LEARNING TO TEACH SCIENCE IN THE SECONDARY SCHOOL

A companion to school experience

3rd edition

Edited by
Jenny Frost

Routledge
Taylor & Francis Group

LONDON AND NEW YORK

First edition published 1998
by Routledge

Second edition published 2004
by Routledge

This edition published 2010
by Routledge
2 Park Square, Milton Park, Abingdon, Oxon, OX14 4RN

Simultaneously published in the USA and Canada
by Routledge
270 Madison Avenue, New York, NY 10016

Routledge is an imprint of the Taylor & Francis Group, an informa business

Typeset in Times and Helvetica by FiSH Books, Enfield
Printed and bound in Great Britain by TJ International Ltd, Padstow, Cornwall

British Library Cataloguing in Publication Data
A catalogue record for this book is available from the British Library

Library of Congress Cataloging-in-Publication Data
Learning to teach science in the secondary : a companion to school experience. – 3rd ed. /
    edited by Jenny Frost.
        p. cm.
    Includes bibliographical references and index.
    1. Science—Study and teaching (Secondary) I. Frost, Jenny. II. School experience.
    III. Title: School experience.
    Q181.L497 2009
    507.1'241–dc22

2009042739

ISBN10: 0-415-55019-X (hbk)
ISBN10: 0-415-55020-3 (pbk)
ISBN10: 0-203-85306-7 (ebk)

ISBN13: 978-0-415-55019-2 (hbk)
ISBN13: 978-0-415-55020-8 (pbk)
ISBN13: 978-0-203-85306-1 (ebk)

CONTENTS

5   TEACHING SCIENCE: SPECIFIC CONTEXTS   175

6 ASSESSMENT IN SCIENCE 259

6.1 Assessment for Learning 260

CHRISTINE HARRISON

■ classroom assessment ■ recording assessment data ■ feedback
■ peer and self-assessment ■ summative assessment

6.2 External assessment and examinations in science 275

JENNY FROST

■ what science examinations are available in schools? ■ understanding the
scheme of assessment in a specification ■ preparing pupils for their public
examinations ■ examining new elements of the science curriculum

7 BEYOND QUALIFIED TEACHER STATUS 285

JENNY FROST AND RALPH LEVINSON

■ getting your first post ■ thinking ahead to the NQT year ■ beyond NQT
■ professional organisations ■ does a PGCE qualify me only for teaching?

INTRODUCTION TO THE SERIES

The third edition of *Learning to Teach Science in the Secondary School* is one of a series of books entitled *Learning to Teach Subjects in the Secondary School,* covering most subjects in the secondary school curriculum. The subject books support and complement the core textbook *Learning to Teach in the Secondary School: A Companion to School Experience* (Capel, Leask and Turner, 5th edition 2009) which deals with aspects of teaching and learning applicable to all subjects. This series is designed for student teachers on different types of initial teacher education programmes, but is proving equally useful to tutors and mentors in their work with student teachers.

The information in the subject books does not repeat that in *Learning to Teach in the Secondary School,* but extends it to address the needs of student teachers learning to teach a specific subject. In each of the subject books, therefore, reference is made to the generic *Learning to Teach in the Secondary School* text, where appropriate. It is recommended that you have both books so that you can cross-reference when needed.

The positive feedback on *Learning to Teach in the Secondary School,* particularly the way it has supported the learning of student teachers in their development into effective, reflective teachers, has encouraged us to retain the main features of that book in the subject series. Thus, the subject books are designed so that elements of appropriate theory introduce each topic or issue, and recent research into teaching and learning is integral to the presentation. In both the generic and subject books tasks are provided to help you to identify key features of the topic or issue and apply them to your own practice. In addition the requirement for material to be available to support student teachers work at Masters level in PGCE courses in England has been met in the latest editions by the inclusion of advice about working at this level and by a selection of tasks labelled 'M'. The core textbook referred to above also has a companion Reader, *Readings for Learning to Teach in the Secondary School,* containing articles and research papers in education suitable for 'M' level study.

Although the basic structure of all the subject books is similar, each book is designed to address the unique nature of the subject. The third edition of *Learning to Teach Science in the Secondary School* retains the strengths of the second edition but has been revised to reflect changes in the standards for newly qualified teachers, the new emphasis in the science curriculum on concepts *about* science, the importance of primary-secondary continuity in science, research into engaging young people in discussion, changes in the guidelines for health and sex education, advances in the use of ICT, developments in teaching citizenship through science, the increased importance of AfL, modifications to the external examination system and, the requirement for Masters level material.

We as editors have been pleased with the reception given to the earlier editions of this book as well as to the *Learning to Teach* series as a whole. Many subject books have moved into their third editions and others are in preparation. We hope that whatever initial teacher education programme you are following and wherever you may be situated you find the third edition of *Learning to Teach Science* supports your development towards becoming an effective, reflective teacher of science. Above all, we hope you enjoy teaching science.

When you move to being a newly qualified teacher we recommend the more advanced book *Starting to Teach in the Secondary School: A Companion for the Newly Qualified Teacher,* 2nd edition (Capel, Heilbronn, Leask and Turner, 2004), which supports newly qualified teachers in their first post and covers aspects of teaching which are likely to be of concern in the first year of teaching.

Susan Capel, Marilyn Leask and Tony Turner
December 2009

ILLUSTRATIONS

FIGURES

TABLES

TASKS

CONTRIBUTORS

Ruth Amos is Lecturer in Education at the Institute of Education, University of London, where she teaches on the PGCE and MA programmes. She previously worked in the chemical industry before becoming a science teacher in London comprehensive schools. Her interests include chemistry education, learning science using ICT, learning outside the classroom in fieldwork and museum settings, environmental education and global dimensions, argumentation and decision-making in school science and curriculum enrichment projects.

Sandra Campbell is Lecturer in Education at the Institute of Education, University of London, where she teaches on the science PGCE and MA programmes. Previous posts include: a science educator for Science Learning Centre London; head of biology in a London school; dentist in a London teaching hospital and in general practice.

Jenny Frost is a retired Senior Lecturer in Education at the Institute of Education, University of London, where she taught on the science PGCE, MA and research programmes. She currently teaches on a Physics Enhancement Course for potential physics teachers.

Marcus Grace is Senior Lecturer in Science Education at the University of Southampton, teaching on PGCE, Masters and research programmes. He taught science at schools in Essex and London. His main research interests are in teaching and learning about controversial socio-scientific issues, particularly in relation to biological conservation, and the science underpinning education for biodiversity, sustainability and citizenship.

Christine Harrison worked in secondary schools teaching science for 13 years before joining King's College, London in 1998, where she became co-director with Paul Black and Dylan Wiliam of the King's-Medway-Oxfordshire-Formative Assessment Project (KMOFAP). She is a Lecturer in Science Education at Kings' and has continued to conduct research into Assessment for Learning alongside her teaching on the science PGCE and MA programmes.

Ralph Levinson is Senior Lecturer in Education at the Institute of Education, University of London, where he teaches on Initial Teacher Education courses and is programme leader of the MA in Science Education. He previously worked at The Open University, after 12 years' teaching in comprehensive schools in London. His research interests centre on studying how beginning teachers explain science, teaching of controversial issues, mixed-mode learning and the pedagogy of risk.

Katherine Little currently teaches biology at a girls' grammar school in Plymouth. Prior to training to be a teacher at the Institute of Education, University of London, she was awarded her doctorate in anthropology, researching the genetics and behaviour of Indian monkeys.

Ian Longman is Senior Lecturer in Education at the University of Brighton, where he teaches on a number of Initial Teacher Education courses. He has been responsible for running a two-year pilot of the TDA's Science Additional Specialism Programme. Previous posts included: head of a science department; LEA advisory teacher for science; science teacher in comprehensive schools in Essex, Kent and East Sussex. He is a past chairman of the Surrey and Sussex region of the Association for Science Education.

Jane Maloney is the Primary Programme Manager at Science Learning Centre London. Up until 2007, she was Lecturer in Education at the Institute of Education, University of London, where she taught on the PGCE Secondary Science course. Previous posts included: Lecturer in Education at King's College, London and at Kingston University; teacher at the Royal Botanic Gardens, Kew; biology teacher, head of year and health education co-ordinator in secondary schools.

Michael Reiss is Assistant Director and Professor of Science Education at the Institute of Education, University of London, Chief Executive of Science Learning Centre London, Honorary Visiting Professor at the University of York, Docent at the University of Helsinki, Director of the Salters-Nuffield Advanced Biology Project, a member of the Farm Animal Welfare Council and Editor of the journal *Sex Education*. For further information see www.reiss.tc.

Pete Sorensen is Lecturer in Science Education in the School of Education at the University of Nottingham, where he teaches on the one-year full-time PGCE, Masters in Learning and Teaching and supervises higher-degree students. Previous posts have included: leader of the science team and the professional studies course at Canterbury Christ Church University College; leadership positions in schools in the UK; science teacher and science education posts in Ghana.

Tony Turner, until retirement, was Senior Lecturer in Education at the Institute of Education, University of London. He is co-editor of *Starting to teach in the Secondary School*, 2nd edition (RoutledgeFalmer, 2004), *Learning to Teach in the Secondary School,* 5th edition (Routledge, 2009) and co-editor in the series *Learning to Teach [subjects] in the Secondary School* (Routledge).

Bernadette Youens is Lecturer in Science Education in the School of Education at the University of Nottingham, where she is Director of Initial Teacher Education. She previously taught science in comprehensive schools in Nottinghamshire. Her current research interests focus on the experiences of beginning teachers on different Initial Teacher Education programmes, and the potential contribution of pupil perspectives to teacher education. She contributed the unit 'External examinations and assessment' in the companion text *Learning to Teach in the Secondary School: A Companion to School Experience,* 5th edition, RoutledgeFalmer, 2009.

PREFACE TO THE THIRD EDITION

As with previous editions, *Learning to Teach Science in the Secondary School,* third edition, is written in conjunction with the generic book *Learning to Teach in the Secondary School* (Capel *et al.*, 2009), to which we assume readers have access. We have attempted not to repeat material in the generic book, although for clarity there is some overlap. Relevant references to the generic book are given in the 'further reading' at the ends of units. Like the generic book, there are tasks for you to do either on your own or in collaboration with mentors in schools, your tutor in higher education or your fellow student teachers. There is the same mix of theory and practical advice, as theory is essential to interpret much of what you experience in your journey to becoming a science teacher. We have adopted the convention of using 'pupils' when referring to people studying in schools, and 'student teachers' for those learning to be teachers, despite the fact that many people use 'students' for the former and 'trainee teacher' or 'beginning teacher' for the latter. We have used 'mentors' for the teachers designated to tutor you in school, although they may be referred to as 'subject co-tutors' or 'school tutors' in your course, and we have used 'tutors' for the people supporting you in your higher education institution.

Since the publication of the second edition there have been a number of developments in education and science education that have necessitated changes to the text. These developments include:

- publication of new standards for qualified teacher status
- a greater emphasis on primary/secondary continuity
- changes in how science departments are organised
- changes in the science National Curriculum
- changes in assessment and examinations
- the introduction of Masters level components of PGCE courses.

We have put advice about working at Masters level in the first unit to alert readers to ways of preparing for this level of work near the start of the course. We have adopted the same convention as in the generic book of labelling some tasks as M-level tasks. **M**

Jenny Frost
October 2009

ACKNOWLEDGEMENTS

The third edition of this book would not have been realised without the willingness of many authors of the second edition to join me in the task of updating contributions. Equally important are the three new authors who joined the team of writers: Ruth Amos, Sandra Campbell and Marcus Grace. All contributors kept to the tight schedule that we were given and delivered the material – more or less – on time. Extended conversations with Alastair Cuthbertson and Ruth Wheeldon on recent changes in science education in schools were invaluable for redrafting some of my own sections. Marcus Grace would also like to acknowledge his helpful discussions with Maxine Farmer, Citizenship Coordinator at Hounsdown School.

Tony Turner, despite being unable to take on the joint editorship of this edition, gave considerable help by providing feedback on early drafts of my own units, as did Ruth Amos. I owe a deep debt of gratitude to Mike Turner, who willingly gave of his time to read and comment critically on a large portion of the book.

My thanks are extended to all of them.

My thanks also go to the people and institutions who have given permission for material used in the book: Cengage Learning Services Ltd for the reproduction of Figure 1.2.1; Caroline Allen for her drawing of a scientist in Unit 3.1; Ivybridge Community College for the outline of schemes of work and an example of a lesson plan in Unit 4.2; Pam Bishop, formerly of the University of Nottingham, for the ideas which contribute to Figure 4.3.5; Nick O'Brien, Satomi Saki and Jamie Styles for ideas and drawings which appear in Unit 5.3; and the pupils and student teacher who appear in the photographs in Unit 5.6.

Finally, I am indebted to Catherine Oakley, Helen Pritt and Sophie Thomson of Routledge for their professional advice, support and patience, to Alan Worth for his careful copy-editing and to Mark Livermore and Karl Harrington of FiSH Books for the typesetting.

Jenny Frost
October 2009

ABBREVIATIONS

A level	Advanced level (GCE)
AAIA	Association for Achievement and Improvement through Assessments
ACCAC	Qualification Curriculum and Assessment Authority for Wales
ACT	Professional Association for Citizenship Teaching
AfL	Assessment for Learning
AIDS	Auto Immune Deficiency Syndrome
APP	Assessing Pupil Progress
AQA	Assessment and Qualifications Alliance
ARG	Assessment Reform Group
AS level	Advanced subsidiary level (GCE)
ASE	Association for Science Education
AST	Advanced Skills Teacher
BEI	British Education Index
BTEC	Business and Technical Education Council
CASE	Cognitive Acceleration in Science Education
CAU	Centre Assessed Unit
CCTV	close circuit television
CLEAPSS	Consortium of Local Education Authorities for the Provision of Science Services
CLISP	Children's Learning in Science Project
CPD	Continuing Professional Development
DARTS	Directed Activities Related to Texts
DCSF	Department for Children, Schools and Families
DfEE	Department for Education and Employment
DfES	Department for Education and Skills
DNA	deoxyribonucleic acid
DoH	Department of Health
EAL	English as an Additional Language
ECM	*Every Child Matters*
EPPI	Evidence for Policy and Practice Information and Coordinating Centre
ESTA	Earth Science Teachers Association
EVC	Educational Visits Coordinator
EVS	Electronic Voting System
GCE	General Certificate of Education

GCSE	General Certificate of Secondary Education
GP	General Practitioner
G & T	Gifted and Talented
GTC	General Teaching Council
GTP	Graduate Teacher Programme
GUM	Genito-urinary Medicine
HEI	Higher Education Institution
HIV	Human Immunodeficiency Virus
HoD	Head of Department
IDEAS	Ideas, Evidence and Argument in Science project
IEP	Individual Educational Plan
IoB	Institute of Biology
IoP	Institute of Physics
ISA	Investigative Skills Assignment
IWB	interactive white board
KS	Key Stages
LA	Local Authority
LRS	Learner Response System
LSD	lysergic acid dyethylamide
MA	Master of Arts/Management Allowances
MI	Multiple Intelligences
MedFASH	Medical Foundation for Aids and Sexual Health
NHSS	National Healthy School Status
NQT	Newly Qualified Teacher
OfQual	Office of the Examinations and Qualifications Regulator (This has taken over the regulatory functions of QCA.)
PACKS	Procedural and Conceptual Knowledge in Science project
PDP	Professional Development Portfolio
PHSE	Personal Health and Social Education
PSMSC	Personal, Social, Moral, Spiritual and Cultural
PLTS	Personal Learning and Thinking Skills
PSA	Practical Skills Assessment
PSHE	Personal, Social and Health Education
QCA	Qualifications and Curriculum Authority
QCDA	Qualifications and Curriculum Development Agency (QCA was subsumed into this in 2009.)
QTS	Qualified Teacher Status
RSC	Royal Society of Chemistry
SASP	Science Additional Specialism Programme
SATs	Standard Assessment Tasks
SEN	Special Educational Needs
SEP	Science Enhancement Programme
SoW	Scheme of Work
SRE	Sex and Relationship Education
STEM	Science, Technology, Engineering and Mathematics
STI	sexually transmitted infection
TDA	Training and Development Agency for Schools
TGAT	Task Group on Assessment and Testing

TIMMS	Third International Mathematics and Science Survey
TLR1	First Teaching and Learning Responsibility
TLR2	Second Teaching and Learning Responsibility
TLRP	Teaching and Learning Responsibility Payments
TTA	Teacher Training Agency (now replaced by TDA)
VAK	Visual, Auditory, Kinaesthetic

BECOMING A SCIENCE TEACHER

INTRODUCTION

Learning to be a science teacher involves a complex mix of knowledge and skills, which are combined in a profession that involves working closely with other people. You will start with your own image of science, with your own view of what knowing about science has contributed to your life and with your own thoughts about how you will engage your pupils in science. In becoming a science teacher, you learn new ways of thinking about science, predominantly because you are learning to see it through the eyes of young people.

Unit 1.1 provides an overview of the knowledge and skills you need and how these are related to the way the book is organised. Unit 1.2 gives advice on managing your professional learning and making best use of the support available. Learning to be a science teacher is demanding emotionally, intellectually and physically. The emotional pressure arises from concerns many student teachers have about their capacity to complete the year successfully, facing success as well as failure in teaching and managing a diversity of pupils. The intellectual demand arises from teaching across the sciences, learning to cope with different levels of achievements of pupils and changing disciplines from science to education. Physically, the course requires complete attention. Classrooms are busy places and you need to be alert to a variety of needs of your pupils. Managing pupils – encouraging some, controlling others, supporting the lower-achieving pupils, maintaining safety for all while promoting their learning – is demanding. These tasks, coupled with the need to prepare several lessons daily and to try out new activities, make a teaching day extend far beyond its mythical '9–4' span.

Unit 1.3 helps you understand science departments as a whole, i.e. how they function, what roles and responsibilities teachers and technicians have and the policies they develop. From it you should learn more about the science-teaching profession as a whole and how to make best use of the support and guidance available in schools. It should also help you to think ahead to career paths you want to take in the future.

LEARNING TO BE A SCIENCE TEACHER

Jenny Frost

INTRODUCTION: A DIVERSITY OF STARTING POINTS

People who come into science teaching do so from vastly different backgrounds, in terms of culture, age, educational experience, work experience, attitudes, levels of confidence, languages and religions. The age profile is wide, with many people having worked in research, science-based industries or finance, before turning to teach science. Some come with teaching experience of, say, English as a foreign language, or of science in schools, where a teaching qualification was not required, or working as learning support assistants. Many have worked with young people in clubs and youth groups. Their own educational experiences of science can vary widely, not only in the type of school they went to but also in the different teaching styles they experienced and the different resources to which they had access. The prominence given to practical work in UK schools can come as a surprise to many graduates from other European countries, from the Middle East, Africa and Asia. Qualifications vary considerably; there are those who came into science via vocational qualifications, possibly going to university for their first degrees in their mid- to late-twenties, as opposed to others who went to higher education straight after school. There is diversity also in studies at university, so that people with degrees as diverse as astrophysics, genetics, sports science and geology can all be training for the same job of science teacher. Different religious beliefs may put creationists and evolutionists side-by-side as colleagues.

The range of backgrounds and perspectives can be a valuable resource to everyone on the course. Different perspectives, knowledge and experience are useful in developing your own knowledge and in challenging your assumptions and preconceptions. But in the end each person has to make their own personal journey in the process of learning to be a science teacher. This unit is concerned with what has to be learned and how it is to be learned.

OBJECTIVES

By the end of this unit you should:

■ be aware of the range of knowledge needed for successful science teaching

■ know the enquiry skills needed to acquire that knowledge

■ know how to begin to prepare for submitting work at Masters level.

THE PROFESSIONAL KNOWLEDGE OF SCIENCE TEACHERS: WHAT NEEDS TO BE KNOWN?

To consider what needs to be known by science teachers, we start first with what you should be able to achieve in the PGCE course, written in the form of objectives of a PGCE science course (Figure 1.1.1). Items a–g refer to the teaching to be undertaken in school and items h–l refer to the skills required for professional learning.

Students should:

a   deploy a wide range of techniques in teaching science in general (which include biology, chemistry, physics, astronomy, geology and the nature of science), effectively and safely to pupils in Y7, Y8 and Y9 (11–14 age range), and possibly Y10 and Y11 (11–16 age range)

b   use similar techniques to teach their specialist science to pupils in Y10–Y11 and to pupils in Y12–Y13 (16–19 age range)

c   assess, record and report pupil progress and achievement professionally

d   develop appropriate provision for students with special educational needs (SEN), for students for whom English is an additional language (EAL), for those with mobility problems and those designated as gifted and talented (G and T)

e   be aware of health and safety legislation and be safe in the practical activities which they do themselves and which they ask pupils to do

f   make use of information and communications technology for the teaching of science

g   work within the statutory guidelines for science teachers

h   make use of the results of educational theory and research that are relevant to the teaching of science

i   develop their classroom observation skills progressively through the course

j   evaluate their own practice through different perspectives in order to extend and improve it

k   map their developing skills as science teachers onto the national or other standards for their course. In England this is the TDA Training and Development Agency for Schools (2008) *Professional Standards for Qualified Teacher Status and Requirements for Initial Teacher Training*

l   enter into the process of becoming a teacher by engaging in high-quality enquiry, reflection and consultation.

■ **Figure 1.1.1** Objectives for a science teacher education course

High-quality enquiry: the student teacher as researcher

We shall start with the last item on Figure 1.1.1, high-quality enquiry. Bishop and Denley in their book *Learning Science Teaching* write: '1) learning science teaching is an intellectual pursuit and 2) the path to accomplishment is found by those science teachers whose mission is to be continuously-learning teachers' (2007: vi). Intellectual pursuits require dedication and a willingness to seek out information and to revise ideas and actions, in the light of new findings. The knowledge that teachers have is not just knowledge that can be written in books and articles (although that is an important component), it is also knowledge-in-action. So your high-quality enquiry will not only require research in books, but also research into your own and other people's practices. You need to bring your investigatory skills, which you have learned through science, to the task of learning to be a science teacher. You are not, however, required to develop these skills on your own. Unit 1.2 outlines strategies that you can use and Unit 1.3 shows how to access the help and information you need within the working environment of a school and a science department. Tasks throughout the book are designed to help you to pursue your enquiries.

We turn now to the components of knowledge that you need to achieve the objectives. These are summarised in Figure 1.1.2.

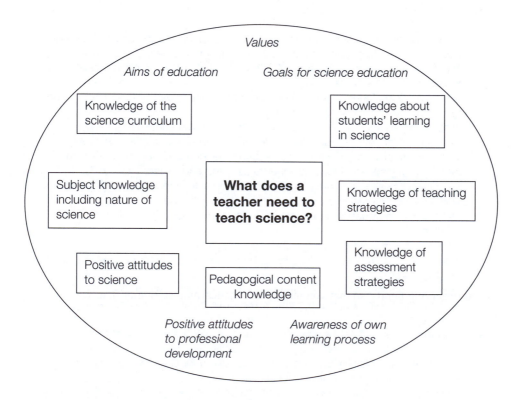

■ **Figure 1.1.2** What does a teacher need to teach science?
Source: adapted from Glauert and Frost, 1997: 129

Knowledge of the science curriculum

Knowledge of the science curriculum makes teachers aware of their responsibilities to work within agreed parameters and to understand the rationale for priorities given to different parts of science. The recent introduction of *How Science Works* into the curriculum has required teachers to include not only known scientific ideas but also ideas about the nature of science and advice about careers in science.

Knowledge of science

Teachers with good subject knowledge encourage pupils to ask more questions and are more flexible in their teaching approaches. Given the normal practice of science teachers teaching the whole of the science curriculum to the 11–14 age range, confidence and competence is required across the sciences. Initially, this breadth of knowledge requirement is seen as one of the main 'hills' to climb when people start science teaching, but students also find it rewarding. This knowledge extends to the nature of science. Possibly those of you who have already studied history and philosophy of science may find it relatively easy to understand this area.

Positive attitudes to science

A teacher's enthusiasm and passion for a subject can have a profound effect on pupils. It is rare for any science graduate, however, to feel equally enthusiastic about all areas of science. As a professional you need to find ways of developing an interest and enthusiasm for sections that you previously disliked.

Chapters 2 and 3 deal explicitly with these three areas. Chapter 2 gives information about the science curriculum and its statutory frameworks. Chapter 3, with separate units devoted to the nature of science, biology, chemistry, physics and astronomy, and Earth sciences, is aimed at an overview of key 'explanatory stories'. The writers are enthusiastic about their areas, and the hope is that their enthusiasm can be shared.

We turn now to the other areas of knowledge in Figure 1.1.2.

Knowledge of learners and learning in science

Your own learning of new areas of science may give you an insight into difficulties others have with the subject. Be honest about your difficulties and remember the ways you get round them – they may well be ways that will be helpful to pupils. An important source of information about pupils' learning in science will come, however, from your listening to and observing pupils, so that you understand the learning strategies that work best for them. The most accomplished teachers are constantly learning and relearning about individuals in their classes and thinking about how to improve the learning experiences of every pupil. In addition, the work of a number of psychologists and researchers from the science education community has strongly influenced our understanding of pupils' learning in science and their progressive understanding of different aspects of science.

Knowledge of teaching strategies

There is a wide range of well-documented teaching strategies that you will be encouraged to learn about and try with your classes. You need to be able to select the ones most suitable for the learners with whom you are working and the learning outcomes that you want to achieve. Management of strategies, of course, goes hand-in-hand with the strategies themselves.

Chapter 4 draws together knowledge about young people's learning in science and the need to identify desired learning outcomes (Unit 4.1). Units 4.2 and 4.3 focus on bringing that knowledge to bear on the processes of planning and evaluating lessons, while Unit 4.4 explains a wide range of teaching strategies and the rationale for choosing between them.

In Chapter 5, we have selected a range of situations in science to highlight strategies in context. Unit 5.1 describes the role language plays in learning science and identifies reading, writing and talking activities which involve pupils in actively sorting out their own ideas. The other units address areas of science teaching that can cause considerable anxiety, because of safety issues or organisational issues (Unit 5.2 'Practical work', and Unit 5.8 'Beyond the classroom'), because the success of the strategy can depend on the reliability of equipment (Unit 5.3 'Using ICT for learning science') or because they involve dealing with personal, social and moral dilemmas (Unit 5.4 'Science for citizenship' and Unit 5.5 'Sex and health education').

Knowledge of assessment

Knowledge of assessment strategies is an essential part of the repertoire of teachers. Assessment is an intrinsic part of teaching, in that teachers listen to pupils and monitor their learning in every lesson and adapt their teaching accordingly – this is Assessment *for* Learning (AfL) that takes place *during* a lesson and feeds back into teachers' knowledge of learners. Well-tried and -tested strategies are explained in Unit 6.1. This is different from assessment *of* learning that is done after the teaching. Unit 6.2 deals with assessment of learning through external assessments and examinations in science.

Pedagogical content knowledge

Pedagogical content knowledge is the amalgam of all the other knowledge we have described so far. It involves knowledge of how to turn the knowledge of content, curriculum, pupils, strategies and assessment into appropriate, well-managed, instructional activities for the particular learners with whom you work. It includes your store of analogies, models, illustrations, resources and examples. All this knowledge on its own is, however, not sufficient. Ability to select appropriately from this large store of resources at the right time is important. It is knowledge-in-action, which has to be drawn upon when you are planning lessons, when you are 'on the hoof' in the classroom and when you are evaluating what learning has occurred. The whole of the book, therefore, is about pedagogical content knowledge and how to develop it.

Other features in Figure 1.1.1

All this knowledge is overlaid with your values, those that you hold and those that you are expected to hold. This goes much wider than science education and in thinking through your own values, we recommend that you start with Unit 4.5 in Capel *et al.* (2009). Likewise your understanding of the aims for education will develop throughout the course, even though you may have fairly definite ideas at the start. Unit 7.1 in Capel *et al.* (2009) will help you to explore your aims against a wide spectrum of beliefs. Positive attitudes to professional development and an awareness of your own learning processes are essential. Attitudes are difficult to teach; perhaps the best advice is to maintain your commitment to high-quality enquiry in the pursuit of becoming an accomplished science teacher, but remain realistic in your expectations (see Unit 1.3 in Capel *et al.,* 2009).

You need, also, to think through your aims for science education, which will influence how you teach and what you prioritise. Your aims may not be the same as the aims embedded in the science curriculum you have to teach; a professional task for you is to reconcile these two sets of aims. Task 1.1.1 asks you to think about your aims for science education at the start and end of the course.

Task 1.1.1 **Thinking about your aims for science education**

Reflect on the ways your science education has been of value to you. From this, think about what you regard as the importance of science education for everyone. Discuss your ideas with fellow student teachers and write a short statement, which should be included in your professional portfolio. Return to this at the end of the year and write about how your thoughts have changed, and why.

SUBMITTING WORK AT MASTERS LEVEL

Finally, we turn to the fact that as part of your initial teacher education programme you will be asked to submit assignments that will be marked against criteria for Masters level. For these assignments it is likely that you will be asked to draw on evidence from your teaching in school and view it through some theoretical perspective. For the M-level tasks suggested in this book, we made the simple rule that there should be a critique of practice in the light of theory (or the other way round – the critique of theory in the light of practice). Similarly, the same should apply to any M-level work you undertake. Initial preparation, therefore, involves three main steps: deciding an area of investigation (if you have a choice), checking that there is sufficient academic literature in that area to provide you with theory or theorising and deciding what sort of evidence of practice is needed. Think of the task of linking theory with practice as looking at practice through theoretical spectacles. You will be familiar with this process in science. Theory is not an afterthought; it is an intrinsic part of the way that observations are structured.

Make decisions as early in the course as possible. For an area of investigation, select something that has begun to intrigue you (for example the role of field work; how ICT can aid learning in science; pupils' understanding of risk; the use of investigations for understanding concepts of evidence; cross-departmental activities to enhance research skills in, say, history and science; involving pupils in assessment; the role of pupil talk in learning science; developing creativity and imagination in science; the development of your use of questions). You can initiate a literature search by going to the library and finding and scanning relevant references, although it is now more common to do a literature search electronically. Your university/college library will have access to digital research databases, such as the British Education Index (BEI), which allow you to access articles (though books will mostly still require a library visit) by typing in a few keywords. Alternatively, Google Scholar will also bring up relevant literature quickly although it is likely to be less comprehensive than accessing a research database. This helps to give you a broad overview of the research that has been done. When using previous research, you have the possibility of adapting the methods or making use of the theory.

Finally, think about the feasibility of gaining usable evidence from your practice. Avoid, if possible, the use of questionnaires; they are notoriously difficult to construct, the quantity of returns are usually too low to make any sensible judgements and they need to be vetted carefully before they can be administered. Classroom products, such as written work or presentations from the pupils, can be ideal, as they are collected as part of routine teaching and can be analysed at leisure. There will be many items in your professional portfolio that may be useful sources of evidence. Whatever you decide to use as evidence, quality is more important than quantity. If you are examining your own teaching techniques, you could record just two or three of your lessons and ask a teacher working with you (or a fellow student teacher in the school) to make appropriate observations; then analyse your techniques and make observations later in your teaching.

Do not make your enquiry too broad. Focus in on a very small area of investigation and analyse it in detail. Discuss your plans with your tutor as soon as possible and with your mentors. They may well be able to help you focus your study.

Read in Capel *et al.* (2009) the 'Guidance for writing' in Appendix 1 and advice on practitioner research in Unit 5.4 and start as soon as possible. Writing as you go along is essential, as the process of writing shapes your thoughts. Writing is not an activity that can be done 'at the end'.

Beyond Qualified Teacher Status (QTS)

The Masters credits from initial teacher education courses form, at most, half the credits for the award of a Masters degree. To ensure that you continue to approach the development of your teaching through high-quality enquiry, we would strongly recommend that you take the opportunity to gain the further credits for the award of Master of Science Education, Master of Education, Master of Arts (Education), Master of Teaching or Master in Teaching and Learning (a government-sponsored Masters course for teachers) within the first five years of your teaching career. Institutions vary in the numbers of credits they accept and how their courses are delivered. It is very important to choose the one that supports most closely your professional context. An increasing number of courses are now on line. This can be an advantage for you as a busy teacher but when you are getting to grips with new knowledge, personal access to a tutor can be very important. You should do some shopping around, reading course literature and looking at websites and, if possible, talking to course leaders.

Continuing with Masters level study is only one part of your continuing professional development. Chapter 7 explores additional routes for continuing professional development.

SUMMARY AND KEY POINTS

Whatever your background, becoming a teacher will involve a steep learning curve, but if you learn to approach your learning in the spirit of high-quality enquiry you will develop the skills to continue your learning throughout your teaching career. There is a range of different types of knowledge to be learned; it is the effective use of that knowledge in action that characterises the successful teacher.

FURTHER READING

Capel, S., Leask, M. and Turner, T. (2009) *Learning to Teach in the Secondary School: An Introduction to School Experience*, 5th edition. London: Routledge.

■ Green, A. and Leask, M. Unit 1.1 'What do teachers do?', 9–21.

■ Turner, T. and Heilbronn, R. Unit 4.5 'Values, education and moral judgement', 217–232.

■ Bartlett, S. and Leask, M. Unit 5.4 'Improving your teaching: an introduction to practitioner research, reflective practice and evidence-informed practice', 300–309.

■ Haydon, G. Unit 7.1 'Aims of education', 369–378.

■ Capel, S. and Moss, J. Appendix 1, 'Guidance for writing', 463–471.

Other books written for science student teachers

Parkinson, J. (2002) *Reflective Teaching of Science 11–18*. London: Continuum Books.

This is a clearly written book, with easily accessible ideas and information.

Wellington, J. and Ireson, G. (2008) *Science Teaching, Science Learning.* London: Routledge.

Each chapter of the Wellington and Ireson book ends with 'Points for reflection' in the form of questions. These could be a good source of questions to investigate at M-level.

Wood-Robinson, V. (ed.) (2006) *ASE Guide to Secondary Science Education.* Hatfield: The Association for Science Education.

This book covers many of the debates in science education alongside practical guidance.

Books useful for M-level work

Bennett, J. (2003) *Teaching and Learning Science: A Guide to Recent Research and Its Applications.* London and New York: Continuum.

This book is, sadly, out of print, but you are still likely to find it in libraries as it forms an excellent basic text for people thinking about Masters level work in science education.

Bishop, K. and Denley, P. (2007) *Learning Science Teaching: Developing a Professional Knowledge Base.* Maidenhead: Open University Press.

This is a report of research into the pedagogical content knowledge of 12 accomplished science teachers. It contains examples of good pedagogy, alongside teachers' reflections on how they learned to develop their skills and knowledge. The introductory discussion on the nature of professional knowledge is helpful. Good references to other research in the field are included.

Monk, M. and Osborne, J. F. (eds) (2000) *Good Practice in Science Teaching: What Research Has to Say*. Buckingham: Open University Press.

A collection of articles on different topics, much of which is still relevant.

Parkinson, J. (2004) *Improving Science Teaching*. London: Routledge.

This is written for practising teachers, but will be a useful resource for interrogating your practice and working at Masters level.

Sears, J. and Sorensen, P. (eds) (2000) *Issues in Science Teaching.* London and New York: RoutledgeFalmer.

> This book contains accessible short articles where authors thoughtfully discuss key issues, many of which are still current. It may offer ideas that could be the basis of studies you undertake in your schools.

Wallace, J. and Louden, W. (2002) *Dilemmas of Science Teaching: Perspectives on Problems of Practice.* London: RoutledgeFalmer.

> A series of case studies addressing issues that face science teachers. The dilemmas raised are discussed by experienced practitioners providing a theoretical foundation for the discourse. The individual studies may provide good material for mentor–NQT discussion or, alternatively, provide new teachers with a chance to read in more depth about a particular issue facing them.

Professional journals

Journal of Chemical Education: Royal Society of Chemistry
Journal of Biological Education: Institute of Biology
Physics Education: Institute of Physics
School Science Review: Association for Science Education
Education in Science: Association for Science Education

Academic journals

International Journal of Science Education
Science Education
Science and Education
Studies in Science Education
Research in Science Education
Journal of Research in Science Teaching

USEFUL WEBSITES

Masters in teaching and learning

> http://www.tda.gov.uk/teachers/mtl.aspx (accessed 20 September 2009).

See also the websites of higher education institutions for information about their own Masters courses.

Google scholar

> http://scholar.google.co.uk/ (accessed 20 September 2009).

UNIT 1.2

MANAGING YOUR PROFESSIONAL LEARNING

Jenny Frost

INTRODUCTION

Each year, one or two potential student teachers say at interview, 'I am sure I shall be a good teacher when you have trained me', implying that learning to be a teacher is something done to student teachers, thus undervaluing their own role in the process. The majority, however, have already thought carefully about the nature of teaching and the characteristics of a teacher and have begun to identify the extent to which they believe they have the qualities to succeed. They have begun the process of taking responsibility for their own learning and are aware of the need to do so. This unit is aimed at helping you to manage your own professional development from the varied experiences you will have on the course.

OBJECTIVES

By the end of this unit you should:

- understand a model of professional development that helps you to learn from experience
- recognise how to use the Professional Standards for Qualified Teacher Status as an aid to learning
- know how to work effectively with mentors
- be able to identify your starting points
- appreciate the progressive complexity of learning experiences that will be an intrinsic part of your course.

During an initial teacher education course you have two types of professional base: the schools where you are 'on placement' and the higher education institution (HEI) where you are registered. In the schools, you work as an individual student teacher (or maybe as one of a pair of science student teachers) alongside teachers and technicians. Early experiences in school involve observation of teachers and pupils, working with small groups of pupils, and team teaching. You gradually take over whole classes. One science teacher acts as your mentor and meets with you on a regular basis, with others also giving you advice. A professional studies programme in school allows you to learn about whole-school issues that are not unique to science and in this you are likely to work with student teachers of other subjects also in the school. In your other professional home, the HEI, you are part of a bigger group of science student teachers attending a highly structured programme of lectures, seminars, workshops and tutorials. Here you have access to a strong literature base in education and, of course, your science tutors. This second base provides you also with a community of peers who share the ups and downs of learning to become a science teacher, with whom you can gain a perspective on all your own particular experiences.

To make best use of the resources at these two professional homes, you need to understand the nature of professional learning, and the role not only of yourself but also of the science teachers and tutors with whom you work.

A MODEL OF PROFESSIONAL LEARNING

A useful model for professional learning is represented in Figure 1.2.1, i.e. the Plan–Do–Review–Learn–Apply cycle (Watkins *et al.*, 2007: 27). This cycle involves planning what to do, trying it out (the 'doing' phase), reviewing it, learning from the review and then applying the learning in a new situation. The 'doing' phase is not restricted to teaching in the classroom, but may include observing lessons, working with a tutor group, attending parents' evenings, marking pupils' work, organising a science visit or being a participant in a mock interview.

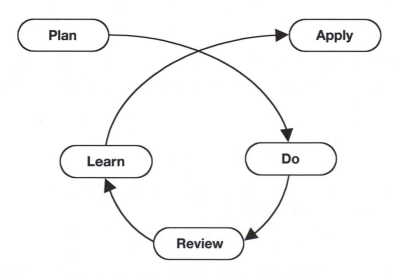

■ **Figure 1.2.1** A model of active learning
Source: Watkins *et al.*, 2007: 27

Reviewing involves standing back, describing the event, analysing it, comparing it with other situations and evaluating its significance. Research shows that reviewing is most effective if done with another person, often a teacher in school or your tutor. In the review, other ideas are brought in to make sense of what has happened and to help in identifying general points that can be applied elsewhere. It is in this phase that links are made to the more theoretical parts of the course, because these provide 'frameworks' for reviewing the event.

In the last phase you ask yourself the question, 'what as a result of this would I do differently next time?'. This leads to new goals and actions. You now go to the next task, apply your new learning and go through the cycle again. This cycle will repeat itself throughout the course and, hopefully, throughout your professional life.

This cycle can be illustrated by the following example:

> A student teacher had prepared a lesson on micoprotein for a bright Y10 class. Her resources were well constructed and consisted of: a worksheet with clear diagrams and information followed by questions which required pupils to interpret the information and apply scientific principles; clear diagrams of the fermenter on a data projector; cooked micoprotein for pupils to taste for 'acceptability'. In the review afterwards her perception was that she had talked for about a quarter of the lesson. Her observer's notes, however, identified that she had, in fact, talked for about three quarters of the lesson. She recognised that she felt under pressure to make sure that she told the pupils all the facts even though she knew this was not how pupils learned. Discussion focused on how she could provide pupils with more time when they were engaged in problems, which would, in turn, provide her with more information about their understanding. The discussion also focused on the personal courage she would need to 'let learners off the leash'. With her mentor she set her goals for the next lesson, to talk for no more than 50 per cent of the time and to use the extra time to monitor pupils' achievements more thoroughly.

Effective mentors will be able to support you in all the phases of the Plan–Do–Review–Learn–Apply cycle. Figure 1.2.2 provides a guide to the sort of support that is known to be helpful. Some people will be better at some parts than another. There may be teachers and technicians who are exceptionally good at helping you find resources and ideas for getting something done. Others may be much better at helping you to analyse what has happened. Your responsibility is to use the varying expertise of the people around you to best effect.

WORKING WITH 'THE STANDARDS'

The publication from the TDA (Training and Development Agency for Schools), *Professional Standards for Qualified Teacher Status and Requirements for Initial Teacher Training (Revised 2008),* sets out the standards which you must meet in order to gain Qualified Teacher Status (QTS) as well as specifying necessary features of the training programmes. The standards form an important framework for your development, so early familiarity with them is essential (see Task 1.2.1). The standards are divided into three main sections:

■   Professional Attributes (Q1–9)
■   Professional Knowledge and Understanding (Q10–21)
■   Professional Skills (Q22–33)

Mentors support action learners in the different phases of their learning in the following ways:

The 'plan' phase

They help students plan what to do by:

- encouraging students to come up with ideas
- acting as a sounding board for ideas
- helping students to work out their ideas in greater detail.

The 'do' phase

They help students get the activity done by:

- supporting motivation
- checking out practical details
- smoothing communication with others.

The 'review' phase

They help students review an experience by:

- encouraging students to make an account
- providing frameworks of questions to consider
- making suggestions for comparisons and evaluations.

The 'learn' phase

They help students to learn from experience by:

- bringing in useful ideas from a range of sources: reading, theories, others' views.

The 'apply' phase

They provide students with tools to promote application by:

- giving support to the question of 'what would you do differently next time?' leading to action planning and goal setting.

■ **Figure 1.2.2** Ways in which mentors can support an action learner

Task 1.2.1 **Familiarising yourself with the standards for QTS**

Read through the standards in detail and discuss with your tutor what they mean and what has to be done by the end of the course to show that you have achieved them. There are likely to be ways in which they are to be used: as an advance organiser; for personal profiling; and as a vehicle for discussion with others; but find out the specific requirements of your course.

Using standards as an advance organiser

The standards show the range of learning necessary and enable you to take stock of your individual starting point. They also help you at various points to recognise short-term goals and project forward to later targets; this will usually be done with mentors or tutors. These processes can guide planning your future learning and anticipating course components later in the year.

Using standards for personal profiling

Using the standards to map the learning ahead goes hand-in-hand with reviewing progress. During your training you will be asked to produce *evidence* that you have achieved (or are beginning to achieve) the various standards. Lesson notes and evaluations, feedback from teachers on your lesson, mark books, reports and your own coursework count as evidence to be kept in a professional development portfolio (PDP). Student teachers often ask what counts as 'sufficient evidence'. Remember that one moment of success does not make a teacher. Some consistency and reliability over a range of contexts will be sought. Development is a gradual process.

A necessary feature of this regular profiling and the need to provide evidence of progress necessitates keeping good documentation of your work. Student teachers soon learn that multiple files are needed and that good administrative and oganisational skills are a necessary part of a teacher's repertoire.

Using standards as a vehicle for discussion

The standards contribute to a shared language with which to discuss educational problems. They help to shape the programme you follow, they affect the way in which feedback to you is structured and the way you review your teaching. They are, however, not sufficient on their own as there are practical and theoretical ideas underpinning each standard. Take, for instance, standard Q25 (b) that requires you to be able to 'build on prior knowledge, develop concepts and processes, enable learners to apply new knowledge, understanding and skills and meet learning objectives' (TDA, 2008: 9). This opens a large agenda: What methods does a teacher use to elicit or find out about prior knowledge? How do you cope when different children in the class have different prior knowledge from each other? What are the appropriate next steps to take to extend understanding and skills? How are these organised with a large class? What constitutes applying new knowledge as opposed to just having new knowledge?

WHAT YOU CAN EXPECT FROM MENTORS AND TUTORS

Which people work most closely with you depends on the pattern of working in the higher education institution where you are registered. It is likely that one HE science tutor has oversight of your progress during the year, and acts as a personal tutor, and that one science teacher in the school acts as your school mentor. In addition, there may be another teacher in the school (often a senior teacher) who has oversight of all the student teachers there and who organises a professional studies programme. You work closely with science teachers whose classes you teach and these teachers give you guidance on your lessons and feedback on your teaching. They are involved in working with you on the

Plan–Do–Review–Learn–Apply cycle, as much as your main science mentor. You form working relationships with the technical teams in both the school and the HE institution.

School-based mentors organise the induction period in school, plan your timetable, and support you as you move from observing classes to working with small groups and then taking over whole classes. They ensure that you have class lists with appropriate information about particular pupils. They meet with you on a regular basis to discuss your learning. They teach you more skills such as how to mark books, how to give constructive feedback and how to monitor practical skills. They discuss feedback you are receiving from other teachers and your own evaluations, to help you identify targets in your next phase of development and ways of reaching those targets. They may well take an active interest in your coursework and reading. You must take a proactive part in these meetings, going to them with the necessary documents and items you want to discuss.

Your HE tutor has responsibility for collating your experiences, monitoring your progress as a whole and ensuring that the course components add up to a coherent experience. Your tutor contributes to the lecture, seminar and workshop programme and is the main supervisor of your written work. Tutors are also involved in periodic profiling with student teachers. When they visit schools, they spend time talking with the mentors about the school programme as well as discussing your progress. They are likely to observe your teaching and to give feedback. The list of 'good practice' in Figure 1.2.3 gives the tenor of conversations you should anticipate with both your tutor and school mentor.

Good practice occurs when:

- student teachers take an active role in the feedback sessions
- student teachers are able to evaluate their own teaching
- the lesson's aims or means of assessing pupil progress and achievement are used to structure feedback
- feedback is thorough, comprehensive and, where appropriate, diagnostic
- there is a balance of praise, criticism and suggestions for alternative strategies
- points made in feedback are given an order of priority of importance, targeting three for immediate action
- student teachers receive written comments on the lesson observed.

■ **Figure 1.2.3** Good practice in giving and using feedback on teaching

WHAT YOU BRING TO THE COURSE: REFLECTIONS ON YOUR STARTING POINT

You can start taking an active role in your own professional development by considering one of your starting points, your ideas about teaching. Your image of what teaching is about and the kind of teacher you want to become are powerful factors in teacher formation. You may also have thought about the way you want to be perceived by pupils. Task 1.2.2 requires you to make explicit the characteristics you associate with a good teacher by reflecting on your experiences as a learner.

Task 1.2.2 **Reflections on your experiences of learning science**

Think back to your own schooling and recall an educational experience, preferably in science, which you remember and value. Why was this a successful learning experience for you? List all the points that you remember as being distinctive about this experience. You may find it helpful to think first of the qualities of the particular teacher, followed by the nature of the learning activities. With other science student teachers, discuss and compare your responses to this task. Collate the positive features identified into a list of the qualities a good teacher of science has.

The second part of this task is to repeat the above exercise, but this time focusing on an educational experience that failed to engage or motivate you. Once again, compare and collate your responses with those of fellow student teachers.

Keep your notes in your Professional Development Portfolio and at the end of the course, consider how much your ideas have developed and how much you have achieved.

The outcome of the first part of Task 1.2.2 is a list of features of a successful learning experience and of the qualities possessed by effective teachers seen from the perspective of individual learners. Science student teachers asked questions similar to those in Task 1.2.2 generate a list that usually includes the attributes listed below.

The teacher:

■ was knowledgeable and enthusiastic about science
■ was approachable
■ knew and treated pupils as individuals
■ had the ability to make science relevant to everyday life
■ was able to explain scientific concepts and ideas clearly and logically
■ adopted a firm, but fair and consistent, approach
■ was patient
■ was willing to give up their time to go over material
■ was well prepared.

One of the challenges of the PGCE year is to incorporate the qualities that learners value into your work as a teacher. Task 1.2.3 helps you identify your starting point.

Task 1.2.3 **Auditing your own starting points**

The range of qualities possessed by good science teachers may seem daunting at the start. You may already have many of these skills through the life experience you bring to teaching, but they may need adjusting to the classroom context. The generic qualities of good teachers can be categorised in three ways:

1   the nature, temperament and personality of the person
2   the commitment to young people and the profession of teaching
3   the professional skills acquired through need and practice.

Use the lists generated above (Task 1.2.2) to audit your personal qualities using these three categories in turn. What qualities do you need to acquire during school experience? In what ways do you expect your school experience to help you to develop these qualities, and how?

USING OBSERVATION AS PART OF YOUR PROFESSIONAL DEVELOPMENT

Observation will undoubtedly be a tool you use as part of your training, but classrooms are complex busy places and observation of anything significant is difficult. This is where observation schedules that focus on different aspects of the teaching and learning can be useful. We have put one observation task here (Task 1.2.4) with a schedule that focuses on the flow of activities in a lesson and on management in Figure.1.2.4. Other schedules can be found elsewhere in this book and in Unit 1.2 in Capel *et al.* (2009). The simple rule for observation is to select only one or two aspects of teaching at a time, so as to build experiences and knowledge systematically and thoroughly.

It is a mistake to think of observation of teachers as something that you do only at the start of the course. It is equally important that you continue to observe other teachers once you have started teaching, because your own teaching experiences help you to identify subtleties that passed you by at the start.

Task 1.2.4 **Watching science teachers: teaching skills**

With the prior agreement of the teacher, arrange to observe a science lesson. Share the purposes of your observation and any particular focus you have. If possible, find a time for a short debriefing with the teacher after the lesson. Use an observation schedule to help in focusing your observation (see, e.g. Figure 1.2.4). After the lesson make a list of questions to discuss with the teacher. Write a summary for yourself identifying the implications of your observation for your lesson planning and those practices that you might adopt.

Being observed

As you increasingly take responsibility for your development, you will be able to explain to anyone observing you what you are working on and how. Most mentors and tutors welcome the student teacher who greets them with, 'I am trying out such and such because I am trying to improve my ... Please give me feedback on that.' If you do not do this, feedback can be unfocused and not as productive as it might have been.

Make notes about how the teacher accomplishes each of the tasks at the different phases of a lesson and about what the pupils are doing.

1   Starting a lesson
■ bringing in the class
■ settling and registration
■ opening up the topic
　□ gaining interest
　□ eliciting prior knowledge
　□ explaining the purpose of work
　□ telling pupils what to do.

2   Equipment/resources
■ location
■ working order
■ distribution
■ collecting in.

3   Main phase of lesson
■ What is the class doing?
■ What is the teacher doing?
■ How does the teacher gain the attention of the class
■ How does the teacher move from one activity to the next?
■ What problems arise? How are they managed?

4   End
■ timing
■ signal to stop/clear up
■ clear up/collect equipment
■ identifying/drawing out/summarising learning
■ setting homework
■ dismissing class.

■ **Figure 1.2.4** Example of a guide for observing a lesson to understand phases of a lesson and management skills (see Task 1.2.3)

YOUR CONTRIBUTION TO THE SCHOOL

You may feel at the start of the course that you are drawing extensively on other people's expertise and may wonder if you can give anything back to the school. You will find that schools welcome the questioning which comes from student teachers, the different ideas that they bring in and the contribution that they make to course development by the end of the year. The majority of student teachers find that some of the resources that they have prepared for their own classes become part of the resources bank for the school.

SUMMARY AND KEY POINTS

Given the unique starting points of student teachers and the different experiences they have in their various placement schools, there is a premium on each student teacher learning to plan and manage their own professional development. Understanding the Plan–Do–Review–Learn–Apply cycle for professional learning makes it easier to seek appropriate help and to make best use of support and input from your tutors, mentors, other science teachers, the technicians and fellow student teachers.

Using standards as an advance organiser, for professional profiling and as a vehicle for discussion contributes to professional development. Progress will be marked by an increasing sophistication of the analyses in which you engage and the move towards a time when you forget about what you are doing and focus entirely on the pupils' learning. This professional learning involves a complex mix of classroom experience and theoretical understanding. One without the other will not be productive.

Above all, remember that you are in charge of your professional development. Your commitment to taking an active part in it is crucial to your success. Learning to teach will take a toll on your personal reserves; it takes stamina and persistence, it requires good administrative skills as well as skills and knowledge needed for the classroom, it will draw on your personal attributes of being able to deal with complex situations, of establishing authority and showing leadership. By the end of the training year you will be aware that you have learned 'a new way of being yourself' (Black, 1987) and will derive a great deal of professional satisfaction from this 'new you'.

FURTHER READING

Capel, S., Leask, M. and Turner, T. (2009) *Learning to Teach in the Secondary School: An Introduction to School Experience*, **5th edition. London: Routledge.**

- ■ Allen, M. and Topliss, R. Unit 1.2 'The student teacher's roles and responsibilities', 22–35.
- ■ Capel, S. Unit 1.3 'Managing your time and stress', 36–46.
- ■ Heightman, S. Unit 1.2 'Reading classrooms. How to maximise learning from classroom observation', 65–78.

Parkinson, J. (2002) *Reflective Teaching of Science 11–18*. **London: Continuum.**

The chapter 'Learning to become an effective teacher' discusses the attributes of good teachers. It outlines issues of professional attitudes and responsibility including the need to review your practice regularly, and suggests ways of doing this.

RELEVANT WEBSITES

TDA (Training and Development Agency for Schools) (2008) *Professional Standards for Qualified Teacher Status and Requirements for Initial Teacher Training (Revised 2008)*. **London: TDA.**

http://www.tda.gov.uk/teachers/professionalstandards/standards.aspx (accessed 20 June 2009)

UNIT 1.3

WORKING WITHIN A SCIENCE DEPARTMENT

Ian Longman

INTRODUCTION

While you are on school experience you become involved in working in a variety of teams, for example subject and pastoral teams. This unit helps you explore the ways in which the science team works in your placement school. The tasks should assist you in demonstrating the necessary professional values and practice required for the award of Qualified Teacher Status (QTS). If you have already spent some time in a primary school you should appreciate the difference between the curriculum structures in the primary school and your secondary school placement, reflecting the different organisation of the respective schools.

OBJECTIVES

By the end of this unit you should be able to:

■ recount how teachers are organised in a number of different teams within a school and know the meetings you are expected to attend

■ explain the structure of the science team and know the key responsibilities which individuals, both teachers and technicians, hold

■ form appropriate professional relationships as a student teacher with other members of the science team

■ appreciate the place of the science team within the workings of the whole school.

ORGANISATION

As part of their professional role, teachers work in a number of different teams within a school. As well as subject teams, other teams are concerned with particular groups of pupils, for example year groups or houses, or certain parts of the curriculum such as PSHE (Personal, Social and Health Education) and Citizenship, whilst others are responsible for other whole-school issues, for example inclusion. It is important for your professional development that you understand the organisation in which you are to work (see Task 1.3.1).

Task 1.3.1 **School staff teams**

Find out how the staff in your placement school is organised into teams. Many schools have a staff handbook that would contain this type of information. Some of these teams would focus on curriculum issues, others on the welfare of the pupils. Examples might include year teams for form tutors and working parties for current initiatives. For each team, where the science department is represented, find out its main role in the running of the school, who its members are, and how often it meets. For example, the head of department is probably a member of a committee with responsibility for the curriculum, another member of the department may link with a team considering the special educational needs of individual pupils, and so on. Ask your mentor or professional tutor which meetings it would be appropriate for you to attend, and the dates of these, during your block of school experience.

Traditionally, the curriculum in secondary schools has been divided up into discrete subject areas leading, unfairly, to the adage that 'primary teachers teach pupils, secondary teachers teach subjects'. Normally this division of the curriculum is mirrored in the organisation of subject teams. Depending on the nature of the school, you may find yourself working within a faculty, for example Science and Technology, a science department or a distinct discipline team, for example a biology department. Factors affecting how subject groupings are organised stem from the ethos of the school and its philosophy, the choice of examination syllabuses, the number of pupils on roll and the management structure of the school. Some schools still retain a traditional, 'hierarchical' headteacher – deputy headteacher(s) – senior teacher(s) – heads of department structure, with teachers of science being organised into separate subject departments. Figure 1.3.1 illustrates this type of organisation in an 11–18 independent school.

A number of schools have moved to a 'flatter' headteacher – assistant headteachers/ faculty managers system. An example of this is a science faculty in a school in the Midlands following reorganisation; previously there had been separate heads of biology and chemistry sections with the head of the physics section doubling as head of department in a co-ordinating role. This would have made the science department relatively top-heavy in terms of managerial posts as well as encouraging the chemistry, physics and biology teachers to operate separately from each other. An Ofsted inspection recommended the move to a faculty structure, where posts of heads of separate departments were replaced by 'senior chemist/biology/physics' within a single large faculty. This particular example is not untypical, with a physical scientist as head of department and other members of the team having senior roles in the management of the school.

Often science and maths or science and technology teachers are organised into faculties in this way. An extreme example of this is given in Figure 1.3.2 where staffs from all curriculum subjects are divided into just three divisions. Science teachers in this particular sixth-form college are in the same division as teachers of mathematics, IT, geography, geology, psychology, and health and social care.

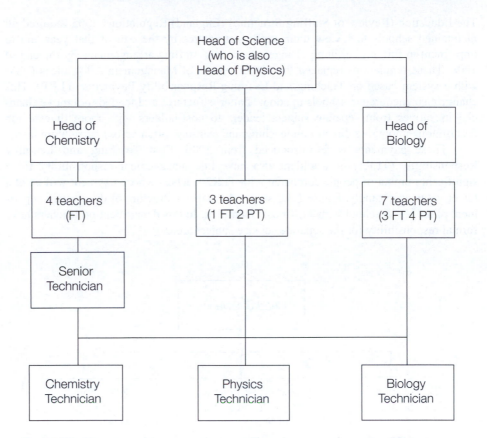

■ **Figure 1.3.1** The organisation of science staff in an independent school in Surrey

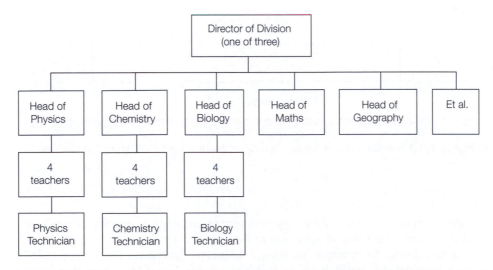

■ **Figure 1.3.2** The organisation of science teaching within a division in a sixth-form college in Surrey

The Education (Review of Staffing Structure) (England) Regulations 2005 required all maintained schools to review their staffing structures by the end of that year and to implement in full any resulting changes to schools' staffing arrangements by the end of 2008. These regulations replaced the earlier system of Management Allowances (MA) with a system based on Teaching and Learning Responsibility Payments (TLRP). This change also encouraged schools to adopt 'flatter' structures and tended to remove financial incentives from separate subject leaders to post-holders with more diverse job descriptions impinging directly on teaching and learning, often across curriculum areas.

These payments were introduced from 2006. First Teaching and Learning Responsibility (TLR1) post-holders also have line management responsibility for a significant number of people compared with TLR2 teachers whose payment will be of a lower value accordingly. Figure 1.3.3 shows the staffing structure of the science department of an 11–16 school with TLR posts identified. In this department no teachers have formal responsibility for the separate science subject areas.

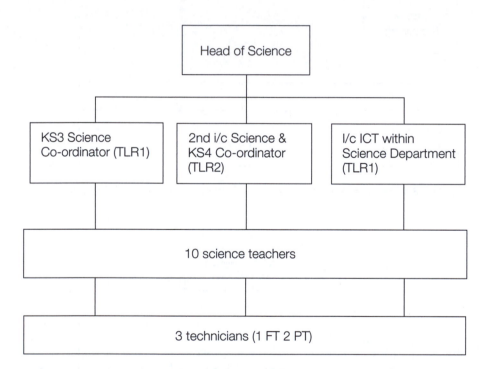

■ **Figure 1.3.3** The structure of the science department in an 11–16 school in Sussex

The development of subject knowledge and related pedagogy is ongoing throughout a teacher's career. You may find a member of the department you are working in is participating in a course, for example the Science Additional Specialism Programme (SASP) to develop knowledge and skills to teach another science discipline such as chemistry or physics.

Task 1.3.2 **The science staff team(s)**

Find out from your mentor how the science team is structured. (This information may also be contained in a departmental handbook.) Try to relate this to factors in the school as a whole, as discussed above. Have there been any changes in this structure, and if so why? It is useful to learn the subject specialisms of each science teacher and which classes they teach. In this way you know from whom to seek advice about subject matters or different groups of pupils.

The science team includes members of the technical staff who provide essential practical support in running the laboratories and often service visual aids and computing resources. To understand how important to teaching and learning these members are, we suggest you spend a day working with them (see Task 1.3.3).

Task 1.3.3 **The role of technicians**

With the help of your mentor arrange to work with members of the technical staff under their guidance for a day. Find out, by observation and discussion, the range of duties and responsibilities they have. They often have roles associated with health and safety, supporting teachers and pupils, as well as departmental admin- istration and information systems, including the use of computers. Find out procedures for ordering equipment, learning materials and other resources for your lessons. You need to be able to practise science experiments well before a lesson. Find out how to get this organised and liaise appropriately with the technicians. Learn about access to computers including their availability, booking systems, particular passwords, technical support and so on. Explore the range of resources that are available to support your teaching. Learn how to book audio-visual equip- ment, for example video-cassette players, laptops and data-projectors. In terms of accommodation you must know which rooms black out, which contain interactive whiteboards, and which contain (working!) fume cupboards.

For the sake of simplicity, this team of teaching and support staff is referred to as the 'science department' for the remainder of this unit. You will find other adults working with teachers in the department in both planning and interacting with pupils. If their contribution is to be effective in supporting pupils' learning in your lessons, then you need to find the time to plan this deployment together. Discuss the purpose and nature of the activities in which they are involved. Adults other than teachers could include teach- ing assistants working with whole classes, librarians supporting pupils' research, visiting speakers, STEM (Science, Technology, Engineering and Mathematics) Ambassadors and learning support assistants. The latter may be working with, for example, pupils with special educational needs, pupils for whom English is an additional language, Traveller children and pupils on catch-up programmes.

CHAINS OF MANAGEMENT

Heads of department (HoD) are usually 'middle managers' in the organisational structure of the school with resulting 'line' responsibility. This usually involves them in the appraisal of a selection of colleagues within the department as part of the school's performance-management procedures. Just as schools are varied, so too are science departments. Science departments are usually the largest curriculum area within a secondary school and many science teachers may have specific responsibilities delegated within a chain of management within the department. Some teachers may have responsibility for a specific science discipline, for example 'i/c chemistry'. Others may have responsibility for the curriculum for a particular age range of pupils, for example 'Key Stage 3 (KS3) Co-ordinator'. In a large department a number of teachers in addition to the HoD may have particular responsibilities for which they receive remuneration. These responsibilities are the subject of a job description and are often outlined in the science department handbook. In addition, all teachers within the department are expected to share in the collective responsibility of ensuring its functioning on a day-to-day basis. You should not only understand the structure of teams in your school and department but also the chains of management (see Task 1.3.4).

Task 1.3.4 **Management structures and responsibilities**

This task is similar to Tasks 1.3.1 and 1.3.2, but here you are focusing on respon-sibilities and *chains of management*.

In science: Discuss with your mentor the structure and management chain of the science team, identifying individual teachers' responsibilities. Record this structure diagrammatically for your future use.

Whole school: Identify the levels of management between you (or a Newly Qualified Teacher (NQT)) and the headteacher of your placement school. To whom would you turn if you needed advice outside your department?

Heads of department also act as 'subject leaders' in their school. In some schools the HoD's job description may be based on the National Standards for Subject Leaders produced by the Teacher Training Agency. These do not have the same status as the stan-dards for QTS or Induction, i.e. they are not mandatory, but provide professional guidance based on how experienced and effective co-ordinators provide leadership in their subject(s).

DEPARTMENTAL MEETINGS

In the drive to raise standards, departments produce development plans which set out their priorities and how they aim to realise them within a whole-school context. The effectiveness of the department in improving the quality of learning for pupils depends in part upon how the plans are developed and agreed – the decision-making process – and the extent to which the agreed decisions are understood and implemented by the whole department.

Such decisions are discussed at departmental meetings where the quality of discussion is crucial to the effectiveness of the department. As a student teacher you are expected to attend departmental meetings in order to understand how departments function and to keep abreast of developments. The issues discussed are often varied, e.g. teaching and learning strategies, issues with curriculum continuity or problems associated with particular pupils.

In schools where there is extensive devolution of financial and policy control you may be surprised at the variety of decisions that need to be made by departments across the school year. These might include decisions about groupings of pupils, choice of examination syllabus, purchase of a published teaching scheme, the provision for pupils with special educational needs, choice of software, health and safety issues, educational visits and other contexts for out-of-classroom learning, homework policy, assessment procedures, professional development opportunities and so on. Departmental policies and much other information are often recorded in the department handbook. You need to be aware of the various policies in place so that you are able to conform to established expectations. For example, what rewards and sanctions for pupils does the department operate and how do these fit in with a whole-school policy on discipline? What are the procedures for communicating with parents?

Task 1.3.5 **Science department policies**

Departments have policies on a wide range of aspects of teaching, for example laboratory rules, discipline procedures, marking of science and literacy, health and safety including risk assessments, equal opportunities, homework, recording of assessments, reporting to parents/carers and so on. Consult the department handbook and other documents to become familiar with these policies. With the help of your mentor, obtain the minutes of recent departmental meetings. Identify current areas of discussion and items of interest of which you would wish to know more. If an agenda for the next meeting is available, read it and brief yourself about selected items.

PRIMARY/SECONDARY LIAISON

Science departments often have policies and procedures in place to ease the transfer of pupils from feeder primary schools. It is important that secondary science teachers are aware of the knowledge, understanding and skills that new entrants have, including their ability to apply key language and terminology in science. Where teachers do not take into account the content of the primary curriculum then pupils' progression in science is likely to be reduced, particularly if this results in repetition of work without additional challenge (Braund, 2009: 22). Some schools have adopted bridging units to improve continuity of teaching strategies across the primary/secondary divide. Other practices to tackle transition issues may include: meetings of teachers from primary and secondary schools and teacher exchanges, induction programmes with pre-visits and/or open evenings, and transfer of assessment data and pupil records. With standardised end-of-key-stage tests in science being discontinued and the introduction of Assessing Pupil

Progress (APP) using levels that should apply in both primary and secondary science contexts, it will be increasingly important that primary and secondary teachers have productive meetings in discussing pupils' assessed work, resulting in more regard being paid by secondary schools to reliable information on primary children's academic progress.

It will also be important that secondary teachers become aware of developments in science in the junior age range following a review of the primary curriculum (Rose, 2009).

Task 1.3.6 **Primary/secondary transition**

Whilst on placement, find out what strategies are put in place to ensure the smooth transfer of pupils from primary to secondary phase. Which features of lower secondary science provide continuity from primary education? Which features provide the desired discontinuity that pupils might seek in changing from children to young adults? How is progression in pupils' attainment maintained from KS2 to KS3?

Compare your findings with a theoretical perspective by Galton (2009: 5–21) on moving to secondary school.

MAKING THE MOST OF THE EXPERIENCE

As a student teacher on school experience you are in the role of 'trainee'. With the help of your mentor and other staff in the science department your priority is to be able to demonstrate the professional standards for the award for QTS. By becoming aware of the workings of the department and by adopting its policies and practices, as set out in the departmental handbook and elsewhere, you should make good progress in achieving Standards Q3 (a) and (b) 'Professional attributes' (TDA, 2008: 5).

Meeting the demands of these standards in this way would be appropriate whatever subject department you worked in. However, there are specific issues related to science teaching that perhaps broaden your responsibilities further. Monk and Dillon (1995:11–12) identified these four issues as safety, fieldwork, sex education and health education. You need to find out how, in the context of your school experience, these demands might impinge on your teaching. Perhaps this is a place in which to raise the effect on your teaching of the diversity of pupils in our schools; how the different back-grounds, expectations, cultures and faiths impinge, in particular, on these four issues. You can find out more about these issues in other units in this book (Units 5.4 and 5.5), but in planning your lessons you need to be aware of and abide by legislation and any local authority (LA) and school guidance, policies and procedures that are relevant in these areas.

Whilst a major part of your placement involves planning, teaching and evaluating your lessons, you also need to gain experience of further aspects of working in a school. Find out to what extent you may be able to assist with extra-curricular activities such as a science club during your block of school experience. It is easy to become immersed in the physical confines of the science department, for example the laboratories, preparation rooms and resource areas. In some schools, members of the science department may have gained a reputation for being a clique, with rare appearances in the staffroom. Do not fall into this trap. You need to gain a broader view of the corporate life of schools to which you can contribute and in which you can share responsibly. In one school in which the author taught, this whole-school approach to working was, in part, achieved by the virtual prohibition of departmental kettles and by providing tea or coffee in the staffroom at break time (although the science department retained a 'steam generator'!).

EXPLORING OTHER DEPARTMENTS

Your block of school experience would be incomplete without an exploration of other departments. One example of where you can put this into practice is if the school open day/evening for parents of prospective pupils, usually held in the Autumn term, occurs during your block of school experience. A notable feature of this event is the effort that goes into displays of pupils' work throughout the school. Certainly get involved with the planning and preparation of the science department's activities, but also negotiate with your mentor that you have time during the event to explore the work of pupils in other subject areas (see Task 1.3.7).

Task 1.3.7 **Display**

Look at the effectiveness of different types of display on show in other departments and consider how you could transfer the best practice, including examples of 3D work to illustrate various scientific concepts in your laboratory in the future. This is important because a number of pupils have difficulties in interpreting and relating two-dimensional diagrams to real objects and structures. Incorporating three-dimensional modelling into science activities can promote learning. Make use of a digital camera to keep a record of the event for your files.

Find out who is responsible for the displays in the science area and how often they are changed. Displays are a means of valuing pupils' work. Discuss with your mentor whether space is available for displays of some of your classes' work and plan accordingly. Again, take digital images for your portfolio of evidence.

During your blocks of school experience you will be observing a number of science lessons and focusing on a variety of professional issues. It is worth pointing out here the value of watching teachers other than science teachers at work. The different ways in which teachers approach their subject is illuminating and helpful in understanding how the same pupils respond to different contexts and teachers. You can often adopt similar strategies to widen the range you use and to improve the effectiveness of your own science teaching.

SUMMARY AND KEY POINTS

This unit has explored the workings of the team of teachers, technicians and other support staff who are responsible for the provision of the science curriculum. In most secondary schools this is the science department, but in some schools other organisational structures exist to teach the science curriculum.

Develop an awareness of the policies and procedures of the department and where you can find reference to these. There is often a departmental handbook which contains this and other essential information. As a student teacher you need to become familiar with your colleagues' expectations of you. You are expected to develop sound professional working relationships within this team, see Standard Q32 (TDA, 2008: 10) and to check your development against the standards for your course. You also need to explore ways of contributing to the life of the school beyond the laboratory.

Check which requirements for your course have been addressed through this unit.

FURTHER READING

Alexander, R. J. (2009a) *Towards a New Primary Curriculum: A Report from the Cambridge Primary Review. Part 2: The Future.* Cambridge: University of Cambridge Faculty of Education.

Alexander, R. J. (2009b) *Children, Their World, Their Education. Final Report and Recommendations of the Cambridge Primary Review.* London: Routledge.
Two reports from a very extensive review of the primary curriculum.
http://www.primaryreview.org.uk/Publications/CambridgePrimaryReviewrep.html (accessed 24 June 2009).

Alexander, R. J. and Flutter, J. (2009) *Towards a New Primary Curriculum: A Report from the Cambridge Primary Review. Part 1: Past and Present.* Cambridge: University of Cambridge Faculty of Education.

Dillon, J. (2000) 'Managing the science department', in Monk, M. and Osborne, J. (eds) *Good Practice in Science Teaching: What Research Has to Say.* Buckingham: Open University Press.
This chapter looks at what research tells us about effective management, particularly at departmental level.

Mitchell, R. (2006) 'Effective primary/secondary transfer', in Wood-Robinson, V. (ed.) *ASE Guide to Secondary Science Education.* Hatfield: The Association for Science Education.
This chapter discusses ways in which transition between schools can be improved.

Peel, C. and Sample, S. (2006) 'Support staff in science departments', in Wood-Robinson, V. (ed.) *ASE Guide to Secondary Science Education.* Hatfield: The Association for Science Education.
This chapter is useful in exploring the variety of job functions which science technicians now undertake, the deployment of teaching assistants and whole-department teamwork.

Rose, J. (2009) *Independent Review of the Primary Curriculum. Final Report.* London: HMSO.
http://www.dcsf.gov.uk/primarycurriculumreview/ (accessed 12 January 2009).

The Wellcome Trust (2009) *Perspectives on Education 2 (Primary–Secondary Transfer in Science).*
http://wellcome.ac.uk/perspectives (accessed 24 June 2009).
This publication contains three articles (two already referenced in this chapter) by well-respected authors giving their perspective on issues related to transition.

RELEVANT WEBSITES

Science Additional Specialism Programme

http://www.tda.gov.uk/teachers/continuingprofessionaldevelopment/science_cpd.aspx for details of SASP, the TDA's science CPD programme (accessed 24 June 2009).

School teachers' pay and conditions

http://www.teachernet.gov.uk/management/payandperformance/pay/2005/ for details of Teaching and Learning Responsibility Payments (TLRP) (accessed 24 June 2009).

THE SCIENCE CURRICULUM

INTRODUCTION

This chapter focuses on the formal science curriculum. Any curriculum involves choices about what is valuable to pass on to the next generation. In the United Kingdom those choices are made at different levels. National bodies provide guidelines through the National Curriculum in Science or through the criteria for science courses leading to qualifications. Science departments in schools interpret these guidelines when producing their schemes of work and individual teachers use their own interpretation when devising lessons from the schemes of work. Pupils, themselves, after the age of 14, make choices about which science courses they follow.

As a science teacher you need to be aware of the national guidelines, to know how these guidelines might be translated into more specific course outlines and to recognise the flexibility that schools and individual teachers still have when creating learning activities for their pupils.

Unit 2.1 gives the background to the National Curriculum in Science, the changes that have occurred in the 20 years since its introduction and the reasons for the changes. We have focused on the situation in England; however, there are sufficient similarities to make the chapter relevant to people in Wales and Northern Ireland, because the early history and principles on which the National Curriculum is based applies to them all. Scotland has an advisory, not a statutory, curriculum for the 5–14 age range. Again, many of the principles apply. Relevant websites for the National Curriculum documents for the four countries are given at the end of Unit 2.2.

Unit 2.2 helps you to understand the detail of the English science curriculum for the 11–14 age range. The tasks are easily adapted for people working with the Welsh, northern Irish or Scottish curricula.

Unit 2.3 examines the diversity of the 14–19 science curriculum. This diversity arises because only one part of the curriculum in England is specified by the National Curriculum; the rest is determined by the choices that pupils make between different courses. Those choices have increased recently with the development of vocationally based courses alongside academic courses. The unit has been written in the context of GCSE (General Certificate of Secondary Education) and GCE (General Certificate of Education) courses, used in England, Wales and Northern Ireland, but the tasks are easily adaptable to the courses leading to Scottish qualifications.

SCIENCE IN THE NATIONAL CURRICULUM

Jenny Frost

INTRODUCTION

People born after 1985 will not have known a time when there was not a National Curriculum, but its significance can pass a learner in school by. As a teacher you need to understand its significance and appreciate that it is still evolving. This unit deals only briefly with the development of the National Curriculum and the debates that have shaped the current form of science within the National Curriculum (NC science). Units 2.2 and 2.3, respectively, give greater detail about NC science for the 11–14 and 14–19 age ranges, respectively.

OBJECTIVES

By the end of this unit you should:

- be familiar, in broad terms, with the aims and purpose of the National Curriculum in science
- be aware of associated assessment
- understand the nature of recent changes, and the reasons for them.

BACKGROUND

The National Curriculum in England, which was first implemented in 1989, provides the statutory educational requirements for the 11–16 age range in secondary schools and the 5–11 age range in primary schools in the maintained sector. It aims for comparability in what is taught in schools in different parts of the country. Despite considerable contemporary controversy at the start about what was of most value and how to define it, the National Curriculum was formulated in a traditional way by a combination of subjects. (Science was treated as one subject.) Teams of experts in the various subjects devised the relevant curricula so, initially, links across the curriculum and co-ordination between subjects were minimal. Now, over 20 years later, several revisions have taken place, giving greater coherence between subjects and more specific guidance on cross-curricular issues.

The National Curriculum brought with it a new language; 'programmes of study' for the content of courses; the numbering of the school years from the entry to school at age 5, called Year 1 (Y1) to the end of compulsory education at age 16 (Y11) and the division of those years into four 'Key Stages': Key Stage 1 for Y1 and 2 (KS1); Key Stage 2 for Y3–6 (KS2); Key Stage 3 for Y7–9 (KS3); Key Stage 4 for Y10 and 11 (KS4). (For a fuller account of the National Curriculum as a whole see Capel *et al.*, 2009: 388–396.)

Science was designated a 'core' subject alongside English and mathematics, and it retains that position today making it compulsory from KS1 to the end of KS4. Arguments for this status varied but included the need for more people in scientific and technical careers, the need for a scientifically literate population in an increasingly scientific and technological society and the importance of passing on a major cultural determinant of the twentieth century. Originally there was pressure to allow science to take up 20 per cent of curriculum time at KS4. A compromise position ensued whereby the programmes of study at KS4 had two versions, one for 'double science', taking up 20 per cent of curriculum time, and one for 'single science', taking up 10 per cent of curriculum time. From 2004, however, only the equivalent of one subject is specified, although it remains a statutory requirement for schools to provide access to a course of study in science leading to at least two subjects.

Since its inception, NC science has undergone several changes: at the time of writing, it is in its fifth version for KS3 and KS4, and its fourth version for KS1 and KS2 (the fifth version to be implemented in September 2011).

NATIONAL CURRICULUM ASSESSMENT

The National Curriculum includes national assessment. At the start, the Task Group on Assessment and Testing (TGAT) was commissioned to develop a model of assessment that would allow monitoring of progress through the whole of schooling. TGAT proposed a model through which progress in learning was to be judged in terms of 'levels' (DES/WO, 1988). The criteria for achieving each level are set out as a series of level descriptors within each 'attainment target'. (There are, effectively, nine levels – levels 1–8 plus 'exceptional performance'.) Originally, attainment targets and their levels applied to all four Key Stages. However, they now apply only to Key Stages 1–3. The expected levels to be attained at the end of each Key Stage by the majority of pupils are shown in Figure 2.1.1.

Range of levels within which the great majority of pupils are expected to work		Expected attainment for the majority of pupils at the end of the Key Stage	
Key stage 1 (5–7 yr-olds) (KS1)	1–3	at age 7, end of KS1	2
Key stage 2 (7–11 yr-olds) (KS2)	2–5	at age 11, end of KS2	4
Key stage 3 (11–14 yr-olds) (KS3)	3–7	at age 14, end of KS3	5/6

■ **Figure 2.1.1** Expected attainment in Key Stages 1–3 in National Curriculum

TGAT also suggested that to meet the government's objective of having a system to allow national monitoring of standards, teachers would be in the best position to make assessments. It proposed that teachers should report on achievement at the end of every Key Stage, with some tasks (Standard Assessment *Tasks* – N.B. not *Tests*, see below) being developed to moderate teachers' assessments. These tasks would only be given to a 'sample' of pupils across the country. The details of what happened to this model are beyond the scope of this book, but very soon tests (Standard Assessment Tests, SATs) were being used to assess achievement in science. SATs were taken by all pupils at the end of KS2 and KS3. There was no national testing of science at KS1. Teachers also made their own assessments of pupils at the end of these Key Stages. It was, though, the results of SATs that were used in school 'performance tables'. The science SATs (along with English and mathematics SATs) were discontinued in October 2008 for KS3. The science SATs for KS2 were discontinued after summer 2009, but not for English and mathematics. New models of assessment, closer to the original TGAT proposal, are in preparation (see Unit 6.1).

THE PRINCIPLES IN THE DEVELOPMENT OF THE NATIONAL SCIENCE CURRICULUM

Breadth and balance in the science curriculum

Breadth and balance were two of the guiding principles of NC science. *Breadth* involved including major ideas from across the sciences, technological applications, social consequences of science and something of the skills of being a scientist. *Balance* referred to giving equal importance to different branches of science (biology, chemistry, physics, earth sciences), such that the curriculum could be the 'jumping-off point' for study of any branch of science later, and to giving equal consideration to the acquisition of scientific knowledge and the understanding of the nature of science.

Historically, this concern with breadth and balance was important. Prior to the introduction of the National Curriculum, pupils had greater choice of subjects from the age of 14. As a result there was a higher proportion of boys selecting the physical sciences than girls and a higher proportion of girls selecting biology than boys. There were pupils who chose to study no science after the age of 14 and those who chose to study only one of the sciences. Science courses varied in the extent to which they included the teaching of investigational skills. There were only isolated examples of the nature of science being part of a course, although many teachers made some reference to it. While the phrase 'breadth and balance' is less frequently used these days, the underlying principles are evident in the existing NC science (see Units 2.2 and 2.3).

Inclusion

The science curriculum is for everyone; for those who like science and those who do not; for those who have a natural talent for it and those who do not. In the 1980s, when the curriculum was first written, there was more concern about the gender imbalance than anything else, with concern that teachers should make the curriculum as appealing to girls as to boys. That concern is still there, but thinking about inclusion goes much wider than gender and requires teachers to have strategies to overcome any potential barriers to learning.

Continuity in the curriculum

The curriculum is structured so that the programme of study of each Key Stage builds on what has been learned before, to prevent overlap of teaching and to provide opportunities for pupils to advance at successive stages. Such linking of the various parts is referred to as 'continuity'. Achieving continuity is not just a case of having a sensibly structured curriculum; it also requires teachers to link what they are teaching to what has been learned and experienced before and what is to come later. Schools have to take stock of primary experience in science. Y7 science might well include a rapid review of what has been remembered, but not a repetition of work that pupils have already done.

Cross-curricular links

Science teachers carry responsibility not only for helping pupils make connections between their science learning and other subjects, but also they contribute to the development of pupils' skills in literacy, numeracy and ICT. In addition, the science curriculum makes contributions to school-wide themes such as health and sex education, citizenship and sustainable futures.

Progression

Progression is about pupil development. A well-structured curriculum supports, but does not guarantee, progression. Learning more information is not really progression although it may be a necessary precursor. Progression is more concerned with being able to link information and use it in more complex situations, being able to deal with increased conceptual complexity and employ more advanced thinking skills. (See Unit 5.1 for a fuller discussion of progression.)

A description of how progression is conceived in the NC science can be gleaned from the level descriptors for each of the attainment targets (see Unit 2.2). You need to appreciate the differences between one level and another because as a teacher you will have to provide the challenges and opportunities for pupils to develop skills of the subsequent levels and be able to monitor their progress.

REASONS FOR CHANGES IN NC SCIENCE

It is reasonable to ask why NC science has changed five times between 1989 and 2008. An initial problem was overload of content. NC science originally included: information technology, which later became a subject in its own right; micro-electronics, which was subsequently taken out; and weather, which was moved to geography. Specific scientific content was specified in too much detail, so that individual facts seemed more important than the concepts they underpinned. Attempts to allow learners to experience the nature of science through open-ended investigations were thwarted by the need for success in investigations in external examinations, and only a limited range of rather closed investigations were used. Exhortations to teachers to teach about science in a social context and to include the nature of science often went unheeded. But probably the strongest criticism was that it was not addressing the needs of all the pupils who were required to study it and it was not passing on to the next generation the features most valued about science.

Many of the criticisms (and successes) of the National Curriculum after the third version can be found in the report *Beyond 2000: Science Education for the Future: A Report with Ten Recommendations* (Millar and Osborne, 1998). This report arose from a series of seminars and debates amongst the science education community during a five-year moratorium on change between 1995 and 2000. Its ten recommendations have strongly influenced what has happened since, so you are recommended to read the report (see Task 2.1.1). Its first recommendation was that the science curriculum should aim to develop scientific literacy and not be modelled on the early preparation of future scientists. It recommended the incorporation of teaching about the nature of science as a subject whose ideas are based on evidence, argumentation and creative leaps. This has resulted in science teachers talking about 'ideas and evidence', 'argumentation' and 'creativity' in science and developing appropriate teaching strategies. More recently, the phrase 'How science works' has entered the science curriculum; it encompasses more than just the use of evidence in science (see Units 2.2, 2.3 and 3.1) and with it has come a different emphasis for teaching and learning science – and for its assessment (see Unit 6.2).

Another recommendation was a new model for KS4 science, at the heart of which was a very different 'single science' curriculum from the one that previously existed. First, it thought of learners as *consumers* of science not *producers* of science. It aimed to enable people to understand science in the contexts in which they meet it in everyday life and to engage in debates that surround science. Second, it would be a core subject for *everyone*. There would then be *Additional Science* for those who wanted to study the equivalent of two subjects in science. Changes to KS4 arrangements were made to allow this new model to apply from September 2004 (QCA, 2004) so that pilot schemes could be trialled. The KS4 NC science was changed to its current form for first teaching in September 2006.

Given that the recommendations from the report for KS3 had been incorporated in the 1999 version, there remains the question as to why there was need for further change at KS3 for implementation in September 2008. This latest change was occasioned by the wish to rewrite the whole of the National Curriculum at KS3 in order to give uniformity to the way subjects were structured, to allow greater flexibility for teachers to adapt the curriculum, to encourage greater cross-curricular work, and to conceive of the curriculum in a more holistic way than the amalgamation of a set of subjects.

Task 2.1.1 Examining the recommendations of *Beyond 2000* (Millar and Osborne, 1998)

Download and read *Beyond 2000: Science Education for the Future: A Report with Ten Recommendations* (Millar and Osborne, 1998).

1 List the successes and failures of NC science that were identified at the time of the report.
2 What were the proposed changes and the reasons for them?
3 Identify which parts of the recommendations might have seemed radical for the science-teaching profession.
4 As you read Units 2.2 and 2.3 and undertake the tasks in them, reflect on the extent to which the recommendations have been implemented.
5 Discuss with colleagues, tutors or mentors your reactions to the recommendations. Are you in sympathy with the ideas? Do they match your own ideas about the purpose of science education for young people?

SUMMARY AND KEY POINTS

The National Curriculum in science is characterised by breadth and balance. It covers all branches of science as well as the nature of science. It includes the link between science and technology and the role of science in environmental and health issues. It is designed to provide continuity from ages 5–16.

Since 2000, the NC science has aimed explicitly for scientific literacy, which has introduced new elements to the curriculum and required a new model for the KS4 programmes in science.

FURTHER READING

Millar, R. and Osborne, J. (1998) *Beyond 2000: Science Education for the Future: A Report with Ten Recommendations.* **London: King's College.**
http://www.kcl.ac.uk/schools/sspp/education/staff/josbornepubs.html and http://www.york.ac.uk/depts/educ/people/MillarR.htm (accessed 25 June 2009).
This report has had a major influence on the current shape of the science curriculum. Implementation of its ideas occurred over the following ten years. Science departments are still working to change resources and practices to match its ideals.

Osborne, J. F. and Collins, S. (2001) Pupils' views of the role and value of the science curriculum: a focus-group study. *International Journal of Science Education*, **23 (5), 441–468.**
This provides an insight into pupils' reactions to the science curriculum. Implications for science education are outlined.

Nicolson, P. and Holman, J. (2003) 'National curriculum for science: looking back and looking forward'. *School Science Review*, **85 (311), 21–27.**
The successes of the National Curriculum in science in terms of the numbers studying science up to 16, the relatively strong performance of UK pupils in international comparisons in science and the breadth of science studied are reviewed in the light of no increase in the number of pupils studying science at A-level.

Duggan, S. and Gott, R. (2000) 'Understanding evidence in investigations: the way to a more relevant curriculum?', in Sears, J. and Sorensen, P. (eds) *Issues in Science Teaching*, **London: RoutledgeFalmer, pp. 60–69.**
This contains useful case studies of why the curriculum needed to change and the direction of the change.

Osborne, J. (2008) 'Engaging young people with science: does science education need a new vision?'. *School Science Review*, **89 (328), 67–74.**
This is a well-argued article that challenges the widely held belief that more scientists are needed. Its extensive literature on research into pupils' attitudes to science and reports on the need for scientists, with international comparisons, is valuable.

RELEVANT WEBSITES

Websites for the National Curriculum documents from England, Wales, Northern Ireland and Scotland are given at the end of Unit 2.2.

UNIT 2.2

SCIENCE 11–14

Jenny Frost

INTRODUCTION

The 11–14 age range is a critical period for maintaining pupils' enthusiasm for science. The curriculum needs to be taught by interesting and knowledgeable teachers who take into account what pupils have already learned in science. The NC science at KS3 provides guidelines that should enable teachers to do this while allowing room for teachers' own creativity and flair. The tasks in this unit enable you to understand the guidelines and to identify areas of expertise that you already have and areas that you need to develop. They also require you to analyse how the guidelines are interpreted in schemes of work in your schools. Finally, there is an M-level task that requires you to reflect critically on achievements in your own teaching.

OBJECTIVES

By the end of this unit you should:

- understand the guidelines for NC science at KS3
- be aware of areas of expertise that you need to develop in order to teach the whole of the science at KS3
- analyse achievements in your own teaching.

FRAMEWORK FOR THE PROGRAMMES OF STUDY AT KEY STAGE 3

All subjects at KS3 now have programmes of study which are constructed under six headings:

- curriculum aims
- the importance of the subject
- key concepts
- key processes
- range and content
- curriculum opportunities.

The 'curriculum aims' are common to all subjects, i.e. that all young people should become successful learners, confident individuals and responsible citizens, which are closely related to the *Every Child Matters* agenda (DCSF, 2009). The 'importance of the subject' is a selection of key features, possibly best thought of in terms of 'if one forgets most of the detail of a subject in later years, what is the abiding memory of it?'. The statement about the importance of science acts as the guiding principle for all that follows.

Task 2.2.1 **The importance of science for pupils**

See *Relevant websites* and download NC science at KS3.

1　Read the paragraph on page 207 about the importance of science. Separate the various aspects into a list so that you can see easily the variety embedded in the paragraph. Underline any words that you think are particularly important.
2　Compare this list with what you remember of your own science curriculum.
3　Share your list and comparisons with other student teachers.

'Key concepts' refer to the nature of the subject not the scientific concepts. 'Key processes' are the skills pupils should learn, which are relevant to the subject. 'Range and content' specifies the scientific concepts to be learned. This section is the closest to a traditional syllabus, but it is written in very broad terms. 'Curriculum opportunities' lists learning activities for pupils.

Key concepts (about science)

There are four key concepts about science listed:

■　scientific thinking
■　applications and implications of science
■　cultural understanding
■　collaboration.

You need to be able to interpret key concepts in terms of scientific concepts being taught and in ways that make sense to your pupils. In the first instance, however, undertake an audit of your own knowledge of these key concepts in relation to various topics in science using Task 2.2.2.

Task 2.2.2 **Audit of prior knowledge: key concepts about science**

1　Download the NC science at KS3 and read the descriptions given for each of the four key concepts and the explanatory notes on page 208.
2　Without recourse to reference sources, list examples from the following topics, which you could use to illustrate each key concept:

■ atoms and molecules
■ extraction of metal ores
■ electricity
■ the structure of the solar system
■ classification of the living world
■ causes of diseases
■ climax communities
■ communication by mobile phones
■ causes of earthquakes.

3 Identify where you need to develop your knowledge and understanding of these key concepts.

4 Put this into your professional portfolio, and throughout the year monitor your increasing knowledge in this area. Talk with mentors about areas you want to develop.

Range and content

The key concepts are taught through a particular specified scientific knowledge, referred to as the 'range and content'. As a teacher you need to be familiar with this content. Task 2.2.3 requires you to judge your confidence with NC science by thinking about the range and content in three ways. First, in relation to the science story or explanation; second, in relation to the evidence on which it is based; and third, in relation to the arguments which link the evidence to the story. For example, the story of the solar system tells of a number of planets circulating round the Sun at different distances and with different periods of orbit. Some planets have moons. The evidence on which it is based includes: observations of the movements across the sky of the Sun, Moon and planets on a daily and yearly (and longer) basis; measurements of distances and periods; views through telescopes of moons associated with planets; eclipses; variation of day length throughout the year; and phases of the Moon. The arguments that relate the story and observations, show how the story of the solar system explains the observations and how other theoretical perspectives are needed (continuous movement of planets without a driving force; theory of gravitational attraction).

Task 2.2.3 Audit of personal confidence on range and content of science

Use Figure 2.2.1 to audit how confident you are in relation to NC science. Do this at the start of your course, but go back to it and modify your responses throughout your training year. By the end you should feel confident in all areas.

Most of the statements in the table of the range and content have been written out in full, just as they appear in NC science (pp. 209–10) but some of the longer statements in the biological section have been abbreviated, so look at the programme of study for the full statement.

Keep your record in your professional portfolio.

Range and content of science at KS3			Science story	Evidence	Arguments
Energy, electricity and forces	a	Energy can be transferred usefully, stored or dissipated, but cannot be created or destroyed.			
	b	Forces are interactions between objects and can affect their shape and motion.			
	c	Electric current in circuits can produce a variety of effects.			
Chemical and material behaviour	a	The particle model provides explanations for the different physical properties and behaviour of matter.			
	b	Elements consist of atoms that combine together in chemical reactions to form compounds.			
	c	Elements and compounds show characteristic chemical properties and patterns in their behaviour.			
Organisms, behaviour and health	a	Cells, tissues, organs and body systems …			
	b	The human reproductive cycle ….			
	c	Conception, growth, development, behaviour and health can be affected by diet, drugs and disease.			
	d	Variation, classification and interdependence …			
	e	Behaviour is influenced by internal and external factors and can be investigated and measured.			
The environment, Earth and universe	a	Geological activity is caused by chemical and physical processes.			
	b	Astronomy and space science provide insight into the nature of observed motions of the Sun, Moon, stars, planets and other celestial bodies.			
	c	Human activity and natural processes can lead to changes in the environment.			

Audit your personal confidence in NC science at KS3 using the simple scheme of ✔, ?, ✗ as explained below.

Examples:	I could give an account of the science story with illustrations and examples.	confident ✔ not sure ? unfamiliar ✗
Evidence:	I know the evidence on which this idea is based.	confident ✔ not sure ? unfamiliar ✗
Arguments:	I can explain the link between the story and the evidence.	confident ✔ not sure ? unfamiliar ✗

■ **Figure 2.2.1** Audit of personal confidence in NC science at Key Stage 3

Curriculum opportunities and key processes

The other two parts of the framework are the key processes and curriculum opportunities. The key processes are the skills that the pupils will gain through learning science and are listed under three headings, namely:

■ practical and enquiry skills
■ critical understanding of evidence
■ communication.

There is, of course, an obvious link with the 'key concepts', e.g. if science is about creativity then pupils need to learn to be creative in science. You can easily track these links for yourself.

Curriculum opportunities are designed to allow pupils to learn these processes. They give an indication of the variety of learning activities that teachers have to create. Task 2.2.4 enables you to cross-reference the curriculum opportunities to the key processes.

Task 2.2.4 **Analysing 'curriculum opportunities' and 'key processes'**

1 Read the list of curriculum opportunities (NC science at KS3 page 212).
2 Analyse:
   a one unit of your school's science course
   b a *different* unit from a KS3 science textbook (see *Further reading*) to find examples of how each opportunity is incorporated and realised.
3 Now read the list of key processes (NC science page 209) and decide whether pupils will have had the opportunity to learn the key processes within the units you studied. (Perhaps score them using the following criteria: *many...,* *some..., few...* or *no opportunities.*)
4 If there are key processes that could not be achieved within the unit studied, find out where in the course they would be learned.
5 Share your notes with other student teachers and with your mentor in school.

In the previous unit, breadth and balance in the NC science were explained. Try the following task to check on the extent to which these have been achieved in the current NC science at KS3.

Task 2.2.5 **Identifying breadth and balance in the NC science**

From your study of NC science at KS3 in Tasks 2.2.1–2.2.4, ask the following questions:

1 Has equal importance been given to ideas about science as it has about the scientific concepts?
2 Is there balance between the sciences? Are geology and astronomy represented as well as physics, chemistry and biology? What about environmental science?
3 Are technological applications and the social implications of science included?
4 Was there anything to help pupils understand careers in science? This is an intended part of *How Science Works.*
5 List other aspects of breadth and balance that are apparent.
6 Identify the extent to which the recommendations of the report *Beyond 2000* (see Unit 2.1, Task 2.1.1) have been incorporated in NC science at KS3.

ASSESSMENT OF PROGRESS: THE ATTAINMENT TARGETS

The other part of NC science that must be understood is the 'attainment targets' section, which gives teachers criteria by which to judge the progress of pupils. There are four attainment targets:

■ AT1 How science works
■ AT2 Organisms, their behaviour and the environment
■ AT3 Materials, their properties and the Earth
■ AT4 Energy, forces and space.

Each attainment target contains descriptors of expected performance at six levels for KS3 (levels 4–8 plus 'exceptional standard'). If earlier levels are needed they can be found on the KS1 and KS2 website. The purpose of the descriptors is to allow teachers to monitor the progress of pupils throughout their schooling with an expectation that, on average, pupils will progress through one level every two years. Task 2.2.6 helps you track the expected progression of some aspects of the science curriculum so that you become familiar with how the attainment targets are organised.

Task 2.2.6 **Tracking progression in NC science attainment targets**

You will need the level descriptors for all the levels of the attainment targets for this task. Download them from the websites (see *Relevant websites*).

1   In AT1, read all the level descriptors and track the progression in the ability to design investigations and collect first-hand data.
2   In AT2–4, read all the level descriptors and track progression in relation to understanding of evidence.
3   Try to characterise how progression is conceived in each case.
4   Cover all levels so that you are aware of what is likely to have been learned in primary school. Write a report (one page) and discuss with your tutor.

WIDER ASPECTS OF THE CURRICULUM

The National Curriculum as a whole has wider objectives than the collection of separate subjects, and lists areas where whole-school strategies are expected to be developed. They are:

■   *general requirements* (inclusion, use of language across the curriculum, use of ICT across the curriculum and Health and Safety)
■   *skills* (functional skills and personal, learning and thinking skills – PLTS)
■   *cross-curricular dimensions* (identity and cultural diversity; healthy lifestyles; enterprise; global dimensions and sustainable development; technology and media; creativity and critical thinking).

Look up these aspects of the National Curriculum (see *Relevant websites*) and find out what strategies have been developed in your school.

Links between science and mathematics

The 'functional skills' are the language, ICT and mathematical skills that people need to function as a citizen. Aspects of language and ICT appear elsewhere in the book, so attention here is drawn to mathematics. Science uses mathematics as a tool, but there are several difficulties associated with this:

■   Pupils do not transfer skills easily from one context to another.
■   Pupils may have acquired a skill without a concept, such as plotting co-ordinates on a graph without understanding why a graph might be useful.
■   The language used in teaching mathematics may not be the same as the language used by the science teacher.
■   Science teachers have often not made a study of the conceptual difficulties that children have with different aspects of mathematics.

There are several steps that an individual science teacher can take to address these difficulties. The first is the obvious one of reading the National Curriculum for mathematics, especially the section on range and content, which is categorised under the following headings:

■ number and algebra
■ geometry and measures
■ statistics.

When you look at the detail under each of these headings you may well find aspects that are unfamiliar, so a second step is to update and develop your own mathematical understanding. The third is to talk to mathematics teachers, and hopefully observe them, to learn how they help pupils to understand mathematical concepts; pay special attention to the language used and the contexts in which problems are set. The fourth is to learn about conceptual difficulties that pupils have in mathematics. A useful start here is an article on 'Numeracy in science' by Lenton and Stevens (2000). The fifth is to anticipate where the mathematical work will occur in science and make sure you have talked in detail with the mathematics teacher or a more experienced science teacher about ways of dealing with the topic.

NATIONAL STRATEGIES FOR SCIENCE

Since 2001/2, the government has financed the gradual introduction of what it called National Strategies to raise achievement, by strengthening teaching and learning across the curriculum (see Capel *et al.*, 2009: 397–405 for an account of national and local strategies). Considerable continuing professional development was supported, and resources generated have subsequently been published on the strategies website of the Department for Children, Schools and Families (DCSF) (see *Relevant websites*). The following list is a selection of resources currently available for KS3 science:

■ frameworks for science (the NC frameworks, with information about progression from Y7–Y11)
■ science objectives, showing year-by-year progression for different topic areas, with associated teaching strategies and 'rich questions'
■ material to support the teaching of science concepts and information about pupils' misconceptions in the section on 'barriers to learning'.

Keep an eye on ideas published on the strategies website as resources are continuously updated.

REVIEWING YOUR WORK WITHIN THE NATIONAL CURRICULUM

It is important to remember that despite all the written guidance, individual teachers' own planning and evaluation are still essential. National guidelines and schools' schemes of work do not tell you how to teach, what to say or how to support students in drawing out the significance of the activities in which they are engaged. Task 2.2.7 (an M-level task) requires you to analyse what you have achieved in terms of NC aims.

Task 2.2.7 **Teaching one of the key concepts**

1 Select **one** aspect of key concepts of NC science that particularly intrigues you – you might select creativity or global dimensions or modelling etc.
2 Explain, in writing, why you chose this aspect of key concepts.
3 Do some reading on the subject so that you have ideas about how others have interpreted it, and some examples to show what it might mean. Locate your own meaning in the context of other ideas.
4 Describe how you have incorporated this aspect of key concepts into a short sequence of lessons with one of your classes.
5 Evaluate the extent to which pupils learned what was intended and identify how you would modify your teaching in the future.
6 Discuss your evaluation with your tutor.

MODIFICATION OF THE AGE RANGE FOR KEY STAGE 3

While 11–14 years is the intended age range for KS3, recently several schools have decided to teach their KS3 programmes in less than three years so that they can start KS4 during, or even at the beginning of, Y9. If this is happening in your school, talk with teachers about the rationale for this and find out the advantages and disadvantages of such a strategy.

SUMMARY AND KEY POINTS

The National Curriculum in science is not just about pupils learning some well-established scientific facts; it extends to their understanding the nature of science as a subject that is based on evidence and imagination and argument. It also points to the need for pupils to develop the confidence to deal with scientific information and to ask appropriate questions in everyday contexts. You need to feel confident that you understand these demands of the National Curriculum so that you can be imaginative in creating the appropriate learning activities for pupils.

FURTHER READING

Lenton, G. and Stevens, B. (2000) 'Numeracy in science: understanding the misunderstandings', in Sear, J. and Sorensen, P. (eds) (2000) *Issues in Science Teaching.* London and New York: RoutledgeFalmer, pp. 80–88.

See also the themed issues of *School Science Review* given at the end of Unit 2.3. These have articles relevant for KS3 as well as KS4.

A selection of Key Stage 3 text books and resources

Association for Science Education, *Upd8 wikid*. Hatfield: ASE.

There is information about the course on: http://www.upd8.org.uk/upd8–wikid.php (accessed 7 August 2009) with sample material and a scheme of work. There is, of course, a fee for the full teaching materials.

Dawson, B. (series ed.), Billingsley, B., Mason, D., van der Welle, S., Butler, R., Lees, D., Lynn, W., Morris, S., Sloane, N., Smith, P. and Ward, H. (2008) *Go Science! 7, 8 and 9*. Harlow: Heinemann, Pearson Education.

The series includes: pupil books; a teacher planning and resource pack with CD-ROM; teacher LiveText with 35 free pupil CD-ROMs (including a VLE version); online assessment.

Gardom-Hulme, P., Large, P., Mitchell, S. and Sherry, C. (2008) *Science Works 1, 2 and 3*. Oxford: Oxford University Press.

This series includes: pupil books; resources and planning pack; interactive resources and planning OxBox CD-ROM; assessment OxBox CD-ROM.

Levesley, M., Clarke, J., Johnson, P., Baggley, S., Gray, S., Pimbert, M., Coates, A., Brand, I., Shepperd, E. and Smith, S. C. (2008) *Exploring Science: How Science Works 7, 8 and 9 for KS3*. Harlow: Longman, Pearson Education.

The pupil books contain a free support CD-ROM. The whole series includes an ActiveTeach CD-ROM with BBC Active Clips; an Assessing Pupils' Progress (APP) Teacher Pack; a Teacher and Technician Planning Guide; a Differentiated Classwork and Homework Activity Pack; a Formative and Summative Assessment Support Pack.

Walsh, E. (ed.), Greenway, T., Oliver, R. and Price, G. (ed.) (2008) *KS3 Science Book 1, 2, 3*. Glasgow: Collins Education, HarperCollins.

RELEVANT WEBSITES

QCA Qualifications and Curriculum Authority website for NC Science in England

http://www.qca.gov.uk

■ DfEE (Department for Education and Employment) and QCA (Qualifications and Curriculum Authority) (1999) *The National Curriculum in Science* (for the KS1 and KS2 science curriculum). http://curriculum.qca.org.uk/key-stages-1-and-2/subjects/index.aspx (accessed 7 August 2009). Note that this publication also contains the KS3 and KS4 programmes for 1999, which have been superseded and should not be used for the tasks.

■ *The National Curriculum in Science at KS3 and KS4*. http://curriculum.qca.org.uk/key-stages-3-and-4/subjects/index.aspx (accessed 7 August 2009).

Welsh Assembly Government (2008) *Key Stages 2–4 Science in the National Curriculum for Wales online*

http://wales.gov.uk/topics/educationandskills/curriculumassessment/arevisedcurriculum forwales/nationalcurriculum/sciencenc/?lang=en (accessed 10 August 2009)

Statutory Rules of Northern Ireland 2007 No.46 EDUCATION – The Education (Curriculum Minimum Content) Order (Northern Ireland) 2007

This gives the outline of the curriculum for all Key Stages (including the foundation stage (pre KS1)), http://www.opsi.gov.uk/sr/sr2007/nisr_20070046_en_1 (accessed 25 August 2009).

■ See also *The Statutory Curriculum at Key Stage 3: Supplementary Guidance*. http://www.nicurriculum.org.uk/key_stage_3/ (accessed 25 August 2009).

Scotland has an advisory, not a statutory, curriculum for the 5–14 age range.

http://www.ltscotland.org.uk/curriculumforexcellence/sciences/index.asp (accessed 12 January 2010).

National Strategies for Science

http://nationalstrategies.standards.dcsf.gov.uk/secondary/science (accessed 6 August 2009).

■ The webpage, 'aspects of learning' contains helpful guidance on each topic of the science curriculum, about teaching and learning, background information and 'barriers to learning'. The latter refer to the common misconceptions related to each topic. You are strongly advised to look at 'barriers to learning' for topics you teach.
http://nationalstrategies.standards.dcsf.gov.uk/search/results/nav%3A46223+facets%3A31768?page=1 (accessed 10 August 2009).

■ Yearly objectives for each of the topics, along with teaching strategies and 'rich questions'. http://nationalstrategies.standards.dcsf.gov.uk/search/results/%22rich+questions%22 (accessed 10 August 2009). You are strongly advised to look at the 'rich questions' for topics that you teach; they are useful for probing understanding and for getting pupils to think critically.

■ *Inclusion in Science.* http://nationalstrategies.standards.dcsf.gov.uk/search/secondary/results/nav:46129 (accessed 6 August 2009).

ASE (Association for Science Education)

http://www.ase.org.uk

ASE has a lot of resources for teachers (see e.g. Wikid, above) and *It Makes You Think*, below.

■ *It Makes you think* is an online set of downloadable resources for teaching the global dimensions of science.
http://www.ase.org.uk/htm/ase_global/ltr2009/itmakesyouthink/about.php (accessed 10 August 2009). See also September 2009 issue of *School Science Review* which is a themed issue on global dimensions.

SCIENCE 14–19

Jenny Frost

INTRODUCTION

The science curriculum in the 14–19 age range is designed to provide choice, have a wide appeal, and lead to a range of further study and employment. The courses provided lead to national qualifications in both applied and academic areas of science. 'Awarding bodies' (they used to be called 'examination boards') form a main source of information. They are responsible for creating and administering the specifications for courses and the related examinations and assessments within nationally agreed criteria. There are currently three awarding bodies in England (AQA, Edexcel, OCR), one in Wales (WJEC) and one in Northern Ireland (CCEA). Scotland has the Scottish Qualifications Authority (SQA), but the pattern of examinations is different there. Information about courses is available on their websites and for tasks in this unit you need to download course specifications (see *Relevant websites*).

While the 14–19 curriculum is increasingly being seen as a continuum (*14–19 Education and Skills White Paper,* 2005), 16 still remains the age limit for compulsory education, and the age at which the majority of pupils first sit for nationally recognised qualifications. For this reason 14–16 science is treated in this unit separately from 16–19.

OBJECTIVES

By the end of this unit you should:

- understand the guidelines of the National Curriculum in science at KS4
- be aware of the range and nature of science courses which are available to the 14–19 age range
- be able to distinguish key features of the different types of courses available.

14–16 SCIENCE

The main qualification that over 90 per cent of pupils in England, Wales and Northern Ireland seek in science is the General Certificate of Secondary Education (GCSE). Figure 2.3.1 gives the GCSE science courses most commonly provided in schools for this age range.

A. Compulsory
   GSCE *Science*

B. Additional Science. Pupils study only one of these additional subjects
   GCSE *Additional Science*
   GCSE *Additional Applied Science*

C. An alternative: Triple Science
   Triple Science: GCSE *Physics*, GCSE *Chemistry* and GCSE *Biology*

Pupils study either just A, or A and B, or just C. Triple Science contains all the course elements of A and B (*Additional Science*) plus some extra material.

Note: at the time of writing, Northern Ireland has 'single science' and 'double science' and is in consultation about changing to the pattern shown here.

■ **Figure 2.3.1** Commonest pattern of GCSE *Science* courses in the 14–16 age range

NC science at Key Stage 4

GCSE *Science*, the compulsory course, is based on the statutory programme of study of NC science at KS4, which is designed to enable young people to feel confident in their interactions with science in everyday life and to understand science as part of their cultural heritage. The 'knowledge, understanding and skills', therefore, relates to *How Science Works*, which has four strands:

- data, evidence, theories and explanations
- practical and enquiry skills
- communication skills
- applications and implications of science.

Task 2.3.1 requires that you analyse the nature of these strands.

Task 2.3.1 **Identifying the ideas in *How Science Works* at Key Stage 4**

Download the programme of study for NC science at KS4 (see *Relevant websites* at end of Unit 2.2). Each of the four strands of *How Science Works* are elaborated, through a series of sub-statements and by 'explanatory notes'.
   Underline key ideas in these.
   For each sub-statement, prepare a three-minute talk to explain it. Think up examples to illustrate your point. (This might work well as a group activity so that you share ideas with others.)
   You may well be able to draw on some of the ideas from Task 2.2.2.

Sixteen major scientific ideas (often referred to as explanatory stories) have been selected as the vehicle for *How Science Works*. Criteria for their selection were that they should allow people to understand, and be involved in, major debates in science and that they should represent our current understanding of how the natural world works. As with the KS3 curriculum, they are drawn from across the sciences. Familiarity with this breadth of science is important (see Task 2.3.2).

Task 2.3.2 **Familiarity with NC science: stories, evidence and arguments**

Judge your familiarity with the 16 scientific stories of NC science at KS4, by thinking about whether you could tell the science story well, whether you know the evidence on which it is based and whether you know the arguments that link the story with the evidence.

Use the Figure 2.3.2 to audit your knowledge.

Keep this in your professional portfolio and update it as the year progresses. Discuss areas for development with your mentor or tutor.

Construction of GCSE *Science*

To understand how a course can be constructed using the National Curriculum you are strongly recommended to look at *21st Century Science (C21)* (see *Relevant websites*), a course that was first developed as a pilot scheme to test the ideas of *Beyond 2000: Science Education for the Future* (Millar and Osborne, 1998). It was tried out in over 70 schools between 2003 and 2005 with sufficient success to support the decision to go forward with the new curriculum. C21 has two strands: 'key science explanations which help us to make sense of our lives'; and 'ideas about science which show how science works'. C21 is now just one of the courses available for GCSE science (examined by OCR) but as it was a pioneer of the new approach, its own website is a valuable source of the rationale behind the construction of the course.

Other examples of course construction can be seen in any of the GCSE *Science* specifications from the various awarding bodies. In the various GCSE *Science* courses you will find several ways of interweaving scientific concepts with *How Science Works*. The details of the specifications indicate both the key science concepts to be learned and the contexts to be discussed. Many include questions that might be useful for starting a topic and intriguing pupils (see, for example, the questions 'Have you ever wondered…?' on the Edexcel GCSE *Science* specification). In all courses, aims are specified, along with suggestions for applications that might be included, and links to publications that have been produced to support the teaching (pupils' textbooks, teachers' guides and associated ICT resources). Task 2.2.3 enables you to extract this information about the course running in your school and to compare it with one other specification.

		Science story	Evidence	Arguments
Organisms and health	a	Interdependence and adaptation to environment		
	b	Variation and evolution; classification		
	c	Functioning related to genes in cells		
	d	Control mechanisms in the body – optimal performance		
	e	Environmental and inherited factors causing variation in health, effect of drugs and medicines		
Chemical and material behaviour	a	Chemical change is caused by rearrangement of atoms		
	b	There are patterns in the chemical reactions between substances		
	c	New materials made from natural resources by chemical reactions		
	d	Properties of a material determines its uses		
Energy, electricity and radiation	a	Energy transfers can be measured and efficiency calculated; economic and environmental effects of energy use		
	b	Electrical power is readily transferred and easily controlled and can be used in a range of different situations		
	c	Radiations, including ionising radiations, can transfer energy		
	d	Radiations in the form of waves can be used for communication		
The environment, Earth and universe	a	Effects of human activity on the environment can be assessed using living and non-living indicators		
	b	The surface and the atmosphere of the Earth have changed since Earth's origin and are changing at present		
	c	The solar system is part of the universe, which has changed since its origin and continues to show long-term change.		

Audit your personal confidence in NC science at KS4 using the simple scheme of ✔ ? ✗ as explained below.

Story: I could explain the science story   confident ✔ not sure ? unfamiliar ✗

Evidence: I know the evidence on which this story is based   confident ✔ not sure ? unfamiliar ✗

Arguments: I know the arguments which link the evidence and the story   confident ✔ not sure ? unfamiliar ✗

■ **Figure 2.3.2** Auditing scientific knowledge and understanding

Task 2.3.3 Comparing the organisation of two different GCSE *Science* courses

Use the specifications of the GCSE *Science* course running in your school and the specification for GCSE *Science* from another awarding body.

1 For the two courses compare (noting similarities and differences):
   ■ the aims
   ■ module/topic headings
   ■ detail given in two or three of the modules/topics.
2 Analyse how confident you are with the content of the topics. What are the areas that you need to develop? Plan how you will develop your knowledge.
3 Find out from your school whether the course is taught by one teacher or whether it is shared between two or three teachers. How do they decide to split the modules/topics between teachers?
4 Are there work-related visits suggested?
5 Are there field work activities identified? What areas of science does the field work cover?
6 From this preliminary perusal of the specifications, is there one that you prefer? What are your reasons? Compare your findings with that of a fellow student teacher.

Keep notes you have made in your portfolio. They may well be useful when you apply for a post later.

GCSE *Additional Science* courses and GCSE *Triple Science*

The model suggested by *Beyond 2000: Science Education for the Future*, was that NC science be a core for everyone and lead to GCSE *Science*, and in addition pupils could study an additional subject that could be either 'concept led' or 'applications led'. The courses that are 'concept led' are referred to as GCSE *Additional Science*; those that are applications led are referred to as GCSE *Additional Applied Science*. There is no compulsion for pupils to take one of these additional courses, but it is obligatory for schools to provide at least one of them. The combination of *Science* and *Additional Science* provides sufficient background for pupils to proceed to the next level of study in science.

Task 2.3.4 Comparing GCSE *Additional Applied* and *Additional Science* courses

For any awarding body, compare the content of the specifications of GCSE *Additional Applied Science* and GCSE *Additional Science*. This is similar to Task 2.2.3.

1 Study and compare: the aims; module headings; resources; suggested contexts; and suggested visits for the two courses.
2 Which course would you like to have studied?

3 Which would you like to teach?
4 Find out whether your school offers both *Additional Science* and *Additional Applied Science*.
5 Who makes the choice about which course pupils take – teachers, pupils, parents…?
6 How is the teaching of these additional courses divided between teachers?

Keep notes you have made in your portfolio. They may well be useful when you apply for a post later.

Despite the recommendation of the *Beyond 2000* report to provide only the equivalent of two sciences at KS4, 'Triple Science' courses leading to qualifications in three separate sciences (GCSE *Physics*, *Chemistry* and *Biology*) are available and there is a belief (not entirely substantiated by evidence) that where pupils study all three sciences it increases the likelihood of them continuing with science later and of being successful. Schools that elect to offer Triple Science may do so instead of or as well as *Science* and *Additional Science*. The Triple Science course contains the material in *Core Science* and *Additional Science*, so that pupils studying Triple Science can be taught with other pupils for a large part of the course.

Task 2.3.5 'Extra science' in Triple Science (GCSE *Physics*, *Chemistry* and *Biology*)

1 Find out what additional material is taught in the Triple Science course. This information is easily accessible on the C21 website, but going to the specifications is another source of information.
2 If your school offers 'Triple Science' as well as *Science* and *Additional Science* courses, how are decisions made about which pupils study which courses? Do teachers or pupils make the decision?
3 How is Triple Science time-tabled alongside *Science* and *Additional Science*?
4 Is material available online via the school's intranet or e-learning environment?

While these courses are the mainstream GCSE courses in sciences found in schools in the 14–16 age range, they are not the only ones available. Figure 2.3.3 gives the list of all science courses that can be examined at this level.

Tiers of entry for GCSE courses

There are two tiers of entry for GCSE courses: foundation and higher. Foundation leads to grades within the C–G range and the higher tier leads to grades within the A–D range. If you have not already done so, look at how the course content for the two tiers is differentiated in the specifications. Talk with teachers about how they decide which pupils enter for which tier.

Science   Human Health and Physiology
Additional Science   Engineering
Additional Applied Science   Environmental science
*Applied Science (Double)   Astronomy
Physics   Health and Social Care
Chemistry   Environment and land based studies.
Biology

*Double applied science covers NC science at KS4

■ **Figure 2.3.3** GCSE qualifications in science subjects

Entry-level science courses

Science courses leading to an entry-level certificate are designed for those pupils in KS4 for whom a GCSE qualification seems inappropriate. They are aimed at the equivalent of NC science levels 1–3. The content of them, however, draws from NC science at KS4, leaving the possibility that pupils who make sufficient progress could be entered for GCSE later. In Task 2.3.6 you study how these courses are constructed. The entry-level course for OCR has been selected for comparison with either Edexcel or AQA entry-level science, because at the time of writing OCR has broken the course into 39 different small units, whereas the other awarding bodies have broken them into about 12.

Task 2.3.6 **Understanding entry-level science courses**

Use the OCR specification and one other for entry-level science. Find the sections on subject content/unit content.

1 Compare the titles of the units. How would you characterise the way the unit titles have been selected? Are they academic, work-related, life-related? Are they written to appeal to teenage culture?
2 What is the rationale for OCR having so many short units?
3 Activities in which pupils might be involved are included in OCR. Are they useful? Does the other specification also have them? Are they similar?
4 Are you familiar with all the subject matter? Where are your strengths? What are the areas you would need to develop?
5 Find out if your school offers an entry-level science course. Find out how decisions are made about who studies it. How often do pupils who start this course transfer later to a GCSE course?
6 Compare findings with those of other student teachers. Keep notes in your professional portfolio.

While courses leading to qualifications at entry level or GCSE are the main qualifications that you are likely to meet in schools, they are not the only ones. Courses leading to

BTEC (Business and Technical Education Council certificates and diplomas) and Diploma qualifications may also be found in the 14–16 age range (see below), and a few schools are offering AS Science (see below) courses to KS4 pupils.

16–19 SCIENCE

Science courses in the 16–19 age range can lead to a range of qualifications. They can include: GCSE; GCE AS and Advanced level; Diplomas, Foundation, Higher and Advanced; International Baccalaureate. There is no National Curriculum for this age group but all qualifications are constrained by national criteria (see *Relevant websites*) in order to provide comparability between courses from the different awarding bodies and to address the framework for the 16–19 curriculum as a whole.

General Certificate of Education (GCE), Advanced and Advanced subsidiary level, sciences

Traditionally, courses leading to GCE Advanced level were two-year courses (typically started at the beginning of Y12, age 16, and completed at the end of Y13, age 18) with an examination at the end. It was common for pupils to study a narrow range of often closely related subjects (e.g. common combinations were physics, chemistry and maths; or chemistry, biology and physics). GCE courses have now been divided into two, with the first-year course leading to an AS level qualification. The addition of the second-year course (referred to as A2) leads to the Advanced level qualification. The rationale for the change included the wish to increase the breadth of education, so pupils might now study as many as five or six subjects to AS and continue with only three or four to A-level. As with GCSE courses, there are national criteria for science courses that are revised every five or six years. They were last changed for teaching in 2008. These changes were partly occasioned by the introduction of *How Science Works* into GCSE; this aspect of science now features more widely in GCE courses as well.

Figure 2.3.4 shows the science courses available for the AS and A-level awards from one or more of the awarding bodies at the time of writing.

Science (OCR, AS only)

Science for Public Understanding (AQA)

Applied Science (AQA, OCR, WJEC)

Electronics (AQA, OCR, WJEC)

Physics (AQA, CCEA, Edexel, OCR, WJEC)

Chemistry (AQA, CCEA, Edexel, OCR, WJEC)

Biology (AQA, CCEA, Edexel, OCR, WJEC)

Human Biology (AQA, OCR, WJEC)

Environmental science (AQA)

Geology (OCR, WJEC)

Human Biology (AQA, OCR, WJEC)

Psychology (AQA, Edexel, OCR, WJEC)

Note 1: There can be more than one specification for each of biology, chemistry and physics from an awarding body.

Note 2: Edexcel offers applied science and engineering through its BTEC higher national programmes, not through GCE programmes.

■ **Figure 2.3.4** Science courses available at GCE A and AS level

The following task will help you identify characteristics of three courses.

Task 2.3.7 **Comparison between three GCE specifications: Physics or Chemistry or Biology with a) Science for Public Understanding and b) Applied Science**

1 Study the specification of a single science A-level (Physics, Chemistry or Biology), related to your own specialism. Look at aims and range of content. How familiar are you with the content? What knowledge and understanding would you need to develop if you were asked to teach it?
2 Compare it with (i) Science for Public Understanding, and (ii) Applied Science.
3 Is there any overlap between the courses? Are there any aims in common? What about content?
4 What are the substantial differences between the three courses?
5 Write a short summary and put it in your development portfolio. Discuss with mentors how decisions were made about which courses to teach.

BTEC, Nationals and Diplomas

BTEC (offered by Edexcel), and Nationals (offered by OCR), and Diplomas (all awarding bodies) are either work-based or work-related qualifications. They aim to provide education through a more practically based, work-oriented experience than has traditionally been available in many schools. Of these qualifications, the Diploma is the most recent and so far the only science-related diplomas are in Environment and Land Based Management and Engineering. There is a proposal for a diploma in science for foundation and higher levels (these are equivalent to the Foundation and Higher levels of GCSE) but at the time of writing the start date has been delayed to beyond 2011 (see *Relevant websites*). In due course, there is an intention to develop diploma qualifications at the Advanced level (comparable with GCE Advanced and AS levels). Like the Applied courses, these will involve visits to places of work, and hence require considerable liaison with industrial and scientific enterprises. The diploma, unlike GCE, is not a single-subject education – it involves a much wider curriculum.

International Baccalaureate and other baccalaureates

The baccalaureate is also not a single-subject qualification, but a more holistic education. The International Baccalaurreate diploma for 16–19-year-olds is composed of a core and six subject groups. The core is compulsory and comprises:

■ extended essay
■ theory of knowledge
■ creativity, action and service.

The subject groups are:

- language A1
- second language
- individuals and society
- experimental sciences
- mathematics and computer science
- the arts.

There are choices within the subject groups. Normally pupils study three subjects at standard level and three at higher level. It is not possible to study three sciences within the IB, but two are possible.

The specifications are only available to schools registered for the IB. However, if you are in a school offering this, find out more about it and the reasons the school has for using these courses. You are more likely to find the IB in independent and internationl schools than in state schools. The IB is not covered by statutory legislation, so information about it is not on any of the government websites.

Wales and Northern Ireland offer the Welsh and Irish Baccalaureate, respectively. Information is available on the respective awarding body websites.

SUMMARY AND KEY POINTS

The aim of the 14–19 White Paper was to open up a range of learning pathways for 14–19-year-olds in order to encourage most 16–19-year-olds to stay in full-time education. Only GCSE science is now compulsory and is governed by the NC science at KS4. The development of a range of science courses, and the increase in applied and vocationally orentied courses provide an illustration of varied learning pathways in science. The story is an evolving one; further developments and changes can be expected in your time as a science teacher.

The external assessment of these courses is dealt with in Unit 6.2.

FURTHER READING

Erduran, S. (2007) (ed.) *School Science Review*, 88 (324), 29–90. Hatfield: Association for Science Education.

The special theme for this edition was 'Argument, discourse and interactivity', a theme chosen in response to new demands of the National Curriculum.

Hanley, P., Osborne, J. and Ratcliffe, M. (2008) 'Twenty-first century science'. *School Science Review*, 90 (330), 105–112.

The authors give an account of research into how teachers and pupils adapted to the demands of a course based on scientific literacy.

Hollins, M. (2006) 'Science education 14–19', in Wood-Robinson, V. (ed.) *ASE Guide to Secondary Science Education*. Hatfield: The Association for Science Education, pp. 56–62.

Hollins, M. (2007) *School Science Review 2007*, 89 (326), 25–91. Hatfield: Association for Science Education.

The theme 'Beyond core science' provides a collection of articles that illuminate the debates about the nature of the science curriculum. It contains arguments for the inclusion of earth sciences, electronics, engineering and psychology.

Murray, C. (2007) 'Reflections on the UK National Curriculum'. *School Science Review*, 88 (325), 119–123.

An interesting account of how it was only through teaching in another country (Zambia) that the author realised how much ideas about teaching and learning in science had progressed in the UK.

Wardle, J. (2009) (ed.) *School Science Review*, 90 (332), 29–94. Hatfield: Association for Science Education.

The theme of this edition was 'Creativity in science'. It was produced in response to the new science curriculum requiring teachers to help pupils understand creativity in science, and to learn to be creative themselves.

RELEVANT WEBSITES

For National Curriculum websites see Unit 2.2.

Science for the 21st Century

http://www.21stcenturyscience.org/ (accessed 30 June 2009).

Awarding bodies in England, Wales, Northern Ireland and Scotland

AQA (Assessment and Qualifications Alliance)

http://www.aqa.org.uk (accessed 25 August 2009).

Edexcel

http://www.edexcel.com (accessed 25 August 2009).

OCR (Oxford, Cambridge and Royal Society of Arts)

http://www.ocr.org.uk (accessed 25 August 2009).

WJEC (Welsh Joint Examining Council)

http://www.wjec.co.uk (accessed 25 August 2009).

CCEA (Council for the Curriculum, Examinations and Assessment)

http://www.rewardinglearning.org.uk/ (accessed 25 August 2009).

Scottish Qualifications Authority

http://www.sqa.org.uk/sqa/1.html (accessed 25 August 2009).

International Baccalaureate

http://www.ibo.org (accessed 18 August 2009).

Ofqual (Office of the Qualifications and Examinations Regulator) for criteria

National Criteria for GCE sciences can be downloaded

http://www.ofqual.gov.uk/743.aspx (accessed 18 August 2009).

National Criteria for GCE sciences can be downloaded

http://www.ofqual.gov.uk/471.aspx (accessed 18 August 2009).

Department for Children, Schools and Families

http://dcsf.gov.uk

14–19 Education and Skills White Paper 2005. **Norwich: HMSO**

http://publications.dcsf.gov.uk/default.aspx?PageFunction=productdetails&PageMode=publications&ProductId=CM+6476& (accessed 13 Aug 2009).

QCA (Qualifications and Curriculum Authority) (2009) *Criteria for the Diploma Qualifications at Foundation and Higher Levels:* **QCA Consultation Document**

http://www.qcda.gov.uk/21855.aspx (accessed 25 August 2009).

QCDA (Qualifications and Curriculum Development Agency) consulation about new criteria for GCSE science (applicable from 2011)

http://www.qcda.gov.uk/21855.aspx (accessed 18 August 2009).

GETTING TO GRIPS WITH SCIENCE

INTRODUCTION

The aim of this chapter is to give an overview of the main ideas that are covered in school science; both how science works and scientific theories and principles. There is no attempt to make this like a textbook because there are plenty of good textbooks (and of course the internet) for more detailed information. The authors have not indicated, either, the levels of explanation that are appropriate for different age groups, but they have directed you to texts that do this. Hopefully, the units, taken as a whole, will help you to keep a sense of the bigger picture of science, so that when you are teaching any particular topic you are aware of where it fits into this larger picture. The chapter has five units: Unit 3.1 The nature of science; Unit 3.2 Biology; Unit 3.3 Chemistry, Unit 3.4 Physics and astronomy; and Unit 3.5 Earth science.

The chapter is also intended to help those of you who are trying to broaden your own knowledge of science, in order to cope with the breadth of the science curriculum. The majority of students find the exploration of areas of science that have been forgotten, or perhaps have never been properly studied, a source of immense personal satisfaction. In the process they often find they become sensitive to the particular difficulties that the different areas present and, as a result, are more aware of the challenges that their pupils face. For more detailed knowledge, go to textbooks and the internet. The authors have listed a few textbooks, but there are many other excellent ones. Explore several to find ones that you like. It is wise to select those with questions to try, and also answers.

THE NATURE OF SCIENCE

Michael Reiss

INTRODUCTION

In the UK, most university students who study science are taught little explicitly about the nature of science. And yet the science National Curriculum in England requires pupils to be taught about 'how science works'. Perhaps unsurprisingly, research evidence suggests that most pupils leave school with a somewhat lop-sided knowledge of this area of science.

This unit explains what is meant by the terms 'how science works' and 'the nature of science'. It looks at whether science always proceeds by the objective and rigorous testing of hypotheses, or whether there are other factors at play in deciding whether one scientific view comes to hold sway within the scientific community over alternatives.

Within schools, there are different views about the nature of science among both pupils and science teachers. These different views are important in terms of how people see scientific knowledge. Ways of getting at people's views of the nature of science are given below. It is hoped that these will be of interest and lead to richer teaching and learning in this area. This is important as it can be argued that long after pupils have forgotten much of the content of science that they are taught at school, they will still hold a view as to how science is done and whether scientific knowledge is trustworthy or not.

OBJECTIVES

By the end of this unit you should be able to:

■ distinguish between alternative understandings of how science is carried out
■ contrast science as undertaken by scientists and science as undertaken in school science lessons
■ help your pupils develop a deeper understanding of the nature of science.

Check the requirements of your course to see which relate to this unit.

WHAT DO WE MEAN BY HOW SCIENCE WORKS AND THE NATURE OF SCIENCE?

In the science National Curriculum, 'how science works' is described under four headings:

■ data, evidence, theories and explanations
■ practical and enquiry skills
■ communication skills
■ applications and implications of science.

This covers a lot of ground. 'The nature of science' refers to a subset of these four bullet points as it is used as a shorthand for something like 'how science is done and what sorts of things scientists research'. It doesn't really cover communication skills or much about the applications and implications of skills, important as these are. These areas of *How Science Works* are covered elsewhere in this book.

WHAT DO SCIENTISTS STUDY?

It is difficult to come up with a definitive answer to the question 'What do scientists study?'. Certain things clearly fall under the domain of science – the nature of electricity, the arrangement of atoms into molecules, and human physiology, to give three examples. However, what about the origin of the universe, the behaviour of people in society, decisions about whether we should build nuclear power plants or go for wind power, the appreciation of music and the nature of love, for example? Do these fall under the domain of science? A small number of scientists would argue 'yes' to all of these, and the term *scientism* is used, pejoratively, to refer to the view that science can provide sufficient explanations for everything.

However, most people hold that science is but one form of knowledge and that other forms of knowledge complement science. This way of thinking means that the origin of the universe is also a philosophical or even a religious question – or simply unknowable; the behaviour of people in society requires knowledge of the social sciences (e.g. psychology and sociology) rather than only of the natural sciences; whether we should go for nuclear or wind power is partly a scientific issue but also requires an understanding of economics, risk and politics; the appreciation of music and the nature of love, while clearly having something to do with our perceptual apparatuses and our evolutionary history, cannot be reduced to science.

While historians tell us that what scientists study changes over time, there are reasonable consistencies:

■ Science is concerned with the natural world and with certain elements of the manufactured world – so that, for example, the laws of gravity apply as much to artificial satellites as they do to planets and stars.
■ Science is concerned with how things are rather than with how they should be. So there is a science of gunpowder and *in vitro* fertilisation without science telling us whether warfare and test-tube births are good or bad.

HOW IS SCIENCE DONE?

If it is difficult to come up with a definitive answer to the question 'What do scientists study?'. It is even more difficult to come up with a clear-cut answer to the question 'How is science done?'. Indeed, there is, and has been for many decades, active disagreement on this matter among academic historians, philosophers and sociologists of science. A useful point to start is with the views of Robert Merton and Karl Popper. In my experience, most working scientists have almost no interest in and know little about the philosophy and sociology of science. However, they do like the views of Merton and Popper once these are explained to them – though they generally think their arguments so obvious as not to need stating. The same working scientists are a great deal less keen on the views of Thomas Kuhn and others, to which we shall come in due course.

Robert Merton characterised science as open-minded, universalist, disinterested and communal (Merton, 1973). For Merton, science is a group activity: even though certain scientists work on their own, all scientists contribute to a single body of knowledge accepted by the community of scientists. There are certain parallels here with art, literature and music. After all, Cézanne, Gauguin and van Gogh all contributed to post-impressionism. But while it makes no sense to try to combine their paintings, science is largely about combining the contributions of many different scientists to produce an overall coherent model of one aspect of reality. In this sense, science is disinterested; in *this* sense it is (or should be) impersonal.

Of course, individual scientists are passionate about their work and often slow to accept that their cherished ideas are wrong. But science itself is not persuaded by such partiality. While there may be controversy about whether the works of Bach or Mozart are the greater (and the question is pretty meaningless anyway), time (almost) invariably shows which of two alternative scientific theories is nearer the truth. For this reason, while scientists need to retain 'open-mindedness', always being prepared to change their views in the light of new evidence or better explanatory theories, science itself advances (though not uniformly) over time. As a result, while some scientific knowledge ('frontier science') is contentious, much scientific knowledge ('core science') can confidently be relied on: it is relatively certain.

Karl Popper emphasised the falsifiability of scientific theories (Popper, 1934/1972). Unless you can imagine collecting data that would allow you to refute a theory, the theory isn't scientific. The same applies to scientific hypotheses. So the hypothesis 'All swans are white' is scientific because we can imagine finding a bird that is manifestly a swan (in terms of its appearance and behaviour) but is not white. Indeed, this is precisely what happened when early white explorers returned from Australia with tales of black swans (Figure 3.1.1).

Popper's ideas easily give rise to a view of science in which knowledge steadily accumulates over time as new theories are proposed and new data collected to discriminate between conflicting theories. Much school experimentation in science is Popperian in essence: we see a rainbow and hypothesise that white light is split up into light of different colours as it is refracted through a transparent medium (water droplets); we test this by attempting to refract white light through a glass prism; we find the same colours of the rainbow are produced and our hypothesis is confirmed. Until some new evidence causes it to be falsified (refuted), we accept it.

There is much of value in the work of Thomas Merton and Karl Popper but most academics in the field would argue that there is more to the nature of science. We turn to

■ **Figure 3.1.1** Black swans (*cygnus atratus*) are native to Australia. Until they became known to people in the West the statement 'All swans are white' was thought to be true. Now we say that it is both falsifiable (i.e. capable of being falsified) and false. Karl Popper argued that scientific statements, hypotheses and theories all need to be falsifiable.

the work of Thomas Kuhn (Kuhn, 1970). Thomas Kuhn made a number of seminal contributions but he is most remembered nowadays by his argument that while the Popperian account of science holds well during periods of *normal science* when a single paradigm holds sway, such as the Ptolemaic model of the structure of the solar system (in which the Earth is at the centre) or the Newtonian understanding of motion and gravity, it breaks down when a scientific *crisis* occurs. At the time of such a crisis, a scientific revolution happens during which a new paradigm, such as the Copernican model of the structure of the solar system or Einstein's theory of relativity, begins to replace the previously accepted paradigm. The central point is that the change of allegiance from scientists believing in one paradigm to their believing in another cannot, Kuhn argues, be fully explained by the Popperian account of falsifiability.

Kuhn likens the switch from one paradigm to another to a *gestalt* switch (when we suddenly see something in a new way) or even a religious conversion. As Alan Chalmers puts it:

> There will be no purely logical argument that demonstrates the superiority of one paradigm over another and that thereby compels a rational scientist to make the change. One reason why no such demonstration is possible is the fact that a variety of factors are involved in a scientist's judgment of the merits of a scientific theory. An individual scientist's decision will depend on the priority he or she gives to the various factors. The factors will include such things as simplicity, the connection with some pressing social need, the ability to solve some specified kind of problem, and so on. Thus one scientist might be attracted to the Copernican theory because of the simplicity of certain mathematical features of it. Another might be attracted to it because in it there is the possibility of calendar reform. A third might have been deterred from adopting the Copernican theory because of an involvement with terrestrial mechanics and an awareness of the problems that the Copernican theory posed for it.

(Chalmers, 1999: 115–16)

Kuhn also argued that scientific knowledge is validated by its acceptance in a community of scientists. Often scientists change their views as new evidence persuades them that a previously held theory is wrong. But sometimes they cling obstinately to cherished theories. In such cases, if these scientists are powerful (e.g. by controlling what papers get published in the most prestigious journals), scientific progress may be impeded – until the scientists in question retire or die!

In a unit of this length there clearly isn't space to provide an account of many other views of how science is done, but there is one philosopher of science whom you will either love or hate – Paul Feyerabend. In many ways Feyerabend anticipated the post-modernists with their suspicion of a single authoritative account of reality. His views are succinctly summed up in the title of his most famous book, *Against Method* (Feyerabend, 1975/1988). Feyerabend is something of an intellectual anarchist (another of his books is called *Farewell to Reason*) and the best way to understand him is to read *him* rather than too tidy a *summary* of him. Here are a few quotes to whet your appetite:

> No theory ever agrees with all the facts in its domain, yet it is not always the theory that is to blame. Facts are constituted by older ideologies, and a clash between facts and theories may be proof of progress.
>
> (Feyerabend, 1993: 39)

> The events, procedures and results that constitute the sciences have no common structure.
>
> (Feyerabend, 1993: 1)

> The success of 'science' cannot be used as an argument for treating as yet unsolved problems in a standardized way.
>
> (Feyerabend, 1993: 2)

> There can be many different kinds of science. People starting from different social backgrounds will approach the world in different ways and learn different things about it.
>
> (Feyerabend, 1993: 2–3)

Task 3.1.1 **Getting pupils to consider the scope of science**

It is all too easy for pupils to take for granted that they get taught different 'things' in their different subjects in school. The aim of this task is to help pupils to become more aware of why there are certain things they study in science lessons as opposed to other lessons.

You can start by having a discussion with pupils about whether there are some things in science that they also learn about in other subjects (e.g. rocks in geography, muscles and breathing in PE, sound in music). Then get them, perhaps in pairs or small groups, to talk about the similarities and differences between what they get taught about in geography and what they get taught about in science. Pupils should end up appreciating that there are overlaps but that science is more interested in experiments, is more universal (so that most science is much the same in any country whereas geography is very interested in differences between countries) and has less to say about human action unless such action can be studied objectively.

Task 3.1.2 **What is your view of the nature of science?**

There have been a number of research instruments devised to enable a person's views on the nature of science to be determined. Probably the easiest for you to get hold of and use is that provided by two leading UK science educators – Mick Nott and Jerry Wellington (Nott and Wellington, 1993). If you quite enjoy reading questionnaires along the lines of 'Does your partner find you boring?' in the backs of magazines while at the dentist, this task is for you. Once you have completed this questionnaire, reflect on *why* the scoring system came up with the result it did. Do you feel content with your view of the nature of science? How would your answers have needed to differ for you to have been classified differently? Discuss whether there is a single ideal view of the nature of science that science teachers should hold.

'REAL SCIENCE' COMPARED TO SCHOOL SCIENCE

There is much in the 5–16 science National Curriculum in England with which to be pleased. However, one of the less successful areas is what is now (July 2009) called 'Practical and enquiry skills'. For one thing, we don't do a very good job of getting children in school science lessons to ask the sorts of questions that scientists actually ask or to ask the sorts of questions that the rest of us ask and to which science can make a contribution. Instead, pupils are too often restricted to uninteresting questions about the bouncing of squash balls or the dissolving of sugar in what are misleadingly termed 'scientific investigations'.

The history of this part of the science curriculum since the first National Curriculum Science Working Group, which published its report in 1987, up to the year 2000 has been analysed by Jim Donnelly (2001). Donnelly argues convincingly that two conflicting understandings of the nature of science can be detected in the battles of those years (and they felt much like battles to those participating in them). One is what Donnelly terms 'essentially empiricist'; in other words, straightforwardly concerned with how factual data are collected with which to test hypotheses. The other stresses social and cultural influences on science. In the language of the first part of this unit, this is a contest between Popper and Kuhn (Feyerabend doesn't get a look in!).

The reasons for this battle need not greatly concern us except in so far as the very existence of the battle indicates the lack of consensus in this area among those responsible for the science National Curriculum. This contrasts with many other parts of the science National Curriculum. There is, for example, little controversy over the inclusion of food chains, melting and series circuits.

Much school science operates on the assumption that 'real science' only consists in doing replicated laboratory experiments to test hypotheses. When I started teaching social biology to 16–19-year-olds in England, the examinations board (it was in the mid-80s, before awarding bodies) that set the syllabus included a project. One of my students was a very fit athlete who lived in Bahrain out of term time. He undertook measurements on himself of such physiological variables as body temperature and body mass just before and just after completing a number of runs both in the UK and in Bahrain under very different environmental conditions. Another student was interested to see whether a person's astrological sign (determined by their birth date) correlated with their choice of school subjects at advanced level (e.g. sciences versus arts) or with their personalities. Accordingly, she carried out a large survey of fellow students.

Both students had their projects scored at 0 per cent. Nor were these marks changed on appeal. I'm not claiming that either of these projects was the finest I have ever seen; but I am convinced that the marks they were given reflected too narrow an assumption in the examiners' minds about what constituted a valid piece of scientific enquiry (Reiss, 1993).

Those who write science curricula and mark students' work are powerful determinants of what passes in school for 'real science'. A more valid approach to finding out what science actually consists of is to study what real scientists do. Careful ethnographic work on this only began in the 1970s – the classic book is Latour and Woolgar (1979). Much of this writing is rather difficult to read and it's much easier to read any really good biographical account of a scientist – though such biographies, in concentrating on individuals, do rather give rise to the 'great scientists' view of scientific progress.

The take-home message from the ethnographic work on science is that while scientific practice is partly characterised by the Mertonian and Popperian norms discussed above, there is plenty of support for Kuhn's views and even for Feyerabend's. For example, school accounts of the science often underplay the political realities of scientific research (not to mention the monotony of much of it). Nowadays governments and companies are far more interested in funding work on genetic modification than research into moss reproduction. Actually, it's the exception that proves the rule. If your moss only lives in Antarctica, the chances are that you will get funding as many countries are keen to undertake research there to stake a territorial claim should the wilderness ever be exploited for natural reserves.

Task 3.1.3 **Get pupils to research how science is done**

Get your pupils to research using books in the school library or internet sources one example of the history and practice of science. For example, at KS4 you might get pupils to research one of:

■ the theory of evolution
■ Rosalind Franklin's contribution to determining the structure of DNA
■ *in vitro* fertilisation
■ the Periodic Table
■ the history of glass
■ plate tectonics
■ the competition between DC and AC among domestic suppliers of electricity
■ the life and work of Galileo
■ the use of X-rays.

This exercise works best if pupils have a choice about what to work on and have some opportunities to work collaboratively.

PUPILS' VIEWS OF THE NATURE OF SCIENCE

In the UK, the most detailed research carried out on pupils' views on the nature of science dates from 1991 to 1993, i.e. in the early years of the National Curriculum. The work was carried out on 9-, 12- and 16-year-olds in England and came up with the following findings (Driver *et al.,* 1996):

■ Pupils tend to see the purpose of science as providing solutions to technical problems rather than providing more powerful explanations.

■ Pupils rarely appreciate that scientific explanations can involve postulating models. Even when they do, models are presumed to map onto events in the world in an unproblematic manner.

■ Pupils rarely see science as a social enterprise. Scientists are seen as individuals working in isolation.

■ Pupils have little awareness of the ways that society influences decisions about research agendas. The most common view is that scientists, through their personal altruism, choose to work on particular problems of concern to society.

One technique that has been used to examine how pupils see science is to ask them to draw a scientist (Figure 3.1.2). The drawings are then examined to see whether pupils tend to draw scientists as male or female, white or black, in laboratories or in other settings etc. It has been suggested that the images produced are becoming less stereotypical, show less gender bias and are more realistic (Matthews, 1996).

Task 3.1.4 **Get pupils to do the 'draw a scientist' test**

Get your pupils to do the 'draw a scientist' test. (This probably works better at KS3 than at KS4.) Explain to them before they start their drawings that this isn't a test in the sense of some people gaining more marks than others and that you aren't interested in the artistic quality of their drawings. Ensure they write their names on the back of the drawing (in case you want to analyse the results by gender, ethnicity, performance in science or something else that requires knowledge at the individual level).

Usually researchers get pupils to do this individually but you might decide that it would be interesting to get pupils to discuss in pairs what they are going to put in their drawings before they do them.

If you want to go beyond what most researchers do you might:

■ require pupils to write a few paragraphs explaining why they drew what they drew
■ interview pupils about their drawings
■ try to untangle whether pupils are really drawing what they think scientists are like or whether they are drawing stereotypes or caricatures.

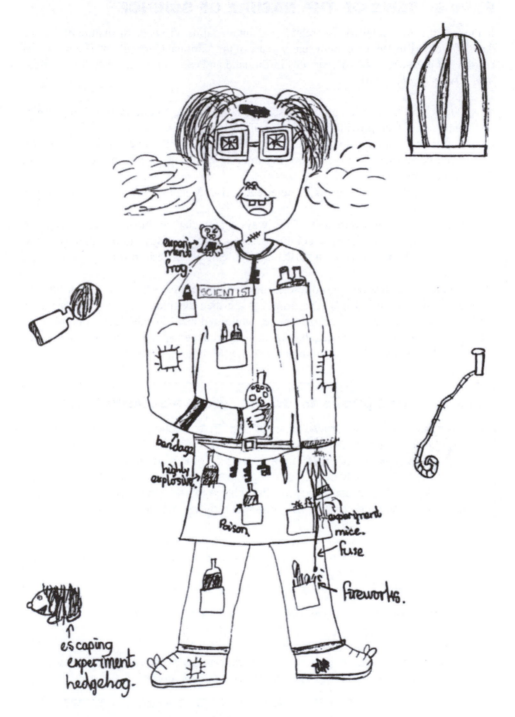

■ **Figure 3.1.2** Caroline Allen's drawing of a scientist

SUMMARY AND KEY POINTS

Science is concerned with the natural world, with certain elements of the manufactured world and with how things *are* rather than with how they should be.

The nature of science is a controversial area and there are several competing understandings of how scientific knowledge is produced. Robert Merton sees science as open-minded, universalist, disinterested and communal. For Karl Popper, the distinctive thing about science is that all its ideas are testable and so falsifiable. Thomas Kuhn goes beyond these views in seeing certain crucial episodes in the history of science as inexplicable within Mertonian and Popperian thinking. Kuhn stresses that when scientists switch from one way of seeing the world to another, i.e. as the paradigm changes, they do so for a variety of reasons not all of which are scientific in the narrow sense of the term.

Pupils generally have rather a limited understanding of the nature of science. The tasks presented here are intended to help deepen their understanding.

Check which requirements for your course have been addressed through this unit.

FURTHER READING

Chalmers, A. F. (1999) *What Is This Thing Called Science?*, **3rd edition. Buckingham: Open University Press.**

An extremely clear and very widely read introductory textbook on the philosophy of science – readable and dealing with the major questions on the nature of science.

Kind, V. and Kind, P. M. (2008) *Teaching Secondary: How Science Works*. **London: Hodder Education.**

A well written and intelligent overview of the various strands of *How Science Works* at both Key Stage 3 and 4. Comes with a very useful CD-ROM that contains pupil worksheets.

Kuhn, T. S. (1970) *The Structure of Scientific Revolutions*, **2nd edition. Chicago: University of Chicago Press.**

A classic in the history and philosophy of science. This is the book which undermined the straightforward Popperian view of science and convincingly argued for the importance of culture in the growth of scientific knowledge. Kuhn introduced the notion of paradigms in science.

Roberts, R. (2009) 'How Science Works' (HSW), *Education in Science*, **233: 30–31.**

A useful introduction to recent research on *How Science Works*.

RELEVANT WEBSITES

National Strategies

http://www.nationalstrategies.standards.dcsf.gov.uk/node/102668?uc=force_uj (accessed 4 July 2009).

Guidance about *How Science Works*.

Qualifications and Curriculum Development Agency

http://www.qcda.gov.uk/7605.aspx (accessed 4 July 2009).

Useful websites about *How Science Works*.

BIOLOGY

Katherine Little

INTRODUCTION

The study of biology in schools is mainly concerned with green plants and animals, meaning that there are only slightly more than a million organisms to come to terms with. However, because life on Earth has a single origin, all living things share common characteristics: they respire, reproduce, respond to their surroundings, move, excrete waste, take in nutrients and grow. Therefore, by understanding some basic concepts, it is possible to extend and apply ideas to a wide range of organisms.

OBJECTIVES

By the end of this unit you should be aware of:

- key concepts in biology
- the distinctive features of living things
- the role evolution plays in explaining how our living environment came to be as it is
- some of the experiments carried out, observations made and theories proposed by natural scientists that have advanced our understanding of living things.

CELLS AND DNA

One of the most fundamental and important ideas in biology is that all living things are made of cells. So called by Robert Hooke, observing that the tissue of cork resembled the regular bare cells of monks under the microscope, it has since been found that, far from empty, cells contain many components. Though contents of cells differ – from mammalian nerve cells to photosynthetic plant cells, muscle cells to sex cells – they all share essential constituents, including a nucleus, cell membrane and cytoplasm.

The nucleus contains a cell's chromosomes along which a complete set of instructions for its life are arranged as beads on a string in the genes, written in the four-letter code of DNA. Genes are translated into proteins, which are responsible for the functioning of a cell.

The genetic code is the same in all organisms, allowing the technology of genetic engineering: for example, a bacterial cell can be induced to produce human insulin by the insertion of the human insulin gene into its DNA strand. Within an organism, different types of cells function differently because different genes are 'switched on'; between organisms there are differences in the forms, or alleles, of genes; for example, that which controls blood group. When genes, chromosomes and gametes become so different that they are incompatible, two different species are considered to exist. However, because of the common ancestry of living things, all living organisms share a wide range of cellular reactions governed by the same genes. For example, we share 98 per cent of our DNA with chimpanzees, our closest relative, but also share 60 per cent with mice. DNA technology is increasingly used in taxonomy, as it is possible to calculate how recently each different species has diverged from another.

DNA is copied faithfully during cell replication by enzymes. The double helix structure, proposed by Watson and Crick in 1953, lends itself to carrying information as one strand complements the other, allowing proofreading of the new strands to occur. Depending upon the type of cell division, the daughter cells may be identical (mitosis), or genetically different (meiosis). In sexual reproduction the number of chromosomes is reduced by half in the gametes (the name given to male and female sex cells, either the sperm and egg, or contents of pollen and ovules). At fertilisation, the full number of chromosomes is restored, giving rise to an organism that has inherited half of its mother's and half of its father's genes. In this way, the genetic essence of an individual can be passed down through generations.

If the sole purpose of an organism's existence is to pass its genes to future generations, then the complexity of life shows the variety of ways in which this can be achieved. There are over 1.2 million named living species of animals, with estimates of 20 times that number still to be discovered. Add to that the other kingdoms – plants, fungi, protists and monera – and numbers of up to a billion species have been proposed. Plants and animals, the kingdoms concentrated on in school biology, represent two main groups of organisms; the first is able to produce its own source of food while the second is dependent upon the first for its supply of nutrients.

PLANTS AS THE POWERHOUSES OF THE LIVING WORLD: PHOTOSYNTHESIS

In 1648, Jan Baptista van Helmont, a Flemish scientist, planted a willow tree in a pot in the first recorded quantitative experiment. After five years, he observed that its mass had increased by 74kg but the soil had only lost 60g. He concluded that water was the source of the extra mass and also the plant's source of life. Subsequent experimentation by Joseph Priestley and Jan Ingenhausz demonstrated that plants produce oxygen and need sunlight to do so. It became apparent that green plants, often overlooked as inanimate and rather dull, are the powerhouses of the living world. Without the ability of these plants to harness the energy in sunlight, the carbon-based living world would rapidly cease to exist. This most crucial of chemical reactions, photosynthesis (literally, building up by light), occurs in every green leaf. Simple molecules of carbon dioxide, from the air, and water, absorbed through the plant's roots, are combined in the leaf using the Sun's energy captured by the green pigment chlorophyll to form glucose, a sugar built around six carbon atoms. The energy in the glucose-oxygen system then becomes available for the plant (a producer) and any animal (a consumer) that might use that plant as a food source.

Additionally, glucose can be polymerised into starch or glycogen for food storage, or cellulose for structural use in plant cell walls. Alternatively, they may combine with other molecules to form either amino acids, the building blocks of proteins, or fats and lipids. Proteins are structurally important (for example, skin and hair contain the protein keratin) and have a vital role as biological catalysts in their action as enzymes. Fats and lipids are the main constituent of cell membranes and are also used for long-term food storage; both walnuts and polar bears depend on their high energy content. Without photosynthesis to capture the Sun's energy, there would be no glucose production, nor its subsequent conversion into more complex biological molecules, and no atmospheric oxygen; hence it is true to say that the natural world is driven by sunlight.

SUPPLYING ENERGY: RESPIRATION

The majority of organisms respire aerobically, that is they combine glucose with oxygen to create a supply of energy that can be used to drive cellular reactions. The reactions of aerobic respiration occur in the mitochondria, organelles dedicated to the oxidation of glucose and the simultaneous formation of adenosine triphosphate, or ATP, the biological currency of cellular energy. Carbon dioxide and water are produced as waste products. This process occurs in every living cell, and the number of mitochondria is indicative of how active a cell is; muscle fibres and intestinal epithelial cells are packed full. Anaerobic respiration can take place under extreme conditions when oxygen is less plentiful, but the amount of energy released is far less. In very small organisms oxygen and glucose needs can be met by simple diffusion of molecules from the external to the internal environment. However, as the size of an organism increases, the surface area-to-volume ratio is reduced, so not every cell can meet its requirements by diffusion. Large organisms have therefore evolved complex systems for the transport of vital molecules to the cells and to remove potentially toxic waste products from them.

TRANSPORTATION OF MATERIAL

Both plants and animals use the process of mass transport to move large amounts of substances. Animals' transport systems are often typified by the example of the mammalian heart (demonstrating the often human-centred view of biology). In this system, the heart, a mechanical pump, moves the transport medium, blood, around the body in a system of arteries, capillaries and veins. These specialised vessels bring the blood's contents into close contact with every single cell, from where it is only a short distance for substances to diffuse into and out of cells. It is in this way that oxygen and nutrients are delivered to cells, brought from the lungs and intestines, respectively, and carbon dioxide, water and other waste products are removed, mainly via the lungs and kidneys.

Plants, being generally less active than animals, do not have such high energy requirements; their rate of respiration can therefore be lower, and delivery and removal of molecules are not as urgent. Nevertheless, plants do need to distribute glucose produced in their leaves to the rest of the plant, and must raise water from their roots to their photosynthesising leaves. Plants have two transport systems; xylem and phloem vessels.

Xylem vessels can be thought of as long, thin tubes that can stretch to the height of the tallest trees, through which, it is hypothesised, water and minerals move from the roots to the leaves as a result of the polar nature of water molecules. Cohesive forces between individual molecules create an unbroken column of water that is pulled up the plant by evaporation from the leaves; no active energy-consuming transport process is needed and so xylem vessels are made of dead cells, containing no organelles. Calculations of the maximum height to which water could be lifted by this mechanism match closely with the recorded heights of the greatest Californian redwoods.

The second plant transport system is the phloem system. Phloem tissue also comprises tubes, but these tubes are living and need to respire. The liquid moving in these tubes is far more concentrated than that in the xylem, being a solution of sugars being transported from the leaves to other parts of the plant, particularly the roots. The direction of flow in the phloem is from a source to a sink and will vary depending on conditions; for example in summer, roots may act as a sink, storing products of photosynthesis, whereas in the spring they will act as a source to feed to growing shoots.

CHANGING LARGE MOLECULES TO SMALL ONES: DIGESTION

Whereas plants can build more complex organic molecules from their synthesised glucose and minerals absorbed from the soil, animals are dependent upon their diet to obtain many essential nutrients. However, food that is ingested is rarely in an appropriate form to be used by cells. It must first of all be digested – broken down mechanically and chemically into its constituent molecules. For example, the energy-rich starch polymer is too large to pass through a cell membrane, so must be digested into glucose monomers before absorption. This breakdown is catalysed by specific enzymes in the human gut – amylase and maltase. Even as the enzymes get to work, mechanical processes of chewing and churning will have begun the physical breakdown, giving the enzymes a greater surface area to act upon.

Surface area is a factor that affects many processes in the living world; so many are dependent on the diffusion of substances across membranes, hence their rate is dependent on the surface area of membrane available. Thus, the rate of absorption of nutrients in the small intestine is maximised by the convolutions of the surface into villi, and further, into finger-like microvilli; plants' absorption of water and minerals from the soil is aided by the fine projections of root-hair cells from the finest of roots; gas exchange in organisms occurs in the spongy, air-filled mesophyll of leaves, across the surface of many-branched air sacs of the mammalian lungs, across the richly blood-supplied feathery gill lamellae of a fish. Equally, the shape of animals and even their behaviour is influenced by heat loss, which increases with increasing surface area:volume ratio. Hence we see the large ears of the desert-dwelling fennec fox to aid cooling, and the huddling of emperor penguins to maintain warmth in the Antarctic chill.

CONTROLLING CONDITIONS: HOMEOSTASIS

To carry out the functions of life, organisms strive to maintain constant internal environments, a process known as homeostasis. To consider a single factor, the water content of cells: if the water content of a cell becomes reduced, the cell will collapse; if the water content is too great, the cell will over-expand, which can result in the membrane of the cell rupturing. The movement of water into and out of cells is governed by the concentration of solutes on either side of the membrane. In humans, two important osmotically active solutes are salt and glucose. If salt or glucose concentration is high in the blood stream, water will be drawn out of the cells causing them to dehydrate; this could occur through the ingestion of salty foods, or in the case of glucose, with the condition diabetes, where glucose is not effectively removed from the bloodstream. To moderate the extremes of solute content, and to eliminate metabolic waste, humans have kidneys that filter the blood to remove excess water and solutes. These organs use mechanisms of high-pressure filtration to remove all particles below a certain size from the blood, then active transport and diffusion to return a correct balance of substances to the body. The final concentration of reabsorbed substances is governed by a hormone – a chemical messenger carried in the bloodstream – released from a gland in the brain, which affects the uptake of water in the kidney.

COMMUNICATION AND CONTROL: HORMONES AND THE NERVOUS SYSTEM

Many biological processes are governed by hormones, and their effects may be both long-lasting and wide-ranging. One dramatic hormone is adrenaline, released from the adrenal glands on top of the kidneys, that elicits the increased heartbeat, raised breathing rate, dilated pupils and sweating palms of fear, preparing the body for 'flight or fight'. Longer-acting hormones include the sex hormones, testosterone, oestrogen and proges-terone, released from the sex organs and responsible for growth and development of sexual characteristics and the development of gametes over months and years. The growth of plants is also governed by hormones, borne out by the use of hormone rooting powder to stimulate root development in cuttings.

The action of hormones is in contrast to the nervous system of animals. Nerve cells carry electrical impulses at great speed to and from the central nervous system. They are typified by their long length, their numerous connections to other nerve cells, and in mammals by their associated Schwann cells, which act as insulation to speed signal transmission. Nerves can elicit lightning reactions in fractions of a second between sensing and responding to a stimulus. For example, whereas a plant will respond to light and grow towards it as a result of a hormone over a course of days, a star-nosed mole will detect prey with its tentacle-like nose and capture it within 120 msec.

EVOLUTION AND GENETICS

The perfectly engineered solutions to problems of maintaining life presented here are the result of millions of years of successive minute changes in design, the designer being the pressures of the environment they inhabit. The theory of evolution by natural selection was famously developed by Charles Darwin, 150 years ago. His work was the result of many years of careful observation of evidence from such diverse sources as fossils from South America, pedigrees of fancy pigeons from London's enthusiasts and observations of weed competition in his own garden. Natural selection explains how changes in organisms occur with clarity and simplicity; subsequent research and evidence continues to support and strengthen the theory, without the need for more complicated explanations for evolution. At the time of publication of *On the Origin of Species*, the mechanism for the inheritance of characteristics was unknown. It was not until the early twentieth century, with the appreciation of Gregor Mendel's formative work on genetics, that the mode of information transmission by 'factors' (now genes) was elucidated. Further advances in the field of genetics sees us, 100 years later, with the understanding and technology to influence our own genes and inheritance.

In a world where resources are finite, it is not other species with whom individuals compete most intensely, but their peers. In a population of similar organisms, some will be better suited to the conditions and be able to produce more surviving offspring than those individuals struggling to survive. For example, in a field that is home to white rabbits and brown rabbits, white rabbits are more likely to be seen and eaten by foxes than their brown counterparts. Of the brown rabbits, those with long legs for fast running will escape the foxes. Only those individuals that are not eaten will go on to breed, and pass on their characteristics; eventually, the field will be home to only brown, long-legged rabbits. Slight changes in species, generation after generation, have led to the living world we see today, and continue to shape it. Evolution is dependent upon there being a diversity of genes within a species to begin with, and the continuing introduction of new genes by mutation. In the present day, when human activity is adversely affecting many habitats, organisms do not have the genes present in their populations that might enable future offspring to adapt to rapid environmental changes. As they cannot evolve to exploit their changing habitats in one or few generations, they are becoming extinct.

ECOLOGY: THE INTERDEPENDENCE OF ORGANISMS AND THEIR ENVIRONMENT

In any study of biology, it is disingenuous to study an organism in isolation from its environment. No plant or animal can exist free from the effect of other members of its community, be it through direct competition for resources within or between species, feeding relationships between successive trophic levels or the alteration of abiotic factors by successive seral stages as an ecosystem progresses to a climax community. An ecosystem is driven by energy from the Sun that is harnessed by photosynthesising plants; this energy, and nutrients, is transferred up the food chain from producer to primary consumer to secondary consumer. Crucially, energy is lost between each level, and only a fraction is transferred up the food chain. There will be energy remaining, for example, in the indigestible fur and bones of animals. Warm-blooded animals, in particular, lose energy as heat to their surroundings, and energy expended as animals move becomes unavailable to higher levels. Even waste, such as dead leaves and faeces, is a rich source of energy. Some of this energy can be considered to move 'sideways' out of a food chain and be used by detritivores (bacteria, fungi and other decomposers), but ultimately all energy will be lost to the environment in the form of heat. Transfer from one trophic level to the next is, at best, 10 per cent efficient, hence the argument for vegetarianism that it is possible to feed the world's population on crops, but not if we persist in growing food crops to feed livestock to satisfy our desire for meat. It is also the rationale behind intensive farming; reducing energy losses by preventing movement means more feed is converted into muscle mass.

Nutrients, on the other hand, follow a cyclical path. Any molecule in an organism is there for a relatively short time, a lifetime at most, before being recycled through the abiotic environment. It is possible to imagine the path of an atom of carbon as it passes from carbon dioxide in the air into the leaf of a photosynthesising plant where it is incorporated into an organic molecule, through the tissues of the animal that eats that plant, until it is respired and returned to the atmosphere. This cycle may take millions of years; it is the carbon that was trapped by plants when the dinosaurs roamed the Earth that is now being released as fossil fuels are burnt, and is causing world-altering climate change.

BIOLOGY: THE HUMAN ANIMAL

Biology is the study of living organisms, among which *homo sapiens* is included. We are part of the continuing evolution of life, a species at present enjoying a successful period thanks to a few spontaneous mutations, including those leading to speech and larger brains. There is no way that we can separate our existence from the influences of the natural world. Plant life provides us with food and oxygen; different habitats influence our available and desirable resources; our drive to propagate our genes drives many individual and cultural practices.

Our application of biological knowledge is amply demonstrated in the field of medicine. For millennia, plant products have been used as drugs to help treat ailments, some passing into folklore and others into the research lab. The spread of infectious diseases has been controlled through our understanding of germ theory. An early proponent of this idea was Ignaz Semmelweis, a Hungarian obstetrician. He observed that many women died of puerperal fever after having given birth attended by doctors, whereas the death rate of those under midwife care was much lower. Doctors came straight to deliveries from autopsies. By insisting that doctors washed their hands before attending labour wards, Semmelweis cut mortality rates to 2 per cent. In other areas, the study of anatomy has lead to microsurgery as opposed to butchery; prophylactic immunisations stimulate our immune system into producing antibodies to pathogens that might otherwise overcome us; endocrinologists have allowed diabetics who would have died in childhood 80 years ago to lead relatively normal lives with the discovery of insulin. As our understanding of biology at a cellular level advances, so technologies such as therapeutic stem cell cloning and treatments for degenerative diseases will become widespread. These future possibilities are necessarily also laden with ethical implications; part of our role as biology teachers is to give pupils the tools to make informed decisions on lifestyle choices: whether to use drugs (legal and illegal); what impact different diets may have on their health and environment; how funding for research should be allocated. Biology has the potential to give rise to some of the most heated debates in science, because as part of biology we find it difficult to maintain an objective viewpoint.

Tasks 3.2.1 and 3.2.2 provide ideas for stimulating thinking and interest in the living world.

Task 3.2.1 **Plants**

1   Take a walk in a wood, or a flight over the countryside in Google Earth. All those trees and plants are made almost exclusively of carbon dioxide and water. That's quite a feat.
2   Grow cress seeds on a damp paper towel. Place them on the windowsill and marvel at the tiny plants' ability to respond to sunlight. Try turning them on their side after a few days – they can sense gravity too.
3   Always effective: stand a white carnation in a small depth of strong food dye, and leave it overnight. The dye will be transported in the xylem to the petals where the intricate network of veins will be revealed in glorious technicolour. For added fun, split the stem and use different colours.

4 Tie a clear polythene bag over a pot plant. After a few hours, droplets of water will start to collect on the inside. This is water that has been transported from the soil through the root hairs, into the xylem vessels and out through the leaves into the air. The process at work here is multiplied a thousand-fold in taking water to the tops of the tallest trees.

Task 3.2.2 **Our bodies**

1 A favourite: stand on your head and drink a glass of water through a straw. Why doesn't it run back out of your mouth? Peristalsis – waves of muscular contraction moving towards your stomach, regardless of gravity.

2 Hold your breath. What caused you to breathe again? Not a need for oxygen, but an urge to rid the body of carbon dioxide. Whilst you do this, think of the abilities of some sea mammals to dive to depths of over 2km for half an hour or more.

3 In front of a mirror, cover one open eye with your hand. The other pupil will expand in response to the darkness experienced by the covered pupil. Tiny muscles in the iris are constantly adjusting the size of the pupil in response to the light level. This represents a fraction of the stimuli from our environment to which our bodies are constantly reacting.

4 Look at a flower. Look at a tree. Look at a snail. Look at birds in the sky. Aren't these the most amazing pictures you have ever seen? Created by a collection of light-sensitive cells on your retina sending electrical signals to the back of the brain, these images enable us to appreciate the natural world.

SUMMARY AND KEY POINTS

From the elephant to the ant to the bacteria that live upon and within the ant, from the giant redwoods of California to the algae in a garden pond, all organisms are performing the processes of living things. They have arrived at a multitude of different ways in which to carry out these processes: remaining in the same place and producing their own food or moving around in search of nutrition; different methods of transporting substances throughout their systems; different mechanisms of sensing and responding to their environments. The diversity of life that is so overwhelming is the result of millions of years of evolution. From the initial single-celled organisms have evolved the wealth of living things upon which David Attenborough has built his illustrious career. Biology provides answers to such questions as: Why are trees green? How do fish breathe underwater? Why do elephants have big ears? Why do animals become extinct? What are we here for? To study biology so enhances our appreciation of our own selves and of the world of which we are both an integral part and self-appointed guardians, that to disregard the discipline would be to go through life blind to the truly awe-inspiring nature of our unique planet.

FURTHER READING

Attenborough, D. (1979) *Life on Earth: A Natural History*. Boston, MA: Little, Brown and Company.

Attenborough, D. (1995) *The Private Life of Plants: A Natural History of Plant Behaviour*. London: BBC Books.

Dawkins, R. (1989) *The Selfish Gene.* Oxford: Oxford Paperbacks.

Diamond, J. (2006) *The Third Chimpanzee: The Evolution and Future of the Human Animal (P.S.).* New York: Harper Perennial.

Goldacre, B. (2008) *Bad Science.* London: Fourth Estate.

Jones, S. (1999) *Almost Like a Whale: The Origin of Species Updated*. New York: Doubleday Publishing.

Reiss, M. (ed.) (1999) *Teaching Secondary Biology*. London: John Murray for ASE.

Ridley, M. (1994) *The Red Queen: Sex and the Evolution of Human Nature*. New York: Macmillan Publishing Co.

Wilson, E. O. (1992) *The Diversity of Life*. New York: W. W. Norton and Co.

RELEVANT WEBITES

Farabee, M.J. (2002)

www.emc.maricopa.edu/faculty/farabee/BIOBK/BioBookTOC.html

An online biology textbook, with more than everything you need to know (accessed 23 July 2009).

Guardian Education

http://education.guardian.co.uk/higher/links . . .

Follow links to biological sciences (accessed 23 July 2009).

Quill Graphics *Cells Alive*

http//:www.cellsalive.com

Lots of interactive diagrams of cells (accessed 23 July 2009).

***New Scientist* magazine**

http://www.newscientist.com/ (accessed 23 July 2009).

The Wellcome Trust's 'Big Picture' magazine

http://www.wellcome.ac.uk/Education-resources/Teaching-and-education/Big-Picture/ index.htm (accessed 23 July 2009).

Lots of animations of cell processes

http://highered.mcgraw-hill.com/sites/dl/free/0072437316/120060/ravenanimation.html (accessed 23 July 2009).

Bank of biology resources and experiments from DG Mackean

http://www.biology-resources.com/ (accessed 23 July 2009).

UNIT 3.3

CHEMISTRY

Tony Turner

INTRODUCTION

In a sense human flesh is made of stardust. Every atom in the human body, excluding only the primordial hydrogen atoms, was fashioned in the stars that formed, grew old and exploded most violently before the Sun and the Earth came into being. The explosions scattered the heavier elements as a fine dust through space. By the time it made the Sun, the primordial gas of the Milky Way was sufficiently enriched with heavier elements for rocky planets like the Earth to form. And from the rocks, atoms escaped for eventual incorporation in living things.

(Calder, 1977: 417–19)

Recycling is at the heart of chemistry. The 92 different types of atom known to occur naturally in the Earth's crust and its atmosphere, group and regroup to form millions of different structures and hence millions of different substances. The sandstones, limestones, granites and clays of the Earth's crust, the soils of the surface, the water and minerals of the oceans, the air we breathe, the tissues of living things and manufactured plastics, drugs and ceramics are simply the result of different combinations of some of the 92 different atoms. There are extraordinarily large numbers of each type of atom, 10^{23} carbon atoms in a 25-carat diamond; 10^{22} gold atoms in a wedding ring; and 10^{21} oxygen atoms in a breath of air. Virtually nothing leaves or enters our planet, so every new material that is made, every new plant that grows, has to be formed from material that is already in the 'spaceship' *Earth*.

OBJECTIVES

By the end of this unit you should:

- appreciate the scope of chemistry
- identify how the microscopic story of particles illuminates the macroscopic phenomena of behaviour of materials
- be aware of applications of chemical knowledge.

PARTICLES AND PHENOMENA

Chemistry is about two stories: the macroscopic world of bulk materials and the invisible particle world of atoms and molecules. They are different but consistent stories and are now so intertwined in our thinking about materials that we often do not recognise when we are moving between the two. We must add to these stories the story of the flow of energy that accompanies chemical change.

The macroscopic story can be fun, messy and very useful. What happens when different substances react together? Are there explosions, as when hydrogen reacts rapidly with oxygen to form water? Are there changes of colour, as when lead nitrate and sodium iodide react? Is there fizzing, as when sodium bicarbonate is added to vinegar? What is the nature and structure of the starting materials and what are the new substances formed, and their structure? How can knowledge of chemical reactions be used to make new substances with properties that we want?

Chemistry, at the macroscopic level, grew out of alchemy, which sought to make gold from base metals. Alchemy provided an experimental basis for progress and identified important substances, such as acids. However, its goal was false and the overthrow of alchemy was an essential step in the development of chemistry (Dixon, 1989: 17). What then is the background to the story at particle level? It was Dalton in 1802 who suggested each element was made of many identical particles (atoms) with a mass characteristic for that element. The idea of atoms goes back to Democritus and Leucippus (fourth century BC, Greece), who were, in turn, influenced by earlier Egyptian science (see Porter and Ogilvie, 2000: 290; Pappademos, 1984: 180 and *Useful websites*). Mendeleyev's realisation of a pattern in the properties of different elements in 1869 led to the idea that perhaps there was some underlying mechanism which explained the pattern. It was not until the early twentieth century, however, that the explanation was found to be linked to the fact that all atoms are made up of different numbers of only three even smaller particles – protons, neutrons and electrons (see Emsley, 2009 in *Useful websites*).

Each of the 92 different types of atom has a different number of protons in its nucleus: one proton in hydrogen, two protons in helium, three in lithium, four in beryllium, five in boron, six in carbon and so on, up to uranium at 92. The number of protons alone does not account for the relative masses of the atoms, but the addition of varying numbers of neutrons does. The shorthand labeling of elements is just a summary. The label $^{12}C_6$, for instance, describes a carbon atom (symbol C) with six protons in the nucleus and with an atomic mass of 12, made up of the mass of the six protons and the mass of a further six neutrons; the symbol $^{235}U_{92}$ represents a uranium atom of 92 protons and 143 neutrons.

The electrons that make up the rest of the atom are the most important components from the point of view of chemistry (see *Useful websites*). These negatively charged particles, balancing the positive charge of the protons to make the atom electrically neutral, mostly determine the way atoms join together for the simple reason that they are the first thing another atom meets in a chemical reaction. (On the scale of the atom, electrons are 'miles away' from the nucleus, the radius of the atom being about 10^{-10}m and the radius of the nucleus about 10^{-15}m.)

Isotopes of the same element such as carbon-14 and carbon-12 ($^{14}C_6$ and $^{12}C_6$, respectively) therefore react chemically in much the same way, because they both have the same number of electrons. It happens in this particular example that while the chemistry is the same, the heavier isotope is radioactive (i.e. a property related to the nucleus and not the electrons), which is useful in the dating of fossils (see Brain, 2003 in *Useful websites*).

Many elements, especially the heavier ones, are unstable and radioactive, e.g. bismuth, uranium. There is a balance needed between the number of protons and neutrons for stability; instability leads to radioactivity. Beyond element 92 (uranium) there are 19 larger very unstable atoms, formed in nuclear reactors by bombardment of the element with other particles, such as neutrons, a fusion process (see Seaborg in *Useful websites*).

One isotope of uranium ($^{238}Ur_{92}$) breaks down naturally to thorium ($^{234}Th_{90}$), losing an alpha particle ($^{4}He_{2}$) in the process. By contrast, another uranium isotope, $^{235}Ur_{92}$, breaks down when bombarded with neutrons, dangerously so, losing much energy as heat. This fission process is one basis for nuclear power for electricity generation and also for atomic weapons.

HOW ARE ATOMS HELD TOGETHER? BONDING OF PARTICLES

The story of the electrons enables us to answer questions such as: How do sodium and chlorine atoms bond together to form salt? How do carbon and oxygen atoms bond together to form carbon dioxide? How do the atoms of gold bond together in a gold wedding ring? There are three fundamental ways in which electrons link atoms: 'ionic bonds' making 'giant structures of ions'; 'covalent bonds'; and 'metallic bonds' forming 'giant structures of atoms' (see 'chemical bonding' in *Useful websites*).

In ionic bonding, one or more electrons are transferred from one atom to another when a compound is formed. The resultant atoms are therefore charged positively and negatively, and are then called ions. The bond between ions is an electrostatic attractive force exerted in all directions, called an ionic bond. Substances bonded in this way are high-melting-point solids, e.g. sodium chloride. The number and arrangement of the ions in the ionic solid is determined by the size of the ion and charge on the ion and the different ways they pack together to preserve electrical neutrality, forming the so-called 'giant structure of ions' characteristic of ionic compounds.

In covalent bonding neither atom becomes charged, and discrete neutral molecules are usually formed. An electron pair is shared between two atoms and lies between the two atoms; this bond is directional. The directional nature of covalent bonds is revealed in a structural model of a substance as shown in the model of water, H_2O (Figure 3.3.1) and methane CH_4 (Figure 3.3.2). In these models a line represents a shared pair of electrons. In the case of methane the carbon atom lies at the centre of a regular tetrahedron and the hydrogen atoms at the four corners.

Covalent bonds also occur in some elements where two or more atoms of the same element form a molecule, as in bromine (Br_2) and sulphur (S_8). Compounds having covalent bonds include octane (C_8H_{18}) and glucose ($C_6H_{12}O_6$). Some very large molecules are often made of repeating patterns of smaller molecules, e.g. cellulose ($C_6H_{12}O_6$)$_n$ where 'n' may be 1000; cellulose is called a polymer (i.e. many parts). Other polymers include DNA, starch, rubber and Teflon. While the atoms within the molecule are tightly bonded, the links between the molecules are weaker, hence a molecular substance is a collection of many millions of molecules each loosely bound to each other. Molecular substances, therefore, melt more easily than do giant structures because the intermolecular forces are

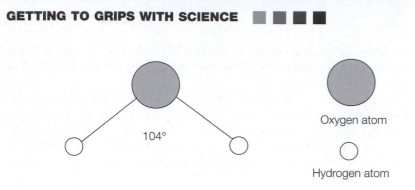

■ **Figure 3.3.1** Structure of water molecule: angle between O-H bonds =104°

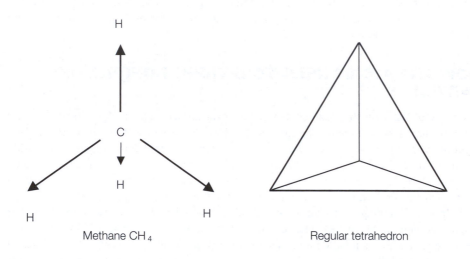

■ **Figure 3.3.2** Directed bonds: the bonds between carbon and hydrogen in a methane molecule point to the corners of a regular tetrahedron

weaker than the forces between the ions in the giant structure. Some molecular substances are gases at room temperature such as hydrogen (H_2) and ammonia (NH_3) or liquids such as ethanol and water.

Molecules formed between two or more different elements may have unevenly distributed charges across the molecule as a whole. Such molecules are said to be polar; water is an exceptional example of a polar molecule. In the water molecule (H_2O or HOH), the electrons in the covalent bond of oxygen and hydrogen are closer to the oxygen atom than the hydrogen atom, so one end of the molecule is slightly negative and the other slightly positive. This uneven distribution leads to intermolecular bonding, causing the molecules to be attracted to each other. In water this causes the melting and boiling point to be higher than expected and allows it to be able to dissolve a wide range of substances. This solvent property includes dissolving many ionic substances, e.g. salt, or causing ionization, e.g. when it dissolves hydrogen chloride gas to make hydrochloric acid solution. Many other molecules have polar properties especially those with an OH group in their structure, such as alcohols, starch and sugars.

Metallic bonding occurs in metals where the outer electrons are loosely held by the atoms and not attached strongly to any one atom. The atoms are held in a 'sea of electrons', maintaining overall neutral charge. The resultant bond is called a 'metallic bond' and the solid is a 'giant structure of atoms'. Metals occur as elements, e.g. gold (Au) and as mixtures (alloys) such as brass (copper and tin). Because of the relative freedom of the electrons, metals are good conductors of electricity in the solid and liquid state (see metallic bonding in *Useful websites*).

Other 'giant structures of atoms' include diamond (C) and silica (SiO_2). In these examples the bonding is covalent, not metallic. In diamond each carbon atom is connected to four neighbours, each by a covalent bond; and in silica the silicon and oxygen atoms are similarly connected by covalent bonds; both diamond and silica are poor electrical conductors. Graphite, also carbon, is exceptional; it has a giant structure, too, but, in contrast to diamond, has some 'free' electrons (as in a metal) making graphite a good conductor of electricity (see 'Structure of diamond' in *Useful websites*). Substances having giant structures have high melting points because the bonding force is exerted in all directions throughout the structure.

There are some important substances that defy our attempt to give exact formulae. Two important 'life substances' comprise large molecules linked to a metal atom. Haemoglobin occurs in mammalian blood and contains iron, but there is no one formula to describe it, differing slightly between mammalian groups. Chlorophyll occurs in green plants and comprises several closely related substances, including so-called chlorophylls A and B, both of which contain a magnesium atom. In both haemoglobin and chlorophyll the metal atom is situated at the centre of a large organic molecule related to compounds called porphyrins. Both substances are responsible for oxygen exchange essential to life in most animals and plants, respectively (see 'Structure of haemoglobin' in *Useful websites*).

ENERGY RELEASED OR ABSORBED IN CHEMICAL REACTIONS

The story of chemical change is not just about the particles and the forces which hold them together, but also the energy which is involved in breaking the bonds between the atoms and the energy released when new bonds are made. When bonds are broken, energy has to be supplied to pull the atoms apart (endothermic change). When bonds are made, energy is released back into the environment (exothermic change). The balance of energy supplied and energy released determines whether the overall reaction is endothermic or exothermic. For example, during photosynthesis sunlight supplies energy to break the hydrogen away from the oxygen in molecules of water, so that the hydrogen atoms can join with carbon dioxide molecules to make large molecules of glucose. The energy released from making the glucose bonds is far less than the energy used in breaking the hydrogen–oxygen bonds in water, so the reaction is overall endothermic. Reactions where the making of bonds releases a lot of energy are often the most dramatic, hence our enjoyment of fireworks, bonfires, the thermite process, and firing of hydrogen and oxygen rockets.

When discussing energy changes chemists talk of enthalpy rather than energy. Enthalpy is merely the energy change for a set number of particles in a particular reaction. If there are double the number of particles then there is double the energy change. The standard number of particles that chemists have chosen as a reference point is the number of particles in 12 g of carbon ($^{12}C_6$), called the molar mass or 'mole'. The number of particles in a 'mole' is 6.27×10^{23}, also called Avogadro's Number. Thus a mole of carbon ($^{12}C_6$) atoms has a mass of 12 grams; a mole of nitrogen *atoms* ($^{14}N_7$) a mass of 14 grams and a mole of nitrogen *molecules* (N_2) has a mass of 28 grams.

When a mole of carbon atoms (12 g) burns in oxygen, 394 kilojoules (kJ) of energy are given out, measured experimentally. If 6 g of carbon were oxidised then 197 kJ would be given out. The equation below describes the energy change when one mole of carbon is burned completely in oxygen. The enthalpy change (ΔH) has a negative sign by convention to show that energy has been lost from the chemical system, although it might have warmed our hands and added to our system!

$C + O_2 = CO_2$; $\Delta H = -394$ kJ/mole.

So by weighing matter it is possible to count particles (atoms or molecules) and know how many moles of substance you are dealing with. By looking up enthalpy tables it is possible to work out how much energy will be released by the amount of substance you are dealing with.

RATES OF REACTIONS

We move the story now from energy change and particle recycling to ask 'how fast?'. Even if reactions are possible, the rate can vary from very slow, such as the change of graphite to diamond (millennia), setting of concrete (days), the browning of an apple (minutes/hour), the setting of superglue (seconds), to very rapid change such as blue litmus changing to red in an acid or the burning of hydrogen in oxygen.

The rates at which chemical reactions occur can be altered in a number of ways. One way is by making the different atoms meet more often by increasing the concentration of particles. Increasing the temperature usually also increases the rate of reaction, because the faster-moving particles meet other particles more often. Grinding solids into a powder increases surface area and exposes more atoms for a reaction, such as between a liquid and a solid.

Many reactions require an 'activation energy' to start them. Once started, the reaction gives out enough energy to supply the activation energy to other atoms. Hence we have to generate enough heat from friction on the chemicals at the tip of a match to make them burn, and as they burn they produce an even higher temperature that provides the activation energy for the wood to oxidise. The first bit of wood to burn supplies the activation energy for the next bit of wood, and so on (see 'Activation energy' in *Useful websites*).

Catalysts can help reactions to go more quickly. They provide an alternative pathway for a reaction, e.g. by allowing the formation of a transitional material with a lower activation energy than the usual pathway. Whichever pathway is used for a reaction the enthalpy change is the same. Common enzymes are catalysts and include those in the mouth and stomach juices, helping digestion.

ENTROPY

We finally add entropy to the story of chemical change. Chemists want to know whether or not a chemical change is possible before they attempt it and the likely conditions for it to occur. Knowing whether enthalpy changes can be positive or negative is only part of the answer. The other part comes from the recognition that the total energy change of a reaction (enthalpy) is made up of two factors, the bond-breaking/bond-making part (already discussed) and a part related to the change in order/disorder (entropy) of the total system.

For example, when salt dissolves in water, ionic bonds are broken and new bonds made between the ions and the water molecules. Ions in a salt crystal are in an ordered state whereas in salt water they are more randomly distributed, i.e. dissolving is accompanied by an increase in disorder of the system. So although dissolving salt is an endothermic change, the change is driven by the increasing disorder of the system. Left alone most systems move in the direction of disorder, i.e. increased entropy.

The idea of 'disorder of a system' was suggested in the nineteenth century by the physicist Wilhard Gibbs. The difference between the total energy change (enthalpy) and the energy factor involving the entropy term is the energy available to do work in a system, i.e. bring about change. This energy was called 'free energy', later named Gibbs Energy. If Gibbs Energy is negative, i.e. lost from the system, then a chemical change is possible. Entropy changes are dependent on the conditions (e.g. temperature, pressure) thus opening the way to predicting the likely condition for a change to occur. Thus both enthalpy change and entropy change in a system are needed to predict whether a chemical change can take place. Note that entropy itself does not have the units of energy but the product 'temperature $\times$ entropy change' does; it is this last term that is used when computing the Gibbs Energy of a system.

Identifying the total system is important; for example, for the photosynthetic process involving light, carbon dioxide and water in a green leaf, you must consider not just the leaf-air system but also the origin of the energy itself, the Sun.

Some aspects of the map of chemistry in relation to matter, energy and change are shown in Figure 3.3.3. For further information see, e.g., 'chemical thermodynamics' in *Useful websites*.

PROPERTIES AND USES

The story of chemistry is one of change, of exploring the properties of natural materials, of changing materials to make new ones and studying new materials to see if they are useful. Iron and bronze were discovered accidentally in domestic fires by our ancestors and their properties of hardness and malleability recognised. The key to making and using materials is to know and understand their properties; that is why the notion of properties has an emphasis in school chemistry. A good example of linking properties to use is found in polymer science, best known through plastics. Natural polymers include lignin, DNA and starch, and early plastics were Bakelite and nitrocellulose.

The properties of a polymer depend on a number of factors. A polymer can be made of one repeating unit (monomer) such as ethane (C_2H_4), to make polythene; or two or more monomers, such as butadiene and styrene, to make rubber, and an organic acid and an amine to make nylon. The size and shape of the polymer molecule can be controlled by the temperature or pressure used, giving different properties such as toughness or hardness. By adding other materials to the polymer (additives), softer polymers can be made suitable for clothing.

Polymer chains can be made linear or branching by adjusting the type of monomer used; linear chains pack closely, branched chains do not pack so well and give less dense, weaker polymers. Incorporating sugars in a polymer gives a biodegradable polymer, reducing their environmental impact; similarly, soluble 'stitches' to aid wound healing can be designed or degradable drug capsules to allow the controlled release of a drug.

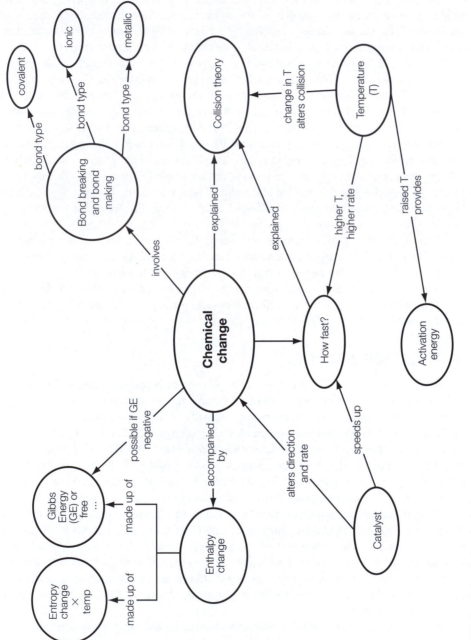

■ **Figure 3.3.3** Aspects of chemical change

Lightweight circuits in information processors can be made from organic polymers (instead of silicon) and use photons to transfer information instead of slower electrons. Silicon-based polymers are used, for example, as hydraulic fluids because of their inertness towards change. For more information see 'Polymers' in the *Useful websites*.

LEARNING ABOUT THE MACROSCOPIC STORY AND THINKING ABOUT THE PARTICLE STORY

Chemistry lends itself to spectacular activities, occasionally with much heat, light and colour. Explosions are enjoyed by most pupils. Many chemists were attracted to chemistry by the element of fun and wonder. Making oxygen and burning things in it is exciting. By contrast, many important changes (to chemists and the curriculum) seem innocuous, e.g. neutralisation, dissolving, oxidation, and are often invisible without markers, e.g. litmus or a thermometer. Practical chemistry often gives tangible results but the explanations of change use invisible particles and invoke hidden mechanisms.

The switch between the particle story and the macroscopic story can, however, make chemistry difficult for many pupils. They often muddle the macroscopic and the microscopic stories such that they talk of water molecules melting when ice melts, instead of talking of them breaking apart so that they are free to move around and hence give an overall 'flowing' property to the bulk material, water. You have to help pupils to distinguish between the observations, what happened, and the explanations given, the theory, and to envisage the scale of the story you are telling. If atoms were the size of small marbles, a mole of them would cover the whole of the surface of the Earth 10 million times. Hence the number in those 10 million layers of marbles is the same number of atoms in an almond-sized lump of coal.

SUMMARY AND KEY POINTS

In telling the story of chemistry it is possible to see how it has illuminated our understanding of numerous processes in living things and has led to the specialised field of biochemistry. It also forms a bridge to the story more often associated with physics of what it is that holds all the particles within the atom together. It provides an insight into the world in which we now live where we take for granted that people make new materials, new drugs, purify our water, supply us with fuels and manufacture the fertilisers used to grow crops. Uses can be found for chemicals with specific properties, and, equally, chemicals with specific properties can be designed to a purpose. Lastly, chemistry provides the understanding to help save our natural resources and undertake the recycling of waste products.

FURTHER READING

Some resources for stories of past chemists

Dixon, B. (1989) *The Science of Science*. London: Cassell.

Carey, J. (1995) *The Faber Book of Science*. London: Faber & Faber.

Daintith, J. and Gjertson, D. (eds) (1999) *Oxford Dictionary of Scientists*. Oxford: Oxford University Press.

Ronan, C. (1966) *The Ages of Science.* London: Harrap.

Porter, R. and Ogilvie, M. (eds) (2000) *Dictionary of Scientific Biography, Volumes I and II.* Oxford: Helicon.
A two-volume series that covers the historical development of science up to the present day. Separate discussions of each science including astronomy and Earth sciences and in-depth biographies of scientists from the Greeks onwards.

McKinney, D. and Michalovic, M. (2004) 'Teaching the stories of scientists and discoveries', in *The Science Teacher*, Volume 71, Number 9 (November 1): 46–51.

Levi, P. (1995) 'The story of the carbon atom', in J. Carey, *The Faber Book of Science*. London: Faber & Faber, pp. 338–44.

Hodgkin, D. (1988) 'Finding what's there', in Wolpert, L. and Richards, A. (eds) *A Passion for Science*. Oxford: Oxford University Press, pp. 69–79. Reprinted as 'Seeing the atoms in crystals', in J. Carey (1995) *The Faber Book of Science*. London: Faber & Faber, pp. 467–74.

Useful school texts

GCSE
Ramsden, E. N. (2001*) Key Science: Chemistry*, 3rd edition. Cheltenham: Nelson Thornes.
Fullick, P. and Fullick, A. (2001) *Chemistry for AQA Separate Award*. Cheltenham: Nelson Thornes.
GCE AS/A2
Conoly, C. and Hills, P. (2008) *Collins Advanced Chemistry*, 3rd edition. London: Collins.
Saunders, N. and Saunders, P. (2009) *AS Chemistry for AQA, Student Book*. Oxford: Oxford University Press.

USEFUL WEBSITES

Activation energy
www.youtube.com/watch?v=VblaK6PLrRM (accessed 26 June 2009).

Avogadro, Amadeo contributions to science
www.bulldog.u-net.com/avogadro/avoga.html (accessed June 26 2009).

Brain, M. (2003) *How Stuff Works: Carbon Dating*
http://www.howstuffworks.com/carbon-14.htm (accessed 26 June 2009).

Chemical bonding
www.visionlearning.com(library)module.viewer.php?mid=55 (accessed 26 June 2009).

Chemical thermodynamics
www.shoclor/UNchem/advanced/thermo/index.html (accessed 26 June 2009).

Emsley, J. (2009) 'Period drama', in *Science Course: Part IV Building Blocks*. London: *The Guardian* and Science Museum
www.guardian.co.uk/theguardian/2008/may01/sciencecourse (accessed 26 June 2009).

J.J. Thomson: Discovery of the electron
www.outreach.phy.com.ac.uk/camphy/electron/electron_index.htm (accessed 26 June 2009).

John Dalton: Atomic theory
www.chemistryexplained.com/Co-Di/Dalton-John.html (accessed 26 June 2009).

Metallic bonding
www.chemguide.co.uk/atoms/bonding/metallic.html (accessed 26 June 2009).

Oxford Dictionary of Scientists
http://www.oxfordreference.com/pages/Subjects_and_Titles__2D_GS10 (accessed 26 June 2009). A subscription service; see also Resources for stories 'Daintith and Gjertson'.

Pappademos, J. Africa's role in the history of physics

http://books.google.co.uk/books?id=ea-dgkryq7AC&pg=PA177&lpg=PA177&dq=Africa's+role+in+the+history+of+physics&source=bl&ots=GRNgtdyNJP&sig=tX8NvwpmP8–VTTz__USK9DvzvGs&hl=en&ei=hvZESuv0E5PLjAfB9Nhi&sa=X&oi=book_result&ct=result& resnum=1 (accessed 26 June 2006).

Polymers: different kinds and their structures

http://pslc.ws.macrog/kidsmac/kfloor2.htm (accessed 26 June 2009).

Seaborg, Glenn T. 'Identification of transuranic elements', in *Contributions to Advancing Science*

www.osti.gov/accomplishments/seaborg.html (accessed 26 June 2009).

Structure of chlorophyll

http://www.ncbi.nlm.nih.gov/books/bvfcgi?rid=cooper.figgrp.305 (accessed 26 June 2009).

Structure of diamond and other carbon allotropes

http://home.att.net/~cat6a/allot_carbon-I.htm (accessed 26 June 2009).

Structure of haemoglobin

www.elpmanchester.ac.uk/pub_projects/2001/MNQC7NDS/haemoglobin.structure (accessed 26 June 2009).

PHYSICS AND ASTRONOMY

Jenny Frost

INTRODUCTION

We had stopped for lunch, a late lunch, as we had lost the route and been forced to do a fairly difficult scramble down steep rocks. We were still way up a mountain and the mist was thick. One of the group pulled out a bag of hermetically sealed crisps from her rucksack – it was blown up like a balloon. Nobody bothered to explain, but ate the crisps with the added satisfaction of knowing why the packet was like that.

(Notes from the author's trip to the Tatras mountains in Poland, 2002)

Behind most of physics is a need to explain events like this. Physics attempts to understand the 'rules' by which the universe works; the way in which matter holds together, how energy interacts with matter and how changes occur. There is a drive, perhaps for elegance or simplicity, to work with as few rules as possible, so that each rule has implications for many phenomena.

At the macroscopic level, the tautness of the crisp bag can be attributed to the pressure difference between the air inside the bag (filled in the factory at a lower level) and the rarefied air high on the mountain. At the so-called microscopic level, the pressure difference can be explained in terms of the different number of air molecules bombarding the inside and the outside of the bag.

Both macroscopic and microscopic explanations are important in physics and will be used in the context of the following topics:

- forces and fields
- the nature of matter
- electricity
- electromagnetic radiation
- radioactivity
- change and energy transfer
- the earth in space
- the expanding universe
- the made world.

Physics and astronomy have been put together in this unit because the development of theories of the solar system and the universe, has relied on the laws of physics which apply as much 'out there' as they do on Earth.

OBJECTIVES

By the end of this unit you should:

■ be aware of the scope of physics and astronomy
■ have some insight into the ways of thinking characteristic of this area of science
■ be confident to explore the area further.

THE SCOPE OF PHYSICS AND ASTRONOMY

Physics and astronomy cover a wide variety of phenomena. The movement of stars and planets; the behaviour of light and heat, of sound, of electricity and magnetism; the discovery of less easily detectable phenomena such as radio waves, ultra violet light, X-rays and radioactivity; the behaviour of the 'stuff' of which the world is made; the forces which exist and the way they determine what happens; and energy transfers which accompany change.

In size terms alone the scope is impressive, from the universe to the smallest of particles. The universe is a million trillion times larger than we are, and quarks (the particles of which protons and neutrons are made) are a trillion times smaller. Physics, like all science, involves detective work, with people *imagining* how the natural world works if only they were the appropriate size and had the appropriate detectors to 'see' everything. This imagining brings into existence a range of 'entities' – particles, current, voltage, gravity, electrons, density, power, energy, work, forces – which become not just end points in their own right but the ingredients of other explanations.

FORCES AND FIELDS

Forces form an important ingredient of explanations in physics. Forces, which in everyday terms we think of as pushes and pulls, all involve interactions between two objects: either through the so-called 'contact forces' (experienced by two objects touching) or through non-contact forces (such as magnetic attraction and repulsion between two magnets; electrostatic attraction or repulsion between electric charges; gravitational attraction between two masses). The contact forces are temporary, i.e. they exist only while the objects are touching, while the non-contact forces are permanent (although their strengths reduce as the distance between the objects increases). A significant part of this account is that both objects experience the same magnitude of the force, but in opposite directions; that is you cannot have one pull without the other.

However, in many situations the concern is for the effect of a force (or forces) on one object (like worrying about the effect of a collision on a car, but not about the effect on the wall it hit). Forces on a single object can have three effects: they can balance other forces on the object, they can change the movement of the object and they can distort the object.

For the first effect imagine a person holding a bucket of water stationary in one hand. The upward pull of the person's hand and arm must have the same magnitude as the weight of the bucket, but acts in the opposite direction. The two forces cancel each other out, they are said to be 'balanced' and there is no resultant force on the bucket. On the other hand, where a person starts pushing a child along in a toy car, there is a resultant force as the push must be greater than the retarding frictional forces, to get the car started.

This leads to the effect of forces on the motion of an object. There is a simple rule with respect to motion and resultant forces: if there is a resultant force on an object then the object's movement will change (its speed or direction); if there is no resultant force the object will carry on moving as before (Newton's first law of motion). This is counter-intuitive because it is saying that an object which is already moving will carry on moving in the same way if there is no force on it to accelerate it, change its direction or slow it down. This is not our everyday experience as cars, for instance, without engines pushing them, soon come to a stop. (In this case, while there is apparently no force on the car, there is, of course, the force of friction that slows it down.) Accepting this idea takes time, but it explains why there is no need for an engine to keep the Earth and planets moving, why sky-divers reach a terminal velocity (i.e. a steady speed when the drag upwards of the air balances the downward pull of their weight) and why air particles keep moving without stopping.

The third effect of forces, distortion, can be seen in forcemeters, where the strength of a force can be measured by the extension of a spring or the twist of a torsion balance.

Related to forces are fields. Fields are areas of influence such as magnetic fields round magnets, electrical fields round electrical charges and gravitational fields round masses and are associated with the non-contact forces.

THE NATURE OF MATTER

The particulate nature of matter is another important theory in physics. Bernoulli in the early eighteenth century imagined gases to be made of swarms of particles which moved according to Newton's laws of motion, hitting the sides of a container and bouncing off, without losing speed. As gases get hotter the particles move more rapidly, and as they get cooler the particles slow down. Eventually the particles slow down enough to be unable to move far from nearby particles because of the forces holding them together, and then liquids are formed. As the temperature drops still further they stay in the same position relative to neighbours and solids are formed. This model explains many phenomena such as change of state, pressure of gases, compressibility of gases and non-compressibility of liquids and solids, and the expansion and contraction of materials.

The later discovery that the particles that Bernouilli had imagined, and that we now know as atoms and molecules, are made up of three more fundamental particles (protons, neutrons and electrons) is explained in Unit 3.3. More recently still, the protons and neutrons are known not to be as fundamental as originally thought; they are each made up of even smaller particles, called quarks. There is now the question as to whether quarks and leptons (electrons and associated particles) are the most fundamental particles or whether they are manifestations of something even more fundamental.

Forces between atoms and molecules, and between protons and electrons inside the atom, are described in Unit 3.3. They are electrostatic forces (forces between charges). Forces holding the protons and neutrons together in the nucleus are of a different nature.

They are referred to as nuclear forces; these have to be much stronger than electrostatic forces, otherwise the positive charges on the protons would push the nucleus apart.

ELECTRICITY

Electrical phenomena arise from some constituents of matter being charged, either negatively (e.g. electrons) or positively (e.g. protons). Electrostatics refers to the study of stationary charges and current electricity refers to where the charges are moving. The two phenomena are not, of course, distinct: build up of electrostatic charge in clouds results eventually in an electric current flowing from the cloud to the ground in lightning.

Positive and negative charges attract, and like charges repel each other. A well-known instance of electrostatics is brushing recently washed hair; the hair sticks to the brush or stands up on end. The brush removes some of the outer electrons from the molecules of the hair, making the brush negatively charged and leaving the hair positively charged. So the brush is attracted to the hair and the hair stands on end, with the positively charged strands of hair getting as far away as possible from each other.

The most common form of electric current is the flow of electrons along a wire, but it can also be the flow of positive and negative ions through a liquid as in electrolysis. In a circuit, say of a bulb connected by two wires to a battery, a current will only flow if a) there is no gap in the metal path anywhere (broken filament or poor contacts) or b) if there is an energy supply (e.g. a battery or other power supply). If there is no current in a circuit, it is not caused by an absence of electrons but by the fact the electrons are not moving. The electrons that form the current are the outer electrons of the atoms that make up the wire. The electrons are not stored in the battery; they do not pour out like water from a water tank. The battery merely supplies the energy to move the electrons and as the electrons are negatively charged they repel each other, and so when one moves, its neighbour moves, and so on right round the circuit. The signal to move travels at the speed of light round a circuit (300,000 km/second), (which is why when a device is switched on it comes on, what seems to be, immediately), while the velocity of the electrons through a copper wire is more like a tenth of a millimetre/second.

Electric currents can produce several effects, but here I deal with two: heating and production of magnetic fields. Wires get hot when electricity passes through them. Sometimes this is a desired effect (electrical heaters) and sometimes it is just a waste of energy. If, for instance, we are running an electric motor it is a pity some of the energy ends up warming the environment. This reduces the efficiency of the motor, but there is nothing that can be done about it.

Magnetic fields are produced round wires carrying a current. Again there is nothing we can do about it; the associated magnetic fields are simply electrical phenomena. We use them, however, to good effect in electromagnets and electric motors. In a similar way, if a wire is in a changing magnetic field, then an electric current will be produced in it; this is the basis of the production of electricity in dynamos and in alternators in power stations.

ELECTROMAGNETIC RADIATION

One of the puzzles that people often have is why the term 'electromagnetic' is linked to phenomena like light and heat that do not seem to have anything to do with electricity and magnetism. Radio waves, microwaves, infrared light, visible light, ultra violet light,

X-rays and gamma rays (the components of the electromagnetic spectrum) all turn out to be electromagnetic waves generated by the acceleration of electric charge. (The excitation of electrons in a heated filament produces light and the oscillation of an alternating current produces radio waves.) The waves travel out from sources (like water ripples travelling out from a stone thrown in a pond) until they encounter some obstacle, when they might be reflected, transmitted or absorbed. If they are reflected or transmitted they carry on travelling. If they are absorbed they transfer their energy to the object, which may get hotter or react in some other way. Obviously, what counts as an obstacle varies for each type of radiation; skin, which reflects light, is transparent to X-rays.

While we talk of 'visible' light, it is no more visible than, say, radio waves or X-rays, in that we cannot see it in transit. Our sensation of 'seeing' comes from when light, reflecting off an object, enters the eye and, on being absorbed, triggers a reaction in the cells in the retina.

All these forms of radiations, while having wave-like properties, also have particle-like properties; when they transfer energy during absorption, they do so only in discrete 'packets', which are called photons. The energy of a photon is inversely proportional to the wavelength, so the photons of radio waves (long wavelengths) have lower energy than those of gamma rays (short wavelengths). The photons of X-rays, gamma rays and ultra violet light have sufficient energy to knock electrons out of the atoms of material they hit, causing the atoms to be ionised. This increases the likelihood of chemical reactions taking place and the absorbing material changing, hence the concern for preventing exposure of animal tissue to these rays. This effect can be used beneficially to destroy unwanted cancerous growths, but the process has to be monitored carefully to reduce damage to other parts of the body.

RADIOACTIVITY

A small number of elements have nuclei which are unstable and which emit high-energy rays (alpha, beta and gamma rays) (see Unit 3.3). These are radioactive elements. Alpha and beta rays are streams of particles (alpha rays are helium nuclei – two neutrons and two protons; beta rays are electrons). Gamma rays are part of the electromagnetic spectrum (similar wavelength to X-rays – the main difference between them being their source: X-rays are created in X-ray machines). Alpha and beta rays can also cause ionisation like gamma rays, and may be used in medical treatment.

CHANGE AND ENERGY TRANSFER

Energy, a concept used in all areas of science, is difficult to define. It is a property of a system; it can be measured, but it is not 'stuff'. There are two ways of talking about energy, one using *energy transfer* and one using *types of energy*. The *energy transfer* model focuses on sources of energy, mechanisms for transferring energy from place to place and efficiency of transfer. The *types of energy* model, on the other hand, identifies types (kinetic, potential, heat, light etc.) and focuses on changes from one type to another. You will find one or the other (or a hybrid of the two) in different textbooks. The transfer model is used here.

The key to the transfer model is to think about *change* in the physical world. Any change requires a transfer of energy from one place (the source) to another place (e.g. transferring the energy in the food and oxygen system in your body to a bike you are riding). Examples of systems that can be sources of energy are:

- chemicals that can be made to react (petrol and oxygen – note that petrol on its own is not a source of energy)
- objects displaced in a field, e.g. a gravitational field (water that is in a mountain lake)
- temperature differences (Sun with respect to the Earth)
- reversible deformations (stretched springs)
- moving objects (wind, running water, fast-moving particles).

Mechanisms of transfer include:

- mechanical devices (water wheels, car engines, muscles and joints)
- radiation (solar heating of the Earth)
- mechanical waves (sound, water waves, earthquakes)
- electric current (this is a major means of energy transfer in the world).

The energy available in a system and the amount transferred from place to place can be measured. When a change has occurred (say the lifting of building materials to the top of a building) the energy is not lost but transferred to another place. Here the building materials have gained some energy by being higher (and hence capable of falling down and gaining speed), some energy is dissipated as sound and some energy goes to heating up the electric motor and pulley ropes, which, as they cool, dissipate it to the atmosphere. From a 'usefulness' point of view only some of the energy remains, but from a 'total energy' point of view it can all be tracked. This is the law of conservation of energy. The efficiency of the transfer is the percentage of available energy that goes into the intended work.

The tendency of all energy transfers to end up with general heating of the environment is significant. The Earth does not, however, get hotter and hotter as a result. The heating causes a temperature difference between the Earth and the outside and much of the energy is radiated out, most noticeably at night. Given that the Earth is transferring energy out to the rest of the universe, life could not continue here if it were not for the Sun transferring energy back into the Earth. At the moment, however, the flow out is not balancing the flow in and hence we have global warming (see Unit 3.5).

THE EARTH IN SPACE

The model that we now have of the Earth and its place in the solar system is very different from our everyday perceptions. What appears to be a cool, flat stationary Earth is in fact a large spherical ball of rock, so intensely hot inside that much is molten. This rocky ball is spinning with a surface speed at the equator of 1000 km/hr and is hurtling through space at 100,000 km/hr as it orbits the Sun, its axis of spin tilted at about 23° to the plane of the orbit. It is covered with a thin layer of air confined to about the first 15 km from the surface, held there by the gravitational pull of the Earth. The Earth stays in orbit 'attached' by the gravitational attraction between it and the Sun. The Earth, with its companion moon, is one of eight planets orbiting the Sun. The belief in this model comes from its ability to explain, amongst other things, why we have day and night, why there are seasons, why we have eclipses of the Sun and Moon, and the phases of the Moon.

THE EXPANDING UNIVERSE

The Earth, large and important to us, turns out to be but a speck in an enormous universe. It takes light, travelling at 300,000 km/second, four years to reach the next star, and 100,000 years to travel across our galaxy. Beyond that there are millions of other galaxies. Everything is moving away from everything else (detected by the red shift in the light from distant stars). The universe is finite, but with no edge. There is no one centre – every point disappearing from every other point.

How did it all begin? The story goes something like this. The universe started with a big bang, which occurred in an extremely short space of time – far too short a time for much material to coalesce, so only small atoms were made, mostly hydrogen, a little helium and a lot of separate particles. These coalesced and formed stars. The Earth formed at a much later date, from an explosion of a star, which took place more slowly than the Big Bang and so allowed time for larger atoms to form from the coalescence of smaller ones.

THE MADE WORLD

It is easy to give an account of physics that makes it seem that the theoretical understanding of the world came first and the practical applications came afterwards. Technological development, however, is an intrinsic part of physics. There is as much science in the design of the particle accelerator at CERN as there is in the study of the particle collisions that occur within it. Theories of thermodynamics developed hand-in hand with the development of steam engines. Since 1945, development in radio technology and, latterly, space travel, have shifted astrophysics from optical astronomy to radio, microwave, and X-ray astronomy, revealing features of the universe not previously known.

Ask young people what they think are the main scientific advances of the last 100 years and it is technology which will dominate their answers: space travel; computers and iPods; mobile phones; cars; aeroplanes; surveillance equipment; surgical techniques; medical imaging; refrigerators; television; CD and DVD players; SATNAV systems. In thinking about physics it is as important to think about the made world as about the world of abstractions.

STRANGENESS OF THE STORIES IN PHYSICS

There is a contradiction in physics. On the one hand, when we get the hang of an explanation we recognise how 'logical' it is because the pieces fit. When gadgets work reliably, which most of them do for long periods at a time, we are aware of our mastery over the 'laws of physics' and the world seems an ordered place. On the other hand, the models and explanations are usually counter-intuitive and are not 'obvious' or 'common sense'. They seem far removed from the everyday word 'logical'. It is not obvious that the table at which I am typing this is really made up mostly of empty space and that the chair on which I am sitting, and which I believe I am touching, is really holding me at a distance by electrostatic forces between my molecules and those of the chair. It is not obvious that when I look out of the window at the green leaves, they are not really green, they are merely reflecting the green light into my eyes and absorbing all the other wavelengths.

A POSSIBLE NEXT STEP

The suggested reading will help you extend your knowledge of physics. Task 3.4.1 contains some questions that invite explanation. Work on them with colleagues, always trying to come up with the cause for particular effects – you may well have explanations at macroscopic and microscopic levels – or perhaps just one.

Task 3.4.1 **Finding explanations for phenomena**

Try to find explanations for the following. Discuss answers with your colleagues:

- Why does the Moon not fall down onto the Earth?
- Why can eggs be beaten faster with a mechanical egg whisk than without?
- Where do the stars go during the day?
- Why is it difficult to turn corners on ice?
- Why do sprinters start their races from starting blocks?
- What is the difference between being radioactive and being irradiated?
- Why does helium make your voice go high?
- How do we know how far away the Sun is?
- Why do land-line phones still work during a power cut?

Collect other physics questions that could be used in your teaching. File them appropriately.

SUMMARY AND KEY POINTS

Physics is the most fundamental of the sciences as it tries to answer questions about the basic constituents of matter, the forces between them and the exchange between matter and energy. Its theories and models, while powerful explanatory tools, for a wide range of phenomena from the tiniest particles to the universe, are often not intuitive and require suspension of common sense to appreciate them.

FURTHER READING

Bowdley, D. (2009) Active in space. Special edition. *School Science Review*, 2009, 90 (333), 43–103.

Driver, R., Squires, A., Rushworth, P. and Wood-Robinson, V. (1994) *Making Sense of Secondary Science: Research into Children's Ideas*. London: Routledge.
     This provides an insight into learners' particular difficulties in thinking through the ideas in science – select the physics and astronomy topics.

Sang, D. (ed.) (2000) *Teaching Secondary Physics*. London: John Murray for ASE.
     This book gives useful explanations of the physics of KS3 and KS4 as well as providing teaching strategies and further reading.

Some school textbooks

Johnson, K. (2006) *New Physics for You*. **Cheltenham: Nelson Thornes Ltd.**
  Aimed at GCSE. There are of course many other GCSE texts.

Adams, A. and Allday, J. (2000) *Advanced Physics*. **Oxford: Oxford University Press.**
  A GCE Advanced level textbook, with a good combination of explanation, application, historical detail, worked examples and practice questions. Traditional categorisation of topics.

Ogborn, J. (ed.) (2008) *Advancing Physics AS* and *Advancing Physics A2*.
  GCE Advanced level resources, containing teachers' and students' guides, and supporting CD-ROMs. Non-traditional organisation of topics, which provides an exciting approach to physics. For more information go the Institute of Physics. (http://advancingphysics.iop.org/).

Science of everyday life, everyday phenomena and technology

Brain, M. (2001) *How Stuff Works*. **New York: Hungry Minds.**

Brain, M. (2003) *More How Stuff Works*. **New York: Hungry Minds.**
  Easy-to-read collection of answers to a host of questions about technological inventions. http://www.howstuffworks.com

Naylor, J. (2002) *Out of the Blue. A 24–hour Skywatcher's Guide*. **Cambridge: Cambridge University Press.**
  A book that can be dipped into at any time you see something interesting in the sky – halos round the Sun and Moon; double rainbows… Explanations are given for them all.

Biographical texts

Sobel, D. (1996) *Longitude: The True Story of a Lone Genius Who Solved the Greatest Scientific Problem of his Time*. **London: Fourth Estate.**

Porter, R. and Ogilvie, M. (2000) *The Hutchinson Dictionary of Scientific Biography, Volumes I and II*. **Oxford: Helicon.**

Ellis, P., Ryan, R. and Macdonald, A. (2003) *Reading into Science: Physics*. **Cheltenham: Nelson Thornes.**
  This book, along with similar ones for biology and chemistry, was produced to support the ideas and evidence part of the National Curriculum. It contains short articles about development of science through both contemporary and historical case studies.

RELEVANT WEBSITES

Brain, M. (2004)
  http://science.howstuffworks.com/ (accessed 17 August 2009).

Institute of Physics
  http://www.iop.org/ (accessed 17 August 2009). Range of support for teaching physics from KS3 to Advanced level. Register online at their website (www.talkphysics.org) to download materials.

New Scientist
  http://www.newscientist.com/ (accessed 17 August 2009). *New Scientist* is useful for keeping you up-to-date with ideas and developments in science.

North American Space Agency

http://www.nasa.gov/ (accessed 17 August 2009).

A good website for up-to-date information about space exploration. Good pictures and explanations.

Bescenta

http://www.bescenta.co.uk/home.cfm (accessed 17 August 2009).

This gives information about a lot of physics and technology (see sections on: space; our planet; transport; and gadgets).

Google search engine

http://www.google.com (accessed 17 August 2009).

EARTH SCIENCE

Tony Turner

INTRODUCTION

Earth science deals with the structure and composition of the Earth, its origins, physical features, changing aspects and all of its natural phenomena. It uses chemistry, mathematics and physics to build a quantitative understanding of the planet.

Aspects of the Earth have long puzzled humans. How did the mountains form and why are there deep canyons beneath the sea? How can the pattern of volcanic activity and earthquake sites over the Earth's surface be explained? The occurrence of fossils high in the mountains well above sea-level challenged both scientific understanding and cultural mores. Likewise the appearance of rocks at high altitude that clearly had once been beneath the sea offered a similar challenge.

Rocks are usually thought of as solid, unbending materials but some rock faces show clearly that rocks have been bent as a result of huge forces acting on them; and lava from volcanic activity shows that rocks can melt. Some island groups have been shown to contain islands with young rocks and adjacent islands with older rocks, e.g. the Galapagos Archipelago. How could that be?

The explanation of these phenomena and many others is the result of advances in the sciences mentioned above, of careful and painstaking observation over a few hundred years and the development of an explanatory model by J. T. Wilson, the Plate Tectonic Theory.

OBJECTIVES

By the end of this unit you should:

- understand how the materials of the Earth undergo continuous change
- be able to describe the nature of the different layers of the Earth from the crust to the core
- understand aspects of the Plate Tectonic Theory and how it explains features of the Earth's crust.

THE ROCK CYCLE

Rocks on the surface and inside the Earth undergo continuous change. As you go deeper into the Earth the temperature increases, largely due to radioactivity. Inside the Earth rocks melt, move and solidify; material from within the Earth comes to the surface either as magma (molten rock) or new rock. Over long periods of time, surface rocks are eroded by the action of water, temperature changes and wind. Particles from eroded rocks are moved around by water and wind and then deposited elsewhere on the Earth's surface. Most deposition takes place on sea or lake beds, although there is some surface deposition.

See Figure 3.5.1 and 'The rock cycle' at BBC Schools Chemistry in *Relevant websites*.

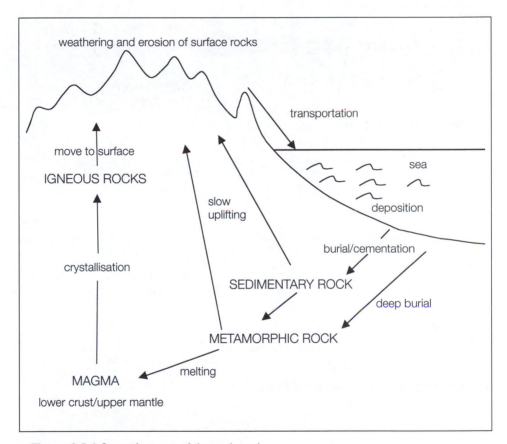

■ **Figure 3.5.1** Some features of the rock cycle
Source: Adapted from McDuell, 2000: 200

Evidence for the rock cycle comes from careful observation of the surface of the Earth. This includes the analysis of rocks and minerals for their chemical composition, their physical appearance and evidence of fossil remains as well as from the study of the patterns of rock distribution across the surface, including the seabed, and of the molten rock thrown up in volcanoes.

STRUCTURE OF THE EARTH

A major task facing geologists is to understand the state and composition of the Earth's interior without being able to go there. Evidence about the interior of the Earth comes from seismic studies, i.e. the study of waves passing through the Earth, usually generated by earthquake activity but also by humans in seismic surveys where the waves from controlled underground explosions are analysed. The different ways in which these waves pass through the Earth show evidence of solid or liquid phases and the boundaries between them. The picture of the Earth's interior that emerges is shown in Figure 3.5.2.

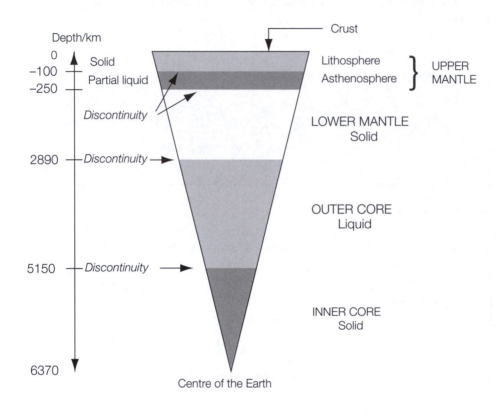

■ **Figure 3.5.2** Segment cross-section of the Earth
Source: Adapted from King, 2000: 60

The Earth's crust and the lithosphere below is solid rock about 100 km thick, although the lithosphere is largely igneous rock (see 'surface rocks' below). Beneath the crust is another layer, the asthenosphere, which is largely solid rock with some liquid. The lithosphere and asthenosphere form the upper mantle. The solid lower mantle is about 2500 km thick and sits above the liquid outer core. The inner core is solid. The motion of matter in the liquid core, which contains liquid metals such as iron, is believed to be the source of the Earth's magnetism although this is disputed by some scientists.

Earthquakes, or controlled explosions, are used to build the picture in Figure 3.5.2. Earthquakes release enormous amounts of energy, which is transferred through the Earth and can be detected at many parts of the Earth's surface. The energy is carried by waves that either travel *on* the surface, where they do a lot of damage, or pass *through* the Earth. There are two types of waves that travel through the Earth, the faster (5 km/sec) longitudinal Primary waves (P), which travel through solids, liquids and gases, and the slower (3 km/sec) transverse secondary waves (S), which travel only through solids. Both S and P waves undergo reflection and refraction. Using seismometers located around the Earth, the position, strength and time of arrival of the S and P waves are recorded from which the structure of the Earth's interior is inferred.

SURFACE ROCKS

Rocks are made up of minerals. Some rocks contain just one mineral, such as marble (calcite) or diamond (crystalline form of carbon); small amounts of impurities may change the appearance of the rock giving, for example, the decorative coloured marbles. Minerals often have characteristic features, such as a colour and regular crystal shape, for example quartz, diamond and many precious stones. Other minerals appear amorphous, such as opal and graphite. Many rocks are mixtures of minerals, such as granite, the constituents of which were formed by crystallisation from a liquid. Other mixed rocks arise from the way they were deposited, e.g. as sediments in rivers such as sandstone, mudstone and conglomerates.

In order to make some sense of the bewildering number of rocks, they can be classified by origin. Igneous rock is formed by magma cooling: slow cooling underground produces larger crystals, e.g. as in granite; rapid cooling on the surface produces small crystals, e.g. as in basalt. Both rocks are made of interlocking crystals of different minerals. Some rapid cooling produces glass-like substances, e.g. obsidian, or powdery rock with air pockets as in pumice stone.

Most of Earth's rocks are sedimentary, formed by the erosion of other rocks and subsequent deposition of the eroded material (see The rock cycle, discussed earlier). The eroded particles are carried by water and deposited on a lake or sea bed (Figure 3.5.1). Characteristics of sedimentary rock include strata (the layering of successive types of sediment), often a cement holding together the particles, e.g. quartz particles bonded by calcite in some sandstone and, sometimes, the presence of fossils, e.g. in limestone such as Portland stone. Some sedimentary rocks are the product of deposition of dead animals, e.g. chalk (calcium carbonate, $CaCO_3$) or dead plants, e.g. coal (largely carbon) or kieselguhr (largely silica, SiO_2).

A third type of rock is metamorphic rock (literally 'changed' rock). Both igneous and sedimentary rock change as conditions of temperature, pressure or chemical environment alter. Marble was once limestone, slate is altered mudstone and diamond is metamorphosed graphite.

To identify a rock you need to know its location and the environment in which it was found, e.g. the strata or the presence of fossils and, in addition, to be able to examine its structure, e.g. type or size of crystals, and know its chemical composition and the constituent minerals. Other helpful factors include physical characteristics such as colour, density and hardness. A generalised rock key is given in 'Peck, D. The rock identification key', listed in *Relevant websites*.

TECTONIC PLATE THEORY

If most of the Earth's rocks are sedimentary, and most of these were formed by deposition on sea beds, how is it that they are now above (sometimes thousands of metres above) the sea? The Tectonic Plate Theory, developed by J.T. Wilson in the 1960s, provides the basis for understanding how the Earth's features have come to be as they are, the mountains and trenches, volcanoes and earthquakes, continents and islands, faults and folds (see Wilson, J.T. in Porter and Ogilvie, 2000). The word 'tectonic' refers to the processes of building. The Earth's crust sits on the lithosphere; the crust and lithosphere are both solid and subject to forces from below. The lithosphere is a rigid layer divided into moving 'plates' – six major plates and a number of minor plates, all of which diverge, converge or slide past each other. They fall into two main types, oceanic plates and continental plates. Oceanic plates are thinner but denser than continental ones. Figure 3.5.3 shows the large plates and some smaller plates and their boundaries. Maps such as these may be found on the internet. A useful one is 'Earthquake patterns and tectonic plate distribution' (see *Relevant websites*). Similar maps can be found for patterns of volcanic activity.

Plates move at about 2–3 cm per annum. Plate movements have given rise to the features of the Earth mentioned above and explain how continents move. At the plate boundaries, earthquakes and volcanoes occur and mountains are formed. The mapping of sites of earthquake and volcanic activity across the globe and the resulting patterns contributed to the development of the Tectonic Plate Theory. The plates move because the lithosphere sits on the asthenosphere, where the mantle is hotter and less rigid and the convection currents in this region 'carry' the plates.

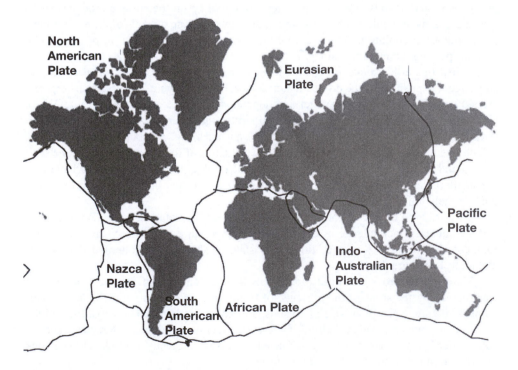

■ **Figure 3.5.3** Map of the Earth showing plate boundaries

The evidence for the Tectonic Plate Theory comes from many sources including:

■ the continents fitting together in a similar way to a jigsaw puzzle
■ the same rock sequences appearing in continents now separated by oceans
■ similar distribution of fossils appearing in continents now separated by oceans
■ the alignment of magnetic particles in the ocean crust on either side of the mid-ocean ridges
■ the pattern of distribution of volcanoes and earthquake zones on the Earth's surface.

Tectonic plates interact in different ways:

■ Where two oceanic plates are moving apart (a divergent, or constructive, boundary), magma rises, solidifies and becomes a mid-ocean ridge. The new material moves away from the ridge at equal rates on each side causing sea-floor spreading. The mid-Atlantic ridge separates the Eurasian plate from the North American plate in the northern hemisphere. Iceland straddles that plate boundary and is one of the few places where you can see an active spreading ridge above sea level (see Figure 3.5.3).
■ When an oceanic plate meets a continental plate (a convergent boundary), the oceanic plate moves beneath the less dense continental plate (in a 'subduction zone'), melts and becomes part of the mantle; this is a destructive boundary. Such regions generate earthquakes and volcanoes, and mountain ranges form, e.g. the Andes. In this case the Nazca plate is moving beneath the South American plate.
■ When two continental plates collide (another type of convergent boundary), neither plate slides beneath the other but upheaval of the crust occurs to produce earthquakes and fold mountains, e.g. the Himalayas. This feature occurs on the boundary between the Eurasian plate and the India Australia plate.
■ If two plates try to slide past each other (a transform boundary), the movement is restricted until the pressure overcomes the frictional forces. This situation produces sudden damaging earthquakes, e.g. along the San Andreas fault in California. Fault lines in rocks on the Earth's surface show evidence of past events.

Sometimes the hot asthenosphere (Figure 3.5.2) finds a weak place in the lithosphere to allow magma to rise from beneath the ocean floor, often forming islands in the sea, such as the Hawaiian Islands. These events are thought to occur when a narrow column of hot mantle, a 'mantle plume', reaches the surface, though there are alternative explanations. The Galapagos Islands were also formed in this way; as the plate on which they rest moves one island moves away from the hotspot; later another island is formed above the hotspot and so a chain of volcanic islands is formed. Other features of hotspots are the appearance of hot springs such as those found in Hot Springs National Park, USA, in Iceland and in New Zealand.

TIME

The Earth is believed to be 4600 million years old; mammals appeared about 65 million years ago and humans much later. An analogy helps in understanding the immensity of time, sometimes referred to as 'deep time'. If one year represents the time since the Earth came into being, humans appeared at 6 p.m. on 31 December.

Geological time is divided into eons, which are progressively sub-divided into eras, periods and epochs. Deciding the boundaries between these is based on a range of evidence, including significant differences between rock types and fossil population. Figure 3.5.4 gives an outline of eons, eras and periods (see *Relevant websites* for further details). Given the complexity of sorting evidence, it is not a surprise that there is controversy amongst geologists about the most suitable categorisation. Note that the naming of eras and periods often refers to significant features or the place where strata were first recognised.

Eon	Era	Date (mya)	Periods	Origin of name – feature or place
Pre-Cambrian *(Now divided into several eons)*	See websites for details	Beginning of universe 4500–542		
Phanerozoic	Palaeozoic (Ancient life)	542–251	Cambrian	Wales (old name Cambria)
			Ordovician	Ordovicas – ancient Welsh tribe
			Silurian	Silures – ancient British tribe
			Devonian	Devon
			Carboniferous	Coal bearing
			Permian	Perm – Russian area
	Mesozoic (Middle life)	251–65	Triassic	'Three layers', outcrop in Germany
			Jurassic	Jura Mountains
			Cretacious	Chalk
	Cenozoic (Recent life)	65–now	Paleogene (Tertiary)	Birth of distant past
			Neogene (Tertiary)	'New born'
			Quaternary	Follows Tertiary period

■ **Figure 3.5.4** Geological eons, eras and periods

DATING ROCKS AND FOSSILS

Two methods are used for dating materials, relative dating and radiometric dating, both of which may be supported by fossil evidence. Relative dating identifies the order of geological events without assigning a date. Sedimentation studies predict that younger rocks lie above older rocks, the law of superposition. Faults and intrusions, lifting and folding complicate interpretations. Experience has given further guidance to sequencing rocks; for example, if a rock stratum has another material introduced into it, e.g. an intrusion of quartz, then the intrusion must be younger than the rocks of the main stratum.

Fossils are found in sedimentary rocks and are often unique to particular eras or periods of the Earth's history. They help to correlate rock sequences and interpret past environments.

Radiometric dating uses radioactive decay (see Unit 3.3). It is important for this process that the half-lives of radioactive elements are known accurately (half-life is the time taken for half the atoms to decay). Two elements used for this type of dating are carbon and uranium.

Radiocarbon dating is used for materials up to 50,000 years old. Carbon exists naturally as two isotopes, carbon 12 ($^{12}C_6$) and carbon 14 ($^{14}C_6$) and the normal ratio of the two isotopes in atmospheric carbon dioxide is known. Only carbon 14 is radioactive with a half-life of 5730 years, decaying into nitrogen and releasing electrons (beta particles). When a plant makes food by photosynthesis it uses carbon dioxide containing both carbon isotopes. When the organism dies, no further carbon is incorporated into the material. After many years the ratio of the two isotopes changes as carbon 14 decays and the radioactivity of the material changes. The remains of plant, animal and products made from them can be dated by this method, e.g. pollen, bones, Turin Shroud.

Other radioactive systems can be used to date older materials. Some rocks, e.g. granite, can be dated from their uranium content. Natural uranium contains uranium 238, which decays into a lead isotope with a half-life of 4.47 billion years.

ENVIRONMENTAL CHANGE

There is evidence that the climate of the Earth has changed several times throughout geological time, including several ice ages. During the last ice age, about 20,000 years ago, much of northern Europe was covered in sheet ice. The causes of an ice age are several and may be related to changes in atmospheric gases, changes in the Earth's orbit about the Sun or changes in the motion of tectonic plates. Dinosaurs, believed to exist from between 250 million years ago (250 mya) to about 65 mya, may have become extinct through an altered climate caused by one or more meteorite impacts. The Earth's climate may be altered by many natural events, including volcanic eruptions and changes in the level of solar radiation. However, the current climate change – global warming – is different from those mentioned above because it is linked to human population growth and the increase in carbon dioxide and other gases in the atmosphere resulting from industrialisation and the use of fossil fuels.

Associated with these issues, there are many pollution problems that are being addressed by legislation or changing people's habits, e.g. the recycling movement; the removal of sulphur oxides from flue gases to minimise acid rain; the banning of domestic coal burning to reduce atmospheric particle pollution. However, the warming of the atmosphere is a problem on a different scale, potentially changing the environment of the whole planet.

The effect of the growth in the burning of fossil fuels has been to increase the amount of carbon dioxide in the atmosphere and, where inadequate combustion has occurred, an increase of hydrocarbons in the atmosphere. The increase in the concentration of these two gases, together with nitrous oxide (a product of combustion of nitrogen from air in hydrocarbon burning engines) are the main contributors to the rise in the average global temperature (see Figure 3.5.5). These gases are the main contributors to global warming.

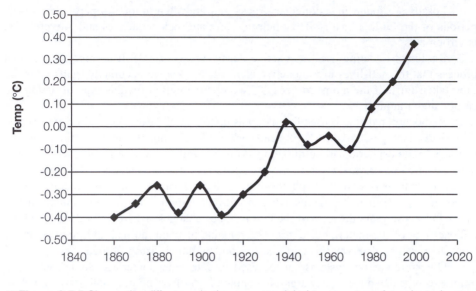

■ **Figure 3.5.5** Shows the difference in the average global temperature, for selected years from 1860 to 2000, from the average global temperature in the period 1961–1990

Source: Adapted from Houghton, 2001: 3

Worldwide temperature readings for each year show that the average global temperature rose by about 0.6°C over the last 140 years. The data for the years post-1860 are more reliable than earlier periods and, in addition, industrialisation in the west was in full swing.

Data from tree-ring samples, corals, ice cores and historical records have been analysed and northern hemisphere average temperatures inferred from them. These analyses suggest that in the 800 years prior to 1860 the average 50-year global temperature was some 0.2°C below the average global temperature in the period 1961 to 1990, with equally small fluctuations in each 50-year period, a pattern quite unlike that post-1860 (for further information see Houghton, 2001: 3).

The changes in the concentration of the gases mentioned above are similar in pattern to the temperature changes and are listed in Figure 3.5.6. Over approximately 200 years, the carbon dioxide concentration grew by about 32 per cent, methane by 133 per cent and nitrous oxide by 16 per cent.

The evidence for global warming does not rely solely on temperature changes. Other changes linked with global warming include:

- glacier retreat, melting of the ice caps and ice-covered seas at the poles
- changing climate and increase in the intensity of severe weather conditions, together with greater rainfall
- thawing of the permafrost
- lengthening in the growing seasons in mid to high latitudes
- earlier flowering of plants, budding of trees and emergence of insects.

Gas	Period 1000–1800	Year 1998
CO_2 (part/million) carbon dioxide	280	370
CH_4 ppm methane	750	1745
N_2O ppm Nitrous oxide	270	314

■ **Figure 3.5.6** Changes in selected gas concentration in air in the millennium 1000 to 2000
Source: Houghton, 2001: 6

An evocative image of global warming is the melting of the snows on Mount Kilimanjaro, which has lost 82 per cent of its snow since 1912 and about one third of that since 1990.

The possible changes that occur vary according to region and the effect global warming has in that geographical area. Some benefits of global warming may include:

■ increase in crop yields in some mid-latitude countries
■ possible increased timber supply
■ increased water resources in some regions, e.g. south-east Asia
■ fewer winter deaths
■ reduced energy consumption in winter time in some regions.

Set against this are possible negative effects such as:

■ a reduced crop yield and a reduced water supply in tropical and semi-tropical countries
■ greater population exposure to insect-borne diseases such as malaria and water-borne diseases such as cholera, associated with warmer climate and increased rainfall
■ flooding in low-lying regions and sea-level rise because of ice melting and increased rainfall
■ greater energy consumption where summer temperatures rise, requiring air conditioning.

For further detail and elaboration of these effects, see Houghton, 2001.

MECHANISMS OF GLOBAL WARMING

The Earth receives radiation from the Sun, absorbs some and re-radiates the rest back to space; the balance of 'energy in' and 'energy out' gives a steady average surface temperature of the Earth. The main radiation warming the Earth is infra-red, at wavelengths just beyond the visible. Most of the energy re-radiated is also in the infrared region.

The presence of water vapour in the Earth's atmosphere is the cause of the Earth's life-supporting conditions (without water the Earth would be much cooler). Water vapour is a trap for infrared radiation and there is a lot of water vapour in the atmosphere. The amount of water vapour in the atmosphere varies across the Earth's surface but human activity does not disturb the overall balance, although the chopping down of rainforests does alter the amount of atmospheric water vapour locally.

However, carbon dioxide, methane and nitrous oxide also absorb radiation and changes in their concentrations are affecting the balance of 'energy in' and 'energy out' of the planet. It is the changes in the concentration of these gases that has led to the trapping of more infrared radiation by preventing some radiation from escaping to space, thus raising average surface temperature of Earth. These gases are often referred to as 'greenhouses gases'. Although the mechanism is not actually the same as a greenhouse, the term has stuck.

Global warming appears to be accelerating since $c.1970$ and could be self-sustaining. For example, energy is radiated back into the atmosphere and space by reflection from the ice- and snow-covered areas of Earth. The loss of snow (white) allows increased absorption of radiation on the darker Earth, accelerating the global warming effect.

The great majority of climate scientists believe that global warming is caused by the increase in 'greenhouse gases' although there is no unanimity on this theory. If true, however, it means that carbon emissions must be reduced soon to stop further warming. Thus the use of fossil fuel must be reduced and replaced by alternatives. This process is not just a technical problem but also has economic and social consequences. The way we generate and use electricity must change, affecting, e.g., our landscapes (wind farms, tidal barriers), our houses (energy conservation, private energy generation) and our travel (commuting and leisure). The last brings into question the huge rise in car ownership, the balance between car use and public transport and the growth in air travel.

This section has touched on aspects of the environmental challenges facing human beings in this century, focusing on aspects of global warming. We have said little about the supply of water, especially clean water, or the need for increased and sustainable agriculture to feed the growing population without destroying more of the flora and fauna of the world. For further development of ideas about global warming and related environmental problems, see *Further reading*.

SUMMARY AND KEY POINTS

This unit has outlined the scope of Earth Science and indicated the importance of chemistry, physics and mathematics in developing an understanding of the Earth's structure and its changing face. The rock cycle has been introduced and its importance for understanding how the present structure of the Earth's surface has arisen, and that it is an ongoing process. An outline of the Plate Tectonic Theory has been given, with evidence for its acceptance and described features of plate movements. How rocks and fossils are dated has been included together with the associated theory. The ways in which the internal structure of the Earth is being understood have been outlined.

Finally concerns of environmental change have been raised and information given about the evidence for global warming and a brief mention of the mechanism. The possible advantages and disadvantages of global warming have been suggested.

FURTHER READING

Ramsden, E. (2001) *Key Science*, **3rd edition:** *Chemistry*. **Cheltenham: Stanley Thornes.**

> The section on 'The Earth' covers: the structure of the Earth; earthquakes; volcanoes; seismology; plate tectonics (with maps and diagrams); rocks and the rock cycle (including linking rock types to landscape). A similar account in greater detail can be found in her book *Chemistry for GCSE*.

Sergeant, S. and Smith, S. (2007) *Earth and Space Book 2*, **in S104 Open University course exploring science (Science Level 1). Milton Keynes: Open University.**

> A detailed discussion of the Earth and phenomena related to it and of seismology and Plate Tectonic Theory. There is also a substantial section on space science. Sample material is accessible online at http://www.ouw.co.uk/pdfs/S104_02.pdf (accessed 23 June 2009).

Open University Open Learning (2007) *Climate Change S 250_3*. **Milton Keynes: Open University.**

> A discussion of many aspects of global warming including the evidence for the theory, possible causes and implications for humanity. Strategies for combating climate change are identified and their implications for the way we live.
>
> http://openlearn.open.ac.uk/course/enrol.php?id=2805 (accessed 25 June 2009).

For more detail and discussion on climate change see

Houghton, J. T. (2001) *Climate Change 2001: The Scientific Basis*. **Third Assessment Report of the Intergovernmental Panel on Climate Change. Cambridge: Cambridge University Press.**

Intergovernment Panel on Climate Change (IPCC) (2007) *Fourth Assessment Report: The Physical Science Basis*. **Cambridge: Cambridge University Press.**

> http://www.ipcc.ch/pdf/assessment-report/ar4/wg1/ar4–wg1–frontmatter.pdf (accessed 25 June 2009).
>
> See also related publications by the IPCC (2007) 1. Impact, adaptations and vulnerability 2. Mitigation of climate change.

RELEVANT WEBSITES

Earth Science Teachers Association (ESTA)

> http://esta-uk.org

Earthquake patterns and tectonic plate distribution

> http://www.earthquakes.bgs.ac.uk/earthquakes/education/eq_booklet/eq_booklet_why_where.htm (accessed 22 June 2009).

Intergovernment Panel on Climate Change (IPCC) (2007) *Fourth Assessment Report: The Physical Science Basis.* **Cambridge: Cambridge University Press**

> http://www.ipcc.ch/pdf/assessment-report/ar4/wg1/ar4–wg1–frontmatter.pdf (accessed 25 June 2009).

Open University Open Learning (2007) *Climate Change S 250_3*. **Milton Keynes: Open University.**

> http://openlearn.open.ac.uk/course/enrol.php?id=2805 (accessed 25 June 2009).

Peck, D. The rock identification key

> http://www.rockhounds.com/rockshop/rockkey/index.html#slate (accessed 20 June 2009).

Radiocarbon dating

> http://www.bbc.co.uk/dna/h2g2/A637418 (accessed 21 June 2009).

The rock cycle at BBC Schools 'bitesize' chemistry

> http://www.bbc.co.uk/schools/ks3bitesize/science/chemistry/rock_cycle_9.shtml (accessed 20 June 2009).

PLANNING FOR TEACHING AND LEARNING SCIENCE

INTRODUCTION

Being able to plan a lesson, a sequence of lessons or a whole course involves being able to construct, ahead of time, a set of events for yourself and 25 to 35 pupils. Learning to plan is an iterative process, where problems that arise as plans are put into action in the classroom, inform the planning process. There are guidelines which can be followed which help to minimise these problems. Nevertheless, you will find planning to be a time consuming part of your work, and you may not feel that you are planning with any degree of confidence until well into your course.

We have started with pupils' learning in Unit 4.1. Lessons may be entertaining, properly organised, with the pupils well disciplined, but if the pupils are not learning science then the lessons are not effective. An introduction to cognitive development in science provides guidelines on pupil progression in science as a basis for planning for individuals within a group and for assessing learning.

Your first lesson will seem 'a big event', such that it is easy to lose sight of the fact that individual lessons are only one tiny step in a long learning process. You must engage early on, therefore, with at least medium term planning of whole topics so that you can recognise how ideas are built up step by step. The need to understand even longer term plans quickly impinges on your work, because of the need to know what pupils have learned previously and what they will learn in later years. Good schemes of work in schools, and the National Curriculum in science, help you gain a long-term perspective. There is a strong warning, however, of the dangers of imagining that well developed schemes of work remove the need to plan. Unit 4.2 helps you to use schemes of work to support your planning while Unit 4.3 takes you through the detailed process of planning individual lessons and evaluating how effective they are.

The teaching strategies you use will be determined by the learning outcomes you want for your lesson. A rich description of a wide range of strategies is given in Unit 4.4, from which you can select what you deem to be appropriate. The underlying rationale will help you make your selection.

PLANNING FOR PROGRESSION IN SCIENCE

Ralph Levinson

INTRODUCTION

What is unique to learning science is that the learner comes across strange ideas that defy experiences of everyday life and common sense. Invisible charges drift through wires, invisible forces hold matter together, the massive trunks of oak trees are made up of building blocks that come predominantly from the apparently immaterial air, balls moving upwards have only a downward force acting on them, the invisible products of a combustion engine have a greater mass than the petrol that is burned, electrical impulses constantly surge through our body. Electrons, atoms, cells, fields, neurones are the invisible or microscopic stuff of nature. Osmosis, entropy change, and radiation are some of the processes that have to become real so that they have an explanatory power. Pupils can only start to understand these things, if they are constructed on the back of experience and knowledge they already have.

Progression 'describes the personal journey an individual pupil makes in moving through the educational system' (Asoko and Squires, 1998: 175). To understand how pupils' learning of science is structured you need to understand progression. But what is involved in this personal journey? Do pupils move from simple to more complex ideas? Is there a pattern in the way all pupils progress which might help us organise their learning more systematically? How personal is the journey – what is the role of teachers? This unit attempts to address these questions and to identify ways in which you can help pupils progress in their understanding of science.

OBJECTIVES

By the end of this unit you should be:

- able to describe examples of progression
- aware of the complexity of progression
- able to start planning for progression
- able to identify the kinds of activities that enable progression.

DESCRIBING PROGRESSION

Imagine a two-year-old at bath time playing with bath toys. Playing is hopefully a pleasurable experience for this infant although she is unlikely to make any distinction between toys which float and those which sink. Even if an adult intervenes and tries to draw the child's attention to these distinctions they are likely to go unremarked. When the child is a little older, say four or five, she starts to categorise objects by certain properties, such as shape, size, colour, soft and hard. She begins to notice that shells, coins and pebbles sink to the bottom of the bath but other objects like polystyrene toys don't, even if they are pushed down – they bob back up to the surface. This might prompt the child, possibly with the support of a helpful older person, to see what happens when a further range of objects are dropped into the water, all of which might be characterised as 'floaters' or 'sinkers'. Once the child has had a range of experiences and has been able to talk about them, she might be able to generalise that 'sinkers' have attributes different from those of 'floaters' and to predict what happens when an object is dropped in water. According to the experiences from which the child generalises, 'sinkers' might be heavy, hard, compact, lacking air. It does not matter at this stage whether these generalisations are correct or not; the point about generalisations is that there are exceptions which might prompt the child to rethink the basis of her reasoning. Contradictions, for example a hard heavy object like a boat that floats, might generate further trials either in the bathtub or, by this time, at primary school. The child might see what happens when she tries to submerge in water a bottle filled with air and then filled with water.

By this time the child's earlier generalisations are becoming refined, and through guided observations, the data collected is more directed. She begins to test certain things out – for example, to find out what happens when the bottle is half-filled with water. As well as being able to predict with some accuracy whether objects float or sink she might notice now that water seems able to 'push up' on an object. She develops a language, with support, where the scientific meanings are very specific, that an object *weighs* less in water than it does in air, that there are *forces* acting on the object, that the upward force acting on the object is called *upthrust*. She begins to test whether the same objects float or sink when placed in different liquids and ask why some objects which sink in fresh water float in salty water. To test her ideas she begins to make measurements, to use equipment to make the measurements (for example a measuring cylinder to find out the volume occupied by the object in water), to record her data, make inferences and test these inferences further.

Of course, this is an idealised case. We have assumed that all the ideas follow on one from another, that the child does have baths in her early years, and has bath toys (some only have showers or don't always have the time to play), and that there's a helpful older other person who intervenes appropriately and knows the right kinds of questions to ask. Some children may have very particular experiences, interest in boats, for example, from an early age, while others might not have seen natural watercourses. Whatever the circumstance of the child, the elaboration of one idea depends on an earlier idea. For example, a child cannot generalise about floating and sinking until she can recognise the difference and has thought about explanations for the differences. Children may go through these stages at different times and at different rates but the point is that all children go through the earlier stages. What we have described is progression, the child's developing ability to make increasing sense of the world, in this case floating and sinking. This developing ability can be mapped through a number of different routes:

■ an increasing sophistication of explanations, from the everyday to using scientific explanations (these objects float while these sink to how ships float when they weigh thousands of tonnes). This also includes argumentation in using relevant data and warrants to support claims (Simon and Maloney, 2007).

■ moving from hands-on activities in familiar situations to applying ideas in less familiar contexts (observing things floating and sinking in a bath to testing ideas using laboratory equipment such as a measuring cylinder or 'Eureka' can).

■ terminology becomes more precise and scientific ('water seems to be pushing on my hand' to 'water is exerting a force on my hand and my hand is exerting a force on the water').

■ moving from qualitative to quantitative explanations (these objects float, these objects float in liquids above a certain density).

■ developing practical and mathematical skills to underpin understanding.

■ developing of procedural skills (making simple observations, planning experiments to test hypotheses, using models as ideas).

Task 4.1.1 **Describing progression in different topics**

Find another context or topic, for example photosynthesis, chemical reactions or light. Map the main stages in progression from Key Stage 1 to Key Stage 5 using about four main stages. For example, the more detailed account about floating and sinking above can be mapped:

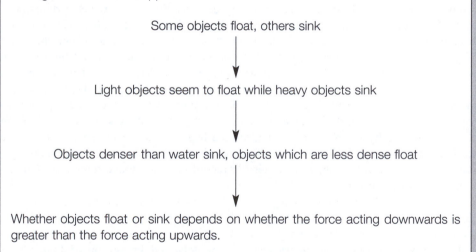

Some objects float, others sink

↓

Light objects seem to float while heavy objects sink

↓

Objects denser than water sink, objects which are less dense float

↓

Whether objects float or sink depends on whether the force acting downwards is greater than the force acting upwards.

THEORISING PROGRESSION

From the previous section you would have a sense of progression of a moving forward from simple everyday ideas to more complex situations or to contexts requiring abstract concepts to explain them. Progression in all these situations may require the use of new scientific terminology and procedural concepts. But as a teacher you need to know how to enable and recognise this progression. Progression presupposes development, i.e. that, with maturity, the child can assimilate more experiences. Piaget produced the most widely recognised explanation of cognitive development as development through a number of age-related stages. In these stages knowledge is actively generated as the learner explores her world. In the first years of life the child understands the world through her senses and moves on to begin to categorise and describe objects through their characteristics. These first stages are known as the sensory-motor and pre-operational stages, respectively (see Burton, 2009) and correspond to the child's playing followed by categorising and classifying as described for floating and sinking in the previous section.

Two further stages were recognised by Piaget, the concrete operational and the formal operational. As the child moves from the stage of concrete operations to formal operations she moves from a manipulation (both mental and physical) of specific experience to generalising and to logical, mathematical reasoning about events not seen. For example, pupils working at the concrete operational stage may be able to measure the time period of a pendulum and show that it is dependent on the length of the pendulum; the longer the pendulum the slower the time period. If presented with the challenge of finding the effect of length and mass of the bob of a pendulum have on the time period, pupils unaided may not be able to separate and control the two variables until they are working at the stage of formal operations. Furthermore, until they have progressed to this higher stage they may not recognise the shortcomings of their approach and the validity, or otherwise, of their conclusions.

Piaget argued that children progress from one stage to the next as they encounter cognitive conflict and have to assimilate new explanatory models and more complex thinking. Although Donaldson has pointed to problems in Piaget's theory – because research shows that children can manipulate more complex variables than Piaget originally supposed – this was not a repudiation of the basis of general stage theory (Donaldson, 1978). (It is worth noting that there have been cogent critiques of the basis of developmental psychology from social constructivist (O'Loughlin, 1992) and feminist perspectives (Burman, 2008).) Intelligible and fruitful learning experiences assist this progression (Posner *et al.*, 1982), hence the teacher has to be aware of the appropriate point to present material and explanations which will advance understanding.

The picture so far is one of the child constructing knowledge of the world about her with occasional facilitation by the teacher. However, the child lives in, and partakes of, a social world in which she is interpreting diverse forms of communication, mainly through talk (Vygotsky, 1978). The child, her peers and teachers generate meanings by interpreting what is said and co-construct new meanings together. The teacher, responding to detailed knowledge of the child's cognitive and social development, presents learning experiences which are beyond what the child already understands but gives enough support to move on to a 'higher rung of the ladder', a process teachers call 'scaffolding'. For further discussion of scaffolding see Wood (1998).

A third explanatory model is that of the child as information processor. The mind acts to transform the information it receives but care needs to be paid to the capacity of the processor at any one time. Information overload inhibits learning and too little information results in lack of stimulation. Knowledge of how much information the child can process is crucial to effective teaching and learning (Kempa, 1992; Burton, 2009).

All three models of learning come under what is broadly termed 'constructivist' theory, because the learners are seen as actively constructing their knowledge. In the UK there have been two particular developments in teaching related to progression in science based on constructivist theory, one is the Children's Learning in Science Project (CLISP) and the other is the Cognitive Acceleration in Science project (CASE).

The Children's Learning in Science Project (CLISP) takes as its basic assumption that many children have conceptions about scientific phenomena that are different from the scientifically accepted explanations (Driver *et al.*, 1994). Thus, for example, younger children and some older children think that when you add a substance to a beaker of water and the substance dissolves, the mass of the beaker and water stays the same, clearly contravening the principle of the conservation of mass. You can't see it so it's not there. Many examples of children's everyday thinking have been identified, and a few are given below:

- heavier objects fall faster than light ones
- electric current is used up as it passes through a circuit
- whales are fish
- plants get all their food from the soil
- when fossil fuels burn there is no product.

Research into children's conceptions about scientific phenomena began in the 1980s, largely influenced by research work in New Zealand (Osborne and Freyberg, 1985). Since then, many articles have been written about children's explanations of events across the science curriculum. These explanations have been termed 'prior conceptions', 'misconceptions' or 'alternative frameworks' according to the viewpoint of the author. 'Prior conceptions' suggest that children have conceptions about nature before they are inducted into the accepted framework of science. 'Misconceptions' implies that children's ideas are often mistaken and need challenging and changing as they begin to understand correct scientific explanations. When children have 'alternative frameworks' the emphasis is that children have another way of explaining the world that is coherent to them and that science is another explanatory framework.

If children do have conceptions that do not accord with the accepted scientific explanation, how can teachers help them to understand something that challenges their way of thinking, particularly when many scientific explanations are counter-intuitive? Under normal circumstances we don't see the gases produced when fuels burn so how can they be recognised as products? When an object rests on a table how can the table be pushing up with an equal and opposite force? A table is a static object which doesn't appear to be doing anything let alone exerting a force when an object is put on it. A whale lives in the sea and looks like a fish so it is a fish. Mammals are hairy and live on land. It just doesn't make sense to say a whale is a mammal.

The challenge for the CLISP project was to provide a strategy, based on constructivist principles, which allows teachers to support pupils through these transitions in their thinking. To plan the learning tasks it is important to know what ideas pupils do have and how dissimilar they are to the accepted scientific ideas. Much of this information can now be accessed from the literature but the starting point is to provide opportunities for pupils to make their own ideas explicit (Driver *et al.*, 1985). Two stages are involved when children make their ideas explicit; the first is 'orientation' – setting the scene – where pupils are given stimulus material relating to the topic, recording what they already know; the next is to induce cognitive conflict by introducing students to discrepant events which may promote 'restructuring' of ideas. In doing so the teacher is promoting in the learner an awareness that there is a difference between their ideas and the scientific idea and that there is a strategy for bridging the difference. Socratic questioning can be used where the teacher helps pupils to identify inconsistencies in their thinking. The last stage is that pupils try out these new ideas in a variety of contexts involving 'application' of ideas and they finally 'review' what they have learned. This strategy is by no means watertight because pupils have experiences which are consistent with their commonsense thinking and teachers are often exasperated to learn that pupils repeat their original conceptions when there was every reason to suppose they had assimilated the new scientific ideas. Think about the way people often say 'close the door or you'll let the cold in' rather than 'close the door otherwise the temperature gradient will mean that there will be a flow of heat from indoors to outdoors'. Everyday language is not very well suited to school science concepts. That is why these ideas are periodically revisited in different contexts. An example of this type of strategy is discussed in Task 4.1.2.

Task 4.1.2 **Understanding conservation of matter**

Context: Pupils are given a situation in which they are asked to choose between two possible explanations of an event; see Figure 4.1.1. In Figure 4.1.1 pupils have to decide whether the mass of the system changes or remains the same. This situation provides orientation by introducing a context and provides the second stage, elicitation, by asking questions. The third stage provides a situation where pupils are asked to carry out tasks which may challenge their preconceptions.

Your task: Go through this problem yourself identifying:

■ concepts pupils might already hold (Driver *et al.*, 1994; Driver *et al.*, 1985)
■ the scientifically acceptable conception
■ how the tasks might help restructure pupils' thinking about the topic
■ how you might run this activity in a Key Stage 3 classroom.

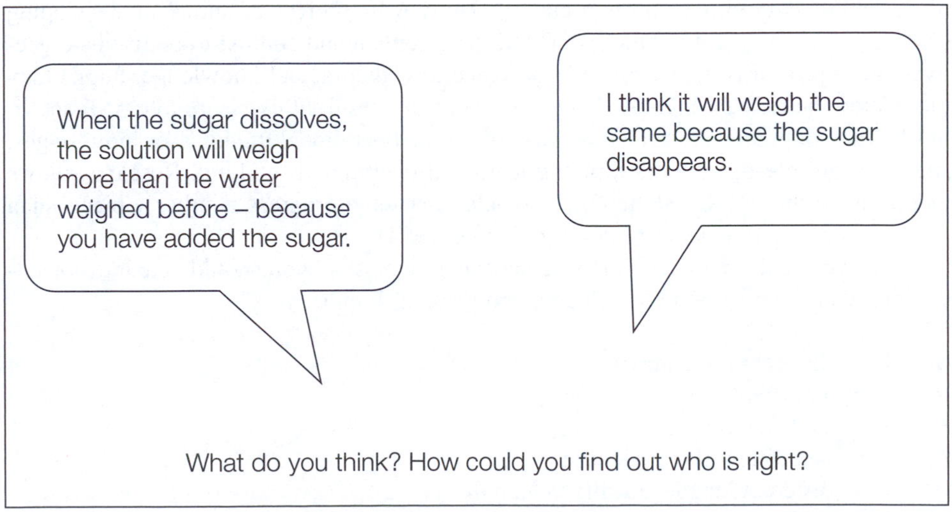

When the sugar dissolves, the solution will weigh more than the water weighed before – because you have added the sugar.

I think it will weigh the same because the sugar disappears.

What do you think? How could you find out who is right?

■ **Figure 4.1.1** An orientation exercise

The CASE project has the aim of helping pupils to progress faster in their thinking skills by promoting cognitive conflict and through reflecting on their own thinking. The theoretical model for CASE is based on the learning theories of both Piaget and Vygotsky (see Burton, 2009). As we have seen in Piaget's work, children move through a sequence of stages as their understanding about the world develops. In Piaget's model the child interacts with the environment where new stimuli are *assimilated* into the child's mental model. Where the child's cognitive structure has expanded so she becomes aware of discrepancies, there is cognitive conflict and the cognitive structure shifts to *accommodate* the new stimuli. The processes of *assimilation* and *accommodation* are intrinsic to Piaget's theory. For Vygotsky, the role of a peer or teacher (which he calls an 'other') is crucial in enabling a child to complete a task successfully. Here the teacher becomes a mediator in framing the task in such a way that the learner can make the necessary jump to success.

The CASE materials are based on the 'five pillar teaching model', which are stages in enabling progression (Adey and Yates, 2001). These pillars are listed below.

1   *Concrete preparation*: pupils become familiar with the practical context of the task and the relevant terminology. The teacher and pupils develop a shared language through questioning and group work.
2   *Cognitive conflict*: pupils are led towards observations which occasion surprise and do not meet their expectations. The conditions have to be right for cognitive conflict to occur. Some children may simply not be ready for it, very able children may be able to assimilate and accommodate new observations with relative ease.
3   *Construction*: the pupil actively puts bits of information together to build new knowledge and make it her own.
4   *Metacognition*: the pupil not only solves a problem but can articulate how it was solved and can therefore use their thinking skills much more flexibly.
5   *Bridging*: applying the skills they have learned to a variety of contexts – for examples of bridging strategies, see Shayer and Gamble (2001).

Activities across all five stages encourage children towards formal operational thinking through such characteristic reasoning programmes as classification, probability, control of variables, equilibrium, proportionality. The CASE project is aimed at developing scientific reasoning skills. Although CASE uses content and context to realise its objectives the approach is not specifically designed to widen factual knowledge. Pupils may move more quickly through the Piagetian stages as a result of exposure to CASE activities but not all pupils may reach the level of formal operational thinking, or jump stages, such as from pre-operational thinking to formal operational thinking. Research shows that progress through CASE activities transfers across to progress in other subjects such as English and mathematics (Adey and Shayer, 1994).

As well as the main cognitive elements in progression, you should take into consideration other factors that may influence progression. Pupils:

■   have different motivations
■   learn in different ways
■   learn at different rates
■   have had different experiences
■   have different language skills to help them
■   have different emotional responses to the topic.

PLANNING FOR PROGRESSION

To support progression in learning in all your pupils you should consider the following points:

a   What is it that you want the pupils to know, understand and do, i.e. to have learned, in this topic by the end of the course, module or lesson?

b   What is it that the pupils know, understand and can do at the start of the topic?

c   What sequence of learning activities will help pupils progress from their present understanding to the objective?

d   How will you know when pupils have reached where you want them to go?

e   Remember that pupils are individuals and will need a range of strategies to support learning.

One way to think about planning for progression is to consider points a to e in turn.

What do you want pupils to learn? Learning objectives and outcomes

What you want pupils to have learned by the end of an activity, lesson or topic is known as the learning objective. An objective at Key Stage 3, for example, could be 'pupils understand that chemical reactions can either be exothermic or endothermic' or 'pupils know how flowers help a plant to reproduce'. But stating objectives in this way begs a further question: How do you, as the teacher, *know* when pupils have achieved these objectives? How can you *tell* a pupil knows or understands something?

To answer these questions, the pupils have to provide evidence of their understanding or knowledge. You need 'doing' words that describe this evidence, for example 'sort these reactions into exothermic and endothermic', 'label the male and female parts of the flower', 'explain the differences between exothermic and endothermic reactions', 'draw what happens when pollen travels from one flower to another'. Statements like these are called learning outcomes, i.e. objectives that can be assessed. Outcomes contain terms like: *explain, design a poster, sort out, discuss, interpret, use the model to show (use the particle model to show the differences between solids and liquids)*. Finding out if pupils do understand the differences between exothermic and endothermic reactions, they could:

■   describe what happens in terms of temperature change in exothermic and endothermic reactions

■   complete schematic diagrams showing where heat is being gained and lost

■   interpret data from an experiment to show that a reaction is exothermic or endothermic

■   identify the thermicity of a reaction from an energy diagram

■   suggest ways of finding out how exothermic or endothermic a reaction is.

Most outcomes and objectives will only be partly achieved. Pupil A may answer a homework question by describing an exothermic reaction as one that gives out heat and an endothermic reaction as one that takes in heat. Pupil B might respond 'Exothermic reactions such as the burning of a candle and the reaction of magnesium with acid lose heat

to the surroundings. We can tell it is an exothermic reaction because the temperature of the surroundings rises as a result of the reaction. If we put a thermometer in the reaction mixture of magnesium and acid, the temperature rises until the reaction is complete...'
Clearly, pupil B has been able to meet the outcome more precisely than pupil A. You could therefore help pupil A to progress by giving a short exercise to help them identify instances of exothermic reactions and see if they can report what happens in terms of temperature change (see Unit 6.1 Assessment for Learning). Pupil B can be superseded by pupil C who relates the temperature change to particle motion. Thus there are opportunities for progression within a particular outcome.

Some teachers identify several levels of learning outcomes to cater for different levels of achievement in the class. They might state their outcomes as follows:

■ All pupils will be able to recall that heat is lost to the surroundings in exothermic reactions and that heat is gained from the surroundings in endothermic reactions.
■ Some pupils will be able to identify exothermic and endothermic reactions and to state what happens to the surrounding temperatures.
■ A few pupils will be able to translate energy diagrams into exothermic and endothermic reactions.

Task 4.1.3 **Identifying three learning outcomes for one objective**

Take the following objectives and break each one down into three outcomes, i.e. what all, some and a few pupils can do:

■ plan an investigation to find out the best anti-acid remedy
■ understand that light can travel through a vacuum but sound cannot
■ know that habitats support a variety of plants and animals that are interdependent.

What is it that pupils know, understand and can do at the start of the topic?

To help pupils to meet learning objectives you must have some idea of where the pupils are starting from. There are at least two reasons for this – pupils may have done much of the topic before and may become bored going over old ground. Secondly, you may assume knowledge which the pupils don't have and if this is the case they may become quickly disaffected. Of course, pupils won't all be starting from the same point so you need a means of finding out what pupils do and don't know before starting a topic. The list below gives guidance on how you can find the relevant information.

1 Pupils ought to have covered something of the topic at Key Stages 1 and 2 if you are starting at Key Stage 3. Starting at Key Stage 4, there ought to have been some coverage at Key Stages 2 and 3. Find out from the National Curriculum and the QCA schemes of work what they are likely to have covered.
2 Ask more experienced teachers who can tell you about the kinds of things pupils know well and what gaps in knowledge to look out for.

3   Acquaint yourself with the literature on children's ideas (Driver *et al.*, 1994; Driver *et al.*, 1985) so you can anticipate ideas pupils may bring to the topic.

4   Use diagnostic tasks and starter activities to find out what pupils know. These activities can be given at the beginning of a topic. They should be:

■   short
■   easy to administer
■   engaging for the pupil
■   able to give you the information you want
■   quick to mark.

What sequence of learning activities helps pupils to progress from their present understanding to the next learning objective?

Starter activities and diagnostic tasks not only tell you what pupils already know and don't know, they also reveal a wide range of understandings within the classroom. The instruction and learning opportunities you give pupils within the lesson must then have two characteristics:

■   offer sufficient challenge for all the pupils
■   allow the pupils to develop scientific ideas, skills, terminology etc. (this is likely to involve active instruction).

Whether you are teaching in a setted, streamed or mixed-ability class there are always differences in knowledge and understanding, although the range of knowledge and understanding may be (but not necessarily) narrower in a streamed or setted class. Differences need not necessarily be vertical, i.e. one pupil knows more than another; they may simply be different and have knowledge in different types of context. Because all pupils are different there is a tendency to think that the best way out would be to give each pupil individualised work. This approach is clearly impossible and probably undesirable; pupils can learn from each other so devising activities for them which encourage discussion and exchange of ideas assists progression.

You need to ensure that you are starting from the appropriate level for those pupils who have clear misconceptions and that you are setting a sufficient challenge for those pupils who have clear understandings. Most departments have a bank of activities which you can adapt for your own purposes. You can support the lower attainers by giving them guided help. Suppose you ask pupils to explain how condensation appears on the outside of a cold, stoppered conical flask, which contains ice (a can taken out of the fridge rapidly gains condensation). Some pupils say that the water seeped through the flask. You might want to help them by showing them a flask containing water where condensation doesn't appear on the outside of the flask, or dyeing the ice red and demonstrating that the water on the outside is colourless.

Don't expect pupils to accept your explanations immediately because you are challenging beliefs they might hold quite strongly. When pupils come to realise that the explanations they have held up to now contradict new explanations which they are beginning to own intellectually, we call this situation cognitive conflict. Resolution of this cognitive conflict can take some time and needs reinforcement; this is why you need to revisit concepts and widen experience. Some pupils will need help to reinforce the concept to help them progress. For others you will need to ensure that they have sufficient challenge. Pupils are progressing through the topic but there are opportunities at various stages for reinforcement for some pupils and extra challenge for others.

Teachers rightly want to ensure that all their pupils are challenged but it is important not to be too ambitious and to devise too many activities. As a starting point, try the approaches listed below:

■ For each idea taught, devise three or four distinct activities, all of which underpin the understanding of the idea. For example, one activity might involve a short practical exercise such as finding out how quickly different liquids evaporate, another discussing a concept cartoon, a third answering questions on a short written piece and finally analysing a piece of data from a website.

■ Devise an activity which all pupils can do but at different levels. For example, it might be answering questions on a piece of data, or a short extract from a video, where successive questions become more demanding.

■ Ask pupils to plan an investigation where you set different demands.

Task 4.1.4 **Planning differentiated investigations**

If we take the example of evaporation, the following tasks could be set:

■ Find out the order in which these four liquids evaporate. You will need a measuring cylinder, stopwatch and evaporating basin. Start off with the same volume of each liquid.

■ Plan an experiment to show how surface area of a liquid influences the rate of evaporation.

■ Devise an experiment to find out if there is a relationship between particle size and rate of evaporation of a liquid.

Devise a set of similar graded investigations for the topic of seedling growth, electrical circuits or acids and bases.

How do you know when pupils have reached where you want them to go?

Pupils provide evidence of outcomes in the work they produce such as written exercises, drawings and analysis of practical work, but much of pupils' understanding is ephemeral, captured quickly in off-the-cuff remarks or contributing something to a discussion when they are not aware of being watched. It is important for the progress of individual pupils that you are able to record the necessary information. While you cannot record the progress in a single lesson of each and every pupil, focus on a sample of three pupils for each lesson and make any notes on points that they appear to have understood or that they find difficulty with. An example of how you can do this is given in Figure 4.1.2. These notes should then be transferred to the register where you keep pupil records.

Self-assessment is another way in which pupils can keep a record of their own progress. When the teacher makes explicit to pupils the stages in their learning the pupils can check how well they have understood each stage. This helps both the pupils and the

Context: Comparing the rates of marble chips dissolving in acid		
	Group 1 John, Paul and Mary	Group 2 Laura, Pamjit and Anwar
Making predictions	Paul could with reasons. John and Mary struggled.	Laura/Pamjit, good predictions but not sure why.
Devising procedure	All gave good response, but John not sure why.	Laura and Pamjit OK. Anwar only understood when told.

■ **Figure 4.1.2** Keeping notes of pupils' progress

teacher. Helping the pupil to develop the skills needed for self-assessment is discussed in Unit 6.1.

Remember that pupils are individuals and will need a range of strategies to support learning.

Selecting teaching strategies to meet needs of individuals is explored in detail in Unit 4.4.

SUMMARY AND KEY POINTS

This unit has discussed the ways in which progression may be described and the theories that underpin such discussion. Children do not always progress in the same way and effective teaching has to maintain a balance between challenge and support, pitching the work at just the right level of demand to encourage participation and success. The keys to enabling progression are two-fold: a sound knowledge of the topic in hand and a sound knowledge and understanding of the pupils in your class. The first can be prepared for; the second develops over time, with increasing confidence and trust developing between you and your pupils. The main thrust of this unit has focused on planning for progression and suggested the kinds of activities that you can try out in the classroom. The *Key Stage 3 Strategy for Science* (DCSF, 2009a) has many useful ideas which complement the material in this unit.

FURTHER READING

Harrison, C., Simon, S. and Watson, R. (2000) 'Progression and differentiation', in Monk, M. and Osborne, J. (eds) *Good Practice in Science Teaching: What Research Has to Say*. Buckingham: Open University Press.
This examination of progression draws on research literature and helps the reader tease out several meanings of 'progression' that are appropriate to different contexts.

Jarman, R. (2000) 'Between the idea and the reality falls the shadow', in Sears, J. and Sorenson, P. (2000) *Issues in Science Teaching*. London: RoutledgeFalmer.
Ruth Jarman addresses continuity and progression across Key Stage 2 and 3 and raises important issues about acknowledging what prior learning pupils have and how that can be assessed and recognised.

Johnson, P. (2002) 'Progression in children's understanding of a "basic" particle theory: a longitudinal study', in Amos, S. and Boohan, R. (eds) *Teaching Science in Secondary Schools: A Reader*. London: RoutledgeFalmer for the Open University, pp. 236–49.

This is a report of a longitudinal study into secondary pupils' (aged 11–14) understanding of particle theory. Useful examples of strategies for discussing ideas with pupils and the types of understanding pupils' display at different levels of progression.

Simon, S. and Maloney, J. (2007) 'Activities for promoting small group discussion and argumentation'. *School Science Review*, 88 (324), 49–57.

USING SCHEMES OF WORK TO SUPPORT PLANNING

Jenny Frost

INTRODUCTION

Most departments have schemes of work to guide teachers and you are likely to be given relevant sections when you join the school. Schemes of work are, however, complex documents that take time to understand, but, if used wisely, can be a valuable resource for your own preparation of lessons. They do not, however, remove the need for your own careful planning for each lesson (see Unit 4.3).

OBJECTIVES

By the end of this unit you should:

- be aware of the levels of planning incorporated into schemes of work
- understand the strengths and limitations of schemes of work
- realise the need to gain an overview of the content of a topic prior to planning individual lessons
- be aware how you can contribute towards curriculum development in a department.

PLANNING AND RELATIONSHIPS TO SCHEMES OF WORK

Planning is usually done as a joint, collaborative activity by a team of teachers in the preparation of schemes of work that are used by all members of the science staff. A scheme of work contains different levels of planning: the long-term focusing on the whole of schooling and then on each Key Stage; medium-term planning for each year group showing the objectives for that year and listing topics to be taught; and short-term planning of topics and of individual lessons. Figure 4.2.1 indicates what a reliable scheme of work is likely to cover.

A scheme of work should:

■ cover the relevant National Curriculum programmes of study
■ meet externally set specifications related to public examinations
■ provide aims for science teaching at several levels (for the whole of pupils' schooling; for each Key Stage; for each year; each topic)
■ include objectives and learning outcomes (for topics and individual lessons)
■ include assessment tasks to provide evidence for learning, especially at lesson level
■ suggest lesson and topic timings
■ suggest suitable activities and teaching techniques
■ draw attention to safety practice, including risk assessment for lessons
■ offer strategies for differentiation, including support for pupils with SEN
■ give references to prior knowledge you may anticipate, e.g. previous teaching of the topic
■ provide evidence of common misconceptions or learning difficulties associated with the topic
■ give opportunities for scientific enquiry and progression of enquiry skills
■ give opportunities for the use of evidence in science
■ give opportunities for links to scientific enterprises, and global scientific activities
■ give opportunity for learning functional skills (literacy, numeracy and ICT)
■ suggest homework activities
■ give references to books, resources and websites
■ refer to the *Every Child Matters* (ECM) agenda (see *Relevant websites*, Unit 2.2).

■ **Figure 4.2.1** Features to be found in a scheme of work

Schools vary as to how strictly they expect teachers to keep to a scheme of work. Below is the rationale for the schemes of work for Ivybridge Community College, a large comprehensive school:

> The Department's *Schemes of Work* are a planning aid for staff as professional teachers, i.e. to support their planning. They are intended to encourage quality and variety of teaching and learning. They are not intended to be prescribed recipes for standard lessons, though they should reduce the need to 'reinvent wheels'.
>
> (Ivybridge Community College, Scheme of Work, 2009)

This school sees schemes of work as an aid particularly to student teachers and new teachers to allow them to teach lessons successfully the first time round, and as a means of sharing professional expertise between colleagues. It encourages everyone to try out new ideas to achieve the same objectives and to feed these ideas into the ongoing curriculum planning and evaluation that the department undertakes. Schemes of work also enable technicians to undertake professional planning of the resources that are likely to be requested at different times of the year.

Figure 4.2.2 gives the headings used for the topic plans used by Ivybridge CC. Topic plans quickly give teachers an overview of what has to be learned, what resources are available, what demands will be made on pupils, the new vocabulary to be learned and what homework is to be set. The topic plans at this school typically run to four pages.

> **Introduction** – the rationale for the topic, especially how it should link to work already undertaken (see below)
>
> **KS2 pupils should have been taught** – list of skills and knowledge from KS2 on the topic
>
> **KS3 pupils should be taught** – list of skills and knowledge to be taught
>
> **Lesson titles** – a list of 12 lesson titles
>
> **Possibilities for investigations** – a list of feasible investigations in the topic
>
> **Skills** – an analysis of practical skills and data-handling skills such as drawing tables and graphs, to be learned – analysed lesson by lesson
>
> **Homework to be set** – one or two pieces per week
>
> **Word list** – (divided into 'basic', 'core' and 'extension')
>
> **ICT opportunities** – list of ICT activities for each lesson
>
> **Opportunities in the workplace** – links between processes learned in the laboratory and commercial or industrial processes

■ **Figure 4.2.2** Headings used for Key Stage 3 topic plans for a scheme of work
Source: Ivybridge Community College

The introduction for a Y7 topic on solids, liquids and gases reads:

> Much traditional KS3 SLG and solution work is now KS2 … This means that we have to introduce KS3 lessons with a rapid review, assessing the need for more thorough revision … This topic is vocabulary-heavy – suggesting one approach to reviewing would be an introductory word test!
>
> N.B. to fit in with the PoS, this scheme starts with the uses of the word 'particle', and towards the end brings in the word 'atom'. This module is designated to provide the full science challenge for Year 7. In theory, the basic ideas of separating mixtures has been covered by KS2 but don't count on it! If it is clear that they **have** done it thoroughly, set some separations as a challenge or give longer to science investigations.

Individual lesson plans accompany the topic plans. Figure 4.2.3 gives an example of one from the Y7 topic on solids, liquids and gases.

You need to be aware of the level of guidance and prescription in the scheme of work in your own school. Task 4.2.1 guides you to do a preliminary analysis.

Task 4.2.1 **Understanding your school's scheme of work**

1　Examine your school's scheme of work, identifying which of the features listed in Figure 4.2.1 have been included. Are there additional features?
2　Read topic plans. Do they contain the same features as in Figure 4.2.2? Have they additional features?
3　Look at lesson plans. Do they contain the same features as in Figure 4.2.3? Have you a fair idea of what you would need to do? What extra preparation is needed?

4   Is the scheme of work built on a 'spiral curriculum' – i.e. periodically are the same ideas revisited but with their scope and complexity widened and deepened? If so, how does the school avoid simple repetition?

5   Does the department have an explicit (documented) view about what makes effective learning? Is it about mastering facts, developing skills, learning to co-operate, other? You may find this in a departmental handbook rather than in the scheme of work itself.

6   How prescriptive is the scheme of work? Are teachers encouraged to try out new ideas and to share these ideas with others?

7   Discuss with your mentor the advantages of having a prescriptive or non-prescriptive scheme of work.

Well-structured schemes of work reduce the anxiety about lesson planning, but do not remove the need for each teacher to undertake their own planning. It is probably helpful to think of a departmental lesson plan as a blueprint that teachers tweak to suit the characteristics of the pupils they are teaching and in so doing might transform it.

PREPARATION PRIOR TO SPECIFIC LESSON PLANNING

When you take over a class you are given certain topics to be taught. Schools vary as to how they break the curriculum into topics, but often there are two topics each half-term. This means that you will be carrying one theme through for several weeks. An important first step in planning is to have an overview of the whole topic so that you have a broad picture of what the pupils are to learn. We suggest here three aspects to pay attention to as preparation before you do the detailed planning of individual lessons, which is described in Unit 4.3. Those aspects are:

1   understanding the scientific content of a topic and developing pedagogical content knowledge
2   gaining an overview of key concepts in science
3   identifying the key processes and curriculum opportunities.

1 Developing scientific knowledge and pedagogical knowledge

It is impossible to plan sensibly, let alone teach, unless you have a clear understanding of the key ideas yourself, not only the ideas you are teaching at a particular time but how they link with ideas that come later, and those learned earlier. One strategy for summarising understanding of the scientific concepts in a topic is to draw concept maps. Examples of concept maps for four topics – the solar system, sound, hydrocarbons and genes – are given in Figures 4.2.2–4.2.5. The first might be applicable for Y7, the second for Y8 or Y9, the third for Y11 and the fourth for a post-16 class. Try developing your own concept maps for topics you have been asked to teach.

You also need to think about your pedagogical content knowledge such as drawings you might put on the board; models, ready-made ones, or ones that pupils make; analogies 'imagine it is like…'; stories 'there was a soldier who had a hole blown in his

Unit Title TC1.3   Lesson Title: **Datalogging changes of state**

HSW / Enquiry/ Skills / Num / Lit		KS3 Programme of Study
Skill – Collect data, create table correctly to display data clearly, process data to determine more information.		3.2a the particle model provides explanation for the different physical properties and behaviour of matter.

Learning Objectives: Basic		Learning Objectives: Core		Learning Objectives: Extension	
To use a datalogger and get a printout of the resulting graph	4b 4c 3a 3b 3c	To get it right! To link shapes on the graph with events that happened (e.g. ice still present/all melted)	5b 5c 4a 4b 4c	To explain why the graph has the shape it does, in terms of maintaining temperature during changes of state.	6b 6c 5a 5b 5c

Suggested Learning Experiences	AFL
• **Starter:** pupils to use their true/false statements from previous lesson • **Main activity:** Demo: how the datalogger works for melting by showing how ice straight from the freezer is below 0°C but warms up to, and stays at, 0°C until it is all melted. Class: to warm ice *gently*, mixing thoroughly, and datalog for at least 2 minutes after it boils. Record the results and plot on graph paper. Illustrate the advantages of datalogging. Heat vs Temp. What is the difference between heat and temperature? Give definitions. • **Plenary:** questions on the graphs produced – what do you notice about the graph? Why do you think it looks the way that it does? What do you think is happening at each of the changes of state? **Differentiation** B: Quality of results, probably! C: Realisation that temperature doesn't rise during a change of state, even though it is being heated. E: Explanation of why temperature doesn't rise during a change of state, even though it is being heated.	Peer-assessment can be completed as pupils can use their true/false statement for previous lesson to test each other's understanding of the lesson

Possible ICT
B/C: C/E: Use of dataloggers to identify changes of state

Homework: Basic / Core	Homework: Core / Extension
Label the states of matter and their changes on a (supplied) cooling or heating curve. VLE: C1.3	Explain, in terms of particles and energy, why melting ice does not warm up as it is heated. VLE: C1.3

Resources and References	Risk Assessment
Dataloggers (temperature probe) Computer on a trolley (for demo) Deliver ice straight from icemaker (i.e. <0°C) Sand as cheap antibumps	Scalds – use tongs to move hot/cold items

■ **Figure 4.2.3** Example of a Y7 lesson plan from a scheme of work
Source: Ivybridge Community College

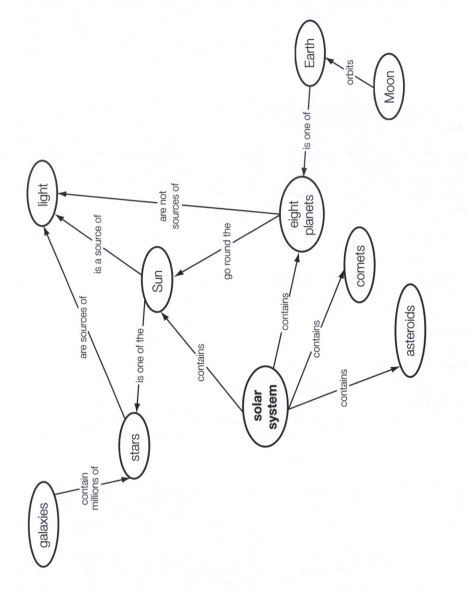

■ **Figure 4.2.4** Concept map for the solar system

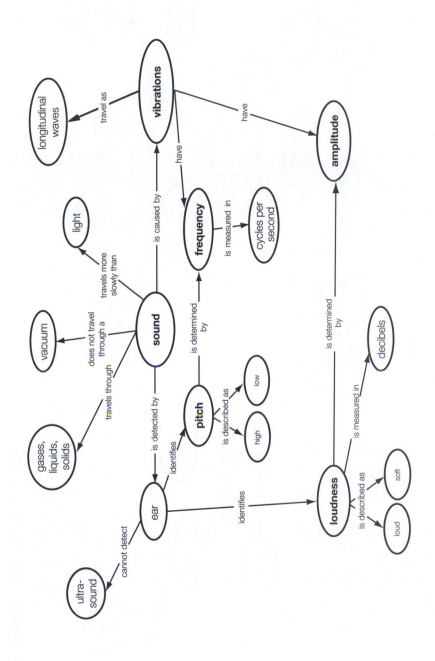

■ **Figure 4.2.5** Concept map for sound

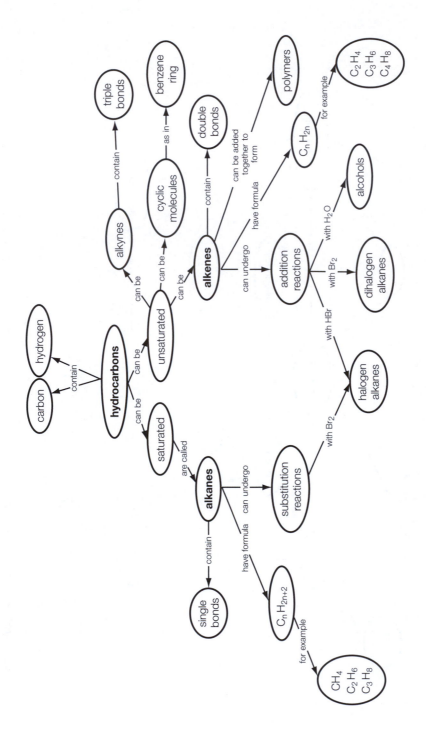

■ **Figure 4.2.6** Concept map for hydrocarbons

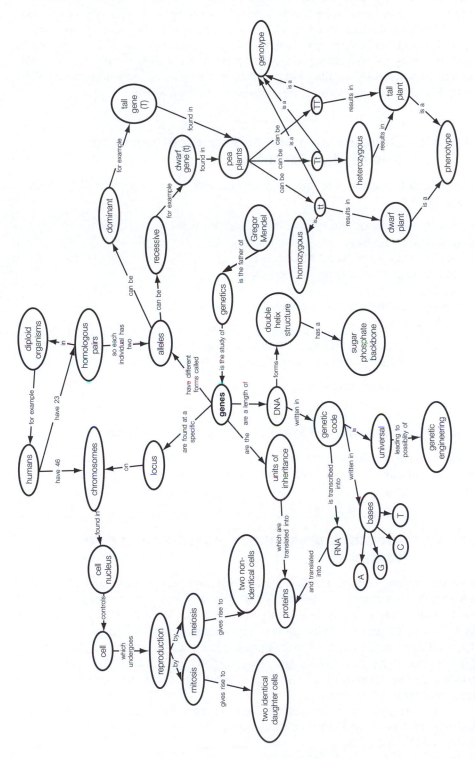

■ **Figure 4.2.7** Concept map for genes

stomach and while it was healing someone studied the effect of digestive juices…'; intriguing demonstrations 'I have here a hand warmer that you can buy in camping shops…'; bridging devices 'Imagine being pushed off a tall building on bathroom scales, the scales would not register any weight while you dropped … Now these people in spacecrafts…they are also falling freely…'. Teachers rarely write these down. You will find that you develop some quite quickly in the act of explaining but you can add to your store by listening to, and watching, other teachers (see Task 4.2.2).

Task 4.2.2 **Developing your pedagogical content knowledge for a topic**

Start a collection of ideas to support your teaching. This collection might include examples of:

- everyday examples which are relevant – applications, related careers
- useful demonstrations
- helpful analogies to explain a concept
- background information about scientists
- bridging activities
- stories about how an idea or new understanding developed
- useful questions.

Plan a file to collect these resources and a reference system for easy access. Be on the lookout for ideas when you are watching teachers.

---

2 Gaining an overview of key concepts about science

Key concepts about science are as important as the scientific concepts. Again you need an overview of what is to be learned about science in the topics that you are asked to teach.

Task 4.2.3 **Identifying key ideas about science to be taught**

From the scheme of work, check which ideas about science pupils will be learning in the topic. These ideas may be clearly identified or you may have to infer them, or create them yourself. It depends on the specificity of the scheme of work. Refer back to units 2.2 and 2.3, to the sections on key concepts about science and *How Science Works*, and to Unit 3.1 on the nature of science, to remind yourself of the array of ideas that might be included. (You may find it helpful to refer to Task 2.2.2 in Unit 2.2.) The scheme of work may be cross-referenced to the textbook being used, so check this as well.

Are there aspects that you would like to augment? Are there aspects where you need to develop your own knowledge? Discuss your thoughts with the teacher responsible for the class.

---

3 Identifying the key processes and curriculum opportunities

In a similar manner you need to identify the key processes that are to be developed in the topic and the curriculum opportunities to be offered (see Unit 2.2 to remind yourself of these).

Task 4.2.4 **Identifying key processes and curriculum opportunities in a topic**

For a topic you are about to teach, use the scheme of work to identify the key processes the pupils are to learn and the curriculum opportunities you are expected to provide (see Task 2.2.3 for more details).

Make a list and ensure that the teaching strategies that you select (see Unit 4.4) are appropriate.

CONTRIBUTING TO CURRICULUM DEVELOPMENT

Remember that curriculum development in a department relies on teachers sharing their successful ideas and incorporating them in the rewriting of the schemes of work. You may well have ideas that can be shared with teachers and that the department will, in the future, weave into their schemes of work. Do not assume that because you are a beginner you are not the one to have the novel ideas. Task 4.2.5 suggests a larger curriculum development task that you could undertake.

Task 4.2.5 **Contributing to curriculum development in a school department**

This task should be tackled towards the end of the course. Schools often identify parts of schemes of work that need improvement. Offer to work with a teacher to improve a particular topic in the scheme of work that the school has identified as in need of revision (This may not mean rewriting the whole topic.) Let other teachers know that you are doing this so they can feed in ideas and tell you the difficulties they had with the topic.

For your topic, address each of the following points in turn:

1   Identify the classes for whom it is intended and time available.
2   Identify the content in the topic and draw a concept map.
3   Use the headings in Figure 4.2.2 to guide the writing of the topic plan (or use the school's own headings).
4   Use the format for the lesson plan shown in Figure 4.2.3 (or the school's lesson plan format) to write the individual lesson plans.

Check objectives and learning outcomes for balance between knowledge, skills, understanding and attitudes. Finally, justify key features that you have included in terms of a) progression (see Unit 4.1), b) teaching strategies (Unit 4.4) and c) curriculum aims (see Chapter 2) and explain how these features are built into the scheme of work. Discuss the finished task with your mentor and then share it with other teachers.

SUMMARY AND KEY POINTS

Schemes of work provide you with starting points for lesson planning. It is your responsibility not only to prepare lessons that reflect the departmental scheme of work, and that respond to the needs of your pupils, but also to be prepared to bring your own individuality and flair to the interpretation of those schemes of work. Before embarking on the planning of individual lessons ensure that you have an overview, and understanding, of the content of the topic in terms of scientific knowledge, ideas about science, processes which pupils are to learn and the variety of learning activities which are suggested.

Later in the course you may well be able to contribute ideas to the department's curriculum development. Be prepared to work with other teachers on the development of a section of a scheme of work, to enhance one aspect of it.

FURTHER READING

Capel, S., Leask, M. and Turner, T. (2009) *Learning to Teach in the Secondary School,* **5th edition. London: Routledge.**

■ Davison, J. and Leask, M. Unit 2.2 'Schemes of Work and Lesson Planning', 79–90.

The following two books are both based on research and focus on the pedagogical content knowledge of science teachers:

Bishop, K. and Denley, P. (2007) *Learning Science Teaching: Developing a Professional Knowledge Base.* **Maidenhead: Open University Press.**

Ogborn, J., Kress, K., Martins, I. and McGillicuddy, K. (1996) *Explaining Science in the Classroom*. **Buckingham: Open University Press.**

Short extracts of Ogborn *et al.* are reproduced in Amos, S. and Boohan, R. (eds) (2002) *Aspects of Teaching Secondary Science: Perspectives on Practice*, London: RoutledgeFalmer for the Open University: Chapters 4 and 13.

PLANNING AND EVALUATING LESSONS

Bernadette Youens

INTRODUCTION

Planning is about having a clear idea of what you want your pupils to learn and why this learning is important to your overall aims. It must address assessment strategies to check what has, and has not, been achieved and must respond to what pupils know and can do now, and to where you want to lead them. The ideas discussed in units 4.1 and 4.2 provide the foundation for lesson planning. In this unit we consider how to plan individual lessons and show how the different components of planning, together with evaluation and reflection, form part of a cyclical process.

OBJECTIVES

By the end of this unit you should be able to:

- identify the elements of a lesson
- distinguish between objectives and learning outcomes
- set achievable learning outcomes for pupils
- understand that some objectives are difficult to assess
- begin to plan activities and select resources to enable pupils to achieve the learning outcomes
- address differences between pupils when planning lessons
- know how to assess pupils' learning with reference to lesson outcomes
- understand the role of assessment in lesson evaluations
- recognise the use of evaluations to inform future planning.

IDENTIFYING THE MAIN FEATURES OF A LESSON PLAN

Good planning results in a well-structured, well-paced and well-resourced lesson that is appropriate for all the individuals in your particular class. Good planning reflects the nature of the class, the individuals within that class and, of course, the quality of the relationships that you have established. How you manage that lesson is dependent upon your personality and style of teaching.

You can learn about the structure of a single lesson by observing a lesson of an experienced teacher and analysing it in terms of its overall plan (see Task 4.3.1). Figure 4.3.1 gives a guide for such observations. In the left-hand column are the main features of a lesson. The right-hand column gives you questions to focus on when observing. If you have forgotten the differences between objectives and learning outcomes turn back to Unit 4.1.

Main features of a lesson plan	Relevant questions
Lesson objectives	What are these? Are they shared with the pupils? How?
Learning outcomes	What are these? Are these also shared with the pupils? How?
Means of assessing the learning outcomes	How does the teacher get feedback on what pupils have learned? When does this occur – throughout the lesson or only at the end?
Phases of lessons Phase 1 – setting the scene	How does the teacher set the scene? How long does it take? Are there activities for the pupils?
Phase 2 – main and subsequent activities	What activities are used? How long do they take? What does the teacher do when pupils are working on their own?
Phase 3 – drawing ideas together – plenary	How are ideas drawn together? How does the teacher gain information that all the pupils have learned?
Phase 4 – clearing up, setting homework and dismissal	How long does clearing up take? Does the homework consolidate the learning from the lesson? Does the homework anticipate the next stage in the learning? How is the class dismissed?
Transitions between phases	How did the teacher manage the transitions between phases?
Resources	What resources were needed? How were they organised and managed?

■ **Figure 4.3.1** Main features of a lesson plan and questions for observation
(see Task 4.3.1)

Task 4.3.1 **Watching other science teachers: lesson planning**

Negotiate with a teacher in your placement school to observe a lesson using questions in Figure 4.3.1 for guidance. Before the lesson, talk with the teacher to establish the context of the lesson and the planned learning objectives and outcomes.

From your observations draft a lesson plan using the headings in the left-hand column of Figure 4.3.1. Show the completed plan to the teacher and discuss how your inferred plan differs from his/her plan.

PLANNING THE MAIN FEATURES OF A LESSON: MAKING A START

There is a limit to what you can learn about planning by analysing another teacher's lesson until you have had a go at planning yourself. Once you have done that, you will, of course, benefit from watching other teachers again. To make a start on planning individual lessons, we suggest you think about:

■ lesson content
■ subject knowledge and subject pedagogical knowledge
■ objectives and learning outcomes
■ learning activities and resources
■ assessment opportunities
■ management of pupils and resources
■ timing and pace
■ planning what you want to say
■ homework.

Lesson content

The science content of a lesson is informed by statutory requirements, the departmental scheme of work, as well as any relevant specification. Statutory requirements are often minimum requirements and your scheme of work may offer additional ideas or content. Make sure that you know what is to be learned in a lesson and remember that you have only an hour or so for any one lesson. You have to make efficient use of the time.

Your subject knowledge and your pedagogical content knowledge

Your subject knowledge must be secure in the subject of the lesson so that you can explain the science to your class in an accessible, relevant and informative manner. Make whatever notes you need, try out problems which you might set a class, make sure you can answer standard questions. It is important, too, that you know how that knowledge is linked within the whole topic so refer back to your concept map for the topic (see Unit 4.2). If you have not already done so at the topic planning stage, refer to books such as

Reiss (1999), McDuell (2000), Sang (2000), Kind and Kind (2008), Sang and Wood-Robinson (2002) and Sang and Frost (2005) to understand the level at which key ideas are to be treated at KS3 and KS4. You need to be able to transform your scientific knowledge into a form that pupils can understand and to select resources and activities to achieve this. If you are having difficulty explaining an idea, talk with colleagues in school and fellow student teachers, or go to several books until you find explanations with which you are comfortable. Find teaching aids that will support your explanation.

Objectives and learning outcomes

You need to 'set challenging teaching and learning objectives which are relevant to all pupils in [your] classes' and that you 'use these teaching and learning objectives to plan lessons and sequences of lessons' (DCSF, 2009a). Identify the objectives for the lesson, for example, 'pupils are to understand how the eye works' or 'pupils are to be acquainted with the Periodic Table'. Objectives may refer to skills and attitudes as well as to knowledge and understanding such as in 'pupils should be able to use a microscope accurately' or 'pupils should be able to work cooperatively on a joint research project' for skills, and 'pupils should show sensitivity towards living things' or 'pupils should respect other people's ideas in discussion' for attitudes. You might have aims for science education that include making pupils curious as well as knowledgeable; if so you may have objectives for your lesson such as 'pupils should show curiosity about the working of the eye'.

Learning outcomes, as explained in Unit 4.1, are *assessable* objectives and are written using *active verbs that refer to the pupils*. For example, for the objective that pupils should understand the working of the eye, you have to ask yourself the question, 'How will I know they will understand?'. You might decide that if pupils can:

■ *label* a diagram of the eye
■ *explain* the functions of the different parts of the eye
■ *relate* the parts of the eye to the parts of a camera.

then they probably do understand the working of the eye. If you wish to add the objective about pupils being curious about the eye, your learning outcome might be that pupils should:

■ *ask* questions about how the eye works.

It is good practice to share objectives with the class, so write them in language suited to your pupils. In the example above, pupils should be told that by the end of the lesson they should understand how the eye works. Most people argue that there is no need to share the more detailed learning outcomes, but there are no hard-and-fast rules. Writing lesson objectives and learning outcomes is not easy; Task 4.1.3 in Unit 4.1 gave practice in doing this.

Preparing activities and selecting resources

Designing appropriate activities to achieve your learning outcomes is one of the creative tasks of teaching. Ready-made worksheets, commercial texts and other teachers are sources of ideas. Selection, however, needs care and adaptation is often necessary. A variety of teaching and learning activities to develop a range of skills and cater for different learning styles is important (see Unit 4.4).

> Although many science lessons are well planned and purposeful, and often include a single main activity of class practical work, some of the best lessons contain a variety of linked activities. This approach frequently helps develop pupils' understanding and caters for a range of learning styles.
>
> (Ofsted, 2002: 13)

Unit 4.4 gives detailed guidance on teaching and learning strategies and activities you can use.

Designing, selecting and adapting activities is only the first step. Activities may look ideal but you must try them out to ensure that they achieve what you want and are manageable by you and the class. Work through the tasks yourself, e.g. complete the worksheet, carry out the web-based research task, perform the demonstration or class practical, or make the poster. This will highlight potential difficulties, give a clearer picture of what you expect of your pupils and provide an estimate of how long activities might take.

Expect to be spoilt for choice as far as resources are concerned. For the lesson on the eye, for instance, you may have available a fluorescein eye (5-litre round-bottomed flask full of water and fluorescein, with lenses stuck on the front which focus a beam of light on the other side); a demountable biological model of the eye; bulls' eyes that can be dissected; jelly lenses which focus differently when flattened a bit; a video of how the eye works; images of the eye from the internet; pictures and explanations in the pupils' books; ideas for pupils making their own model of an eye (tennis balls with holes cut on opposite sides, to hold a short-focus lens and tracing-paper screen). For practical activities carry out a risk assessment and record the outcomes of that assessment on your lesson plan (see Unit 5.2).

Assessment opportunities

Assessment opportunities are places during the lesson when the teacher is able to gain feedback from the pupils about the extent to which they understand the science being taught. From the example of the lesson on the eye, above, a possible activity for the first outcome is to give the class a drawing of the eye and ask them to label it. You still have to decide whether you give pupils a drawing of the eye or they draw it themselves, and whether a list of labels is given or pupils have to remember them. For the second outcome you have to decide whether they explain the working of the eye in writing or orally; whether they do it from memory or match functions to parts from a given list; or whether they correct a faulty account of the working of the eye. In a similar way you need to think of possible opportunities to assess all the learning outcomes. Unit 6.1 gives a much fuller discussion of assessment strategies that you can use.

Task 4.3.2 provides an opportunity for you to watch for assessment opportunities in another teacher's lesson.

Task 4.3.2 **Objectives and learning outcomes: identifying assessment opportunities**

Observe a lesson taught by an experienced teacher in your school.

1 Before the lesson ask the teacher to share with you:
   - ■ the objectives of the lesson
   - ■ the learning outcomes.
2 Classify the objectives as knowledge, understanding, skills or attitudes.
3 During the lesson, identify how each activity or learning opportunity contributed to achieving a stated objective.
4 List the opportunities taken by the teacher to get feedback about successful learning.
5 After the lesson ask the teacher to explain how successful each activity or learning experience was in contributing to the objectives and to assess whether or not the pupils had achieved the learning outcomes and the evidence for that judgement.
6 Later, compare your notes on the lesson with the post-lesson discussion with the teacher and list implications for your lesson planning in terms of learning outcomes, choice of activity and lesson evaluation.

Management of pupils and resources

A key feature of successful lessons is good management, e.g. how to organise the movement of pupils or how to utilise the resources. For example, if you want your pupils close to you, during a plenary or a demonstration, where do you seat them and what instructions do you give about moving? If equipment is to be used by pupils, plan where it is to be placed and how it is distributed, e.g. by you or by selected pupils. Record these decisions on your plan. It is often in deciding about the management of pupils and resources, that you make the final decisions about all the resources you need. Whatever resources you use, whether video, worksheets, practical activities, models, posters, computers etc., you have to think about how many are available, as this determines the size of working groups. If pupils are to work in groups, decide beforehand whether they are allowed their own choice in forming groups or whether you determine groups. Well in advance of the lesson, give your requisition list to technicians.

Timing and pace

Once you have selected activities and resources how do you package them into a well-structured, well-paced lesson? As Marland notes:

> The pupil in a school is in a time-structured environment and expects that the component elements of the day should similarly be time-structured. There is no escape from this demand of a use of time, which is complete, intense and varied. The pupil is stimulated by a good use of time and bored and irritated by bad use.
>
> (Marland, 1993: 122)

By rehearsing the tasks yourself, you have an idea how long each task or activity might take. You also need to judge how long it takes to change from one activity to another, i.e. the transitions between activities are events in their own right that have to be planned and timed. They may involve a change not only in task but also in focus for the pupils and these have to be explained and orchestrated.

Each lesson needs a definite beginning and ending which introduces and summarises, respectively, the substantive content of the lesson (sometimes called 'starters' and 'plenaries'); these are elaborated in Unit 4.4. Leave sufficient time at the end of the lesson to review and consolidate learning and to link forward to the next lesson.

Planning what you say to pupils

Teachers spend a lot of time talking to pupils, including telling, explaining, describing, summarising, eliciting, as well as talking for management purposes. It is important to plan what you want to say. Do not rely on checking your knowledge and understanding in a book or scheme of work, nor assume that the right words are 'in your head'. The process of writing out what you want to say clarifies key points for you. Think about each phase equally carefully; it is as important to plan what to say in the concluding part of the lesson as in the introduction and main phase. It may, in fact, be *more* important, as ends of lessons are typically short of time.

When you are planning to introduce a new topic, your script should include what the topic covers, what pupils can expect to learn, how it links with what they have learned before and its relevance to their lives.

As well as planning and writing what to say, *practise* it, either to a friend or to your mirror. Preparing in this detail is especially important when teaching a topic new to you. By rehearsing the ideas you want to share with your pupils you gain a better understanding of the material yourself.

Homework

Most schools have a homework policy and you need to know what the policy is in your placement school and your departmental guidelines. You should know why homework is set and the learning outcomes you expect. Homework is a part of your lesson planning. Homework can be used to:

- consolidate learning
- extend understanding
- promote study skills
- address differentiation issues
- promote interest and intrinsic motivation
- involve the home and parents in pupil development.

The purpose of the homework must be clear to the pupils. Homework should be timetabled into your lesson, an episode in the lesson plan (see below), so that you can explain the task and say when and where it is to be submitted. Outline the assessment criteria and provide information about your expectations. Check that your pupils can complete the task and that you are not making false assumptions about access to resources, e.g. books or the internet.

If you expect pupils to treat homework seriously then you must set the example by sharing your expectations with them. Do not set homework orally just as the bell is to go; this practice sends a negative message to the pupils about its importance.

KEEPING A WRITTEN RECORD OF YOUR PLAN

Only when your planning is complete do you summarise it in a written 'lesson plan' (see Figure 4.3.2). There are many ways teachers summarise their lesson plans and no one way is best. Your training institution or placement school may provide you with a pro-forma for lesson planning.

A lesson plan should have a structure with which you are comfortable and space for notes you can consult as necessary during the lesson. The format may change as you gain confidence and acquire expertise. Use highlighter pens to remind you of particular issues, e.g. safety and management strategies. Figure 4.3.2a effectively gives a checklist of headings for a lesson-plan summary and Figure 4.3.2b gives a summary of the action as the lesson progresses.

CHECKING LESSON PLANS

Plans need checking and this may be achieved in many ways. Two ways are suggested below: using a list of questions to review the lesson and reviewing the lesson from the pupils' point of view.

Questions to ask yourself when checking a lesson plan

One way to check your plan is to ask yourself whether you have planned:

- how to greet the class and settle them
- how to share the learning objectives and lesson outline with the pupils
- a starter activity to engage the attention of the pupils
- that pupils are actively engaged throughout the lesson, e.g. is there dead time while you organise books or equipment?
- how to talk to the class about a new topic and for how long
- opportunities for pupils to discuss and assimilate new ideas
- assessment opportunities
- an activity for pupils to reflect on what they have learned
- a plenary activity to reinforce the key learning points
- how to anticipate the next lesson
- homework and when it is to be handed in
- how to praise pupils for the way they worked and set standards for next lesson.

You may wish to add to this list.

Checking lesson plans by thinking from the pupils' perspectives

Another way to check your plan is to visualise the whole lesson through the eyes of the pupils.

Name Class Date Time Venue Pupils with SEN Pupils with EAL	Topic NC or other ref. e.g. PoS and level Lesson no...... of ......lessons
Learning outcomes	Personal professional targets
Assessment opportunities and strategies	Prior knowledge Link to previous teaching

Key questions and important words

Learning issues to be addressed from previous lesson

Resources and their management, e.g. named pupil to distribute tray of equipment per bench

Risk assessment

Administration, e.g. collect books from prep room; hand back homework

Homework, e.g. details including assessment criteria

■ **Figure 4.3.2a** Lesson plan summary: a checklist

Activity	Time	Pupil activity	Teacher activity	Resources
Episode 1				
Transition				
Episode 2				
Transition				
Episode 3				
Transition				
Episode 4				

■ **Figure 4.3.2b** A sample lesson plan summary: activities and timing

To do this, think about, What exactly will the pupils be doing at any moment? How are you going to ensure that the pupils know exactly how you want them to complete a task? If, for example, you find that you have planned for the pupils to be listening to you for over 20 minutes, is this too long? Once you know your classes, this strategy can be particularly effective if you have one or more pupils in mind as you visualise the lesson. What is effective for those pupils may be effective for most pupils.

Task 4.3.3 **Checking a lesson plan using two approaches**

Review a newly prepared lesson plan using the two approaches described above, i.e. using a checklist of questions, or reviewing the lesson from the pupils' perspective. Modify your initial lesson plan as necessary.

Which approach will be useful to your future planning, or should you use a combination of approaches?

Planning for differentiation

As you become more accustomed to planning lessons, you are able to focus on more difficult aspects of planning. These deal almost entirely with thinking about the learning of each individual and not just of the class as a whole. Planning for differentiation is about creating and adapting lessons so that they are suitable for all learners in the class. Recognising, and planning for, different levels of achievement are discussed in Unit 4.1, especially the task of setting differentiated learning outcomes (see Task 4.1.3). How to differentiate for different learning styles and different motivations is explored in Unit 4.4 along with the theories that underlie the recommended practice.

Other factors to take into account

As your teaching progresses other factors make demands on your planning. Figure 4.3.3 provides a list of such factors. It is important to recognise that you cannot address all of these all of the time. Incorporating one or more of these factors in your lesson plans widens your choice of objectives.

---

1 Individual Education Plans: Are there pupils in the class with IEPs? Do my plans consider their needs?
2 Additional adults: How many pupils have in-class learning support? Have I planned how to help teachers giving learning support.
3 Learning styles: Have I varied the strategies I use in the lessons across the topic to address different learning styles? See above, preparing activities and Unit 4.4.
4 Equal Opportunities: For example, are there opportunities in the lesson to use examples from different cultures? Is the content of the lesson relevant to the everyday experiences of the pupils in this class? Do boys and girls get an equal share of my attention?
5 Cross-curricular links: Are there any opportunities to make explicit links with work in maths, geography, citizenship, personal, social, moral, spiritual and cultural (PSMSC) etc.?
6 Literacy and numeracy: Are there opportunities in the lesson to develop pupils' literacy and numeracy skills set out in the National Strategy?
7 ICT: Are there opportunities in the lesson to develop pupils' ICT skills. How can learning be enhanced by the use of ICT?

■ **Figure 4.3.3** Additional factors to consider when planning science lessons

---

Task 4.3.4 **Lesson planning: widening your aims**

Review one or more recent lesson plans using the notes on widening your aims above and Figure 4.3.3. Identify the extent to which you have addressed any of these factors and check your achievements against the standards for your course. Select one or more factors that you have not yet considered and plan ways to incorporate them in a future lesson(s). Plan and teach a lesson in which you have included one such factor and evaluate your lesson.

Monitor your inclusion of these wider aims and review your progress towards meeting the standards for your course.

SETTING PROFESSIONAL DEVELOPMENT TARGETS

The lesson plan *pro-forma* has a place for your professional development targets. The objectives and learning outcomes discussed above refer to pupil outcomes. You have aims of your own about your development as a teacher. When you plan a lesson, in addition to setting learning outcomes for pupils, it is also important to remember to set objectives for yourself. These are sometimes referred to as professional development targets. Examples of targets might be to:

■ *learn the names of five pupils*
■ question the whole class effectively, that is *'involve the whole class in answering questions by using true/false statement questions, and using true/false cards which everyone holds up'*
■ provide challenging work for a named pupil, i.e. *identify when the pupil has completed the main activity and provide her with an extension activity*
■ manage a whole class practical safely, e.g. *plan and give instructions about the safe use of chemicals in an activity, how to dispose of them after use and to wash their hands afterwards.*

Professional development targets are important for your progress and should be specific and manageable. They should be shared with the person observing you and you should ask for feedback on them specifically. Priorities will change as you progress. To begin with you are likely to focus on management issues, but you should find yourself moving to more sophisticated targets such as changing the style of your questioning to require higher-order thinking skills, monitoring the achievements of six individuals in great detail, helping a class to assess their own learning.

LESSON EVALUATIONS

The process of evaluation is one key to making good progress as an effective classroom teacher. Throughout your training year you are expected to evaluate each lesson carefully, to record your evaluations and to file them along with your lesson plans.

Evaluations should respond to the professional development targets you set. They should be recorded the same day and a routine developed. It is of little benefit to you, and an ineffective use of your time and effort, to write up three weeks' worth of evaluations frantically before a meeting with your mentor or tutor. Lesson evaluations do not need lengthy prose; concise, well-focused bullet points can be more helpful. Figure 4.3.4 provides an example of a format that you might use. One effective strategy for managing this is to copy this format on to the back of the lesson-planning summary sheet.

Evaluating your lesson must go beyond a 'good feeling'; whether pupils have learned anything is your 'litmus test'. Pupils may or may not have stayed on task, the

Class		Date	Time
Number of pupils		with SEN	with EAL
Topic		Lesson title	

Personal response
Record how you felt at the end of the lesson: what went well, what went less well?

Learning outcomes
What did your pupils learn? Have the learning outcomes you set been met? What evidence have you gathered to make this judgement?

Next learning?
What should be taught?

Pupils
Identify those needing special attention (learning/behaviour).

Management and control
Identify achievements and issues to be addressed.

Personal professional targets
Include skills of communication, explanation, using resources, assessment.
Cite evidence for your judgement. Record feedback by an observer.

Personal targets for development
Short-term targets that you plan to use to inform your planning for the next lesson with this class.

■ **Figure 4.3.4** Example of an evaluation pro-forma

practical may not have worked as planned and, as a consequence, you ran out of time. Record facts such as these. Record your perceptions on the learning of the whole class, groups of pupils and individuals *with the evidence you have* from the classroom or you expect to have (e.g. when you have marked homework). Identify and record which factors influenced the success, or otherwise, of the lesson. Review your professional development targets in a similar way to assessing learning outcomes.

Lesson evaluation is an important stage in planning and teaching but only if the issues identified by the process are used to inform future lesson planning and your own progress. Figure 4.3.5 summarises the position of evaluation in the lesson planning cycle, emphasising the importance of assessment and evaluation in the planning of teaching.

KEEPING RECORDS: TEACHING FILES

Keep written records of lesson plans and evaluations in a teaching file adhering to the guidelines of your own institution. Your files should typically include:

■ a timetable of classes taught, including venue and name of class teacher
■ class lists, annotated to show special needs, disability, etc.
■ a chronological record of lessons taught, for each class
■ a chronological record of homework set
■ mark lists and other records of pupil progress
■ lesson plans including subject content notes and copies of resources used
■ your lesson evaluations
■ a record of all written observations of your lessons made by teachers, mentors and tutors.

Your file provides evidence of your teaching skills and progress in meeting the standards for QTS. Files form important professional documents. Student teachers frequently comment that they are expected to produce detailed lesson plans whereas qualified teachers do not appear to do so; experienced teachers have internalised many aspects of the planning process and therefore their plans will be much more succinct.

A WORD OF CAUTION

A frequently quoted model of lesson planning describes teachers starting with the learning objectives and working systematically through; this is often referred to as a rational linear framework. Planning is, in practice, a more untidy process, partly because it is a creative activity. A mixture of experience, knowledge, available resources, including the scheme of work and the advice of other teachers, interact in a complex way to contribute to a lesson plan. Indeed, learning outcomes may crystallise towards the end as the plan is realised. (Research shows teachers rarely start from lesson outcomes (John, 1993)). For this reason, do not attempt to fill in the pro-forma until the end of the planning process; a large sheet of paper on which you brainstorm ideas is likely to be more useful at the start.

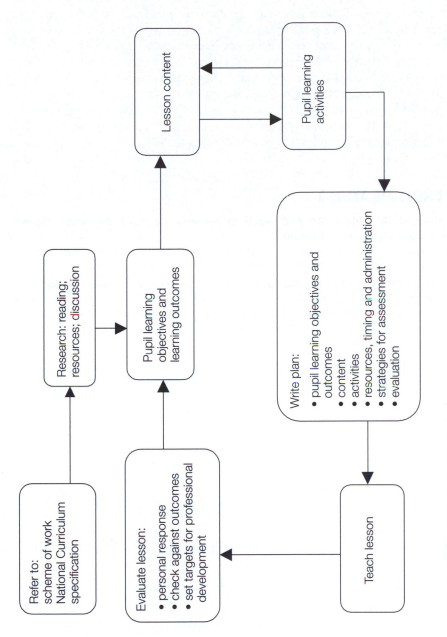

■ **Figure 4.3.5** Lesson planning cycle
Source: adapted from Bishop, 2005

SUMMARY AND KEY POINTS

Effective lesson planning is the key to successful teaching. The final lesson plan is the product of planning and the orderly simplicity of that document suggests that planning is a logical process. In practice, the interplay of many factors make planning a complex and creative process, summarised in the lesson planning cycle (Figure 4.3.5).

Although schemes of work provide a guide to the essential content of a lesson, the way you teach it and the pace of the lesson depends on what your pupils know and can do. Thus assessment of your pupils' learning and skills, and evaluation of your teaching are important aspects of future planning. The cyclical nature of the process highlights one of the most important qualities of a teacher: the ability to reflect critically on one's own practice and identify targets for future practice.

FURTHER READING

Wood-Robinson, M. (ed.) (2006) *ASE Guide to Secondary Science Education*. **Hatfield: Association for Science Education.**

Contains advice on lesson planning, concept maps and developing schemes of work. The chapter on safety in the laboratory should be read by all intending science teachers.

Parkinson, J. (2002) *Reflective Teaching of Science 11–18*. **London: Continuum Books.**

An extensive chapter on 'planning your teaching' includes a section on writing lesson plans. Several types of pro-forma are given, explaining how they contribute to effective teaching and learning. A most useful text for the new teacher.

TEACHING STRATEGIES AND ORGANISING LEARNING

Pete Sorensen

INTRODUCTION

'Miss, I'm bored!' 'Can't do science, sir, it's too hard!' 'What's the point of doing this? I'll never need to know it!' Most teachers have heard similar such cries over the years. Worry about pupils' lack of interest and the implications for the future has been one of the factors lying behind the changes seen in the science curriculum, as discussed earlier, in Chapter 2. Reports such as those of the House of Commons Science and Technology Committee (2002), the Elton Report (DES/WO, 1989), and the influential report *Beyond 2000: Science Education for the Future* (Millar and Osborne, 1998) noted pupils' perceptions of science as irrelevant and boredom as factors, with blame pointing to dull teaching methods, poor planning, lack of match to pupils' needs and little variety in approaches used.

In contrast to this gloomy picture, inspection reports in recent years have indicated that the quality of science teaching was high in many lessons. In reviewing the period 2004–2007, Ofsted noted many positive features, highlighting that 'the best teaching and highest standards were found in schools where staff drew on a rich range of resources to support a wide variety of activities. These were carefully planned to match pupils' needs and stimulate their interest' (Ofsted, 2008: 30). At the same time they expressed concerns about some poorer practices and asserted that overall progress had slowed. A particular worry was that:

> In too many primary and secondary schools, teachers were mainly concerned with meeting narrow test and examination requirements and course specifications. This led them to adopt methodologies which did not meet the needs of all pupils or promote independent learning.
>
> (ibid: 6)

Thus, while the previous unit has focused on planning in general terms, here we look in more detail at the teaching strategies chosen and the manner in which these are implemented. These are crucial factors in gaining interest and maximising learning.

TEACHING STYLES

In Capel *et al.* (2009: 285, Unit 5), teaching style is defined as 'resulting from the combination of your underlying behaviours (personality plus characteristics), your microbehaviours (ways you communicate through speech and body language) and the teaching strategies you choose'. *Teacher behaviour* refers to the way that the teacher relates to the pupils. You may choose a very formal approach or a friendlier one; you may decide to use a more formal mode of behaviour in some instances (e.g. to give instructions for a practical) than in others (e.g. in facilitating class discussions). *Teaching strategy* concerns the actual teaching approach or method used. The teaching style chosen depends on particular views on how children learn, the group or individuals you are working with and the intended learning outcomes for a given teaching episode.

Task 4.4.1 **Analysing different teaching approaches**

Consider the three different approaches to teaching about corrosion outlined in Table 4.4.1.

1 List the strategies used by each teacher.
2 Identify possible strengths and weaknesses associated with each approach.
3 What differences in behaviour might be required of the teachers using each approach?
4 How do these approaches impact upon the requirements for the organisation of learning?
5 Which approach do you prefer and why?

The approaches in Table 4.4.1 roughly accord with the three broad bands of teaching styles described in Capel *et al.* (2009: 289) with the first 'closed', the second 'framed' and the third 'negotiated'. One particular style may be more applicable to teaching

■ **Table 4.4.1** Three outline approaches to teaching the corrosion of metals

1	2	3
Four test tubes containing nails in different conditions present at start. Title: 'Corrosion' on board and diagram displayed on OHT. Class brought round front and teacher explains that each nail has been left for several weeks. Results explained to the class. Pupils return to seats and copy the diagrams and results from the board. Teacher explains nature of the processes taking place and dictates notes for the class to copy down. Class given some questions for homework as a preparation for a short test next lesson.	Class given a brief introduction to the lesson, with an outline of the activities and objectives for the lesson. Worksheet distributed and discussed. This includes photographs of heavily corroded samples of 'iron' and others that have remained shiny and questions as prompts for suggesting hypotheses to explain differences. Class shown possible equipment that they might want to use and divided into small groups to suggest hypotheses and plan experiments. Plans shown to teacher and groups set up experiments to leave for next time. Class asked to complete plans for homework.	Question on board: 'Why does Mr Turner's car have holes in?' Class brought round front. Discussion of question linked to title of 'corrosion'. Task set: 'investigate the factors that affect the corrosion of metals'. Class brainstorms possible factors and ideas to be investigated using flipchart. Class divided into small groups to investigate their chosen factors and prepare presentations. Some groups use the Internet; others decide to do a corrosion survey across the school; some opt for experiments. Class asked to gather information from home that might help as their homework.
Short test completed at start of lesson. Teacher goes over answers. Class given textbook showing results of corrosion experiments with different metals. Teacher explains results to group and writes notes on board to copy. Questions from book given to complete. Teacher concludes lesson by summarising work covered and relating to earlier work on the reactivity series. Second set of questions given for homework.	Short Q&A at start on last lesson. Objectives set. Group check nails. Changes noted. Teacher introduces idea of corrosion of different metals using video extract. Pupils set questions from book linking corrosion and the reactivity series. Lesson concludes with a Q&A to establish learning, and questions set for homework.	Teacher checks each group properly planned at start. Timings given. Support sheets provided to some pupils. Librarian and LSA work with groups who leave the classroom for surveys/research. Lesson finishes with group discussion of progress and further decisions on presentations. Some experiments shown to the whole class. Each pupil asked to write one thing they've learnt on posters stuck on wall by next time.
Homework questions discussed at start of lesson. Title 'methods of protecting against corrosion' given and slides of famous landmarks shown and discussed. Notes written on board for class to copy. Textbook with sections on 'factors that speed up/slow down corrosion' and 'uses of metals' discussed. Class asked to revise for test on corrosion next week as homework.	Pictures used for short Q&A at start, revising ideas covered so far. Nails checked. Teacher introduces set of nails left previously for longer period. Class discussion of findings. Pupils write conclusions based on class and teacher's results. Pupils' nails left set up to return to in 3 months' time. Class set small-group tasks to research 'factors that speed up/slow down corrosion' and 'uses of metals'. Class asked to research area for homework, to support posters for presentations.	Posters on wall at start with 'things learnt'. Time limit set of first half of lesson to be ready to present. Teacher supports group preparation. 5-minute presentations given. Some involve rap, some posters, some plays, one a PowerPoint presentation. Teacher annotates flipchart from first lesson. Homework to prepare ready to teach others next time. Posters used to identify key areas for teaching: necessary factors; slowing/speeding up; nature of metal; link to uses all included.
Past exam-paper questions used for test. Last part of lesson used to discuss answers. Formal test signalled for end of year.	Class continue work on group tasks. Each group presents poster. Teacher summarises key points covered and pupils make notes. Q&A used to test understanding. Formal test to be given at end of year, with nails revisited part way through.	Jigsaw activities used for pupils to teach each other the different aspects. Pupils asked to produce revision tools for their portfolio. Whole-class concept map produced for display, updating flipchart. Some experiments left running. Signal that corrosion will be revisited later.

specific aspects of the topic or particular pupils or classes and we consider these issues further within the unit. However, whatever the style there are other aspects of your behaviour that are crucial to gaining the interest of the pupils. Thus an enthusiastic teacher, using the 'closed' approach, might start: 'Now, everyone! Look at this nail! Underwater for 20 years and it still hasn't corroded! How can that be?' Compare this to a tired teacher, using the 'negotiated' approach: 'We're looking at corrosion over the next few lessons. You've done a bit of stuff on this before but we need to do some more. I know it's not very exciting but you need it for your exams. OK, let's brainstorm what you know to find out where the gaps are and together we can try and find a painless way to get the boring bits done.' I think you would agree that the first teacher is more likely to gain the pupils' interest. However, many would argue that the *potential* to stimulate interest and meet individual needs is higher in the negotiated approach. We return to such aspects of behaviour later in the unit. In the next section we focus on teaching strategies, looking in particular at the range of methods available, their relationship to learning outcomes and the importance of using a range of strategies in your teaching.

TEACHING STRATEGIES: THE NEED FOR VARIETY

There are a number of reasons why it is important to use a variety of strategies in teaching. These include the need to:

- meet a variety of learning outcomes
- cater for pupils' different backgrounds and attributes, including preferred modes of learning (drawing on evidence from learning theory and advances in neuroscience) – see Units 5.5 and 5.6 of Capel *et al.*, 2009
- motivate and interest pupils.

Let us consider the implications of each of these considerations for your practice.

1 Learning outcomes

There are many possible teaching methods that can be used in a lesson. Thus, in seeking to teach the reactions of metals with acids, the teacher may choose to start with a demonstration, run a class practical in the main body of the lesson and conclude with a group discussion of the results and some note-taking. In deciding which methods to employ it is important to identify the desired learning outcomes first, as indicated earlier in Unit 4.1.

Task 4.4.2 **Activities and learning outcomes**

Table 4.4.2 contains a list of activities used by student science teachers during their course. Add to this if you can think of other examples. Now, imagine that you have been asked to teach 'The Eye'. Pick out a few examples of activities that you judge may be suitable for meeting each of the following learning objectives:

- to be able to name the parts of the eye
- to be able to research information about problems with sight
- to understand the role creative thought processes and use of data played in developing our understanding of the eye

---

■ to make accurate observations
■ to work effectively with other people.

In each case explain why you have chosen the particular activities. Are any of them capable of being used to try and meet all five of these learning outcomes?

■ **Table 4.4.2** Ways of learning: possible activities to use with pupils

1 Assessments	26 Experimenting	51 Presentations
2 Blogging	27 Fieldwork	52 Problem-solving
3 Brainstorming	28 Film	53 Projects
4 Card sorting	29 Flow diagrams	54 Quiz
5 Case studies	30 Games	55 Radio
6 Classifying	31 Group discussions	56 Reading
7 Concept cartoons	32 Inductive approaches	57 Recitation
8 Concept maps	33 Interactive whiteboard	58 Records
9 Creative writing	34 Internet searches	59 Reports
10 Critical incidents	35 Interviews	60 Role play
11 Crosswords	36 Investigations	61 Simulations
12 DARTS	37 Jigsaw activities	62 Slides
13 Data analysis	38 Lectures	63 Spider diagrams
14 Data bases	39 Mind maps	64 Spreadsheets
15 Data logging	40 Mobile learning	65 Surveys
16 Debate	41 Modelling	66 Tape work
17 Demonstrations	42 Multimedia	67 Thought experiments
18 Design tasks	43 Music	68 TV
19 Diaries	44 Mysteries	69 Video
20 Dictation	45 Note-taking	70 Visitors
21 Discussion	46 Observation	71 Visits
22 Displays	47 Paired work	72 Web-page development
23 Drama	48 Photography	73 Word searches
24 Drawing	49 Posters	74 Workshops
25 Evaluation	50 Practical work	75 Writing

In completing Task 4.4.2 you may have noted that some:

■ activities are better suited to meeting particular learning outcomes (e.g. practical work is better suited to meet the learning outcome 'improvement of observational skills')

■ objectives may be achieved just as well by different activities (e.g. knowledge of the parts of the eye may be equally well learnt through producing posters or writing notes)

■ activities may only lead to superficial knowledge acquisition (e.g. recitation) whilst others may support deeper-level understanding and the attainment of higher cognitive goals (e.g. discussion or thought experiments)

■ objectives *cannot* be met by certain activities (e.g. 'the ability to work with other people' through 'dictation').

The need to link methods carefully to learning outcomes is one reason why it is important for you to use a variety of strategies in your teaching. Moreover, some learning outcomes may be missed altogether without careful thought about methods. For example, the learning objective which mentions the role of 'creative thought processes' is now a specific part of the *How Science Works* section of the National Curriculum but has rarely featured in many teachers' planning until quite recently.

2 Pupil differences, learning styles, learning strategies and cognitive development

In selecting teaching strategies it is clearly important to recognise the needs of the learners. Materials to support teachers, which have been developed as a result of research outcomes, suggest that people have a range of preferences in the way they use their senses to explore ideas and construct their views of the world. For a fuller discussion of these ideas see Capel *et al.*, 2009: 262–5. Here we consider two of the most influential ways in which learners have been characterised and their implications for teaching: 'VAK' and 'MI'.

(I) VISUAL, AUDITORY AND KINAESTHETIC LEARNERS (VAK)

You will encounter many teachers and other educationalists who suggest that learners may have preferences for either visual or auditory or kinaesthetic modes of learning. Indeed, in recent times some schools have started to set or group pupils on this basis. The rationale for this rests on assumptions about a link between preferences for particular types of activities and ways of thinking (representing). Visual learners prefer to learn through seeing and tend to set up visual images that help them to remember ideas. Auditory learners prefer listening and have a tendency to set up 'internal dialogues' to help develop their thinking and understanding. Kinaesthetic learners prefer to learn through doing, often remembering the feelings accompanying the tasks undertaken. It has been claimed that, on average, roughly 29 per cent of people have a visual preference, 34 per cent auditory and 37 per cent kinaesthetic (Smith, 1996). This VAK model suggests that it is important to pay attention to the different preferences in selecting teaching strategies. Boredom for some may result from a lack of opportunity to engage using their own preferred mode. Various reports have suggested that the mode most often neglected is the kinaesthetic one. Thus specialist teachers, working with pupils manifesting poor behaviour in mainstream classrooms, have found that changing teaching strategies to incorporate kinaesthetic modes of learning can lead to significant improvements in engagement and, thus, learning.

Task 4.4.3 **Learning modes**

Imagine that you have been asked to teach 'Cells' to a Year 7 group. Consider ways to introduce this topic that will help to ensure that pupils with each of the three preferred learning modes are engaged early in the first lesson.

(II) GARDNER'S MULTIPLE INTELLIGENCES MODEL (MI THEORY)

The multiple intelligences model of Gardner (1993) is also regarded by many educators as helpful in examining ways to support learning. Gardner initially identified seven components of human intelligence and suggested that a given individual will have some intelligences more highly developed than others. In later versions of the model this has since been increased to eight, maybe nine, components. Table 4.4.3 includes brief descriptions of each intelligence and examples of activities that might link to each intelligence. However, it is important to note that in selecting activities it is not being suggested that learners be allowed to work entirely in a learning mode that draws on their most highly developed intelligence or intelligences. Rather, it is important to select activities that allow access to all of the multiple intelligences over time, as we often use groups of intelligences together to solve problems and develop thinking. In this way there are likely to be gains in each of the intelligences and learning is likely to be maximised (see Capel *et al.*, 2009, Unit 4.3).

■ **Table 4.4.3** Gardner's multiple intelligences

Intelligence	Description	Example activities
Linguistic	Adept with language	Word games, listening to stories
Mathematical-logical	Like organisation, logic and structure	Number work, problem-solving and sequencing
Musical	Recognise rhythm and tunes, react to mood	Design raps to learn sequences
Visual-spatial	Good sense of direction, create mental images	Concept maps, multimedia presentations
Body-physical (kinaesthetic)	Good control of movement, like to use touch	Role play and practical work
Interpersonal	Relate well to others	Group work, collaborative learning
Intrapersonal	Strong self-knowledge, metacognitive approach	Learning diaries, reflective evaluations
Naturalistic	Skill of recognition in natural environments	Classifying organisms
Existential	Awareness of place in the cosmos and significance of self	Considering purposes of scientific endeavour

Task 4.4.4 **Multiple intelligences**

You have been asked to teach the topic 'Energy Resources' to Year 7, based on the *QCA Scheme of Work* (DfEE/QCA, 2000).

http://www.standards.dfes.gov.uk/schemes2/secondary_science/

List possible methods that you could include in lessons under each of Gardner's multiple intelligence headings and link these to particular learning outcomes indicated in the scheme of work.

> Is it possible to use all 8/9 ways of learning to meet any one particular learning outcome? If so, explain how this could be done. If not, identify a learning outcome that can be met by most methods.

There have been some strong critiques of the way work on learning styles and multiple intelligences has been applied in schools, including a tendency to conflate the two. Thus, Sharp, Bowker and Byrne (2008) caution against 'the casual acceptance and promotion of VAK' (p. 293) and assert that 'the labeling of children in schools as visual, auditory or kinaesthetic learners is not only unforgiveable, it is potentially damaging' (p. 311), and White (2005) questions the evidence for the theory of multiple intelligences. A systematic review of the learning styles field was carried out by Coffield *et al.* (2004). This review indicates that all those models commonly used for educational purposes fail to meet one or more basic tests of reliability or validity. A particular concern is expressed over the way simple inventories and self-report questionnaires may be used to classify learners and hence influence teaching approaches.

Many of the critiques of VAK, multiple intelligences and learning styles concern their application in ways which seem to deny the complexity of teaching and learning and its context dependency. However, many also point to the positive impact of these ideas, especially when they lead to more careful consideration of the need to include more variety in lessons in seeking to meet the needs of a range of pupils. One important debate concerning the application of learning styles is whether the argument is for teaching 'to' learning styles or to develop pupils' facility to work in other modes. It is important to be aware that both Gardner and Smith have been critical of some of the ways in which their work has been applied.

Task 4.4.5 **Evaluating learning styles**

Consider the possible benefits for including learning styles as an important consideration in planning teaching and organising learning together with critiques from those who counsel caution. Where do you stand in relation to this debate and why? Why do you think learning styles are so popular with a lot of teachers? This is an area of considerable controversy and it will be important for you to think carefully about your stance throughout your practice as you seek to draw positively on the work in this field. Seek to try out strategies with your groups on teaching practice in the light of discussions with tutors and mentors. In evaluating impact take care to consider other possible explanations.

Whatever the stance you take on issues of learning styles, taken together with the constructivist arguments examined in Unit 4.1 and in Capel *et al.*, 2009: 254–9, there are clear implications for differentiation in the application of teaching strategies. The attendant organisational issues that arise are discussed later in this unit. However, it is important to include a further reference here to pupils with additional needs. Thus, for example, various forms of physical impairment may make it difficult or impossible for some pupils to learn if a particular teaching strategy is used. In such cases it is also important that a variety of strategies are developed in order to meet such needs. There is also the need to seek to remove barriers to the inclusion of pupils with particular needs when planning teaching strategies, as the National Curriculum makes clear (DfES/QCA, 2008). Difficulties can be overcome with the right support or modifications to course materials, equipment or buildings. In science practical work this could include resizing and providing unbreakable apparatus (where sight impairment or dyspraxia is an issue), providing adjustable tables (for example to assist wheelchair users) or supporting a pupil's upper arms (where pupils have weak muscular control). Unit 4.6 of Capel *et al.*, 2009 gives sources of support for helping to meet particular additional needs. Also, note that ICT can often help overcome difficulties. For example, computer simulations of experiments that allow variables to be manipulated can enable a pupil to 'carry out' an experiment where the actual experiment is not possible.

3 Motivation and interest

Here we simply point out the importance of variety in maintaining interest and concentration. Psychological research shows that an individual's attention span on single tasks is limited, even when the motivation is there in the first place.

THE ORGANISATION OF LEARNING AND TEACHER BEHAVIOUR

Thus far, we have concentrated mainly on teaching strategies. It is now important to bring in the second part of the teaching style definition mentioned at the start of the unit, that of teacher behaviour. This factor is crucial if interest is to be generated and maintained and learning is to be organised in an effective manner. In considering the organisation of learning we focus firstly on (A) the different sections of lessons, including transitions between sections; secondly on (B) questioning; thirdly on (C) differentiation issues; and finally; (D) 'awe and wonder'.

(A) Different sections of lessons

Local authority advisers and others working to support teachers in schools through various stages of national strategies have, in recent years, sought to stress particular features and structures of effective lessons (see Capel *et al.*, 2009, Unit 7.4). This has been interpreted by some as meaning that you must have a 'three-part', 'four-part' or even 'six-part' lesson for it to be effective. This is not the case. The key is to structure in a way that is flexible and geared to meeting the learning needs of the pupils. Thus the subsections that follow are not intended to be read as fixed sections, rather as guides to approaches.

1 STARTS OF LESSONS

The starts of lessons are crucial (DCSF, 2009a). It is here that expectations are established and the correct atmosphere for learning developed. Although this unit does not focus on it, it is worth remembering that the learning environment itself is important (see Unit 1.3).

There are a number of actions to consider at the start of lessons:

■ Seek to create a positive learning environment through the way you greet pupils. This means being at the door and being positive in the way you interact on arrival.

■ Share the purpose of the lesson, indicating how it links to previous lessons.

■ Share the learning objectives or outcomes with the pupils *when this is appropriate* – you may wish to hide these until later, let them emerge over time or encourage individual pupils to make their own decisions about priorities. It is often a good idea to have objectives displayed somewhere in the room so they can be referred to at different points in the lesson.

■ Use formative assessment strategies to establish prior learning (see Unit 6.1 for examples of these as well as a discussion of broader assessment issues).

■ Use techniques to help relax the class (e.g. closing eyes and focusing thoughts; repetition of instructions to relax at progressively lower and slower rates; breathing exercises). Share these explicitly with the class, explaining their purpose with groups unused to this sort of approach.

■ Use music to help establish a positive working atmosphere. There is evidence that particular music (e.g. Mozart) supports preparedness for learning through activating different parts of the brain, and different music can be used to stimulate specific learning atmospheres (Smith, 1996). However, take care! For some people background music can be irritating and it is best to avoid more recent popular music as this can provoke off-task discussion and argument.

■ Use activities which require co-ordination of physical and mental activity, often called 'brain gym' (Dennison and Dennison, 1989). A well-known example of this is 'rub a dub'. This involves rubbing the stomach with one hand (using a circular action) whilst patting the head with the other one, switching hands, then the direction of rotation. There are claims that activities such as this have been shown to help develop co-ordination and stimulate the brain, thus preparing pupils for learning. Others would simply say that they help to create a good atmosphere in which to start work.

It is obviously not possible or sensible to use all of the different techniques each time. However, establishing routines that include scene-setting and short activities to generate interest is important.

2 STARTER ACTIVITIES

Aspects of many of the activities included in Table 4.4.2 can be drawn on to develop starter activities. A typical starter will last from 5 to 10 minutes but there are no rules. The one chosen depends on a number of factors, such as the objectives of the lesson and the nature of the group. Examples of starters include:

■ brain gym (for examples see Dennison and Dennison, 1989)

■ thought experiments – examples can be found in the CASE materials (Adey and Yates, 2001); for a discussion of some famous examples see Brown (1991)

■ 'science in the news' items (the internet is very helpful here). Present an article or headline relevant to the topic and ask for opinions or explanations

■ controversial statements – present and start the lesson by taking sides

■ diagnostic tests using 'show me' strategies for answering questions (e.g. answers written on small whiteboards; yes/no cards; 'traffic light' cards to indicate confidence/agreement (red indicates no idea/wrong; amber some idea/maybe; and green sure/right)

■ short video clips, e.g. volcanic eruption; cheetahs stalking their prey; car braking at edge of cliff

■ key-word games, e.g. loop cards, word dominoes.

Many commercial books and web-based resources are available to support you with developing further ideas.

Task 4.4.6 **Starting a lesson: identifying strategies**

Observe the start of a number of lessons on teaching practice. Make a note of any useful techniques. Ask the pupils their opinions of particular strategies and use these to help inform your judgements. Build up a database of starter activities and use them to inform your own lesson planning.

---

3 MAIN BODY OF THE LESSON

The main body of the lesson, termed 'development' in National Strategy materials, can itself include a number of different parts that depend on the nature of the activities being included. However, even if there is one main activity, such as a practical, it is important to ensure that this is broken down into parts to help maintain pace and check on learning. Thus short plenaries within lessons, with a focus back to objectives, may often be important. Other approaches, such as jigsaw activities, simulations and role play may contain more natural breaks; for details of the thinking behind such approaches, see Joyce *et al.*, (2002); for some practical examples in science see Parkinson (2002, Chapter 5). For some pupils it is helpful to use activities that last for relatively short periods in order to help maintain concentration, keep on task and generate pace. If you have the expected learning outcomes displayed in the room you can refer individuals back to these without interrupting the main flow. This will help with approaches to AfL (Assessment for Learning) (see Unit 6.1).

4 ENDS OF LESSONS

The end of a lesson is as important as the start. A plenary at the end of a lesson might typically last for 5 to 10 minutes. It is here that you can have an overall check on whether or not learning outcomes have been met. You can also reinforce expectations, share achievement and set targets. Again, strategies that promote the active involvement of pupils are important. A whole range of activities may be included here as well, with a focus on determining the learning that has taken place. Examples include key-word matches, sharing mnemonics, pupil presentations and concept-map development. It is sometimes good to dismiss the class in parts according to their responses to questions on learning, especially prior to break or lunchtime when there is no risk of delaying the next lesson.

5 TRANSITIONS BETWEEN PHASES

A crucial point of lessons is the transition between activities. There are two important aspects of transitions to consider: organisational issues and learning considerations. Careful management and organisation of transitions is vital. It is important to establish clear routines and ensure that expectations are met. Aim to develop signals to use with your group. These could involve a clap, drum roll, loud bang, particular snatch of music or an announcement of 'statues!'. Such techniques can also be used to introduce breaks in activity (e.g. for brain gym or relaxation exercises) when pupils seem to be drifting off task. This is often important in longer lessons. However such signals are used, there is also a need to give clear time warnings in advance of transitions, sometimes counting down ('five minutes left now!'; 'one more minute only!' etc.), so pupils are prepared for the point when you want everyone to stop. Such time warnings may also be accompanied by organisational instructions, such as: 'turn bunsens off now!'; 'return equipment to trays and clear up the bench'; or 'discuss results with your partner ready to share with the class'. These, again, help to ensure pupils are ready for the change of activity or focus.

The second aspect of transitions focuses on intended learning outcomes and is equally important. This concerns the need to ensure that the links between possible learning outcomes from one activity and learning targets in the next part of the lesson are made explicit to the pupils. If this is not done it is likely that many pupils may miss the point of the activities and simply remember what they *did* rather than what they were supposed to learn. It is also possible that they will not draw on earlier parts of the lesson appropriately in later tasks. The cues needed to help with this aspect of transition are provided by phrases such as: 'now we've got those two factors identified, we're going to find out why they're important'; 'hold on to that idea, you are going to use it to try and solve the next problem'; or 'keep those results in mind, we are going to see if they fit with Newton's ideas'. As mentioned earlier in the unit, it is sometimes useful to focus back on any intended learning outcomes shared at the start of a lesson at key transitions.

(B) Questioning

One generic aspect of teaching that is important to cross-reference here is that of questioning. This is a vital part of many teaching strategies. It is particularly important in science if targets associated with higher-level thinking and enquiry are to be achieved, for example in the *How Science Works* strand of the National Curriculum.

Task 4.4.7 **Types of questions science teachers ask**

Read pages 112–18 of Capel *et al.*, 2009 and the article on the types of questions asked by science teachers (Koufetta-Menicou *et al.*, 2000). Observe one or more questioning sequences used by teachers during your observations on teaching practice and classify the questions according to the categories identified by Koufetta-Menicou and Scaife (2000). Draw up a questioning sequence of your own for use whilst teaching objectives from the *How Science Works* or enquiry parts of the science curriculum. Ask your mentor to provide you with feedback about the sequence used.

(C) Differentiation

The need to differentiate in order to meet particular needs raises a number of issues. Thus whilst most people using the term would accept that 'differentiation concerns how we manage the learning of individual pupils in order to maximise the progress each makes' (Chapman *et al.*, 2000), there are differences in the models applied to support differentiation. One much-used model of differentiation (Dickinson and Wright, 1993) focuses on four aspects of differentiation that are in the hands of the classroom teacher:

■ by resource – different resources may be selected to meet particular needs, e.g. tape/video/posters/materials/texts/CD-ROM

■ by task – this could involve differentiating the demands of the task given to particular pupils; alternatively, through different tasks for the same objectives, e.g. knowledge and understanding of the structure and function of parts of the ear through either making a poster, a DART activity, producing a model using plasticine/clay or making a video presentation

■ by support – using other adults/individual teacher/co-operative approaches

■ by response to outcomes – various forms of feedback may be used by the teacher or other response partners involved.

For other approaches, see Capel *et al.*, 2009, Unit 4.1.

Task 4.4.8 **Differentiation strategies**

During early school experience keep a log of the differentiation strategies you observe being used by practising teachers. Where possible, discuss these strategies with pupils and note their response. How effective are the strategies seen?

Keep a log of the differentiation strategies you make use of during the early part of your school experience and in the later part experiment with any strategies you have not already had the opportunity to trial. Ask experienced teachers to observe and give feedback. Again, seek to determine pupils' responses and use these to inform your future practice.

Apart from differentiation by outcome, it is perhaps differentiation by 'task demand' that has been most prevalent in schools. This often involves judgements being made about a student's innate 'ability' or 'intelligence'. However, theories of multiple intelligences, as opposed to 'general intelligence', and studies that have indicated that some of the main determinants of pupils' examination achievements are class, sex and ethnicity, have challenged the validity of differentiating (or grouping) on this basis. Thus Chapman *et al.* (2000) have highlighted the risks associated with teachers using the 'notion of ability as a major determinant for differentiation' and argue instead for differentiating by 'approach to learning', a form of differentiation that they have termed 'non-judgemental differentiation'. They suggest a six-stage model of learning which involves:

■ *Right Frame of Mind*: involving the establishment of prior knowledge – including advance organisers, setting targets and creating a relaxed learning environment.

■　*Getting the Facts*: involving the use of multisensory inputs, with choice for learners as their independence grows.

■　*Exploration*: including individual/pair/small-group activities with differentiation based on multiple intelligences.

■　*Memorising*: using review techniques to support long-term memorisation.

■　*Show You Know*: with opportunities for learners to demonstrate new knowledge and understanding through group and whole-class activities.

■　*Evaluation of Learning*: including reflection and discussion with peers and teacher, that is, metacognitive reflection (see later section 'Metacognition').

Task 4.4.9 **The six-stage learning model**

Return to this model during your school placement, following completion of Task 4.4.6 above. Select a class with which you feel most comfortable. Identify the challenges and any barriers you perceive in implementing this model with the class. Evaluate the model in terms of your own teaching experience and observations. Do you think this is a good model for learning? If so, what changes to your practice would be needed to implement this with the class and how would you go about introducing them? If not, how would you modify the model to support the needs of particular groups of learners?

(D) Awe and wonder

Awe and wonder cannot be taught, but maybe they can be caught. How can you as a teacher convey a sense of the excitement of science to your pupils? This comes back to the enthusiastic teacher mentioned earlier. Is it really amazing (as well as counter-intuitive) that bulb after bulb can be placed in parallel and still shine as brightly as the previous one? Can a dull grey rock really contain that shiny metal? Or is Earth science really boring? A tree – from thin air? Imagine journeying to Mars! On paper it's hard to convey the behavioural attributes of a teacher who is seeking to generate such feelings of wonder without sounding crass or resorting to multiple exclamation marks. Yes, generating awe and wonder does require using a variety of teaching strategies, including those that allow feelings to be expressed and shared. Yes, appropriate use of ICT can help. Yes, it is important to know about the pupils' needs. However, it is your behaviour as a role model that is most important. Without showing that you are an enthusiast you stand little chance of gaining the interest of many pupils. This is especially important in motivating pupils at the start of lessons, as noted earlier in the unit. Many of us were motivated to become scientists by either the subject or the teacher, or possibly both, or a parent or friend. Richard Feynman attributes his way of looking at the world to the influence of his father, who had no direct scientific training but who appears to have had a sharp eye, an inquiring mind and a sense of wonder about the natural world (Feynman, 2000: 4–5).

METACOGNITION

In conclusion let us return to the learners. There is growing evidence that when pupils are taught about how to learn, encouraged to think about their own learning and given choices about the strategies they use, then their learning is enhanced (see Unit 5.5 in Capel *et al.*, 2009). The development of thinking skills is an important part of the Secondary National Strategy, and the QCDA's (2009) Framework of Personal, Learning and Thinking Skills (PLTS) includes the development of 'reflective learners' as a key goal for schools. In terms of the focus of this unit, this means going further than simply selecting and implementing particular teaching strategies. It also means sharing with pupils the *reasons* why you are using the strategies chosen and the way you are implementing them. It also means sometimes giving *them* the opportunity to work in ways they choose themselves. You might like to look back now to Task 4.4.1 and the implications of ideas on metacognition for deciding between the three approaches outlined.

SUMMARY AND KEY POINTS

In this unit we have discussed different teaching strategies and the way that these can be used to achieve particular learning outcomes and meet the needs of different pupils. We have also considered the importance of teacher behaviour in generating interest and enthusiasm. The important stages of a lesson have been highlighted and strategies that can be employed to help maximise learning discussed. Models of differentiation have been considered and arguments presented in support of strategies involving differentiation by approach to learning. In employing such strategies it is suggested that you should seek to do these *with* pupils rather than *at* them.

FURTHER READING

Ginnis, P. (2002) *The Teacher's Toolkit*. **Carmarthan: Crown House Publishing.**
  A very useful generic book containing a wealth of strategies to support teaching and learning, together with their rationale.

For reading on specific strategies for teaching particular science concepts and aspects of the curriculum, there are two main series of publications available to support student teachers:

The ASE series, published by John Murray/Hodder:

Reiss, M. (ed.) (1999) *Teaching Secondary Biology*. **London: John Murray.**

McDuell, B. (ed.) (2000) *Teaching Secondary Chemistry*. **London: John Murray.**

Sang, D. (ed.) (2000) *Teaching Secondary Physics*. **London: John Murray.**

Sang, D. and Wood-Robinson, V. (eds) (2002) *Teaching Secondary Scientific Enquiry*. **London: John Murray.**

Kind, V. and Kind, P. M. (2008) *Teaching Secondary How Science Works.* **London: Hodder.**

The Hodder and Stoughton series:

Winterbottom, M. (2000) *Teaching Biology to KS4*. **London: Hodder and Stoughton.**

Wilson, E. (2000) *Teaching Chemistry to KS4*. **London: Hodder and Stoughton.**

Jerram, A. (2000) *Teaching Physics to KS4*. **London: Hodder and Stoughton.**

RELEVANT WEBSITES

In terms of national expectations and initiatives it is clearly important to consult DCSF and QCDA websites regularly.

The National Strategies site (http://nationalstrategies.standards.dcsf.gov.uk/secondary/science) has become an increasingly important one. Here you will find the latest Framework for teaching science and a whole host of materials to support teaching strategies, including those associated with *How Science Works* developments.

TEACHING SCIENCE: SPECIFIC CONTEXTS

INTRODUCTION

In this chapter you will find guidance on specific aspects of teaching science. We have started with a consideration of the role language plays in learning science (Unit 5.1). This is not only about the very large new vocabulary that pupils have to learn but also how an active involvement in activities associated with reading, writing and talking in science lessons can help pupils shape and refine their ideas.

Unit 5.2 addresses many of the issues associated with practical work: the purposes of practical work; the organisation of it; ensuring that pupils learn some science from it; and safety considerations. Like any part of teaching, the practical work has to be tried out beforehand, but this involves talking with the technicians ahead of time, so that you have access to the equipment on *two* occasions – once to try it out and once for the lesson.

There is commitment nationally to the use of ICT in learning. Student teachers can easily be anxious about this because of technical problems that might arise. Unit 5.3 gives straightforward advice about contexts in which ICT can be used for teaching science, ways to ensure that the outcome will be successful and ways to evaluate the contribution it can make to learning science.

Citizenship is a cross-curricular theme involving all subjects. For many science teachers this brings into their teaching different sorts of concepts to those with which they are most familiar. In Unit 5.4 the author explores socio-scientific topics that might be included in the science curriculum and explains concepts such as rights and responsibilities. He describes strategies that teachers can use to help students to explore the issues and to make informed decisions about courses of action that they might take.

Much of the advice in Unit 5.4 about how teachers manage discussion of socio-scientific issues applies also to sex and health education (Unit 5.5). Here teachers have to deal with potentially sensitive and personal issues that require 'distancing techniques' and ground rules. The unit also gives guidance on the law relating to sexual activity and to the use of drugs.

The last context (Unit 5.6 'Beyond the classroom') addresses the task of using the world outside the classroom for science: lessons in the school grounds; in the locality; in museums or further afield on residential field trips. There are enormous benefits to be had provided that activities are thought through carefully, adequate preparation is done and the necessary organisation is put in place.

LANGUAGE IN LEARNING SCIENCE

Jenny Frost

INTRODUCTION

Any subject has its own discourse, its vocabulary, its assumptions and its ways of think-ing. If pupils are to feel comfortable with scientific discourse, they need not only an introduction to it but also opportunities to practise using it.

OBJECTIVES

By the end of the unit you should:

■   be aware of the range of language used in science and how it is connected to the conventions of scientific discourse

■   recognise that learning science involves entering into, and participating in, the discourse of science

■   be able to select and create a diversity of active learning tasks that involve pupils in reading, writing and talking science

■   know how to explore the teacher's roles in these activities.

LEARNING SCIENCE INCLUDES LEARNING A NEW LANGUAGE

Science teachers are inevitably teachers of language, because they are teaching pupils to write, read and talk about science and to listen to other people talking about science. Science has its own rich vocabulary and language conventions, which must be taught (and practised) as a component of science lessons.

What are some of the features of the language of science? Think first about the nouns that are used in science explanations. They have been classified in Figure 5.1.1 into three groups: naming words, process words and concept words.

The naming words are the simplest to acquire, because they relate mostly to objects that can be seen. It does not mean that these words will be learned quickly, because

---

Naming words – nouns that give the names of objects which can be seen:

spider, thermometer, ammeter, measuring cylinder, metal, eye, chlorine, sodium…

Process words – words that refer to a process:

dissolving, life-cycle, respiration, cooling, evaporation, energy transfer, radiation, transpiration, osmosis, diffusion, erosion, homeostasis, Krebb's cycle…

Concept words – nouns referring to abstract concepts:

electron, atom, polymer, entropy, energy, density, acceleration, enzyme, species, community…

■ **Figure 5.1.1** Categories of nouns
Source: Adapted from Wellington and Osborne, 2001: 22

people take time to learn new names and use them routinely. Devices for helping pupils to memorise words include vocabulary lists, posters, exercises where words are matched to pictures, diagrams to be labelled, models and objects with labels. Of course, being in an environment where the words are routinely used is a major factor.

The process words are ones that involve a sequence of events. Some refer to processes that occur in a relatively short space of time, such as dissolving or freezing, which can be demonstrated easily. Others take place over a long period, such as erosion. Some, such as evolution, not only take place over a long time but also rely on a great deal of theoretical knowledge to understand them. Timelines, and diagrams with arrows, are used to represent many of the processes, but they themselves are conventions that need to be learned.

For the concept words there is a need to make 'entities', such as atoms, energy, etc., seem real in the first place, and having done that to use them in explanations as if they were as real as the objects in the naming words list. Teachers have, for instance, to make the idea of an atom seem real and then use it in the explanation of differences between elements and compounds. They persuade pupils to imagine unseen entities by using analogies, simplifications and models (see Ogborn *et al.*, 1996b).

Naming words may in time become concept words. The word 'heart', for instance, moves from the label for one particular object to a label for a range of objects that pump blood, so that it can be used for things as widely different in size and shape as the heart of a cow and the heart of a daphnia.

Words associated with investigations

To these nouns we must add words and phrases associated with investigations, such as: accuracy, average, pattern, anomalous, correlation, data, reliability, sampling, trial run, variables. These are all associated with procedures necessary to obtain reliable data and to make conclusions out of the data. Pupils do not just pick up such 'procedural knowledge', they have to be taught it explicitly (see Unit 5.2).

Connecting words, verbs, adjectives

Science is about causal relationships, which have their own language conventions, particularly in the use of connecting words and phrases:

■　'*Because* the lungs expand, the pressure goes down, *consequently* air is pushed in from outside…'
■　'Carbon is not a metal, *nevertheless*, it conducts…'

There is a vast array of verbs that are used to describe events:

■　'The liquid *effervesces*'
■　'The diode *emits* light'
■　'Copper *accumulates* on the anode…'
■　'Hydrogen is *liberated* at the cathode…'

There are adjectives and adjectival phrases…

■　'The decay of radioactive material is *random*…'
■　'The difference in the temperatures is *negligible*…'
■　'This is *comparable to* what happens in …'
■　'This material is *translucent*'.

Most of these words are not part of the everyday language of many pupils even though they are not specifically scientific words. They can therefore act as a barrier to learning if a teacher is not aware of the difficulties they may cause.

Scientific words with everyday meanings

Science also uses many everyday words that are given a specialised meaning. 'Properties of materials' does not, for instance, mean 'houses owned by rolls of cloth'. Collect your own list of words that have both scientific and everyday meanings to add to this starter list: plant, energy, force, dense, material, property, characteristic, field, compound, current, power…

As an adult you are able to judge the meaning of a word from its context, and have no trouble in distinguishing the meaning of, say, 'power' in a scientific context (joules per second) from a political context. Think of words which pupils use quite easily in different contexts ('cool' for instance) and make explicit this use of the same word to mean different ideas, so that pupils become aware that it is not so odd to have the same word with different meanings.

Task 5.1.1 **Listening to scientific language**

Read Chapter 2 in Wellington and Osborne (2001: 9–23) 'Looking at the Language of Science' for a much fuller description of the language of science and the difficulties pupils have with it than that which is given above.

1 When observing a class, record a sample of the scientific vocabulary that is being used. Record for perhaps 5 minutes only, listening first to the teacher and then to the pupils. Don't worry if you record only a fraction of the vocabulary.

Classify the words being used into:

■ scientific nouns
■ scientific verbs
■ connecting words
■ scientific adjectives

2 Use the classification in Figure 5.1.1 to classify the nouns that have been used.
3 List any words that have both scientific and everyday meanings.
4 Make a comparison between the teacher's and the pupils' language.
5 If possible, observe the same teacher with a class of a different age (if you can switch from Y7 to Y13, this would be ideal). Compare the language use of both pupils and teacher in the different classes.
6 Reflect on the language you heard, in the light of Wellington and Osborne's account of language difficulties.

Summarise your findings and discuss with your mentor. Make notes of implications of your findings for your own practice.

LANGUAGE ACTIVITIES FOR LEARNING SCIENCE

Central to many activities for learning science is the conviction that pupils must be *actively* involved in the construction of their ideas through reading, talking and writing. Wellington and Osborne (2001) provide a rich variety of language tasks that engage pupils actively. Key points from their book are summarised here but you are strongly advised to read it.

Reading activities

Reading material that is used in science usually falls into one of the following categories:

■ instructions (how to do a practical activity)
■ structure text and pictures (explaining the structure of things)
■ mechanism text and pictures (explaining how something works)
■ process text and pictures (explaining a process)
■ concept-principle (explaining a concept or principle)
■ hypothesis-theory (explaining a hypothesis and a theory).

Pupils need considerable help in using different texts and learning to extract information from them. Pictures may need as much deciphering as words; pictures are as much about language as text. Tasks that constitute *active* reading fall into two categories:

1   deconstruction of a complete text
2   reconstruction of a broken text.

In both cases the reader has to do something with the text other than just read it. Deconstruction exercises might be:

■   drawing a concept map or spider diagram to summarise a complex text
■   underlining key ideas
■   extracting specific information in response to questions
■   summarising a paragraph in one sentence
■   tabulating information from a written text
■   rewriting for a different audience.

Reconstruction exercises are ones created by presenting learners with text that has been broken up in some way. This may be:

■   diagrams that have labels missing
■   texts with gaps in them
■   jumbled sentences which have to be re-ordered (e.g. instructions for a practical activity in the wrong order)
■   a set of statements that have to be put together in a flow chart
■   sentences that have to be made up from separate elements
■   incomplete text where the last paragraph has been taken out and pupils have to predict what it will be.

All these activities are referred to as DARTs (Directed Activities Related to Texts). They require pupils to go to texts with a specific purpose, and have much in common with good study techniques that you will have used for note-making when extracting information from texts and for revision purposes.

Newspaper reports are discussed as a resource in Unit 5.4, particularly for debates on social and ethical issues. Whether you are using them to stimulate debate, or as a source of information, they need to be read actively, and lend themselves to deconstruction activities. It is difficult to provide generic questions for a newspaper article but the following provide a possible selection:

■   Why is it deemed newsworthy? Why has it been written now?
■   What are the facts reported?
■   What is the evidence on which the article is based?
■   How was the evidence collected?
■   Who are the writers? What authority do they have?
■   What conclusions do the writers come to?
■   What relevance does the article have for you?
■   Do the title and article convey the same message? (They often do not).

Also, a structured comparison of articles on the same subject from different newspapers can be very instructive (see Unit 5.4).

Before you tackle Task 5.1.2, on creating your own DART, discuss with the teachers responsible for supporting pupils with special educational needs (SEN) and pupils for whom English is an additional language (EAL), what sort of texts, layouts and pictures are accessible to the age group you have in mind (see also Wellington and Ireson, 2008: 225–30).

Task 5.1.2 **Creating your own DART**

1 Read Wellington and Osborne (2001: 45–62) and review their samples of DARTs.
2 Collect a range of DARTs that you have used, or seen used in school. What type of DARTs are they? Is there a range or are they all the same, e.g. text completion where words have been omitted?
3 Construct a new type of DART to be used in your next topic, in four forms, one for pupils with special educational needs, one for pupils who have limited English, one for middle-attaining pupils and one for the high achievers.
4 Discuss your DART with your science mentor, with the special needs co-ordinator in the school and the teacher responsible for pupils with EAL.
5 Use the DART with a class and evaluate what pupils learned from it. Would you make any changes to it?

Talking activities

Sorting out ideas through discussion is an important way of learning. Many DARTs can be, and often are, done as collaborative activities in pairs or small groups and hence provide an opportunity for discussion.

Ideas for discussion activities, such as concept cartoons, have also been developed from the literature on children's ideas in science (see Unit 4.1 and Driver *et al.*, 1985 and 1994). These cartoons show different people voicing their ideas, and pupils are asked to decide who might be correct – or to suggest how they could find out. They can be used in more than one way. For instance, a concept cartoon which appears in the collection by Naylor and Keogh (2000) has a picture of two snowmen with the sun shining, one wrapped in a coat and scarf and the other one not wrapped up. The children in the cartoon are arguing about which snowman would melt faster. This cartoon could be used before much work has been done on insulation and pupils could decide how they would investigate to come to a decision – or it could be used at the end of a topic on heat transfer, where the pupils were expected to bring to bear their new understanding of insulation to argue the case about which would melt first.

It is also possible to develop true/false lists, card-sorting activities and multiple-choice questions from these ideas. Figure 5.1.2 shows a concept cartoon and a true/false exercise developed from the same material. (Incidentally, the statements were all ones that I heard during a session about the Earth in space with adults. You will similarly learn to collect ideas from conversations in the classroom.)

There's no air on the Moon; that's why they wear spacesuits.

There's no gravity on the Moon – if spacemen didn't have boots they'd float away.

When astronauts drop things they fall to the ground.

There's no air; that's why there's no gravity.

There is gravity on the Moon, it's less than on the Earth, so they can jump higher.

Statements	True	False	Not sure
There's no gravity on the Moon.			
There is gravity on the Moon.			
The gravity on the Moon is less than the gravity on the Earth.			
The Moon is smaller than the Earth.			
There's no air on the Moon.			
If spacemen did not have big boots, they would float off the moon.			
Astronauts have to carry air with them to breathe, when they walk on the Moon.			
When astronauts let go of objects on the Moon they fall to the ground.			

▪ **Figure 5.1.2** Alternative ideas developed into a concept cartoon and into a true/false table

ARGUMENTATION IN SCIENCE LESSONS

A particular type of discussion referred to as 'argumentation' has received a great deal of attention in science education over recent years (Newton *et al.*, 1999; Mortimer and Scott, 2003; Osborne *et al.*, 2004; Erduran *et al.*, 2004; Simon *et al.*, 2006; Simon, 2008). Argumentation differs from the everyday meaning of 'to argue' (see Unit 5.4) as it involves providing evidence for a claim that is made and showing how the evidence supports that claim (and does not support counter-claims).

One of the reasons for the interest arises from the inclusion of *How Science Works* into the curriculum. In Unit 3.1, scientific knowledge was described as being the product of a community of scientists who debate alternative theories, and eventually agree which theory best fits the available evidence. It follows, therefore, that if pupils are to learn about how science works, they need to learn about argumentation and to acquire its skills.

The essential component of any activity that requires argumentation is the making of an *informed* choice. Pupils might be asked to:

■ choose between two theories on the basis of available evidence
■ choose the best artefact for a particular purpose
■ choose a course of action in light of the risks associated with it
■ choose a course of action where there are different ethical or moral issues involved
■ justify choice of experimental procedure
■ decide whether data is valid or invalid and whether it is reliable.

Figure 5.1.3 is an example of an argumentation task of the 'choice between two theories' type, developed from the true/false statements in Figure 5.1.2.

In pairs, study the evidence below about the Moon and the two theories about gravity on the Moon. Which evidence supports theory 1? Which evidence supports theory 2? Is some evidence irrelevant?

Theory 1
The Moon does not have a gravitational pull.

Theory 2
The Moon does have a gravitational pull.

Evidence
The Moon orbits the Earth.
The Moon orbits the Sun.
The Moon is smaller than the Earth.
There is no air on the Moon.
Astronauts who walked on the Moon carried air supplies with them.
Astronauts jumped higher on the Moon than on the Earth.
When astronauts let go of objects on the Moon they fell to the ground.
Astronauts wore space suits when they walked on the Moon.

■ **Figure 5.1.3** An argumentation task

There are now many sources of ideas for argumentation lessons. The IDEAS project (Osborne *et al.*, 2004) developed and pre-tested a range of activities related to competing scientific theories and socio-scientific issues (see *Further reading* for details) and four of these are produced in Wellington and Osborne (2001: 92–4). For many teachers the skills required for teaching argumentation are new and it is for this reason that reports and analyses of teaching strategies are useful. Such reports can be found in a collection of articles in the issue of *School Science Review* devoted to the theme of argumentation, discourse and interactivity (Erduran, 2007). You will also find advice in Unit 5.4 on strategies necessary for managing argumentation of socio-scientific issues. See *Further reading* at the end of Unit 5.2 on the use of investigations and the interpretation of data as another source of discussion material related to the nature of evidence in science.

Task 5.1.3 **Planning a discussion activity**

When you are familiar with discussion activities plan a lesson using one of the following as stimulus material for discussion:

■ concept cartoons
■ competing theories, with evidence given
■ artefacts for a particular purpose
■ anomalous data
■ controversial issues.

Pupils should be directed to draw on evidence to support their position. Evaluate the lesson, focusing on the learning outcomes gained from the discussion activity. Discuss with your mentor the strategies you adopted and any critical incidents that occurred.

MODELS AS A SOURCE OF DISCUSSION ACTIVITIES

Pupils learn *from* models, but they need also to learn *about* models, because modelling is intrinsic to science. Models are not the real thing – but an aid to help focus on particular aspects of an object or phenomenon. Parkinson (2002) defines four types of models: *scale models*, such as biological models, of the eye, the ear, kidneys, human bodies; *analogue models*, such atomic and molecular models, or a string of beads representing electrons in an electric current; *mathematical models* which allow people to manipulate a situation and find out what will happen if parameters are changed; and *theoretical models*, which bring together a range of experiences and theories such as plate tectonics, the existence of quarks or the theory of evolution.

Having introduced models to pupils, encourage them to discuss their limitations, i.e. the extent to which they match the evidence and the extent to which they do not. Pupils need to become familiar with the function of models as an aid to thinking. With scale models, such as models of the eye and ear, this is relatively easy. Analogue models are a little more difficult and mathematical and theoretical models even more so.

Writing in science lessons

The act of writing is a form of discovery. It helps to shape ideas. This should be one of the main, if not *the* main, reasons pupils are asked to write. There are conventions of written language as there are of spoken language. Writing in science is essentially non-fiction. The KS3 Literacy Strategy (DfES, 2001) identified eight different types of non-fictional writing. These are listed in Figure 5.1.4.

Information – writing which describes how things are in a logical order

Instruction – writing which describes how a task should be carried out

Explanation – writing which explains a process or how things work

Persuasion – writing which argues for a particular point of view

Recount – writing which presents events in chronological order

Discussion – writing which presents different points of view

Analysis – writing which examines, for example, statements or data and makes a reasoned response

Evaluation – writing which describes the strengths and weaknesses of, for example, an experimental procedure.

■ **Figure 5.1.4** Types of non-fiction writing identified in the Key Stage 3 Literacy Strategy

Think back to your own school days and identify what sort of writing in science you did. Which were the types you used most often? Now look at what is being done in your present school (Task 5.1.4) to consider to which areas of non-fiction writing science lessons contribute.

Task 5.1.4 **Identifying types of non-fiction writing used in school science**

Read: Staples, R. and Heselden, R. (2001) 'Science teaching and literacy, part 1: Writing'. *School Science Review*, 83 (303): 35–46, for an analysis of the language used in different types of writing.

1   Which sort of writing (use the list in Figure 5.1.4) do you most commonly see in pupils' books?
2   Create a writing task that creates opportunities to use two of the types that are missing and try them with your classes. Think how you will introduce the tasks and how you will explain what is expected.
3   Plan carefully how you will respond to the writing ensuring you use Assessment for Learning (AfL) (see Unit 6.1).
4   Evaluate the activity in terms of the learning that occurred.
5   Discuss with your mentor what you have learned from this activity about presenting and responding to written tasks.

If pupils are to become competent in using the different writing modes they need guidance in understanding the different conventions of each type of writing, support in adopting them and opportunities for practising them. One such form of support is a 'writing frame'. Writing frames are documents which highlight the key features that have to be addressed. Many schools use them for investigations. Wellington and Osborne (2001: 69–74) offer four others, namely:

- a frame for supporting the writing of reports
- a frame for writing explanations
- a frame for writing up experiments
- a frame to support an argument.

As well as thinking about the type of non-fictional writing, think carefully about the 'voice' in which you expect pupils to write, namely personal and transactional, exemplified in Figure 5.1.5.

Personal writing

I ground up the rock salt. I poured water on it. I then filtered it. I then heated it and it dried up and salt was left behind.

Transactional writing

Salt can be extracted from rock salt by the successive processes of dissolving, filtration and evaporation.

▧ **Figure 5.1.5** Transition from personal to transactional scientific writing

Pupils need support to make the transition. You could provide pupils with different audiences for their writing. There is a tendency for science writing to be done for the teacher as an adjudicator. Do pupils ever write instructions for a younger child? Do they ever write a science newspaper or newsletter? Do they ever exchange their findings with people in another school or with people in another country? Do they prepare posters of projects that inform parents about the work they have been doing? Do they write collaborative posters? Are they ever asked to write in a genre more associated with fiction: write poems; imagine being a red blood cell and write about a day in your life; imagine what life would be like without electricity; write a story about being part of a space mission. Whatever you do, expect the transition from personal to transactional writing to be slow, but like any other learning, it can be helped if you make the learning explicit and do not expect it to happen on its own.

INTERACTIONS IN THE SCIENCE CLASSROOM

Activities described in this unit give pupils opportunities to try out their own ideas, transform them into different genres, adapt them for different audiences and engage in scientific reasoning. Dealing with the diversity of ideas that might be expressed poses a challenge for science teachers. It requires the teacher to engage pupils in uncertainty and debate.

The M-level task suggested in Task 5.1.5 asks you to analyse how you cope with opening up ideas, allowing everyone to contribute their ideas and still arrive at what you regard as a respectable scientific understanding. As an aid to achieving this we suggest that you use the four classes of communicative approach suggested by Mortimer and

Scott (2003: 33–40). They derive these approaches by looking at two different dimensions of classroom talk, whether it is interactive or non-interactive and whether it is authoritative or dialogic. Their four approaches are summarised below:

- ■ *interactive/dialogic*: many people discussing and debating different points of view
- ■ *non-interactive/dialogic*: one person pays attention to more than one point of view (maybe the teacher summarising different ideas which have been raised by the class)
- ■ *interactive/authoritative*: more than one person involved, but one person has authority as in a teacher asking closed questions to which there is only one right answer
- ■ *non-interactive/authoritative*: one person talking, as in a teacher explaining an idea or giving instructions.

All these communicative approaches can be found in science lessons, but there is a tendency for the non-interactive/authoritative to dominate (Mortimer and Scott, 2003: 24).

Task 5.1.5 **Evaluating interactions in your own teaching**

Read Chapters 1–3 of Mortimer and Scott (2003). Make sure you understand the communicative framework. (They give examples of episodes from classrooms to exemplify the framework.) Then read Chapter 4 where they use the framework to analyse teaching episodes.

Become familiar with the communicative approach framework by trying to identify episodes in lessons you observe which fit the different types of approach.

Plan a lesson (or a sequence of two or three lessons) where you use some of the activities suggested in this unit to encourage pupils to use their own ideas. You may be using a combination of writing, discussion and reading tasks. After you have taught the lessons reflect on the communicative approaches that you have used.

This may be a task where you can ask for help from a mentor or tutor observing you to give you feedback. Alternatively, you can tape-record a lesson and make your analysis from that.

SUMMARY AND KEY POINTS

Learning a subject involves entering into the discourse of the subject. This involves not just learning about the specialist language but also understanding the way the subject is constructed. By involving pupils actively in writing, talking and reading in science lessons, they are more likely to understand the nature of the subject as well as the substantive knowledge. You are encouraged to try out the range of activities suggested and to reflect on their value in your teaching, and the strategies that you need to adopt to make them successful.

Finally you are encouraged to use a framework of communicative approaches to evaluate the extent to which you are giving pupils opportunities to express and use their own ideas in the science lessons.

FURTHER READING

Capel, S., Leask, M. and Turner, T. (2009) *Learning to Teach in the Secondary School*, 5th edition. London: Routledge.
■ Allen, F. and Taylor, A. Unit 5.2 'Active learning', pp. 267–84.
■ Zwozdiak, Myers, P. and Capel, S. Unit 3.1 ' Communicating with pupils', pp. 107–23. See particularly the section on questioning, pp. 112–17.

Amos, S. and Boohan, R. (2001) *Aspects of Teaching Science: Perspectives on Practice*. London: RoutledgeFalmer.
This is an Open University 'Reader'. Of particular relevance are:
■ Section 1 Talking about science
■ Section 3 Imagined Worlds (especially Chapters 12 and 13)
■ Section 4 Communicating science.

Erduran, S. (ed.) 'Argument, discourse and interactivity'. *School Science Review*, 88 (324), 24–90.
This collection of articles provides: examples of classroom activities; teaching strategies; and analysis of classroom discourse.

Jarman, R. and McClune, B. (2007) *Developing Scientific Literacy Using News Media in the Classroom*. Maidenhead: McGraw-Hill/Open University Press.

Mortimer, E. F. and Scott, P. H. (2003) *Meaning Making in Secondary Science Classrooms*. Maidenhead: Open University Press.
Report of research into the discourse that occurs in science classrooms, with a particular focus on the interactions between teachers and pupils. Types of classroom talk effective for learning are identified.

Naylor, S. and Keogh, B. (2000) *Concept Cartoons in Science Education*. Sandbach: Millgate House Publishers.
These concept cartoons covering a wide range of science topics provide an invaluable start for discussions.

Ogborn, J., Kress, G., Martins, I. and McGillicuddy, K. (1996) *Explaining Science in the Classroom*. Buckingham: Open University Press.
This is a report of a research project studying the nature of explanation. Selected portions are reproduced as Chapters 4 and 13 in Amos *et al.* (2002) and these may form the best starting points.

Sutton, C. (1992) *Words, Science and Learning.* Buckingham: Open University Press.
This is a study of the role of language in the creation of science, as well as in the learning of science. It is a delightful read.

Wellington, J. and Osborne, J. (2001) *Language and Literacy in Science Education*. Buckingham: Open University Press.
This is an invaluable resource. The authors have brought together research from the last 40 years on language in science education, supplying many examples of activities that can be adapted for your own lessons, with the theoretical underpinnings.

Selection of the publications on argumentation from the group at King's and the Institute of Education:

Erduran, S., Osborne, J. F. and Simon, S. (2004) 'Enhancing the quality of argument in school science'. *Journal of Research in Science Teaching*, 41(10), 994–1020.

Osborne, J., Erduran, S. and Simon, S. (2004) *Ideas, Evidence and Arguments in Science* (IDEAS project). London: King's College.
(This pack is available from King's, see Jonathan Osborne's website.)

Simon, S., Erduran, S. and Osborne, J. (2006) 'Learning to teach argumentation: research and developments in the science classroom'. *International Journal of Science Education*, 28(2), 235–60

Simon, S. (2008) 'Using Toulmin's argument pattern in the evaluation of argumentation in school science'. *International Journal of Research and Method in Education*, 31(3), 277–89.

The evaluation of argumentation as a learning tool in science is the subject of a current research project 'Talking to Learn, Learning to Talk in School Science' based at King's College and the Institute of Education in London, directed by Jonathan Osborne and Shirley Simon. Reports of the research will emerge in due course.

LEARNING SCIENCE THROUGH PRACTICAL WORK

Jenny Frost

INTRODUCTION

In the UK most science lessons take place in laboratories, which reflects a long-held assumption that practical work plays an essential part in helping pupils to learn science. As a beginning teacher, your first objective in practical classes is to run them effectively and safely. Pupils and equipment have to emerge undamaged. Pupils must also come away with increased confidence in their scientific skills and understanding, which come more from discussing the significance of the practical work than from just 'doing' it. Developing and managing such discussions is your second task or objective.

OBJECTIVES

By the end of this unit you should be able to:

■ identify the various purposes of practical work
■ recognise the different roles of the teacher in each type of practical work
■ organise practical work sensibly and safely in a laboratory
■ plan the work so that pupils engage with the thinking associated with practical work as well as the doing.

PUPILS' RESPONSE TO PRACTICAL WORK

There is evidence that many pupils enjoy practical work (Nott and Wellington, 1999) though boys are more enthusiastic about it than girls (Murphy, 1991), that 11–13-year-olds enjoy it more than older pupils (Denny and Chennell, 1986) and that higher-achieving pupils often find it tedious and unnecessary (Woolnough and Allsop, 1985). It is important therefore to think carefully about the purpose of any practical work that you provide and ensure that it is both motivating and worthwhile.

Facets which many pupils report as liking are:

■ dramatic or unexpected events (the whizzes, bangs and intriguing puzzles of science)
■ autonomy in working – often working for 20 minutes at a time on their own with limited intervention from a teacher
■ open-ended investigations where they can make their own decisions (Simon, 2000)
■ working together – the co-operative nature of working in pairs or groups
■ having a sense of achievement
■ handling materials and seeing things happen for themselves.

TYPES OF PRACTICAL WORK

The term 'practical work' is a generic term for a range of activities which make different demands on the skills of both teacher and pupils and which have different purposes. Various writers have provided classifications for practical work according to purpose. Here is a three-way classification adapted from Woolnough and Allsop (1985):

1 *illustrative* practical work designed to illustrate particular scientific phenomena
2 *exercises* to develop practical skills and techniques
3 *investigative* practical work and problem-solving in order to learn how to investigate and to solve problems.

Practical activities are often called 'experiments'. Most practical work, however, comprises well-tried and tested activities where teachers know what will happen (and the pupils know that teachers know). This certainly applies to illustrative practical work and exercises and, to some extent, investigations.

Illustrative: demonstrations

Demonstrations by teachers frequently fall into the category of illustrative practical work, for example two demonstrations that you are likely to do at KS3:

■ the reaction of alkali metals (sodium, potassium, calcium) with water
■ production of sparks from a Van der Graaf generator, including making your hair stand on end by charging yourself up from the generator.

They are not experiments; they are carefully contrived events that allow teachers to bring phenomena into the classroom. Without the specially prepared chemicals (highly reactive chemicals stored under oil) and a particular machine, such phenomena would be impossible to demonstrate.

The purpose of such demonstrations is to show *and explain* what happens. The practical event acts as a springboard for conversations about abstract ideas such as the relative reactivity of metals, the ability of metals to release hydrogen from water, high voltages breaking down the resistance of air, and the repulsion of millions of negatively charged particles arranged along hair fibres.

To do a demonstration well, you first have to be able to make the event happen with confidence. Your own practical skills have to be well honed, such that you do not have to worry about whether the demonstration will work. Plenty of practice beforehand is needed. Experienced teachers will be able to tell you of obvious pitfalls. A humid day can, for instance, make it difficult to build up charge on a generator; even the moisture from the breath of 30 pupils can affect how well the charge builds up.

Second, you need to ensure safety for pupils and yourself. The alkali metals demonstration requires a safety screen and goggles, and only small pieces of the metals should be used. Stock bottles of sodium and potassium must not be in reach of the class. The small Van der Graaf generators used in schools are safe for teachers to charge themselves up, if standing on an insulated platform.

Third, you need to be aware that much of the equipment can distract attention from the phenomenon itself. Pupils may recall the safety screen, rubber gloves, goggles and tweezers rather than the details of the small pieces of metals that fizzed; or the shiny globe on the Van der Graaf generator and the whirring of the electric motor driving the belt, rather than the sparks. You need to keep pupils focused on the significant observations, not the equipment.

Your fourth task, which is probably the most crucial, is to engage pupils in dialogue about what is happening at the same time as doing the demonstration. For many beginners this is the most difficult part. They find they have long pauses during the demonstration when they do not know what to say. Planning and practising your 'script' is as important as practising the demonstration itself.

The fifth skill is to take the class *beyond* what they can see, and to persuade them of the theoretical story that explains it. This has been described as 'putting meaning into matter' (Ogborn *et al.*, 1996b: 16), making the invisible seem real, the abstract seem tangible and relating the abstract story to the real phenomenon which has just been observed. This requires the art of persuasion on the part of the teacher and the stimulation of imagination in the pupils.

A well-executed demonstration looks effortless, so it is easy not to realise how difficult it is until you try to do one yourself. A good start is to watch an experienced teacher and analyse the various factors involved in organising and running a demonstration. Task 5.2.1 is designed to help you to do this.

Task 5.2.1 **Observing a demonstration**

Watch a demonstration and monitor both the teacher and pupils by using the schedule below. You may need to vary it according to the nature of the demonstration.

Pupil positions: Are the pupils seated or standing? How visible is the demonstration for all the pupils?

Safety: How is safety ensured?

Presentation by teacher: What introduction is given? Are pupils clear about the purpose of the demonstration? Handling of apparatus – is this confident and skilful?

What is the nature of the commentary that the teacher gives during the demonstration?

Pupils' engagement/response: Is interest aroused? Is interest maintained? Any expectancy/surprise?

Pupil participation: Are pupils spectators or participants? Are pupils active through: a) questions and answers? and/or b) making observations/readings?

Place in lesson/topic: How does the demonstration fit with the rest of the lesson/topic?

How is the demonstration followed up? Does the follow-up activity consolidate the learning? Did it require pupils to apply what they had learned? Did it have some other function?

What record of the demonstration did pupils make? Did the pupils take notes during the demonstration? Was there any guidance?

Task 5.2.1 draws attention to demonstrations not being isolated events, but parts of a learning sequence. Follow-up activities must allow pupils to consolidate the key ideas, making sense of the science for themselves.

Seating arrangements are also important. An experienced teacher may say just 'come up for a demonstration' and an orderly process ensues. When you take over, you say exactly the same, but the result may be a 'rugby scrum', with half the class sitting right up against the demonstration bench, leaning on their arms to get a better look, but completely blocking the view of the demonstration for those behind. Why the difference? It is merely that you have not established your routines and expectations with the class. So a sixth skill is to decide, and make explicit, how you want pupils to come up and where you want them to sit or stand.

By way of summary, Figure 5.2.1 provides a checklist to enable you to evaluate your planning and preparation for a demonstration.

Guides for planning and preparing a demonstration:

- Make a risk assessment (see later) and implement the necessary precautions.
- Practise the demonstration so that it runs smoothly.
- Decide what features of the phenomenon you want pupils to notice.
- Decide what explanations you want to build round the demonstration.
- Plan how to move the pupils to their positions for watching.
- Think how you will focus pupils' attention on the key events.
- Make sure there is a board nearby where you can sketch diagrams, put key words, write results.
- Plan the questions, or other conversation starters, which you will use during the demonstration.
- Plan how you will move from the phenomenon to the theories or concepts behind it. Think what theoretical entities you are bringing into play.
- Plan follow-up activities that involve pupils using their new knowledge.
- Make sure you give the apparatus list to the technicians in good time.

■ **Figure 5.2.1** Checklist for evaluating planning for a demonstration

Illustrative: whole-class practical work

Much of the practical work that pupils do for themselves is also illustrative. Teachers hand over to pupils the task of setting up apparatus so that pupils can demonstrate phenomena to themselves. Once set up, there is a host of activities which can safely and productively be given to pupils: displacement reactions, testing leaves for starch, measuring rates of cooling, looking at cells down a microscope and measuring pulse rate before and after activity form just a small selection from a long list.

A well-run practical lesson seems straightforward, but it is not. Watch an experienced teacher analytically to see the different facets of the job (Task 5.2.2).

Task 5.2.2 **Observation of a practical lesson: teacher focus**

Setting the task: How do the pupils know what to do for the practical work? How do the pupils know why they are doing the practical work?

Safety: In what ways is this addressed? Are reminders necessary?

Pupil organisation: Where do pupils sit during the explanation of the activity? Where are they during the practical work? How is the transition organised?

Apparatus/materials: How and where are these assembled? How are they distributed? How and when is the clearing up done? How does the laboratory look at the end of the lesson?

Involvement with the pupils: What is the teacher doing while the pupils carry out practical work? What noise level is acceptable?

Interventions: Does the teacher want to stop the practical work for any reason? Note the reasons for the intervention.

Timing: What proportion of the lesson is used for practical work? Is this enough/too much?

Follow up: How does the teacher use the pupils' results? How does the teacher deal with 'wrong' results? What happens in the rest of the lesson? Is it related to the practical work?

The last part of the schedule indicates that pupils' results might not be as you hoped. For an amusing and thought-provoking account of how teachers deal with such critical incidents read Nott and Wellington (1999). Wrong results, however, can be the basis of some excellent teaching about the importance of repeatability and the rejection of anomalous results. It is relatively easy, but unhelpful, just to ignore them.

Now turn your attention to the pupils. Task 5.2.3 directs you towards differences in their motivation and approach to practical work, their skills and understanding. Use this on a different lesson to Task 5.2.2.

Task 5.2.3 **Observation of practical lesson: pupil focus**

Setting the task: How do pupils find out what to do? Did they read any instructions?

Safety: Do pupils observe safety instructions? Note safe practice and unsafe events. Does safety become an issue?

Purpose of practical: Is the purpose clear to all pupils? Identify and note uncertainties. What do you think is the purpose of the practical work?

Apparatus/materials: Do pupils know where to get apparatus? Do pupils know how to use apparatus? Note problems they experience.

Pupil grouping: Do pupils in groups collaborate? Do boys/girls share equally in tasks? Are some pupils passive passengers? Do pupils stay on task? What off-task behaviour do you see?

Pupil conversations: What do pupils talk about during the activity? Is the 'on-task' talk about procedure or purpose?

Intervention: Do pupils seek teacher help? What for? Do pupils seek peer help? What for?

Timing: How much of the work do pupils complete?

Application: Do pupils obtain results? Are pupils able to interpret results? How are pupils engaged in consolidation? What writing do they do about the practical work?

Just as in demonstrations, teachers need to plan how to interact with pupils during practical work. They have to keep an eye on skills and help pupils in difficulty. Teachers must use questions to help pupils to notice key events: 'Are you getting as many bubbles as before?' 'What might the bubbles be?' Teachers also need to ask pupils to think about why something is happening 'What do you imagine is going on?' 'What made you sure the bubbles were hydrogen?' 'Where might they have come from?'

Practical exercises for the teaching of techniques and skills

Considerable time in science lessons is spent on teaching practical techniques such as lighting Bunsen burners, using pipettes and burettes or interpolating scales on a range of measuring instruments. Most of the necessary skills will be second-nature to you and you may have to think hard how to explain them. Practise your own skills and knowledge so that you can show pupils what skilful handling of equipment entails. Make sure that enough time is allowed for pupils to practise new skills.

While sometimes you will have a whole lesson devoted to such a skill (e.g. how to use a microscope) it is more likely that such skills are taught as an intrinsic part of another lesson. Watch an experienced teacher to see how they monitor practical skills and provide help for those who are having difficulty in mastering them.

The microscope provides a convenient example of a problem common to all practical lessons, i.e. that of ensuring pupils observe what the teacher wants them to observe. It is rare for pupils, even when their microscopes are properly focused, to observe the detail that an experienced teacher would. Teachers have to draw attention to significant features. 'Look in the centre of the slide, do you see cells which look like two little sausages? Now look to the left, can you see others? Now look at some of the other cells, can you see faint green dots inside them?' Where schools have icams, key features can be discussed together before pupils return to microscopes to find them for themselves. Alternatives of sketches on the board, illustrations in books or projected photographs can be equally effective. The more general point is that observations are dependent on the ideas you have in your head; the more you know about a subject the more you observe and register. Teachers have an important role in helping pupils to identify and register significant observations.

Investigations and problem-solving: scientific enquiry

Investigations and problem-solving form the third category of practical work. Learning about science involves learning about how scientific knowledge is built up and how scientists collect and use evidence to support their ideas. Pupils not only have to know about this, they themselves also have to be able to put this learning into practice by carrying out investigations, collecting evidence, analysing it and evaluating the strength of it. This section therefore covers the practical work associated with investigations that can be used to develop pupils' practical and enquiry skills and their critical understanding of evidence (see Units 2.2 and 2.3).

There are several types of investigations that are undertaken in schools. The categories in Figure 5.2.2 are taken from a study by Watson *et al.* (1999).

THE TEACHING OF INVESTIGATION PROCEDURES

Investigations typically involve some or all of the steps shown in Figure 5.2.3. Do not assume that pupils learn how to investigate just by doing investigations. Much more systematic teaching of what has become known as 'procedural knowledge' is required (Lubben and Millar, 1996). Ideas for relevant teaching strategies have now been published (e.g. Sang and Wood-Robinson, 2002; Goldsworthy and Feasey, 1997, 2000a, 2000b). Figure 5.2.4 gives examples of a selection of such strategies. Just as science teachers have to explain scientific concepts such as gravity and homeostasis, they have to explain investigational concepts, such as validity, reliability, significant differences, independent and dependent variables and controlled variables.

WHAT CAUSES DIFFICULTIES WITH INVESTIGATIONS?

Five characteristic difficulties arise from:

1   identifying dependent, independent and control variables
2   the type of dependent and independent variables
3   the number of independent variables
4   the analysis and evaluation stages
5   the degree of openness of the investigation.

The terms 'independent variable' (i.e. the one that the investigator changes) and the 'dependent variable' (i.e. the one *potentially* dependent on the independent variable) need

Type of investigation	Characteristics and examples
Classification or categorisation	Making or using keys to sort out rocks, leaves or a collection of invertebrates.
Pattern seeking	Questions such as: 'What plants withstand trampling?' and 'What plants grow on the beach at different distances from the sea?' would lead to pattern finding. In these, variables cannot be controlled, so cause and effect is difficult to determine. Correlation between one factor and another is, however, possible to identify. Such investigations presuppose that pupils have learned survey techniques in tackling problems such as: 'What is the total number of species growing in this field?'.
Fair tests	Fair tests form the most frequently found type of investigation. They require the control of variables, and the need to identify dependent and independent variables. They may be couched in terms of simple comparisons: 'Compare the insulating properties of five different materials'; 'Compare the tensile strength of different fibres'. They may be in the form of finding the effect of one factor on another: 'What is the effect of the number of layers on insulating properties?'; 'What is the effect of different temperatures on the rate of reproduction of yeast?'. Lastly, they may be in the form of finding the factors which affect another factor as in: 'What are the factors which affect the rate at which an apple turns brown?'; 'What are the factors which determine resistivity of a metal?'.
Investigating models	Here a concept/theory is tested out by modelling a situation, for instance: investigating the rate of water loss from different-sized cubes of 'oasis' in order to explore the effect of surface area to volume ratio on transpiration in plants.
Exploring	These may involve recording something over time: the growth of a plant; the light levels in a building; temperature differences in different parts of a building. Decisions have to be made about how often and for how long the measurements are made.
Making things or developing systems	Testing the accuracy and reliability of a new instrument, e.g. a pulse rate meter; testing the accuracy of thermometers; designing a method of measuring wind speed; make a circuit which will ring a bell when it begins to rain.

(For classification of investigations used here see Watson *et al.*, 1999.)

■ **Figure 5.2.2** Types of investigations

to be explained to pupils. To distinguish the independent and dependent variables they are often referred to as 'what I change' and 'what I observe or measure', respectively; and sometimes the 'input variable' and 'the output variable'.

There are three types of dependent and independent variables:

■   categoric (single categories described in words, e.g. colour, type of material)

---

1 Planning and organising an investigation

■ Find an area of interest which is ripe for investigation.
■ Research to find what others have found before.
■ Formulate a question so that it can be investigated.
■ Make some sort of prediction of what would be the outcome.
■ Decide what data are needed to answer the question.
■ Decide how to collect the data, and ensure that they are valid.
■ Decide which variables are to be controlled, if any.
■ Decide which variables are the independent variables, if any.
■ Decide which variable is the dependent variable.
■ Identify and assemble the necessary equipment and tools to obtain the data.

2 Obtaining the data

■ Do trial runs, and iron out the difficulties.
■ Decide on appropriate recording charts and tables.
■ Obtain and record data.
■ Decide when sufficient data have been collected.

3 Analysing the data

■ Decide which graphical techniques are most appropriate for effective
   representation and analysis of tabular data.
■ Look for patterns in the data using appropriate graphical or statistical techniques.
■ Use the patterns as evidence to answer the question and draw a conclusion.

4 Evaluating the evidence

■ Evaluate the strength of the evidence, by considering the reliability of the
   collecting techniques, the factors which were difficult to control, the accuracy of
   the measuring instruments, mistakes which might have been made.
■ Find a way of expressing the answer to the original question, which reflects both
   the findings and the level of certainty of the findings.

5 Communicating

■ Write a report of the investigation.

■ **Figure 5.2.3** Steps in investigations

■ discrete (whole numbers, e.g. number of legs, number of layers)
■ continuous (any number within a range, e.g. temperature, weight).

Pupils find categoric variables easier than discrete, and continuous variables are the most difficult. The types of variable, of course, determine the types of graph that are appropriate; for instance, using categoric independent variables with numerical dependent variables leads to bar charts (as in: 'Which shoe is the most difficult to pull over the floor?'); continuous variables lead to line graphs (as in: 'How is the volume of hydrogen produced per minute affected by the size of current?'). If, of course, both dependent and

Ask pupils to sort a collection of questions into those that are scientific and those which are not.

Give pupils a set of scientific questions and different ways of investigating, and ask them to match the questions to the appropriate method.

Ask pupils to critique accounts of invalid methods. These don't have to be in written form – you can always demonstrate an unfair test and ask pupils to spot the mistakes.

Provide sets of data and ask pupils what graphical techniques would be appropriate.

Provide sets of data with different interpretations, and ask pupils which interpretation fits the data best.

Provide other pupils' accounts for pupils to mark to a set of criteria.

■ **Figure 5.2.4** Examples of teaching strategies that can be used to teach procedural knowledge needed for investigations

independent variables are categoric (i.e. In which trees are spiders and mites found?), then no graph can be drawn.

Increasing the number of variables to be considered increases difficulty. Asking pupils to study the effect of, say, 'surface area' and 'temperature difference between an object and its surroundings' (two independent variables) on the 'rate of cooling' (one dependent variable) is far more difficult than studying just the effect of one independent variable. It is not just a matter of it taking longer to do; many pupils who have not reached formal operational thinking cannot follow the logic of holding one variable constant at one point and then changing it at the next. It is also possible to have investigations where there is more than one dependent variable, such as in an investigation into 'Which liquid is the most viscous and the most transparent?'. Here pupils would have to test for viscosity and transparency separately.

In analysing data and drawing conclusions pupils find it difficult to decide which data can be used to answer their original question. They also often report the results without any interpretation when writing a conclusion, and they sometimes report what they expected to happen not what actually happened. Teachers need to give guidance by showing pupils how to 'interrogate data' first by looking for patterns. Questions such as 'Which is the highest, which is the lowest number?' 'Are the numbers increasing, decreasing, staying the same, or do they seem to change randomly?' 'Is there any number which is vastly different from the others?' are useful to help pupils look carefully at numerical data. Where graphs have been plotted, again practice is needed in interpreting graphs (see Goldsworthy and Feasey (1997) and Sang and Wood-Robinson (2002) for further guidance). When drawing conclusions, pupils find it difficult to make the switch from description of patterns in data to more generalised statements. To some extent it is a matter of language conventions. Sang and Wood-Robinson (2002: 83) provide an example of '*The more turns on a wire the stronger is the electromagnet. The higher the current the stronger is the magnet*' being turned into '*The strength of the electromagnet depends on the number of turns and the size of the current. Generally the higher the current . . .*'. In some investigations where it was not possible to control variables, pupils will be be asked to look for correlations between two variables rather than cause and effect and their conclusions have to be couched in appropriate language.

Remember, it is all too easy to have a practical lesson where the bell goes just as the class has finished the table of results. 'For homework analyse the results and draw a conclusion' is unhelpful as pupils are being sent to do what for them may be the most difficult part, unsupported.

Evaluation is as difficult as analysis. Here pupils have to think about accuracy and reliability of data. To estimate errors, pupils have to be able to identify: the accuracy with which any parameter can be measured; whether any results have to be discarded and why; situations where is it difficult to judge an end-point (e.g. when a chemical has completely dissolved); whether it is sensible to average all results; whether further investigation is necessary. They have to decide on the validity of data. If they were carrying out a fair test, the data will not be valid if they were unable to control variables sufficiently well. In investigations that required using a sample they have to decide whether the sample size is adequate. Evaluation needs as much guidance and support as analysis.

The degree of openness of the investigation is determined by decisions that are left to the pupils. One technique which is commonly used to support decision-making is providing prompt sheets. These can be written as a series of questions to be addressed as a checklist or as a writing frame with spaces. These 'props' will increasingly be removed the further pupils progress up the school. By Y12, when pupils are undertaking large investigations for advanced-level courses, they will be working relatively independently with only minimal support.

SAFETY ISSUES: RISK ASSESSMENT IN SCIENCE

Risk assessment in the workplace was first introduced as a requirement of the Control of Substances Hazardous to Health Regulations in 1988 (COSHH). Since then requirements have been updated and extended, and you need to be aware of the risk assessments needed for activities in school. Concerns about safety have persuaded some teachers to abandon otherwise interesting practical work. This to be regretted and is not necessary if pupils are taught to handle equipment properly and follow necessary precautions.

It is a *legal* requirement to make a risk assessment of *every* practical activity that you do. Distinguish risk from hazard. Hazard is the potential of something to do harm; risk is the likelihood of harm occurring in a particular set of circumstances. Factors to take into account when assessing risk are:

■ inherent hazards of materials and equipment (things which could cause harm)
■ your own personal confidence with, and knowledge of, the materials and equipment
■ skills and knowledge of pupils
■ behaviour of the class and your ability to control it
■ precautions which can be put in place.

Inherent hazards of materials and equipment are clearly documented. Your department should have the Hazcards available from CLEAPSS (2004). Study these for any practical activity you do, even apparently simple ones. Once you have read them, consider whether, in the light of your ability to manage the class, there is likely to be a problem. If there is, find an alternative way of teaching or gain help from the class teacher.

Frequently met hazards and precautions are given in Figure 5.2.5. DO NOT TAKE THIS AS A DEFINITIVE LIST; it is merely a starter list.

If you are confident and knowledgeable about handling materials and equipment and can explain the reasons for various precautions, then you are likely to conduct the practical work safely. Take into account the skills of the pupils, and adapt accordingly. Independence that you might give to older pupils may not be appropriate to younger ones, who are more likely to be clumsy with equipment which is new or complex. Behaviour is also a key factor. Activities that would have a low risk with one class will have a high risk with another.

	Hazard	Typical precautions
Clutter in the laboratory	Bags, coats, stools in gangways and between the benches	Put stools, bags underneath the benches. Places for coats need to be allocated.
Heating substances	Spitting or spills of hot liquids or solids; hot tripods, test tubes etc.; inflammable liquids; open flames; pupils not used to handling fire	Goggles worn (over eyes and not on some other part of head); you as a role model; Pupils learn to turn bunsen off as soon as chemicals spit; stand when doing practical work; test tubes not pointing to anyone; long hair tied back; luminous flame when bunsen not in use; anticipate a level of excitement, or anxiety, in Yr 7 with flames.
Electrical equipment	Little danger from batteries; low-voltage units are safe as school is required to have them checked on regular basis	Dry hands when using mains equipment; no naked terminals on high-tension units (used further up school).
Acids and alkalis	Alkalis cling to surfaces such as the eye; both can burn clothes and skin if strength and molarity are high	Goggles worn; low-molarity solutions used in lower school; small quantities only available.
Other chemicals	Toxic chemicals; chemicals which cause stains; highly flammable chemicals	Check toxicity; use small quantities; keep control on stock bottles; some reactions can only be done in a fume cupboard.
Glassware	Chipped or broken glassware	Check all glassware; container for broken glass; teacher to clear breakages.
Biological material	Toxicity; infections from animals/animal parts; allergies; cultures of microbes	Check toxicity of any plant material; cultures of microbes to be sealed – some cultures not permitted.
Sharp instruments	Scalpels, knives and pointers can easily cut the skin	Restricted use; safety corks on the end.

■ **Figure 5.2.5** Common hazards and precautions

Use Figure 5.2.5 only as an initial guide, you must follow it up with more detailed reading, for example see 'Health and safety in science education' (Borrows, 2006); and the *Safeguards in the Science Laboratory*, ASE Safety Committee (2006). Note there are specific regulations about the use of ionising radiations, electrical equipment and pressurised systems.

EVALUATING YOUR PLANNING OF PRACTICAL WORK

Figure 5.2.6 gives a checklist of questions to ask yourself to make sure you are fully ready for practical lessons.

Summary of questions to check planning of a class practical lesson:

■ Have I done the practical myself beforehand?
■ What is the purpose of the activity? What are the learning outcomes that I want? How will I explain the purpose?
■ Will the pupils work on their own, in pairs or in larger groups?
■ How much apparatus will I need? Does the school have enough? If not, this may mean altering group size.
■ Have the laboratory technicians been given the list in sufficient time for them to prepare what I want?
■ What are the associated risks?
■ Are there some items that I will distribute myself (for safety or equity reasons)? If so, how will I distribute them?
■ How will I give instructions of what to do? Orally? By demonstration? By written instruction? By pictorial instruction?
■ What decisions will I leave to the pupils?
■ How will pupils record observations? Do they make a table for results, or do I give them one?
■ What would be 'good performance' for this age group?
■ What will I talk about with pupils while they are doing the practical work?
■ How long do they need?
■ How do I stop the practical work? How and when should pupils clear up? Can chemicals go down the sink? If not, where do they go?
■ How do I ensure all the equipment has come in? How do I make a record of numbers of items at the start?
■ Do I need to collect class results? If so, how and when?
■ What is the science I want to draw out of it? How do I do that?
■ How long will this take?
■ Do pupils need to write a report of the activity?
■ What follow-up activity is there which will enable pupils to consolidate their new knowledge by applying it?

■ **Figure 5.2.6** Questions for evaluating planning of class practical work

QUESTIONING ASSUMPTIONS

The unit started with the assumption that practical work was useful in learning science, an assumption that is not universally accepted. Task 5.2.4 addresses this issue.

Task 5.2.4 **Reflecting on the role of practical work**

Several writers have questioned the value that practical work plays in learning science. They pose questions such as:

■ Does practical work improve conceptual understanding?
  To what extent do school investigations model how scientists work?
■ Can pupils learn to interrogate data? What are the significant factors in this process? What is the role of the teacher?

Use the literature (see *Further reading*) to examine debates and research findings related to practical work. Use one of the questions above or find another one from the debates and collect evidence from your school experience to illuminate it.

SUMMARY AND KEY POINTS

Practical work for up to 30 pupils requires a lot of organisation and attention to matters of safety. These factors will dominate your thinking when you first start using practical work. It is important, however, that you analyse the roles that practical work plays in learning science and thus make the time spent as productive as possible. To do this, you need to decide whether you are using illustrative practical work, exercises or investigations. Planning discussions alongside planning the practical work and preparing appropriate follow-up activities will increase the chances of your pupils learning from the practical work.

FURTHER READING

AKSIS Project

> Goldsworthy, A., Watson, R. and Wood-Robinson, V. (1999) *Investigations: Getting to Grips with Graphs*. Hatfield: ASE.
>
> Goldsworthy, A., Watson, R. and Wood-Robinson, V. (2000) *Investigations: Developing Understanding*. Hatfield: ASE.
>
> Watson, R., Goldsworthy, A. and Wood-Robinson, V. (2000) *Investigations: Targeted Learning.* Hatfield: ASE.
>
> These three sets of resources have lots of information about teaching investigations.

ASE Safeguards Committee (2006) *Safeguards in the School Laboratory*. Hatfield: Association for Science Education.

Boohan, R. (2008) 'Innovations in practical work from the Science Enhancement Programme'. *School Science Review*, 89 (328), 85–95.

> The Science Enhancement Programme (SEP) (funded by Gatsby) produces innovative practical activities in the physical sciences. Join the SEP Teacher Associates Scheme (free) to gain their publications. http://www.sep.org.uk (accessed 24 September 2009).

Borrows, P. (2006) in Wood-Robinson, V. 'Health and safety in science education', in *ASE Handbook for Secondary Science*. Hatfield: ASE, pp. 106–13.

> Peter Borrows always provides a measured and informed response to those who say that much school practical work is too dangerous.

CLEAPSS (2004) *Hazcards*. Uxbridge: CLEAPSS School Science Service.

Gott, R. and Duggan, S. (2006) 'Investigations, scientific literacy and evidence'. Wood-Robinson, V. *ASE Handbook for Secondary Science*. Hatfield: ASE, pp. 188–97.

Gott, R. and Duggan, S. (2007) 'A framework for practical work in science and scientific literacy through argumentation'. *Research in Science and Technological Education*, 25 (3), 271–91.

Millar, R., Lubben, F., Gott, R. and Duggan, S. (1994) 'Investigating in the school science laboratory: conceptual and procedural knowledge and their influence on performance'. *Research Papers in Education*, 9 (2), 207–48.

Lubben, F. and Millar, R. (1996) 'Children's ideas about the reliability of experimental data'. *International Journal of Science Education*, 18 (8), 955–68.

These are reports of some of the findings of the PACKS project (Procedural and Conceptual Knowledge in Science) that explored children's ideas about investigation procedures. They provide useful insights into children's thinking in investigations and their approaches to them.

Parkinson, J. (2004) 'Learning through practical work' (ch. 9), in *Improving Secondary Science Teaching*. London: RoutledgeFalmer.

This book is written for serving teachers. Once you are confident in organising practical work you will find this is valuable to help you question and improve the learning that comes from practical work and understand relevant research evidence.

Sang, D. and Wood-Robinson, V. (eds) (2002) *Teaching Secondary Scientific Enquiry*. London: John Murray for ASE.

Wellington, J. (ed.) (1998) *Practical Work in School Science: Which Way Now?* London: Routledge.

This collection of articles provides a range of different perspectives on school practical work. The first two articles (by Jerry Wellington and Robin Millar, respectively) focus on the debate about the value of practical work. An article that not only questions the role of practical work but also gives alternatives is: Osborne, J. 'Science education without a laboratory?' pp. 156–73.

RELEVANT WEBSITES

As a student teacher you will have access to all the publications produced by CLEAPSS Consortium of Local Education Authorities for the Provision of Science Services.

http://www.cleapss.org.uk/secfr.htm (accessed 24 September 2009).

Their resources include a CLEAPPS (2009) *Science Publications* CD-ROM, Uxbridge: Brunel University.

USING ICT FOR LEARNING SCIENCE

Ruth Amos

INTRODUCTION

The technology revolution (Tan and Koh, 2008) continues at what often feels like an alarming rate (indeed by the time this text reaches publication we will no doubt wish we had included other innovative ICT resources for learning science). This section aims to encourage you to build upon your own ICT skills and to use ICT purposefully with your pupils as effective learning and teaching tools.

OBJECTIVES

By the end of this unit you should:

■ be aware of the range of ICT resources available for learning and teaching science and their underlying rationale alongside non-ICT strategies
■ be able to identify those which involve the pupils in active learning.

Check the requirements of your course to see which relate to this unit.

ICT RESOURCES IN SCHOOLS

Exploring the ICT hardware facilities in a school will most commonly reveal suites of computers in bookable computer rooms, and possibly class sets of laptops in the science department. Many schools have installed data-projectors, interactive screens and white-boards (IWBs). Visualisers, digital cameras/microscopes and CCTV cameras may also form part of the science department's suite of resources. Electronic Voting Systems (EVS) are becoming a popular tool for capturing Assessment for Learning (AfL) data. EVS technology is particularly useful in science for eliciting prior knowledge, raising awareness of possible alternative conceptions and tracking individual progress within a single lesson.

There is a vast array of software available for assisting in the development of scientific ideas in the classroom. Discovering, and becoming familiar with, animations, simulations, video clips and images which have the potential to enhance learning for your pupils requires time and a very clear focus on desired learning outcomes for an activity/ lesson. There is a danger that you may 'grab' an ICT resource off the shelf without fully exploring the value that it actually brings to the learning experience. Is an ICT resource appropriate for what you hope to achieve? Always have a non-ICT back-up activity prepared as well, just in case technical support is not available when you need it most!

PLANNING AND STRUCTURING LESSONS USING ICT

Before we consider the various ICT learning strategies that you will want to explore in developing effective learning experiences, review the skills you need as a teacher to include a variety of ICT activities in your teaching repertoire. Familiarity with software applications such as Word, Excel and PowerPoint is very useful in terms of structuring lessons, so ensuring that you move smoothly from an ICT resource to the next activity. PowerPoint is a potentially powerful means of structuring lessons. Slides can be created to present learning objectives, making the return to these at key points in a lesson more purposeful. How proficient can you become in creating simple, clear slides, so that the production of your ICT resources does not become the main focus of your precious plan- ning time? The optimum number of slides in a presentation for an hour's lesson is open to debate but try to be minimalist. Five is a good number to work with – for example:

1   an engaging image to capture attention and ignite curiosity as pupils arrive
2   the learning objectives
3   clear 'what, how, how long' instructions for the main activity(ies), to support explanation/modelling of what pupils need to do
4   some purposeful AfL questions
5   the key learning points, focusing on the learning outcomes.

Try not to fall into the trap of preparing so many slides that you lecture. If you plan activ- ities like quizzes or a series of images, see them as separate, linked presentations. Also, use the projector and screen in conjunction with an 'old-fashioned' whiteboard, which many science departments have retained. You then elicit students' ideas, build upon them and are more open to the serendipitous events that occur. If you structure the lesson so tightly through pre-prepared slides, it can lead to pupils 'waiting for the teacher's answer', rather than thinking for themselves. Used appropriately, PowerPoint can help a great deal with pace of lessons and reminders (for you too!) about such tasks as homework.

ICT STRATEGIES FOR LEARNING IN SCIENCE

The science National Curriculum (NC) for Key Stage 3 (KS3) embodies ICT in its *Key Processes* programme of study (DCSF, 2009a), highlighting the importance of using ICT in cross-curricular approaches to learning. Several current science GCSE courses include CD-ROM resources in their course support, and ICT can assist greatly in aspects of *How Science Works*, such as data collection and presenting scientific information.

There are a number of activities in which ICT can support learning ideas about science. Figure 5.3.1 gives a summary of such activities, in part adapted from a similar list in Rogers and Finlayson (2003).

Activity focus	Examples and resources
Information gathering and examining evidence	Using internet browsers, websites, real time data monitoring and multimedia CD-ROMs
Practical work	Using sensors, interfaces, data-logging software, visualisers, CCTV cameras, video
Data handling	Spreadsheets and graphing software such as Excel, searching ready-made databases
Simulations and animations	Virtual experiments/visual aids, stimulating and helping explain phenomena
Building conceptual links and understanding	Mind mapping using Visio software, interactive whiteboard (IWB) applications, Electronic Voting Systems (EVS)
Use of mathematical models	Exploring relationships, predicting and testing theories using software such as Excel
Communication	Word-processing packages, PowerPoint, publishing, web authoring, digital capture of photographs and images, video-conferencing
Assessment for Learning (AfL)/ exploring ideas	Electronic Voting Systems (EVS)

■ **Figure 5.3.1** ICT learning activities in science

1 Information gathering and examining evidence: using websites and CD-ROMs

Pupils need a carefully constructed task, with specific questions therein, to prevent them wandering vaguely through websites when gathering information. Most sites are heavily text-based, so select ones that are suitable for your class and for the particular learning objectives. Find sites and CD-ROMs that are easy to navigate, and that include video clips, good animations, search facilities and quizzes to test what has been learned. Check the level of interaction of the sites using as a simple guide:

■ low interaction: browsing and reading only
■ medium interaction: with some tasks but only 'click and reveal'
■ high interaction: tasks involve forms/multiple-choice with answers, email access to authors
■ very high interaction: communication, active participation.

A number of interactive sites are included at the end of this unit. If *you* find them difficult to use then so will pupils. At the end of an activity, set up an evaluation of the site or CD-ROM in which the pupils give feedback on key aspects so that you can build upon the original activity. Always evaluate the use of a CD-ROM or website compared with a more traditional resource and decide whether using ICT will be more effective for learning.

2 Practical work: data logging and control

Data logging involves replacing measuring devices, such as thermometers, by a sensor, and replacing people recording results and drawing a graph, by an interface and then usually a computer. In deciding to use data logging, you have to be convinced that there are real educational values to be gained from the ICT approach. Data logging also covers devices called 'data loggers' which log (collect and store) data away from the computer. The data can be downloaded on to the computer at a later time. This can be useful, say, for recording temperature fluctuations over an extended period out in the field.

Commonly, schools have only one set of data logging equipment so it has to be used either for demonstration (projecting the display on the big screen so that everyone can see) or as a component in a circus of activities. Where there are class sets of sensors, interfaces and laptops, then the data logging can be done as a whole-class activity. It is essential to have technical support at hand during a data-logging activity, as sensors and interfaces can often stop linking with each other for no apparent reason.

There is a wide range of sensors available, from a number of suppliers, and a selection of some useful ones and their applications are given below in Figure 5.3.2.

The guidance given about practical work in Unit 5.2 applies here, especially trying it out beforehand. For instance, do your temperature sensors give the same readings as a conventional thermometer for the temperature of boiling water? Trialling data-logging equipment, particularly alongside non-ICT methods, can create useful investigations for pupils in their own right. Encouraging pupils to select appropriate apparatus in planning activities works well. They can discuss the benefits of the sensor method versus the non-ICT method, try out the different approaches and suggest improvements based upon reliability and precision.

Applications for data loggers often need a little extra creative design. For example, the reaction between dilute hydrochloric acid and sodium thiosulfate solutions produces a precipitate of yellow sulfur. The classic method for measuring the reaction time is the 'disappearing cross experiment' and allows exploration of the effects of starting with varying concentrations of acid in terms of reaction time. A great technician I worked with designed a data logging version of the experiment – placing light sensors below a series of reaction mixtures with varying composition to monitor ever-decreasing light levels as the precipitates fall, and capturing data on different channels of the interface to explore the varying rates simultaneously. Pilot runs showed that there was too much 'background light' so the technician designed box housing for the sensors to sit in, which eliminated the problem.

There are four main advantages to using data logging for learning science, namely:

1 Simultaneous graphing offers the opportunity for discussion of what is happening *while* it is happening, and of identifying how the graph relates to the phenomenon, i.e. the phenomenon and the visual representation of the phenomenon are happening together.

2 Both fast and slow changes can be monitored which would be difficult or tedious if done manually.

3 Less time is spent on plotting graphs, which releases more time for interpretation of the graph, a skill which pupils often find difficult (see *Data handling* below).

4 Pupils can have a more realistic understanding of how data might be collected by real scientists. 'Real time' monitoring of changing situations can be followed

Sensors	Examples of application/practical activities
Temperature	Exothermic and endothermic reactions Temperature changes over a day (in a building, in a greenhouse, outside) Investigating why some animals huddle in the winter
Light	Monitoring light levels in different environments Monitoring the rate of a reaction in which a precipitate is formed Investigating light reflected from different materials
Pulse	Investigating fluctuations in resting pulse rate Investigating how quickly pulse returns to normal after exercise
Light gates	Measuring speed using an air track and 'floating' trolleys Measuring reaction times
Voltage and current	Investigating the voltage current relationships of resistors, thermistors, current diodes Charging and discharging a capacitor
Pressure	Pressure change with depth of water Pressure change with altitude (within tall buildings, out on field trips in hilly country)
pH	Investigating acidity in ponds, streams, soil Monitoring acid-base reactions
Oxygen	Monitoring oxygen levels in a yeast culture to indicate microbial growth Monitoring oxygen levels in streams
Position	Investigating whether plants grow faster during the day than at night Measuring distortion of elastic material Monitoring the oscillations in a spring Monitoring the rate of a gaseous reaction, with a gas syringe
Mass (electronic balance)	Monitoring the rate of a gaseous reaction

■ **Figure 5.3.2** List of commonly found sensors and examples of use in practical work
Source: Details of these (and other) activities are given in Frost (2002a, 2002b)

online. For example, the reproductive health of the female giant panda at the Smithsonian Zoo, Washington, USA, is monitored continuously, and her latest relevant hormone levels can be seen at any time via the zoo's website.

3 Data handling

Data-handling packages, including Excel, handle numerical data and can be useful in a number of ways. Pupils can prepare relatively simple databases incorporating maybe only five or six fields. Try using data about themselves, selecting aspects that are not too sensitive (possible fields: hand span, arm length, size of foot, length of forearm, eye colour, hair colour). You can then use the software to draw bar charts and pie charts to review the data (e.g. distribution of people with different-coloured eyes; use search facilities to find those people, say, with blue eyes and large hands; correlation graphs to review whether people with long arms also have large hands; you can test the theory that the size of your foot is the same as the length of your forearm etc.). Similar activities around using data, for example, on the planets or elements in the Periodic Table can help students to look for patterns/characteristics and to exercise higher-order thinking skills. The ability to interrogate a database is important. This is where discussion comes in and the time saved not having to draw all the charts and graphs can be used on interpretation. One drawback of Excel is that it does not plot lines of best fit very well.

An Excel spreadsheet allows pupils to manipulate numerical data in two main ways. First, you can do routine calculations by putting a formula in (e.g. if you are measuring mass and volume, then you can set it to calculate density automatically in the next column). This can allow a whole class set of results to be processed and discussion can focus on their reliability. Pupils investigating rates of reaction can input gradient calculations, or explore the effects of different orders of reactants on rate very easily at KS5. Second, it is possible to graph results, again if class sets are being collected, and to keep an eye on the graph that is building up.

Interactive whiteboard (IWB) software may have the facility to 'drag' graph paper and axes onto the screen, thereby giving pupils opportunities to actively practise building scales and plotting data (Beauchamp and Parkinson, 2005).

Task 5.3.1 **Developing graphical skills**

Investigate the assertion that producing graphs manually can take some pupils 'three to four times longer' than producing computer-aided equivalents (Barton, 2004: 32).

1 Talk with colleagues in your maths/ICT departments about the timing and extent of graphical learning that pupils will have gone through prior to your lessons. Develop a guide for both manual and Excel graph-plotting which your pupils can use.

2 Choose two lessons in which pupils either collect, or are given, data, which requires them to understand the concepts of dependent and independent variables.

3 In the first lesson, set the task of manual graph-plotting. In the second, book a computer room or the science department laptops and ask pupils to create graphs using Excel. (Be prepared to devote an entire lesson to both activities, with extra material ready if a whole lesson is not needed.)

4 Reflect upon and evaluate the successes and drawbacks of both approaches and redevelop your guides to graph-plotting in the light of what you learn about your learners. How much variation was there in times needed for successful graph production? Which skills did students develop successfully during each activity? What was most challenging?

4 Simulations and animations

Simulations cover virtual experiments such as making up electric circuits, altering pressure and temperature in the Haber process and studying changes in a predator–prey relationship. They allow pupils to investigate a phenomenon, focusing on the conceptual understanding, without the clutter of reality slowing them down. They are interactive and provide feedback to pupils about what is happening. They must not be confused, however, with reality and unless pupils have experience of handling the appropriate equipment, they will lose sight of what the simulation relates to. Simulations can also provide virtual experiences like journeys to the planets, or through the blood system or models, say, of the human body or molecules that can be manipulated in some way. Some simulations add 'conceptual labels'; for instance, in showing the movement of a bouncing ball force and velocity arrows will be added so that it is possible to watch what is happening to these parameters as the ball moves.

Software companies have produced a wide variety of animations designed to contribute to pupils' understanding of abstract scientific theories. Moving images of particles in solids, liquids and gases dance before pupils' eyes; but beware!, most animations contain inherent errors and over-simplifications (often as a result of unavoidable limitations in graphic capability). Particles in a liquid are inevitably displayed with spaces in between them, thereby reinforcing a commonly held misconception. Therefore, as mentioned earlier in this unit, examine, and encourage pupils to examine, the limitations of this kind of model as you explore the ideas that it is intended to support (see *Relevant websites*).

5 Building conceptual links and understanding

Brainstorming ideas at the start of a new topic and creating summary concept maps using Word or Visio software gives students opportunities to organise and store their ideas electronically.

Using interactive whiteboards (IWBs) to help build explanations and to assess pupils' progress in understanding ideas can be very effective. Flipcharts (like PowerPoint slides) can be designed easily once you are familiar with the software. The following features are most useful when getting started (don't try to become an expert on all the interactive features at once!):

■ covering up images fully or partly to ignite curiosity or to initiate thinking
■ uncovering key words gradually during assessment activities (but beware of the same 'wait for the teacher's answers' response as is possible with PowerPoint)
■ labelling scientific diagrams in stages using layering techniques (an electronic version of overhead transparencies)
■ using interactive 'drag and drop' assessments
■ saving pupils' ideas and following them up in later lessons thereby looking at progression.

Software comes with instructions on how to build these kinds of interactive activities. Engaging contexts can be used to improve motivation.

What happens to the apple?

■ **Figure 5.3.3** IWB cartoon. Sketch diagram (originally with a famous cartoon character as the top layer) to show how a layering technique can be used to 'reveal' the underlying digestive system. The apple is the 'rubber', allowing pupils to see beneath the skin.

Source: adapted from and reproduced with kind permission of Nick O'Brien. Sketch reproduced with kind permission of Satomi Saki

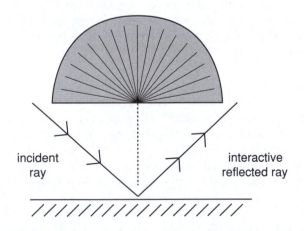

■ **Figure 5.3.4** IWB reflection. Sketch diagram to show how demonstrations such as judging the angle of the reflected ray when investigating reflection can be facilitated

Source: adapted from and reproduced with kind permission of Jamie Styles

6 Mathematical models

There are commercially available mathematical models, such as ones on the predator–prey relationship in ecology, or the breeding rate of rabbits in a limited environment. It is helpful, too, if pupils can set up their own models, however simple, as they then know what the model is that they are experimenting with. Excel is the most accessible modelling tool. They could set up a model of the energy consumption in a house, with columns for 'appliance', 'wattage', 'time it is run', 'cost'. They can allocate a box for total cost over a week, another for budget that they must not exceed, and another for the difference between expenditure and budget. The model allows them to monitor their energy consumption against budget.

7 Communication

Communication technologies give pupils the opportunity to prepare both colourful and imaginative presentations, whether for personal work or for posters and whole-class talks. Adding images to illustrate ideas and concepts can increase the appeal of material. Pupils can capture their own digital photographs of an event to include. They can easily experiment with ideas by writing, reviewing and changing, and this can be a great encouragement to support the writing process. Remember that if you are using 'writing frames' these can be put onto the computers. Pupils need structured guidance about what to include in a presentation, just as you will carefully prepare your own. Give them a clear remit, for example:

- maximum number of slides (keep this low – five or six)
- one image only per slide
- key questions to answer
- everyone must contribute.

PowerPoint presentations need to encourage the audience to actively participate as well. Have evaluation frames for pupils so that when they are watching each presentation they know what to record, and also they can peer-assess one another using agreed criteria. Ask everyone to assess scientific accuracy closely – pupils often copy and paste information into presentations without actually reading/checking it. The presentation itself, then, is not the final outcome.

Digital video and video-conferencing can give pupils access to opportunities to support their learning. Schools are recording experiments/discussions which can be viewed online to follow up lessons. Pupils can link up with their peers in other countries to take part in joint projects/discussions. Exciting opportunities for role play and 'real life' interactions are possible using video-conferencing. It is necessary to have a broadband connection to make this feasible. Pupils can talk 'live' to scientists across the world and take part in simulations of global events. For example, the National Space Agency in Leicester runs a 'Monserrat' disaster simulation in which pupils try to respond to the eruption of a volcano that began in July 1995. They have to make decisions about what to do as scientists relay information about what is happening at that moment.

8 Assessment for Learning (AfL)/exploring ideas

Electronic Voting Systems (EVS), or learner response systems (LRS) as they are often known, have been appearing in many schools for assessment. There are a number of possible applications of the technology, in which individual pupils have a 'pod' or 'clicker' through which they can interact with questions driven through the IWB. Multiple-choice and 'dilemma-style' questions can be created easily and capturing answers immediately allows pupils to see individual and whole-class answers on the big screen. Within the lesson, the same questions can be revisited and pupils can see their own progression after a learning activity has addressed their original ideas. It is possible for users to be completely anonymous but, more usefully, each 'pod' has an identifier, and assessment data can be exported to Excel. For example, you can use the initial assessment results to put pupils into groups where at least one person has a good (accurate) idea, so encouraging peer teaching. You might have a series of questions, which, depending upon the categories of understanding into which pupils' answers fall initially, you give different answers to different groups for different intervention activities. Pupils' confidence levels increase when they see the board go from 'dark' (the shade used for incorrect responses in software package) to 'light' (for correct responses) over the course of a lesson or two (Figure 5.3.5).

Task 5.3.2 **Evaluating the effectiveness of ICT resources**

At some point in your training year, try to use and evaluate the effectiveness of as many of the ICT resources described in this unit as you realistically can. Your task here is to:

1 choose two resources that have conventional, non-ICT equivalents (for example, using data logging versus a non-ICT measuring device; using a drag-and-drop interactive activity versus a card sort etc.)
2 read at least two of the texts recommended below to make some inferences about why the ICT method may enhance pupils' learning about science or process skills
3 run the ICT and non-ICT activities side-by-side (using half the class for one and half for the other, trying to balance higher and lower achievers in each half)
4 critically reflect upon your assessed learning outcomes for the lessons which you focused on, and attempt to diagnose the different contributions of the ICT and non-ICT approaches to pupils' development of ideas and skills
5 use what you learn to develop your next approaches to activities for promoting learning.

You will find more guidance on the use of ICT resources in the June 2003 edition of *School Science Review* that was devoted almost entirely to ICT in science education (Wellington, 2003).

The use of ICT has altered the way in which teachers and pupils interact. Outside bodies, teachers, science departments and schools are setting up websites of key resources for pupils, posting key readings and preparation for the following week for

Q1	Q2	Q3	Q4	Q5	Q6	Q7
T	F	F	F	T	F	F
T	F	F	F	T	F	F
T	F	F	F	T	F	F
T	F	F	T	T	F	F
T	F	T	T	T	F	F
T	F	F	F	F	F	F
T	T	/	T	T	T	F
T	F	F	T	T	T	F
T	F	T	T	T	T	F
T	F	F	T	T	T	F
T	T	T	F	T	F	F
T	T	F	T	F	T	F
T	F	F	T	T	F	F
T	F	F	F	T	F	F
T	F	X	T	T	T	F
F	T	T	F	T	T	T
T	F	F	F	T	T	T
T	T	T	F	T	T	T
T	T	F	F	T	T	F
T	F	F	F	T	T	F

Q16	Q17	Q18	Q19	Q20	Q21	Q22
T	F	F	F	T	F	F
T	F	F	F	T	F	F
T	F	F	F	T	F	F
T	F	T	T	T	F	F
T	F	F	T	T	T	F
T	F	F	T	T	F	F
T	T	F	F	T	F	F
T	F	F	F	T	F	F
T	F	F	F	T	F	F
T	F	F	T	T	F	F
T	F	F	F	T	F	F
T	F	F	T	T	F	F
T	F	F	F	T	F	F
T	F	F	F	T	F	F
T	F	F	F	F	F	F
T	F	T	T	F	T	T
T	F	F	T	T	T	F
T	F	F	F	T	F	F
T	T	F	T	T	T	T
T	F	F	F	T	T	F

■ **Figure 5.3.5** EVS data for a range of seven true/false questions, showing initial and final responses for 20 students exploring ideas about ionisation energy

Source: adapted from and reproduced with kind permission of Ruth Wheeldon

their classes (especially A-level groups), and receiving and responding to homework online. Virtual learning environments are being used for students to study extra GCSEs online.

SUMMARY AND KEY POINTS

Using ICT resources to support the learning and teaching of science is a well-established, commonly used strategy. Specific resources and activities need to be trialled and evaluated thoroughly and technical support needs to be strong to ensure that lesson time is effective. You need to be very clear about the differences between using ICT resources to structure a lesson, and for pupils learning actively.

Check the requirements of your course to see which relate to this unit.

FURTHER READING

Beauchamp, G. and Parkinson, J. (2005) 'Beyond the "wow" factor: developing interactivity with interactive whiteboards'. *School Science Review*, 86 (316), 97–103.
Very pertinent advice about how to promote active learning through the IWB.

Barton, R. (ed.) (2004) *Teaching Secondary Science with ICT*. Maidenhead: Open University Press.
This is a well-balanced review of a number of practical applications of ICT in the science classroom. Ideas are evaluated through research.

Dixon, N. (2008) 'Can data logging improve the quality of interpretation and evaluation in chemistry lessons?' *School Science Review*, 89 (329), 55–62.
A useful article showing how A-level students developed data-analysis skills through data logging.

Frost, R. (2002a) *Data Logging in Practice.* London: IT in Science.

Frost, R. (2002b) *Data Logging and Control.* London: IT in Science.

Rogers, L. and Finlayson, H. (2003) 'Does ICT in science really work in the classroom?' Part 1 'The individual teacher experience'. *School Science Review,* June 2003, 84 (309), 105–11.

Sang, D. and Frost, R. (eds) (2005) *Teaching Secondary Science Using ICT*. ASE, Hodder Murray.
A comprehensive review of how to implement ICT for learning science effectively.

Wellington, J. (special issue ed.) (2003) 'ICT in science education'. *School Science Review*. 84 (309), 39–120.
This review of ICT in action in the science classroom is still current and contains ten articles on the use and evaluation of ICT for learning science.

RELEVANT WEBSITES

National Curriculum
Available: http://curriculum.qca.org.uk/ gives details of the science NC for 2009 onwards.

Becta
The government agency leading the national drive to ensure the effective and innovative use of technology throughout learning. Their website contains a vast amount of information, advice and research about ICT resources for science.
http://www.becta.org.uk/ (accessed 28 June 2009).

National Space Centre, Leicester

http://www.aerospaceguide.net/nationalcentre.html (accessed 28 June 2009).

North American Space Agency, NASA

It is an excellent example of a site in which pupils can have a high level of interaction. Current space shuttle missions can be followed and the latest projects at NASA explored.
http://www.nasa.gov/ (accessed 28 June 2009).

http://nationalzoo.si.edu/Animals/GiantPandas/PandaConservation/default.cfm

Displays real time data for the reproductive state of the female giant panda in the Smithsonian Zoo, Washington, USA (accessed 28 June 2009).

http://www.absorblearning.com/en/Free_online_Absorb_resources/

An online library of simple simulations, animations and other useful ICT resources. It remains (at the time of writing) free to use online (accessed 28 June 2009).

http://www.ewart.org.uk

A simple website containing animations and ICT activity design suggestions and contains examples which are very good for critical evaluation of scientific accuracy (accessed 28 June 2009).

http://www.beep.ac.uk/

Website for the BioEthics Evaluation Project (BEEP) which can be used for online debating of socio-scientific issues for A-level biology (accessed 28 June 2009).

http://www.thenakedscientists.com/

Includes an online science radio show, podcasts, discussion forum, science, medicine and technology news, interviews, medical and health advice, educational resources and articles, experiments, projects and book reviews. It was set up with support from, among others, the Royal Society and Cambridge University (accessed 28 June 2009).

http://revealproject.org/

Reports on a two-year study into the use of Electronic Voting Systems (or learner response systems) in educational settings and has many useful examples for science and tips on how to make the most of the assessment opportunities (accessed 28 June 2009).

SCIENCE FOR CITIZENSHIP

Marcus Grace

INTRODUCTION

Citizenship is a statutory National Curriculum subject at Key Stage 3 and 4. The programme of study (QCA, 2007) proposes that effective citizenship education should develop social and moral responsibility, community involvement and political literacy. The curriculum is based on three key concepts: i) *Democracy and justice*, ii) *Rights and responsibilities*, and iii) *Identities and diversity: living together in the UK*. As practising caring and professional teachers we obviously have an important role to play in promoting these concepts among our pupils. Through our everyday interactions with pupils, we demonstrate 'democratic' values such as working together, listening to each other, respecting other viewpoints, trying to reconcile conflicting differences and appreciating and celebrating that we are all equal yet different. To take the principles of citizenship seriously, we need to acknowledge the importance of pupil 'voice' by giving them opportunities to explain their ideas. Discussing how they plan to carry out an investigation or why they disagree with someone else's findings is part of science, but it is also part of citizenship.

OBJECTIVES

By the end of this unit you should be able to:

- identify opportunities for teaching citizenship through science
- use a range of strategies to teach about controversial socio-scientific issues
- assess citizenship in science
- locate appropriate resources.

WHAT IS CITIZENSHIP?

Citizenship can refer to (a) the status of being a citizen, i.e. belonging to a certain community or country, which brings with it certain rights and responsibilities defined in law, or (b) the expected behaviour associated with being a citizen (Citizenship

Foundation, 2009). Citizenship, as with all curriculum subjects, should have explicit links with the framework of *Every Child Matters* (DCSF, 2009b), and the personal development learning agenda (DCSF, 2005), so that pupils have a secure learning environment which is required to tackle the controversial issues that will continue to confront them through their lives (Crick, 2001).

WHAT IS THE CONNECTION BETWEEN SCIENCE AND CITIZENSHIP?

Citizenship could be seen as an overarching theme linking all other subjects together. As science teachers, it is initially probably advisable to stick to what we know best and concentrate on the science-related components. Science teachers have a specific contribution to make to help develop pupils' ways of thinking and behaving as active citizens of the future. Science lessons provide an opportunity for pupils to learn about the applications of science and about socio-scientific issues, i.e. issues which have a basis in science and have a potentially large impact on society (Ratcliffe and Grace, 2003). There are questions raised in the media every day relating to controversial socio-scientific issues which impact on us all: How conclusive is DNA evidence in a murder trial? Is climate change really as big a threat to humanity as scientists tell us? Should we build a new generation of nuclear power stations?

With the advancement of science, the knowledge base of education for socio-scientific issues is becoming increasingly complex, and making decisions about the issues involves a difficult compromise between many conflicting values. Socio-scientific issues are not purely scientific but might also include aesthetic, spiritual, social, political and economic values.

HOW DO SCIENCE AND CITIZENSHIP FIT TOGETHER AT SCHOOL?

The citizenship programme of study encourages pupils to engage with debate and decision-making about contemporary controversial issues, and ultimately become informed and active citizens. Science teachers have an important part to play when these issues are underpinned by science.

Task 5.4.1 **Linking citizenship and science in the curriculum**

Look at the Key Stage 3 science and citizenship programmes of study. Compare the Curriculum Opportunities sections and look for commonality. For example, how might Citizenship 4f: work with a range of community partners, where possible, and Science 4f: use creativity and innovation in science, and appreciate their importance in enterprise, slot into the science scheme of work?

Perhaps, for example, pupils could consult a local engineering company or university to discuss how to improve the energy efficiency of bicycles. The STEM Ambassadors scheme might help with this kind of project.

There are many different ways in which you can teach citizenship through science. The examples given below are linked to the three citizenship key processes that are set out in the curriculum.

Critical thinking and enquiry

Pupils could:

■ Investigate the accuracy of science stories (socio-scientific issues) presented in the media and the extent to which they influence public opinion. Examples might include 'designer babies', 'superbugs', genetically modified ('frankenstein') foods, and risks from vaccinations or mobile phones. They could examine the reliability of the sources of information upon which the stories are based.

■ Access and evaluate sources of information about the use of electricity or water by the school, to consider how valid and reliable the data is. This could involve consulting utility companies over prices, and surveying related patterns of behaviour among pupils and staff.

■ Analyse and evaluate the variety of opinions surrounding a socio-scientific issue. Issues could range from complex and emotional ones such as fox-hunting, to decision-making about whether the school should have wooden, metal or uPVC window frames.

Advocacy and representation

Pupils could:

■ consider how different people express themselves when putting forward their point of view

■ practise communicating with different audiences, such as writing a letter to the local MP or newspaper, to attempt to get their message across as persuasively as possible

■ give a presentation about a socio-scientific issue, representing the views of others with which they do not agree.

Taking informed and responsible action

Pupils could:

■ create or review the school policy on purchasing environmentally friendly products by carrying out research on the life-cycle of materials

■ plan how to collaborate as a class to communicate their collective view about a socio-scientific issue to a relevant local or national organisation

■ teach younger children about, for example, the value of reusing and recycling of waste materials.

Task 5.4.2 **Citizenship and science in your practice school**

Find out how aspects of science for citizenship are taught in your school. Why has the school decided to take this approach?

Look through your department's schemes of work. What opportunities can you identify for teaching citizenship in science lessons?

HOW DO SCHOOLS TEACH SCIENCE FOR CITIZENSHIP?

It is up to individual schools how they deliver the citizenship curriculum. Hounsdown School in Hampshire runs a particularly motivating citizenship programme, described by Ofsted as excellent and contributing well to pupils' personal development. The programme links with all other curriculum subjects. The school has three Citizenship Focus Days and three Citizenship Theme Days during the course of the school year. On Focus Days, subject teachers teach whatever was already on their timetable, but modify the lessons to focus on key content and processes in the citizenship curriculum as well as those in the science curriculum. A recent example of a focus day science lesson is shown in Figure 5.4.1.

The school has converted the KS3 citizenship attainment targets into levelled statements for the pupils. After each activity, in consultation with the teachers, the pupils level themselves against the statements, and the teachers draw on this at the end of the year to compile a summative review.

On the Theme Days, the whole school comes off the normal timetable and different citizenship themes are arranged for each year group. All pupils work their way through a series of activities through the day, some run by teachers and others by external organisations. Many of the activities consider socio-scientific issues such as junk food, fire safety, fair trade, race and human rights, consequences of vandalism, sexual health, drugs awareness, and being a global citizen.

TEACHING ABOUT CONTROVERSIAL ISSUES

Effective teaching of citizenship in science involves the discussion of pupils' ideas in the classroom. Many of these ideas are controversial, i.e. significant numbers of people argue about them without reaching a conclusion (Oulton *et al.,* 2004a). Stradling defined controversial issues as: issues on which our society is clearly divided and significant groups within society advocate conflicting explanations or solutions based on alternative values (Stradling, 1985: 9).

Pupils will encounter moral dilemmas before and after they leave school, and we as teachers therefore have to help them develop the means to make properly informed decisions.

Lesson title: The problems with polymers
Aims: to understand the environmental impact of making and using polymers
Citizenship content: ■ critical thinking and enquiry: research, plan and undertake an enquiry into issues and problems using a range of information and sources ■ to discuss the environmental aspects of making and disposing of polymers ■ to carry out research to identify these issues ■ to present the findings to the public.
Science content: ■ polymer manufacture from non-renewable fossil fuels ■ the environmental effect of alternative methods of polymer disposal – excessive landfill, toxic combustion, waste of valuable resources
Key vocabulary: polymer, environment, non-renewable resource, combustion, toxic fumes
Starter: short videos made by pupils on recycling to promote ideas about waste management
Development: ■ pupils to research and discuss the problems of plastics from manufacture to disposal ■ pupil groups choose which issue to investigate – manufacture, combustion, landfill, reusing and recycling
Plenary: pupils present their work to the class (in the role of a public audience)
Evidence produced: group posters showing ideas used for their presentation
Resources required: camcorders, science textbooks, A3 paper, coloured pens
Assessment: pupils level themselves against citizenship attainment target levels.

■ **Figure 5.4.1** Outline of a Year 9 lesson on polymers

Class discussion

Class discussion is widely recognised as an effective way to encourage pupils to explore issues. However, pupils are sometimes rushed into making up their minds on the issue, and there is a danger that they might form their opinions too soon, possibly based on the personality of the protagonist rather than the validity and reliability of the evidence being presented.

It is useful to decide what we mean by the terms discussion, debate and argument. All these terms can be used synonymously, generally to mean verbal interaction aimed at resolving a controversy (Newton *et al.*, 1999). However, we need to be clear that we are talking about the kind of verbal interaction in which all participants respectfully listen to each other's viewpoints, involving self-reflection and a clarification of values (Solomon, 2001), not the scenario of frequent heckling as witnessed in the House of Commons, or argument without structure or reasoning akin to that often found in television programmes such as *EastEnders*.

The very process of discussing socio-scientific issues requires pupils to act and behave in a way expected of good citizens, and it is important that they understand basic ground rules for discussion, such as respecting and listening sensitively to each other's points of view. Although the activity may be carried out within a science lesson, pupils should also be considering personal and social values; when dealing with real issues the emotional aspects need to be handled sensitively. This involves finding out (if you can) if there are pupils in the class who might be deeply affected by the issue. Some pupils may prefer not to be present and this is of course their prerogative; on the other hand they may want to talk about their experiences. If pupils have questions they would prefer not to ask in front of their peers, you could use a question box where they can post questions anonymously for discussion in the next lesson.

Managing discussion

In chairing a discussion about controversial issues, we need to consider some main principles – which themselves can be controversial! (QCA, 1998).

Neutrality. Some teachers prefer to act as a neutral chairperson, not declaring their own view while encouraging pupils to express theirs. However, neutrality is difficult to sustain and can undermine the rapport that the teacher has built up with the pupils (Stradling, 1985). Other teachers have a 'stated commitment' approach, where they declare their views from the start, and encourage pupils to agree or disagree on the basis of their reasoning. Oulton *et al.* (2004a) argue that if we really want pupils to be open about what they feel and think, then the teacher should reciprocate to engender trust and transparency among all concerned.

Balance. A 'balanced' approach is where the teacher tries to ensure that all different views of the issue are covered, and one-sided arguments are countered by playing 'devil's advocate'. The difficulty is knowing how to achieve balance. The teacher will need to have some understanding of all viewpoints. The QCA (1998) point out that it is impossible to be completely unbiased, and in some cases undesirable, but we need to avoid indoctrination.

Reason. We must guard against giving pupils the impression that real life issues can always be resolved through reason (Ashton and Watson, 1998), and over-simplifying moral dilemmas, which renders them unrealistic (Kibble, 1998).

The QCA (1998: 56) suggests that we 'teach pupils how to recognize bias, how to evaluate evidence put before them and how to look at alternative interpretations, viewpoints and sources of evidence, above all to give good reasons for everything they say or do, and to expect good reasons to be given by others'.

Task 5.4.3 **Teaching about different controversial issues**

Write down your definition of a controversial issue. If possible, ask someone else to do the same and compare your definitions. Then compare them with Stradling's definition above. List some current controversial socio-scientific issues and note whether Stradling's definition holds true for each. Comment critically on the approaches to neutrality, balance and reason advocated by the authors in the section above. Look at the survey questions in Table 5.4.1 about two controversial issues. To begin with, cover up the figures given in the table and complete the survey yourself. Then compare your responses with the figures given. These are results from a survey of over 200 teachers showing the approaches that they would adopt when teaching the two different controversial issues. There are clear differences among the teachers. Think about why these might both be considered socio-scientific issues, and write down why you think teachers hold a range of opinions about the teaching of different topics (see Oulton *et al.*, 2004b for further discussion of this data).

■ **Table 5.4.1** Approaches teachers would adopt when teaching two different controversial issues. Figures show percentage of respondents indicating their choice.

If I was teaching these topics I would:	Racism	Factory farming
1 (a) present a balanced view	62	83
(b) present a biased view	21	12
(c) explain to pupils that balance is impossible to achieve	17	05
2 (a) not give my opinion	29	33
(b) only give my opinion if asked	29	53
(c) make my opinion clear to pupils	42	14
3 (a) encourage pupils to make up their own mind on the issue	42	82
(b) try to influence pupils to adopt a particular attitude to the issue	34	07
(c) discourage pupils from making up their mind at this stage of their development	02	11
4 (a) discourage pupils from talking about their own attitudes and values	04	03
(b) encourage pupils to talk about their own attitudes and values	38	32
(c) encourage pupils to talk about their own attitudes and values and analyse each other's opinions critically.	58	65

Source: Oulton *et al.*, 2004b

Using and developing pupils' knowledge of socio-scientific issues

Before the class discusses an issue, you should ensure that the pupils have sufficient understanding of the underlying science and social aspects. To establish that pupils have the required knowledge base, you will have to find out what they know already, what they need to know for the discussion, and how they will access this knowledge. With the proliferation of sources of information all purporting to be accurate and based on scientific evidence, it can be extremely difficult to gauge the reliability of the information. This is even more difficult for pupils to disentangle. In their attempts to engage us with issues, journalists may sometimes unintentionally dilute the scientific evidence due to editing, restricted space, their own interpretation of the data, and their use of emotive language. But before we go rushing to scientific reports for reliable data, we should also remember that scientists themselves may also be prone to bias. They are only human, with their own priorities, values, beliefs and role in society. Fortunately, there are now a number of well-established and reliable education sites with excellent resources, enabling teachers to conduct informed discussion about a range of socio-scientific issues. The added value of restricting your pupils to such resources is that you are more able to control the direction the discussion is likely to take.

Task 5.4.4 **Observing an experienced teacher**

New teachers will have fundamental concerns about teaching controversial issues. Pupils might ask 'non-scientific' questions which you are unable to answer or feel uneasy about answering. A good way to learn how to organise and facilitate a discussion is to ask to observe experienced teachers including English and humanities teachers, who tend to use this approach more readily than science teachers. Observe a discussion lesson and try to note down answers to the following questions:

- How is the dilemma presented?
- Does the teacher draw on pupils' knowledge and experiences?
- Does the teacher use a carefully selected set of information and resources for discussion? How are they distributed?
- Are media reports being used? What kind?
- Is this a whole-class discussion or a collection of small-group discussions, or a mixture of both?
- If pupils are grouped, how does the teacher organise the groups? Do the pupils have stimuli to provoke discussion? Does the grouping occur spontaneously or does the teacher allocate groups? Does the teacher allocate roles within the groups?
- What are the aims of the discussion? Are these made clear to pupils?
- Are there expectations/ground rules? What are the intended learning outcomes?
- Do all pupils contribute equally?
- What is the role of the teacher during discussion?
- What is the level of noise? Are pupils overly noisy? Are there uncomfortable silences?
- Do pupils have enough time to think about the issues before and during the discussion?
- How does the teacher manage obstinate, sensitive, emotional or unacceptable viewpoints? How does the teacher deal with dominant or 'opinionated' pupils? Does the teacher press for consensus? Does the teacher try to highlight differences?
- How does the teacher deal with questions he/she is unable to answer?
- How much time is devoted to teacher talk and pupil talk?
- How are the results of the discussion presented?
- Do the pupils seem content or frustrated with the activity and the overall outcomes?

Teaching strategies

As in all teaching situations, the approach you use will depend on factors such as the age, ability and group dynamics of the class, the space available and the general situation at that time. The following is a brief introduction to a range of teaching strategies you may wish to use.

ROLE PLAY

Role play is one of the most frequently used approaches for teaching about controversial issues among secondary school teachers (Oulton *et al.*, 2004b); it offers pupils the opportunity to explore other peoples' perspectives. However, simply putting a pupil in role does not necessarily mean that they can empathise with the viewpoints of others (Lynch and McKenna, 1990), so we should be cautious about its universal effectiveness.

CRITICAL INCIDENTS

'Critical incidents' (Nott and Wellington, 1995) are scenarios of real situations, which are used to help pupils appreciate and articulate their views about issues. They are confronted with an example of an incident and asked to respond by saying what they *would* do (a reactive perspective), what they *could* do (a proactive perspective) and what they *should* do (an ethical/moral perspective) in this situation. How the pupils respond is an indication of their views on the nature of socio-scientific issues, and these are not always forthcoming if simply responding to abstract, context-free questions. What they *could* and *should* do does not always coincide with what they *would* do. Here are some examples of critical incidents:

> What would you/could you/should you do or say in the following situations?

> 1   While talking to your friends about how humans and monkeys are similar because they have evolved from common ancestors, someone says that his family believes that we are all created in God's image and they don't believe in evolution.
> 2   You are on a school trip waiting for a coach. Someone spots a large spider and stamps on it. Someone else is really upset about the incident.
> 3   You are carrying out a practical science investigation involving burning chemicals. Someone says that she would seriously prefer not to take part on the grounds that the work is contributing to atmospheric pollution, and that every bit counts.
> 4   A visitor from an environmental organisation suggests that transferring freight from road to rail is a good way of easing traffic congestion. Someone says, 'But my dad's a lorry driver, he could lose his job.'

HEADS AND HEARTS

This activity (Ratcliffe and Grace, 2003) encourages pupils to recognise the existence of an emotional reaction and a rational response to a controversial issue. Pupils are asked to immediately react to a question, for which you give them up to four choices. Depending on their choice, they move to the relevant corner of the room. Pose a question such as: *Should we have genetic testing to eliminate serious genetic disorders from our society in future generations?*

Designate each corner of the room as: not at all; compulsory for everyone; compulsory for those who have relatives with the disorder; only for those who want to be tested. Some pupils may want to stand mid-way between corners. Then ask them to put their hand on their head if they had made the decision by thinking rationally, or on their heart if it was an immediate emotional response. Ask some to explain their views.

CONSEQUENCE MAPPING

This allows pupils to explore a 'What if…' scenario by considering the consequences of an action. Get pupils working in small groups to write the proposed action in the middle of the large sheet of paper, and then map the possible primary and secondary consequences of this action. For example, the proposal might be: *What if fishing in the North Sea is completely banned?* Other groups could map the opposing view: *What if fishing in the North Sea is completely unrestricted?* The maps could be displayed on the walls for comparison. The activity encourages pupils to identify their own values and those of others in relation to the issue, and appreciate that socio-scientific issues involve considering values as well as scientific evidence.

EVALUATING MEDIA REPORTS

Media reports (from tabloid and broadsheet newspapers, TV, radio, internet etc.) can demonstrate the relevance of science to everyday issues. They can be used to identify scientific terms, the underpinning science concepts, the values and opinions of people involved, and the evidence that is being used to support or challenge claims being made. Pupils can also learn about the nature of media reporting itself by looking at the role of an editor, or by concentrating on 'hooks' which draw in the audience. These might include surprise elements, exciting visual or audio presentation or emotional triggers such as sadness, humour, fighting against almost unbelievable odds, incredible coincidences and so on. One systematic way of evaluating science-related media reports is to get pupils to answer the following questions:

■   What are the scientists/researchers claiming? (i.e. What are their conclusions?)
■   What scientific knowledge did the researchers use to support their conclusions?
■   What evidence is provided to support their conclusions?
■   Does the evidence provided here convince you that the conclusion is correct?
■   What extra evidence is needed? How might this be collected?

To highlight the socially framed nature of scientific research science, additional questions could be posed:

■   Who did the research?
■   Who do they work for?
■   How certain are they about their conclusions?
■   Do other scientists agree with their conclusions?

PROBABILITY AND RISK

In analysing risk, pupils need to understand probability and to recognise that nothing we do is completely risk-free. Risk is a combination of the probability of something going wrong and the cost to you if something does go wrong. Individuals will have different views. You could ask pupils how willing they would be to engage in a range of potentially dangerous activities, and compare their perceptions with risk statistics from the Health and Safety Executive website or the government's UK National Statistics website. Pupils could rate the danger by discussing in small groups how much money (or other benefit) they would require to take the risk. This kind of activity promotes discussion about science and society:

■ how risk statistics are derived
■ how the risks associated with the issues are presented to the public
■ why scientists are unable to state categorically the risks associated with certain issues
■ how we decide whether or not to carry out risky activities – do we always calculate the risk first?

The *Mind Tools* website also provides some useful resources and ideas about probability and risk.

DECISION-MAKING FRAMEWORKS

A way to promote systematic and critical risk-benefit discussions among pupils is to provide them with a decision-making framework of the kind shown in Figure 5.4.2.

Present pupils with some background on a real socio-scientific issue, maybe as brief text with some visual stimulus. Here is an example:

> African elephants are endangered animals, although their numbers are recovering again since the ban on ivory trading, and strict action against poachers. However, elephants are naturally very destructive animals, and can inflict serious damage on crops and property, easily destroying a field of crops in one evening – eating some and trampling the rest. They can also cause human injury or even death. This has resulted in growing conflict between elephants and local people.

What should be done about the problem, *why* and *how*?

Pupils then spend five minutes alone thinking quietly about how and why the problem should be solved. This enables them to start forming their own views to draw on in the subsequent discussion. Then pupils discuss the issue in small groups using the decision-making framework as a guide towards making a decision. Meanwhile you can circulate among the groups observing the group interaction, although you need to decide in advance how much to intervene, bearing in mind that your presence could alter their discussion and even stifle their creative ideas! If handled carefully, this is an excellent means of demonstrating to pupils that an active citizen needs to develop the skill to balance human values and science knowledge to take part in informed decision-making about social issues. At the end of the discussion, some groups may have reached a decision, others may remain undecided. The important purpose of this activity is not to force pupils into making a decision but to take the pupils through the decision-making process.

Follow these steps, consider the questions and complete the table as you go.

1. OPTIONS

   ■ What are the options?
   ■ Discuss the possible solutions to the problem and list them in a table.

2. IMPORTANT THINGS TO CONSIDER

   ■ How are you going to choose between these options?
   ■ Discuss the **important** things to consider when you look at each option, and add them to the table.

3. INFORMATION

   ■ Do you have enough information about each option?
   ■ Discuss what **science** is involved in the problem.
   ■ Discuss what **extra scientific information** you need to help you make the decision.

4. ADVANTAGES/DISADVANTAGES

Discuss the advantages and disadvantages of each option, and add them to the table.

5. CHOICE

Which option does your group choose?

6. REVIEW

What do you think of the decision you have made?
How could you improve the way you made the decision?

OPTIONS (possible solutions) *[as many as you think of]*	IMPORTANT THINGS TO CONSIDER *[for each option]*	ADVANTAGES *[for each option]*	DISADVANTAGES *[for each option]*
1			
2			
3			

■ **Figure 5.4.2** A decision-making framework for learning about socio-scientific issues (after Ratcliffe and Grace, 2003)

ASSESSMENT METHODS

Useful types of assessment in teaching about controversial issues include observation, written open responses, listening to discussions, self-assessment, a portfolio of evidence, and active, participatory approaches. Evaluation of learning from the activities above is perhaps not as straightforward as for the recall of scientific 'facts', development of practical skills or explanation of science concepts and processes. Our main educational aim of education for citizenship is for pupils to develop informed and responsible attitudes and actions when confronted with real issues. Research has shown that there is not a strong correlation between knowledge and attitudes (e.g. Gayford and Dillon, 1995), and attitudes may be modified without corresponding behavioural change. It might therefore not be realistic to expect changes in behaviour, and the best we can do is evaluate opinions and decision-making. Furthermore, we are not necessarily aiming to change pupils' attitudes. Two pupils might have strongly opposing views on using animals in medical research. We are not in a position to judge that one view is better than the other; what we want to assess is pupils' reasoning in reaching this view.

Assessing pupils' understanding of socio-scientific issues can be attempted by constructing a hierarchical scoring system of the kind shown in Table 5.4.2. Give pupils the outline of a controversial issue and then ask them to make a decision about it, explaining their answer as fully as possible. It is, of course, important to make the marking criteria clear to the pupils from the start.

■ **Table 5.4.2** A possible scoring system for assessing decision-making

Score	Pupil response
0	No response given
1	Decision stated but lacking any supporting reasons
2	Evidence used for one side of the issue
3	Evidence used for at least two perspectives
4	Pros and cons of the perspectives are weighed
5	Perspectives weighed and limitations of the evidence highlighted

There are also ways of assessing pupil interaction while they are discussing issues in small groups. For example, Hogan (2002) identified roles that promoted the group's reasoning processes:

■ promoters of reflection
■ contributors to content knowledge
■ mediators of group interactions and ideas

and roles that inhibited the group's reasoning process:

■ promoters of acrimony (outwardly hostile to fellow group members)
■ promoters of distraction
■ participants reluctant to collaborate.

This approach obviously requires the teacher to know the pupils well and can only be conducted in a trusting environment. It is also important that the pupils are aware of the learning goals from the start, and they should have opportunities to self-assess or peer-assess their work (Black and Wiliam, 1998; see also Unit 6.1).

AVAILABLE HELP AND RESOURCES

Many outside organisations will readily help with citizenship days, although you should look out for possible bias in messages being promoted. Excellent help can be sought from local police and fire-safety services, NHS sexual-health nurses, environmental organisations, fair trade organisations etc.

Teaching resources on socio-scientific issues can be accessed through websites associated with the Association for Science Education (ASE), Science Museum, Wellcome Trust, Institute of Biology, Institute of Physics and Royal Society of Chemistry. Several national newspapers have good websites for accessing information on contemporary issues in science. See also the list of resources at the end of this unit.

Task 5.4.5 **Evaluating a resource**

Access information about a specific issue from an organisation's website or pamphlet.

- What views does the organisation advocate?
- What might be the opposite viewpoint?
- Are images used appropriately to support the message?
- Do they give sources of their information?

SUMMARY AND KEY POINTS

This unit has highlighted the challenges facing teachers when dealing with socio-scientific issues as part of the citizenship curriculum. Unfamiliar approaches, like engaging pupils in discussion, can be a daunting prospect for a new teacher. However, when handled well, such approaches can be hugely motivating to pupils of all ages and abilities. When starting out teaching, observe experienced teachers dealing with these issues, look for overlap between the science and citizenship programmes of study and see where controversial issues occur in your schemes of work.

FURTHER READING

Two editions of *School Science Review* are particularly useful and relevant to science and citizenship, and ethics in science, respectively:

Nott, M. (ed.) (2001) *School Science Review*, 83 (302).

Levinson, R. and Reiss, M. (2004) *School Science Review*, 86 (315).

Lynch, D. and McKenna, M. (1990) 'Teaching controversial material: new issues for teachers'. *Social Education*, 54, 317–319.

Newton, P., Driver, R. and Osborne, J. (1999) 'The place of argumentation in pedagogy of school science'. *International Journal of Science Education*, 21 (5), 553–576.

Nott, M. and Wellington, J. (1995) 'Critical incidents in the science classroom and the nature of science'. *School Science Review*, 76 (276), 41–46.

QCA (Qualifications and Curriculum Authority) (2007) *National Curriculum at Key Stages 3 and 4.*
http://curriculum.qcda.gov.uk/key-stages-3-and-4/index.aspx (accessed 15 December 2009)

RELEVANT WEBSITES

Among the best websites for secondary schools are:

BBC

www.bbc.co.uk/schools/teachers/ (accessed 30 June 2009).
Resources and teachers' packs for all subjects.

Citizenship Foundation

www.citizenshipfoundation.org.uk/ (accessed 30 June 2009).
Resources include free downloadable lesson plans.

Health and Safety Executive

http://www.hse.gov.uk/education/statistics.htm#death (accessed 30 June 2009).
UK statistics for education.

Junk food roadshow

www.foodlabuk.com/ (accessed 30 June 2009).
Curriculum-based workshops.

Mind tools

www.mindtools.com/ (accessed 30 June 2009).
Useful resources and ideas about probability and risk.

Professional Association for Citizenship Teaching (ACT)

www.teachingcitizenship.org.uk/ (accessed 30 June 2009).
Free membership for trainee teachers.

QCA

http://curriculum.qca.org.uk/ (accessed 30 June 2009).
Useful resources on sustainable development

Science year

www.sycd.co.uk/can_we_should_we/startfil/home.htm (accessed 30 June 2009).
Information on handling a number of socio-scientific issues.

STEM ambassadors scheme

www.stemnet.org.uk/home.cfm (accessed 30 June 2009).
Links schools with professional scientists and engineers.

TeacherNet

www.teachernet.gov.uk/ (accessed 30 June 2009).
A vast collection of resources for all subjects.

Teachers TV

www.teachers.tv/ (accessed 30 June 2009).
Downloadable videos, podcasts and classroom resources.

UK National Statistics

http://www.statistics.gov.uk/hub/index.html (accessed 30 June 2009).
Useful UK government statistics

Y Touring

www.ytouring.org.uk (accessed 30 June 2009).
A theatre company that presents dramas on contemporary issues for young people.

Acknowledgements

I am very grateful to Maxine Farmer, Citizenship Coordinator at Hounsdown School, for her helpful discussion, and to Ralph Levinson upon whose original work this unit is built.

SEX AND HEALTH EDUCATION

Jane Maloney and Sandra Campbell

INTRODUCTION

Since the implementation of the National Curriculum in 1989, schools have been expected to provide pupils with sex education within the science curriculum and the Personal, Health and Social Education (PHSE) curriculum. Guidance for the provision of sex education in schools can be found in a document entitled *Sex and Relationship Education Guidance* (DfEE, 2000). This guidance makes it clear that sex education needs to be set in a wider context and the focus should be on sex *and* relationships.

Sex and relationship education (SRE) is an important part of the *Every Child Matters* agenda, a green paper published by the government in 2003 as part of the response to the report into the death of Victoria Climbié. Central to the aims of the *Every Child Matters* programme is to give children the support they need to:

- be healthy
- stay safe
- enjoy and achieve
- make a positive contribution
- achieve economic well-being.

Although *Sex and Relationship Education Guidance* provided clear guidance for SRE in schools, the debate about how SRE should be approached in schools continues. It is important for you to know how dynamic the SRE situation is and to be alert to any new guidance and changes in legislation that may affect your teaching. A report published in 2008 (DCSF, 2008) recommended that PHSE should be made a statutory subject in all four Key Stages; this recommendation has been accepted by the government. If implemented, PHSE could become statutory in September 2010. However, you will be expected to teach those sex and health education topics that come under the remit of the science curriculum. Pupils will have had some age-appropriate sex and relationship education and health education in primary school, for example, learning about where babies come from, puberty and keeping healthy. During their secondary education they learn more details of, for instance, adolescence, fertilisation, foetal development and childbirth, contraception, and the effects of drugs, smoking and alcohol. Depending on which examination syllabus your school is following for GCSE, you may need to teach across a wide range of topics including the menstrual cycle, oral contraceptives, *in vitro* fertilisation, the use and misuse of drugs, and drug addiction. It is also worth noting that the subjects taught as a part of a school's sex-education programme may differ across England, Wales, Scotland and Northern Ireland.

Although this unit is about sex and health education, the main focus will be on preparing you to teach sensitive issues in general and most teachers would agree that teaching pupils about sexual matters is one of the most sensitive issues on the curriculum. At least you can be assured of pupils' interest and cannot be accused of teaching a topic that is irrelevant. The separation of 'sex education' from 'health education' is an artificial one but, as the two are subject to different constraints, they will be discussed separately.

OBJECTIVES

By the end of this unit you should be able to:

■ appreciate how science topics related to sex and health education fit in with the whole-school policy on SRE, PHSE and citizenship education and the *Every Child Matters* agenda

■ understand the legal aspects of health-related matters and the teacher's responsibilities in teaching sex education

■ recognise your own concerns about teaching sex and health education

■ identify teaching strategies that are appropriate for teaching about sensitive issues.

Check the requirements for your course to see which relate to this unit.

SEX AND RELATIONSHIP EDUCATION

State schools are legally required to have a sex education policy that should describe how sex education is provided within the school and who is responsible for providing it. SRE is defined as: 'learning about sex, sexuality, emotions, relationships, sexual health and ourselves' (Sex Education Forum, 2005). At the time of writing, those aspects of SRE taught within the science and citizenship curricula are under statutory order (i.e. through the National Curriculum) and those taught within PHSE are non-statutory.

Although SRE cannot be taught entirely by the science department, clearly some aspects of SRE can be provided within the science curriculum. It is important to be clear about the responsibilities of different departments in the school so that pupils receive a coherent and co-ordinated SRE. In this unit we focus mainly on the responsibilities of the science department in the provision of SRE.

The need to teach about sexual health

It is worth checking the statistics on sexual health each year; for example, the number of teenage pregnancies, under-16 abortions and rates of sexually transmitted infections

(STI) in young people. The Department of Health (DoH) produces an annual report that provides such statistics in England (see *Relevant websites*). Another source of statistics on sexual health is produced by the Medical Foundation for AIDS and Sexual Health (MedFASH). Such statistics can help to provide a context for young people learning about sexual health, or may help build your confidence in teaching SRE. Examples of relevant statistics include:

■ the teenage conception rate declined by 13.3 per cent (in 15s–17s) between 1998 and 2006 but there was an increase in 2007
■ the under-16 abortion rate was lower in 2009 than in 2007
■ the number of STI diagnoses at GUM (genito-urinary medicine) clinics has risen steadily over the last ten years and 16–24-year-olds account for nearly half of all STIs diagnosed in GUM clinics.

Secondary-school pupils receive considerable information about aspects of human reproduction but research shows that this can result in 'patchy understanding' (Harrison, 2000) and the DoH report would appear to support this view. A report on the provision of SRE in schools (DCSF, 2008) indicated that the *science* part of SRE was taught well, in fact the survey of young people's views suggested that SRE is *too biological*. It is the broader aspects of SRE that cause concern, i.e. teaching about the skills for coping with relationships and the feelings and emotions experienced during relationships.

You may be expected to teach an SRE-related topic so it is important that you are aware of which topics are taught in science.

Task 5.5.1 **Sex and health-related topics in the science curriculum**

Obtain copies of the science department's schemes of work for KS3 and the examination syllabus taught at KS4 and identify which sex and health topics are in the curriculum.

■ What topics are related specifically to sex and health education?
■ In which year group are these topics covered?
■ Are any of the topics revisited as the pupils get older?

This inquiry should help you to appreciate your responsibilities for teaching aspects of sex and health education. Make a note of any topics you need to revise before you teach them. Note also any resources available in your school that you need to review to assess their suitability for your classes.

Whole-school policy

Before you plan your approach to teaching these topics you need to appreciate how the teaching of sex and health-related issues in science lessons fits in with the school SRE policy. The guidance given to schools by the DCSF makes it clear that effective sex and relationship education is to be firmly rooted in the framework for PHSE. The aim of SRE is to equip pupils with skills, knowledge and understanding and in this respect it is much like any other part of the curriculum. However, sex and health-related issues are often controversial and need sensitive handling at an individual and group level (Turner, 2000).

The pupils in your classes may well represent a wide range of divergent views on contraception. Differences about sexual morality and religious views on sexual behaviour have to be taken into account unless we plan to teach pupils merely the biological facts about sex and reproduction. For a summary of the moral perspectives of six religious groups on aspects of sex education refer to Jennifer Harrison's *Sex Education in Secondary Schools* (Harrison, 2000).

While a small number of new science teachers feel confident about teaching sex and relationship education, for many it is a daunting prospect. Talking to other teachers about their experiences in teaching SRE is often reassuring. Many teachers will have some very funny stories to tell you as well as helpful hints to help you cope with any feelings of embarrassment you might feel when using words such as 'clitoris' or 'penis' in front of a class for the first time. Experienced teachers in your school are likely to have a clear idea about the questions that you may be asked and how you might answer them sensitively. While it is important to understand how to teach the 'plumbing' of sexual reproduction, it is through eliciting and discussing the pupils' questions that the 'relationship' part of SRE is best covered.

The most helpful guidance is to be well prepared, not just in your subject knowledge (and any good biology textbook will help in this respect), but also in the way you intend to handle questions that are not appropriate for you to answer in a science lesson or questions you do not feel capable of answering. It is important, therefore, that you understand in which parts of the curriculum aspects of health and sex education are taught in your school.

Task 5.5.2 **Two aspects of teaching SRE**

For the review of SRE (DCSF, 2008) teachers were asked to comment on current SRE delivery. One of the key findings was that most teachers 'considered that the factual aspects of SRE and contraception were taught well, but that the teaching on the relationship aspects – sexuality, feelings and emotions, skills for coping with relationships and making decisions about sexual activity – was weak'.

Find the school's documentation for PHSE and the *Every Child Matters* programme and select some of the resources used in science and PHSE for one aspect of SRE.

1 Interview a teacher of PHSE and a teacher of science to find out about the approaches used in these lessons.
2 Does what you have found out support the views reported in the survey? Analyse the responses from the teachers to ascertain how much emphasis there is on providing factual information, and how much on discussion of feelings and emotions. Does this emphasis vary between PHSE and science? How do the teaching approaches vary between PHSE and science? Why do you think this might be?
3 Do you think the rights parents have to withdraw their children from SRE should still exist when PHSE is statutory? Justify your answer with reference to both the science curriculum and the PHSE curriculum.

Task 5.5.2 helps you to identify which aspects of the SRE and Health Education curricula come within the remit of the science department. It should also reassure you that even if you feel your teaching in science seems divorced from the discussion and reflection that pupils need to develop a fuller understanding of their sexual health, this need is being addressed elsewhere in the curriculum. It also gives you the confidence to avoid such discussion should you feel ill-equipped to cope with this style of teaching in your class.

The legal aspects

You need to be aware of legal aspects about sex and the law. Below are those that are most pertinent to young people of secondary-school age:

- The age of consent to sexual activity is 16.
- Children under the age of 16 do not commit an offence if they take part in sexual activity with an adult.
- It is an offence of strict liability for an adult to take part in sexual activity with a child under 13. If the offender is under 18 there is a lesser maximum penalty.
- An adult is not guilty of an offence because he takes part in sexual activity with a girl under the age of 16 but not under the age of 13, if he has reasonable grounds to believe the girl to be aged 16 or over.
- A boy aged 13 could be liable for offences of sexual activity with a child.
- Homosexual acts between adults are legal provided that they both consent, are both 16 or over and the act takes place in private.

As legislation changes regularly, you need to keep up to date with any changes in the law. For further information concerning sex and the law, the Brook website is very helpful (see *Relevant websites*). The inclusion of these aspects of the law in this unit is not to suggest that you should be teaching them to your classes but to raise your awareness of their existence and to give you confidence should you be asked by your pupils about such matters.

It is worth noting the guidance on sexual orientation provided by the DfEE:

> The Secretary of State for Education and Employment is clear that teachers should be able to deal honestly and sensitively with sexual orientation, answer appropriate questions and offer support. There should be no direct promotion of sexual orientation.
>
> (DfEE, 2000: 13)

Textbooks and many teaching materials assume intercourse is heterosexual and you need to think about how your use of language might expose your own views on sexual orientation. For instance, are you using language that makes an assumption that all the children you teach are heterosexual or come from heterosexual families? It is important that you consider this point for all matters related to sex and health education.

Unit 12 of the PHSE Key Stage 4 curriculum contains a 'true or false' quiz which you may find helpful. It is reproduced in Figure 5.5.1.

Young people and the law

Mark each statement true or false.

1 Parents have a legal right to withdraw a pupil at secondary school from any sex education that is not part of the science National Curriculum.   T / F

2 It is illegal for a school to teach about homosexuality.   T / F

3 A 16-year-old can get married with the permission of their parent(s)/carer(s).   T / F

4 A pharmacist/chemist is allowed to refuse to sell emergency contraception to a pupil under 16.   T / F

5 A girl under the age of 16 cannot legally have an abortion.   T / F

6 People of all ages can buy condoms.   T / F

7 If a 14-year-old goes to a family planning clinic or their GP for contraceptive services their parent(s)/carer(s) have to be told.   T / F

8 Schools may display information about local and national contraceptive services.   T / F

9 The age of consent for gay men is 18.   T / F

10 If a 15-year-old pupil tells a teacher in confidence that they are having a sexual relationship, that teacher is legally bound to keep what has been said confidential.   T / F

(Adapted from de Meza and de Silva, 2004)

Answers are available online:
http://www.qca.org.uk/libraryAssets/media/qca-05-1695-pshe-unit12.pdf

---

▨ **Figure 5.5.1** True/false quiz

The need for ground rules

It is wise to establish ground rules for any classroom discussions, but this is of particular importance when talking about potentially sensitive topics. Pupils sometimes ask their teachers personal questions because they trust their advice and want the benefit of their experience, but keeping discussions to a theoretical level avoids a number of pitfalls.

Task 5.5.3 **The need for ground rules**

This task requires you to reflect on how many of your personal details you are willing to reveal to your class and to plan the 'ground rules' you expect your class to follow in your lessons.

1 Consider the implications of answering these pupils' questions:
   ▪ Are you married?
   ▪ Do you have a girlfriend/boyfriend?
   ▪ Do you have children?
   ▪ Do you smoke?

■ How much do you drink?

■ Have you ever taken drugs?

2 Consider which questions you would definitely not answer.

3 What does it imply to the pupils if you are prepared to answer some personal questions and not others?

Some of the answers to the questions may be obvious to pupils if you are an established teacher in a school. However, pupils are unlikely to know personal details about you as a student teacher on school experience except that they will probably know whether you smoke or not, and they may feel uncomfortable being told about the hazards of cigarette smoking to their health by someone who is obviously ignoring the advice themselves.

Task 5.5.4 **Developing ground rules**

This task enables you to plan the ground rules to use with your classes. Although you probably want to ask your classes to suggest the rules themselves it is a good idea to have some idea of what you want beforehand. Consider this list and identify the rules that you think the pupils may suggest and the rules you may have to introduce yourself.

■ We must listen to each other's opinions.

■ We must respect different points of view.

■ We must be able to change our minds.

■ We should use the correct biological words whenever possible.

■ We won't ask personal questions.

What other rules do you think should be added?

HEALTH EDUCATION

Ask pupils to draw a healthy person and they are likely to draw someone who has a big smile and looks happy. They appreciate that being healthy is not just about an absence of illness but is also about the state of mind and social wellbeing of a person. Being healthy is about being confident to make informed decisions and being able to function within your own community. It is worth considering a little further what you mean by 'healthy'.

Task 5.5.5 **What does 'being healthy' mean?**

This task helps you to clarify your thoughts on what being healthy means. It is also a useful introductory activity to use with your pupils as it engenders a lot of discussion, always a good start to a topic.

Indicate on the list of statements below whether you agree or disagree with each one.

Being healthy is...	Agree	Disagree
enjoying being with people		
hardly ever taking medicine		
being able to run for a bus		
not smoking		
being the ideal weight		
being able to adapt to changes in my life		
eating the 'right foods'		
being able to touch my toes		
not being ill very often		

If possible, share your decisions with other science teachers or student teachers. Can you suggest how your science teaching can promote the skills pupils need in order that they can choose a healthy lifestyle for themselves?

Teaching about a balanced diet, drugs and alcohol abuse

Although children spend only one fifth of their time in school the contribution of schools to their wellbeing can be highly significant. Many primary and secondary schools have achieved National Healthy Schools Status (NHSS) and have strengthened their policies relating to healthy eating, physical activity and emotional wellbeing within the PHSE programme. A Healthy School provides:

■ a supportive environment, including policies on smoking and healthy and nutritious food, with time and facilities for physical activity and sport both within and beyond the curriculum; and
■ comprehensive PHSE which includes education on relationships, sex, drugs and alcohol as well as other issues that can affect young people's lives such as emotional difficulties and bereavement.

(DoH, 2004: 5–56)

A key issue here for secondary teachers is that the work covered in these topics needs to *build on* what pupils have covered at KS2. In the primary school they learn about the importance of an adequate and varied diet and the effects on the human body of tobacco, alcohol and other drugs. They may have drawn posters to promote giving up smoking and drawn meals on paper plates that promote healthy eating, and the work at KS3 must take this into account.

Legal aspects

Information about the effects and associated risks of drugs and alcohol, including relevant street names for different illegal drugs or controlled substances can be found on the website www.talktofrank.com. This website also contains clear guidelines as to the law relating to individual drugs and, as such laws can be changed, you will need to check the following information is still current:

- Illegal drugs are classified Class A, B or C with Class A considered to be most harmful.
- Class A drugs include ecstasy, LSD, heroin, cocaine, crack and magic mushrooms (whether prepared or fresh).
- The penalties for possession of a Class A drug are up to seven years in prison and/or an unlimited fine.
- Dealing in a Class A drug, which includes giving it to friends for no charge, can result in a life prison sentence and/or an unlimited fine.
- Class B drugs include cannabis and amphetamines.
- Being caught in possession of Class B drugs can result in a five-year prison sentence and an unlimited fine. The actual penalty is likely to depend on the amount of drug that is in someone's possession, their age and whether or not it is their first offence.
- Someone caught dealing in Class B drugs can go to prison for up to 14 years.
- Class C drugs include ketamine, tranquilisers like temazepam and some painkillers.
- Possessing Class C drugs can result in a two-year prison sentence, while the penalty for dealing is up to 14 years.
- Dealing in drugs on or near school premises, at or around the time when young people are present there, is a very serious offence known as aggravated supply.
- Cigarettes and other tobacco products cannot be legally sold to anyone under the age of 18.

The *Talk to Frank* website also gives the complicated details as to the legality of sale and consumption of alcohol, on and off licensed premises.

TEACHING STRATEGIES

There is a range of teaching strategies you could adopt when teaching sex and health education but many science teachers avoid the more creative teaching methods. There is no reason to leave the more innovative methods to PHSE/Citizenship teachers; science teachers need to select appropriate methods for the topic and age of the pupils.

As so much of sex and health education involves pupils engaging in discussion and making decisions about their personal life, it can make lessons uncomfortable for them. To avoid pupils having to give details about their own lifestyle or information that is too personal, you can use 'distancing techniques'.

These techniques enable pupils to question and discuss topics that are of interest to them without having to disclose personal details. For example, they could watch a video where the characters act out a situation that raises questions that the class can discuss. The pupils can talk about the issues regarding the characters and at the same time raise issues that concern them. You may find the Channel 4 sex education programme website 'Let's Talk Sex' useful in this respect (see *Relevant websites*).

Case studies with invented characters, theatre productions and role plays are other examples of distancing techniques. Pupils are able to introduce issues into the discussions without exposing their own ignorance or experiences; they can explore the consequences of certain behaviours without indicating what they would do, or have done, themselves. Nevertheless, pupils need to be able to get the answers to specific questions that trouble them, but how this is facilitated requires careful consideration. Imagine the potential result should a teacher invite pupils to ask *any* questions during a lesson. A common technique used to address pupils' queries is the 'question box' where pupils are allowed to write down any questions they have (without their names on) and place them in a box.

Task 5.5.6 **The 'question box' technique**

This task enables you to reflect on using the question box technique and to consider how you would ensure its successful use in the classroom. Ideally you should be carrying out this activity with a class you teach. However, if you are not scheduled to teach this topic with one of your classes you can still obtain pupils' questions but you will have to agree with the teacher beforehand how the pupils' questions will be answered.

1 Negotiate with the science department to find a class where you can set up a question box at the beginning of the topic on human reproduction. Alternatively, negotiate with the PHSE/Citizenship co-ordinator to set up the box at the beginning of the topic Sex Education.
2 Explain the activity to the pupils and leave the box in a place that is accessible.
3 Empty the box and sort the questions out into these categories:
   a Questions that should be answered in the science lessons and questions that you think would be addressed better in PHSE/Citizenship lessons (see Task 5.5.1).
   b Questions that you don't know the answers to but do think should be answered (consider whether science or PHSE/Citizenship lessons).
   c Questions you don't think are suitable to be answered in class.
4 Discuss with the class teacher how departments need to liaise with one another to answer pupils' questions. How will you deal with questions in category b?
5 What resources are available in the school to help you answer questions in category c?
6 Consider how you would have dealt with all these questions had you opened the box and read the questions out for the first time in front of the class.

Another important aim when teaching SRE is to give pupils the opportunity to rehearse forms of language using technical terminology (see Task 5.5.7). They will certainly be able to appreciate the difference between forms of language when comparing slang names and scientific names for the parts of the body.

Task 5.5.7 **Technical language used in science**

Collect the resources used by the science teachers when teaching sex and health. Look at the materials and study the language used. Consider how many of these terms the pupils might be meeting for the first time, for example, *uterus*, *menstruation*, *ovulation*, *placenta*, *testis*, *scrotal sac*. Pupils may well have an understanding of the concepts but may not use these biological terms in their explanations.

Some teachers adopt a technique known as the 'graffiti board' where the pupils put forward words that they know are commonly used to describe the human reproductive parts and processes and these are written on the board. Then the correct terms are identified and pupils are subsequently expected to use these in lessons. You might feel that this is inappropriate but it is important that we acknowledge that pupils are familiar with a rather different vocabulary from the one we would wish them to use in the classroom.

We must ensure that the pupils can use the correct terminology, for example by having clearly labelled diagrams readily available and having key words on the board or around the room. Familiarity with the new words may help to reduce their embarrassment and enable them to use the terms in the correct way, thereby also reinforcing the correct spellings of the words.

A typical activity used in school is to ask pupils to label the diagrams of the human reproductive systems, copying from a book or from an image on the interactive whiteboard, and then finding out the function of each part. Alternatively, they could be asked to describe, draw the shape or make models of each part so they have to consider the relative size of the various parts, how many there are and where they are located in relation to each other. If pupils then find out the function of the parts it may help them to make associations between structure and function.

Task 5.5.8 **Devising activities for the classroom**

This task requires you to devise an activity that develops pupils' literacy skills. Select a health topic taught in KS3 and devise an activity using one of the following tasks:

■ Analyse teenage letters pages; what knowledge and attitudes are portrayed in the letters?
■ Analyse two newspaper articles on the same topic; which one has the more detailed and accurate scientific content?
■ Role play – make a video of a discussion between two people of opposing views.
■ Using ICT – make a PowerPoint presentation presenting alternative views.
■ Write an article for a school magazine presenting an argument for and against an issue.

An important idea in discussions of health is the concept of risk. Pupils need to understand how health risks can be affected by lifestyle choices, such as the risk of getting lung cancer from smoking.

Using data which helps pupils assess the risks to their health if they smoke, drink alcohol or take drugs (that are not medicines) make the topic more relevant to them and also involve them in using numeracy skills. Causes-of-death statistics for different age groups can be obtained from the Office for National Statistics. You may find it helpful to liaise with the mathematics department to find out when the pupils study probability so that they can appreciate how to estimate risk. (See 'Probability and risk' in Unit 5.4 for a fuller discussion of teaching the concept of risk.)

RESOURCES

Some of the topics that come under the umbrella of 'health and sex education' are controversial and/or the subject of ongoing research. To keep abreast of these developments, you can find up-to-date information, resources and materials supplied by a number of organisations. Among these are:

- The Wellcome Trust
- The Institute of Biology
- The Department of Health
- health education authorities
- television programmes for schools
- *Teachers TV.*

(See *Relevant websites.*)

SUMMARY AND KEY POINTS

Teaching pupils about keeping healthy is a topic that will, hopefully, always be a part of the science curriculum. However, the issues included under this title will naturally always be subject to change.

What changes can you look forward to in the future? The substances identified as commonly used drugs are likely to alter as new drugs become available and the legal status of existing drugs may also change. Links between certain diseases and lifestyle may become more evident.

Of course, not everything is subject to change. The bodily changes at the onset of puberty are unlikely to alter (although the average age at which they begin might). The 'natural way' for conceiving a baby will not change although new techniques for promoting fertility may well be developed.

Our role as science teachers is to ensure that we keep abreast of changes and work with other departments to develop the knowledge and skills of pupils in order that they can become informed and responsible citizens, able to understand issues of risk and to make decisions about their own lives, taking into account how these decisions affect other people.

FURTHER READING

De Silva, S. and De Meza, L. (2004) *More About Life: Sex and Relationship Education in Secondary School.* London: Forbes Publications Ltd.

This is a comprehensive teaching pack for teaching about sex and relationship education in secondary schools within the context of PHSE.

DfEE (2000) *Sex and Relationship Guidance*. **London: DfEE.**

This document clarifies what schools are required to do by law but the most useful section for student teachers is the section on practical strategies for teaching some of the sensitive issues which may need to be tackled. It is also worth noting the guidance concerning confidentiality.

Harrison, J. (1999) 'Reproduction and sex education', in Reiss, M. (ed.) *Teaching Secondary Biology.* **London: John Murray for the ASE.**

This chapter concerns asexual and sexual reproduction in both plants and animals. However, section 6.3 *Human reproduction and sex education*, gives you some useful suggestions for teaching ideas and highlights concepts that pupils often find confusing or difficult to understand.

Harrison, J. (2000) *Sex Education in Secondary Schools.* **Buckingham: Open University Press.**

This book contains a comprehensive background to policies on sex education together with practical guidelines and resources that are particularly helpful for student teachers.

RELEVANT WEBSITES

Brook

A long-established charity offering free and confidential advice specifically to the under-25s. Its website, www.brook.org.uk, contains quizzes and games and gives teachers and young people access to a wide range of relevant publications.

Department of Health

Annual reports on relevant statistics can be found at:
http://www.dh.gov.uk/en/Publicationsandstatistics/Publications/AnnualReports/DH_084908

Medical Foundation for AIDS and Sexual Health

http://www.medfash.org.uk/ (accessed 1 July 2009).

Office for National Statistics

Recent government statistics on, for example, teenage pregnancy and abortion rates can be accessed through the website at:
www.statistics.gov.uk (accessed 1 July 2009).

Every Child Matters

Full details of the agenda can be found at:
www.dcsf.gov.uk/everychildmatters/ (accessed 1 July 2009).

Youth Health Talk

A website about young people's real life experiences of health and lifestyle can be accessed at:
http://www.youthhealthtalk.org/Home (accessed 1 July 2009).

Health Talk

A resource for professional organisations and everyone involved in healthcare teaching and learning can be found at: http://www.healthtalkonline.org/TeachingAndLearning (accessed 1 July 2009).

Talk to Frank

www.talktofrank.com is an independent government funded website where young people can access information about drugs and can also ask questions and seek advice on drug-related matters (accessed 1 July 2009).

Channel 4 *Let's Talk Sex*

http://www.channel4.com/learning/microsites/L/lifestuff/content/up_close/letstalksex/stories.html (accessed 1 July 2009).

Sex Education Forum (2008) *Young People's Charter on SRE*. London: National Children's Bureau

http://partner.ncb.org.uk/dotpdf/open_access_2/sef_ypcharter_a4.pdf (accessed 1 July 2009).

UNIT
5.6

BEYOND THE CLASSROOM

Ruth Amos

INTRODUCTION

This unit encourages you to use out-of-classroom activities for pupils learning science and to be alert to such opportunities. Learning outside the classroom is often described as informal, and in-class experience as formal, learning (Wellington and Ireson, 2008: 319–23) and their definitions are worth exploring for yourself and with other educators.

Learning outside the classroom can give reality and purpose to science lessons (Braund and Reiss, 2006), helping pupils to contextualise their world within school science. Science concepts can make more sense whilst sampling plants in a habitat (adaptation), observing folding in rock strata or discussing objects and artefacts at a museum. Pupils may develop a sense of wonder about the world (Goodwin, 2001). There is growing evidence that 'fieldwork . . . offers learners opportunities to develop their knowledge and skills in ways that add value to their everyday experiences in the classroom' (Dillon *et al.*, 2006: 107).

The Professional Standards for Qualified Teacher status in England require you to be able to 'identify opportunities for learners to learn in out-of-school contexts' (TDA, 2008), thus recognising the importance of contexts beyond the classroom to develop and broaden pupils' understanding. The National Curriculum for Key Stage 3 (KS3, QCA, 2007: 212) states that 'pupils should be offered opportunities to . . . work safely in the field, use real-life examples as a basis for finding out about science . . . and to . . . experience science outside the school environment'. Fieldwork, as well as visits to industry, universities and other sites of scientific interest, gives pupils access to such opportunities. In Unit 3.2, we explored how the current NC focuses upon the global dimensions of science; working with pupils outside the classroom can open up a wealth of opportunities to explore sustainable development and environmental issues, as well as understanding of different cultures. At KS4, fieldwork contributes to a number of strands of *How Science Works*, such as data collection and risk (see Unit 2.3).

OBJECTIVES

By the end of this unit you should be:

■ convinced of the importance of relating science beyond the classroom to the science curriculum
■ aware of the range of resources which enable you to place science in interesting contexts, including fieldwork in the environment
■ able to plan and carry out some teaching outside the classroom
■ aware of the advantages of residential fieldwork for teaching science
■ alerted to the safety and legal factors when undertaking fieldwork.

Check the requirements of your course to see which relate to this unit.

OPPORTUNITIES

Beyond the classroom: why fieldwork?

Fieldwork traditionally forms part of learning science and may be carried out in lesson time, on one-day excursions or residential courses. Fieldwork encompasses investigations done outside, seeing the effects of science or technology on our lives or visiting a site of special interest such as a museum, local graveyard or field centre. Some courses, such as Salters Horners physics (SHAP, 2003), require pupils, as part of AS coursework assessment, to visit a site of industrial and scientific importance and report on their visit.

Fieldwork can also help to raise awareness of the interactions between science and technology with the natural and made environment. However, many schools have excellent in-house resources, and video and the internet can bring a world of images and information into the classroom, so why undertake fieldwork when it is, after all, more challenging to organise than laboratory work? Plants and animals in the wild do not perform to order and successful visits to most sites depend on advanced planning involving a pre-visit.

The broad educational benefits of fieldwork can include:

■ promoting enthusiasm for science and the natural and made environment
■ encouraging a lifelong interest in some aspects of those environments
■ broadening understanding of how science and technology interact and are part of our lives
■ promoting awareness of issues around environmental damage and protection
■ revealing the impact of humans on the environment
■ developing positive attitudes towards the environment
■ encouraging speculation and discussion.

Fieldwork is important because it is, sometimes, the only way for pupils to truly experience some phenomena, e.g. the diversity of living things, the motion of the stars and planets or the effects of pollution.

■ **Figure 5.6.1** Inner-city Key Stage 3 pupils exploring a rocky shore, Pembrokeshire, Wales

In relation to the science curriculum, fieldwork can allow pupils to:

■   increase their knowledge of science
■   develop process skills, e.g. plan and practise inquiries and whole investigations
■   understand how numerical and other data are collected in the field
■   use data-logging equipment (Fearn, 2006)
■   develop small-group work skills
■   bring recordings/observations into school for further study
■   prepare and give presentations.

From a management point of view, pupils have greater freedom to discuss, interact and move outside the classroom. This enhanced freedom can be daunting to inexperienced teachers but usually has a beneficial effect on behaviour and generates motivation. However, a successful visit does need to be carefully organised.

Task 5.6.1 **Joining in a field visit or excursion**

Discuss opportunities with your mentor for taking part in a school visit or excursion during your placement. If appropriate, offer to supervise one or more activities planned for the trip or, with support, plan an activity. Taking part in a science-based field visit would be ideal but taking part in an outdoor activity in another subject area can also be beneficial.

Keep a record of how the trip was planned and carried out; the checklist in Figure 5.6.2 may help you. Collect your impressions of the pupils you worked with. The headings below may help you structure your perceptions:

■ knowledge: what pupils knew about the visit and intended learning before and what they gained from the task
■ understanding: could pupils explain what they were doing and why; could pupils explain how the data and observations they collected would help them meet the learning outcomes for the activity?
■ attitude: were pupils motivated to tackle the task; did they enjoy the experience and consider the activity worthwhile?

Working outside the classroom can involve using normal lesson time in the school grounds or nearby, but more ambitious activities may require a half-day or whole-day visit. Occasionally, a residential field visit may be planned. We turn first to the use of regular classroom time, such as a timetabled period.

FIELDWORK IN LESSON TIME

Most schools have a playground, which is a source of habitats, materials and structures. Others have a playing-field or access to open spaces. Planned carefully, an hour's science lesson can be taught outside the classroom. Some activities are taught outside because they need space to be effective; others can only be taught outside. Ideas for activities and a discussion of associated planning are discussed below.

Activities

A variety of data can be collected in the school grounds or in local sites of interest, for example:

■ measuring the length of a shadow as part of estimating the Earth's size (Ogborn *et al.*, 1996a)
■ identifying building materials
■ estimating animal populations. Some pupils may regard small animals such as insects as insignificant; or be unaware of the diversity of insect population or that some small animals are abundant and economically important, e.g. worms
■ reading instruments in a weather station. Helping pupils to connect physical measurements, such as pressure, humidity etc., to the changing weather patterns and to national weather forecasting

- sampling soils to relate, e.g. differences in plant populations to soil profile
- studying leaves to reveal variation in one plant (Bebbington, 2006), within a species or as part of a wider study of diversity
- following a science trail to identify areas for study (Borrows, 1999; Murphy and Murphy, 2002a)
- examining headstones for evidence of weathering
- monitoring river pollution levels (Sanderson, 2006).

The March 2006 special issue edition of *School Science Review* was dedicated to outdoor science and gives ten good examples of out-of-classroom activities across the sciences.

Task 5.6.2 **Planning a science trail**

Explore the school buildings and grounds to identify sites of interest to include in a science trail that could be experienced by pupils within a period. The stations should have a common focus (see collection of data above).

Identify a topic or short sequence of lessons you expect to teach; or choose a topic of interest to yourself. Identify 4–6 stations that would provide interest and motivation and contribute to understanding of the topic. For each station:

1 Identify the locality and what pupils are expected to look for and record.
2 Explain for yourself the science involved.
3 Prepare an explanation of the science for the pupils, or better still, construct a series of questions which allow them to explore the station and then to explain observed phenomena.
4 Link the pupils' experiences to the topic and hence to the SoW.

Draft a record sheet for pupils to use on the trail. Discuss your notes and record sheet with your class teacher or mentor. Where possible try out the trail with a group of pupils. Creating clues, perhaps involving digital photographs, to lead pupils from one station to another can improve engagement and motivation and add an element of challenge. Evaluate the learning outcomes for the activity and build upon these for your next attempts.

Demonstrating phenomena

Examples of activities that may work well outside include:

- developing a timeline for the age of the universe (Murphy and Murphy, 2002b)
- comparing the speed of sound with the speed of light (needs a very large playing-field)
- modelling states of matter using pupils as molecules
- the Doppler effect (Weaver, 2006)
- launching a water rocket.

Planning

Working outside the laboratory depends partly on your own attitude to teaching, and experience, but also on departmental policy. As a student teacher you cannot take a group of pupils outside on your own, the class teacher or another qualified person must be with you. Your school will have an educational visits co-ordinator (EVC) who will be able to guide you as well.

Successful outcomes depend on checking out the proposed site in advance (not too far ahead, though, as local activity can change sites rather suddenly). When planning your lesson, consider factors such as the:

- length of a period and what is possible
- class size and your ability to supervise the activities safely
- guidelines and routines to emphasise to ensure safe and sensible behaviour
- suitability of sites for outside study
- safety factors, e.g. road traffic, local ponds, unpleasant plants or pupils susceptible to hay fever
- role of the regular class teacher in your activity.

Figure 5.6.2 may help you plan such an activity.

The weather can adversely affect plans so have a non-fieldwork activity ready in case it really is too challenging to go outside. Some activities can actually be undertaken by looking through the window. For example, the Earth Science Education Unit (ESEU) based at Keele University has an excellent range of resources on its website, including various 'through the window' activities (see *Relevant websites*).

GOING OFF-SITE

One-day excursions or residential courses allow opportunities for activities which cannot be carried out in lessons or in school. The new environment often stimulates motivation and greater engagement (Amos and Reiss, 2006). You may get to know your colleagues better and see pupils in a different light. Parental permission is required for all activities outside the school grounds, even if you are only walking to a local site down the road. Be alert to the opportunity to join a field visit and offer to help with planning and preparation. The EVC in your school should have a plan and checklist for fieldwork to which you should refer (see Task 5.6.3).

Pupils need explicit guidance and advice about behaving appropriately in outdoor areas frequented by members of the public. In addition, farm animals or dogs out for a walk can elicit a surprising amount of curiosity, and occasionally unease, amongst pupils who normally reside in urban areas. Clear guidelines are vital to ensure the wearing of sensible outdoor clothing and shoes (not their £90 trainers!), sunhats and sunscreen (or woolly hats and gloves) and so on. Some of the potential problems can be alleviated by preparing a 'kit' checklist for parents/carers. Recommend that pupils bring only small amounts of money on a day/residential field visit and that electronic equipment as far as possible stays at home. Most schools have clear policies on whether pupils can take mobile phones on field visits (this may be different from the usual in-school 'no mobiles' policy as some parents/guardians are keen to be in mobile communication with their children whilst they are away). Any pupils who have to take regular medication need to

Aims

- What are the learning objectives for, and proposed outcomes of, the activity?
- How are the objectives achieved by working outside?
- Are there guidelines for the activity in the SoW or elsewhere?

Legal and safety issues

Have you:

- discussed the proposal with your class teacher?
- carried out a risk assessment on the site?
- identified any special safety issues to be observed?
- planned your briefing to pupils to cover behavioural and safety issues?
- planned adequate supervision by you and the class teacher?
- checked that your pupils can work outside without risk, e.g. none has allergies?

Preparation and planning

Have you:

- tried out the activity yourself and checked that it can be carried out on the chosen site in the time available?
- checked that data obtained can be used to meet your objectives and achieve your learning outcomes?
- prepared briefing for pupils, including instructions and record sheets as well as safety and behavioural matters?
- checked the availability of equipment for the number of pupils in your class and discussed your requirements with technical staff?
- planned how the equipment is to be distributed and returned (using pupils as monitors, for example)?
- checked whether pupils need instruction about how to use the equipment you select?
- planned timings for briefing, departure, work and return?
- ensured that pupils know what to do with data on return to the classroom. Are the data to be followed up immediately or later?
- decided where the data are to be kept between now and the next lesson?
- planned, as needed, an appropriate homework task?
- reminded pupils, prior to the activity, to bring sun/rain protection as necessary?

■ **Figure 5.6.2** Checklist for planning a short outside activity

have it available; often a member of staff will look after all medical treatments but some pupils may need to carry their own so always double-check that everyone has whatever they need with them before you leave school.

Sites of special interest

Many schools arrange activities at a variety of sites. Examples include:

- hands-on science centres (Wellington and Ireson, 2008)
- local or national museums (Griffin, 2002)

- a neighbourhood industry
- waste disposal, recycling and water-treatment sites
- waterways, ponds and bridges.

MUSEUMS AND HANDS-ON CENTRES

Planning a visit to a museum or hands-on centre can be challenging. Falk and Dierking (2000) advise paying attention to three contexts for learning in informal settings: the personal, social and physical. Most museums require pre-booking for school groups so be sure to check, and book ahead in plenty of time. In addition, specific galleries (such as the Launch Pad at the Science Museum in London) allow groups specifically allocated time. Demonstration shows may be on offer, so ask in advance. Where possible, allowing pupils to explore a museum gallery freely first, then bringing them back to the same gallery later in the visit, can help to overcome the initial 'novelty value' (DeWitt and Osborne, 2007). Naturally, adequate supervision has to be in place for all activities but as long as galleries are a manageable size, it is possible for teachers to position themselves strategically to allow pupils to explore freely. Ask pupils to choose a 'buddy' with whom they spend the day (checking that they are in the appropriate place etc.). When planning a museum or centre visit, the guidance for organising fieldwork is broadly applicable and, in addition, think about the following:

- a pre-task at school to help orientate pupils to what they will explore
- a mix of free-choice exploration and semi-structured learning in the gallery/centre ('who am I?' photographs showing part of an object/artefact can help to engage pupils on a trail, but avoid worksheets unless you want the visit to be labelled as being 'just like school'!)
- build in peer discussion or collaborative approaches, where possible
- a post-visit activity to build upon the learning opportunities.

FIELD CENTRES

Many field centres organise teaching programmes for groups of pupils. Pupils generally respond well to a combination of adventure activity and subject-focused work, especially when the latter is subtly woven in. Measuring your heart rate whilst climbing, learning about forces whilst canoeing or examining geological features whilst abseiling alongside a waterfall can create memorable moments, to which learning can be linked in the longer-term. Whilst AS- or A-level coursework has often been the goal of traditional field-centre visits in science, younger pupils can also benefit from a residential experience. In addition to learning science, being away from home contributes to their growing independence and self-confidence. Opportunities for problem-solving and team-building can give a tremendous boost to pupil–pupil, and pupil–teacher relationships back at school.

■ **Figure 5.6.3** A science student teacher working with a group in the Space Gallery at the Science Museum, London

Task 5.6.3 **Planning a field visit**

If the opportunity arises, join in with a field visit. Use the checklist below to guide you through the approaches needed. Much of the guidance in Figure 5.6.2 is also pertinent here.

Educational objectives: identify:

1   the purposes of the trip and links with the SoW
2   the facilities at the field centre
3   how fieldwork is to be initiated and followed up in school
4   the contribution of fieldwork to preparation for coursework and possibly public examinations
5   the suitability of the field-centre resources.

Legal responsibilities: you should:

1   read the school (and Local Authority) regulations which apply to field trips
2   identify how the Health and Safety at Work Act applies
3   carry out risk assessments for travel and fieldwork
4   identify the responsibilities and rights of parents while their children are on residential courses

5   collect medical-requirement data for all participating pupils
6   collect contact details for parents/carers during the visit
7   know the agreement to which parents consent when they sanction a field visit for their child and how that consent is obtained
8   know the adult–pupil ratio which applies to travel and working in the field
9   know how insurance is effected for the trip
10 know how pupils can be helped financially to attend the course.

Advance planning: find out:

1   how pupils are briefed and prepared for the trip, including the Country Code of Practice
2   the equipment needed from the school and how that is identified, collected and delivered to the site
3   what pupils need to bring with them, and prepare the checklist for parents/carers
4   who prepares the written course materials
5   the domestic arrangements during the course
6   how to cost the trip and assess the parental contribution
7   the transport arrangements.

Safety: obtain copies of documents which identify:

1   guidelines for working and behaving at the field centre
2   special precautions/hazards associated with the particular field centre
3   arrangements made for pupils and parents to contact each other in an emergency
4   staff responsibilities, including responding to injured or unwell pupils.

Guidance on health and safety is given by the Health and Safety Executive (http://www.hse.gov.uk/schooltrips/).

What happens while you are away? Find out what you do about your teaching responsibilities; normally you will set cover work for all your classes and leave it with your head of science or subject mentor.

OTHER OPPORTUNITIES: PEOPLE WITH KNOWLEDGE OR EXPERTISE

It is highly motivating for pupils to listen to and talk with people whose specialist knowledge enriches the science curriculum. Outside speakers are particularly useful for controversial issues. Many professional and learned societies provide speakers, e.g. Institute of Biology, Institute of Electrical Engineers and the Medical Research Council. Parents and governors of the school may be a source of expertise. The Widening Participation Initiative (www.dcsf.gov.uk/hegateway/uploads/EWParticipation.pdf) has created more links between higher education institutions (HEIs) and schools. Many HEI science departments provide ambassadors (often research students) who go out to school to give demonstration lectures, master classes and careers advice. Also, as part of your teacher education course, you may be involved in out-of-classroom learning projects with pupils from partnership schools.

SUMMARY AND KEY POINTS

How planning for out-of-classroom learning proceeds is determined by teachers' attitudes and the contexts involved. Whatever your circumstances, there are often opportunities to go beyond the classroom when planning your lessons. Some schools promote cross-curricular field studies, e.g. geography and science, which can be very effective. What is possible depends on the local environment, your ability to identify opportunities and the support you get. In this unit we have made suggestions of ways to go beyond the classroom and suggest you regularly monitor the publications of your professional associations for further ideas.

Check the requirements of your course to see which relate to this unit.

FURTHER READING

DfES (2006) 'The learning outside the classroom manifesto'. London: Department for Education and Skills.

The manifesto was launched by the DfES (now the Department for Children, Schools and Families) to demonstrate renewed commitment to outdoor experiences. The website developed from the manifesto can be found at http://www.lotc.org.uk/ and contains advice and guidance on a whole range of issues. (Accessed 24 Sept 2009.)

Braund, M. and Reiss, M. (2004) *Learning Science Outside the Classroom*. London: Routledge Falmer.

A practical guide to using a wide range of informal, non-classroom-based contexts for science education. Risk assessment and safety issues are addressed.

Glackin, M. (2007) 'Using urban green space to teach science'. *School Science Review*, 89 (327), 29–36.

A very useful article for teachers in urban areas.

Lock, R., Slingsby, D. and Tilling S. (special edition eds) (2006) 'Outdoor science'. *School Science Review*, 87 (320), 23–111.

A very good collection of ideas and activities for outdoor learning in science.

Reiss, M. (ed.) (1999) *Teaching Secondary Biology*. London: John Murray for the ASE.

An excellent resource addressing many important topics in the teaching of biology. Chapter 9 discusses ecology and provides valuable advice about using the environment and undertaking fieldwork.

SHAP (Salters Horners Advanced Physics) (2003) *Exemplar Coursework: Visits*.

Downloadable from: http://www.edexcel.com/quals/gce/gce-leg/physics/salters/Pages/default.aspx (accessed 15 December 2009)

QCA (Qualifications and Curriculum Authority) (2007) *Programmes of Study, National Curriculum for Science at Key Stage 3 and Key Stage 4*.

Wellington, J. and Ireson, G. (2008) *Science Learning, Science Teaching*. London: Routledge.

Chapter 12 contains discussion on formal and informal learning and about using secondary sources in science lessons. There is an interesting and practical section on interactive science centres.

RELEVANT WEBSITES

Earth Science Education Unit (ESEU) based at Keele University

http://www.earthscienceeducation.com/ (accessed 3 July 2009).

This has an excellent range of online resources and ideas for teaching earth sciences.

Health and Safety Executive

http://www.hse.gov.uk/schooltrips/ (accessed 3 July 2009).

Provides advice and guidance on risk assessment for fieldwork and out of school visits.

The National Curriculum (2009)

http://curriculum.qca.org.uk/ (accessed 3 July 2009).

The Training and Development Agency for Schools

http://www.tda.gov.uk/ (accessed 3 July 2009).

Salters Horners Physics

http://www.york.ac.uk/org/seg/salters/physics/ (accessed 3 July 2009).

ASSESSMENT IN SCIENCE

INTRODUCTION

This chapter describes and contrasts two types of assessment: formative and summative. Formative assessment is that carried out by teachers to enhance learning and is known as Assessment for Learning (AfL). It also includes self-assessment by the pupils. In contrast, summative assessment (assessment *of* learning), is associated with certification and selection and is used to inform pupils of what they have achieved at the end of a course. Results of summative assessment may also be used for selecting people for jobs or higher education, and as data in the published annual 'performance tables' of schools.

Assessing for learning is an essential part of teaching and it has been a strong theme in earlier units (particularly in those in Chapter 4 on planning), so do not be led into thinking you can leave worrying about assessment until after you have mastered teaching. Christine Harrison, in Unit 6.1, describes a range of assessment strategies that can be used as part of your routine teaching and explains the underlying rationale. The unit is based on research and in-service work with teachers.

Another important task for teachers is to prepare pupils for external assessments and examinations such as GCSE. Examination results are high-stakes assessment; they provide individuals with a sense of achievement and influence future action. For similar reasons they are important to parents. Examination results affect the standing of the school locally and nationally and influence the popularity of the school to prospective parents. For these reasons, preparing pupils for external assessments and examinations receives high priority in schools. Finding out about the scheme of assessment associated with any course you teach has to be done as soon as possible.

ASSESSMENT FOR LEARNING

Christine Harrison

INTRODUCTION

Assessment in schools has three main purposes:

1 to support learning
2 for review, transfer and certification
3 for informing on school improvement and accountability.

The first of these purposes, to support learning, is by far the most important in the day-to-day work of teachers and students in schools. Yet, when people hear the word 'assessment', they generally think of the second purpose and see assessment as tests and examinations and for many, assessment is associated with stressful times either revising and sitting examinations or waiting for results. At the present time, children in England face around 80 high-stakes examinations or tests, the first within seven weeks of starting school. The burden of testing and the perceived need to keep written records of attainment to satisfy the second and third purposes of assessment has skewed how some teachers and some pupils think about assessment. Testing and the documentation of achievement have taken time and focus away from quality interactions between teacher and pupils and have undermined the role and importance of AfL.

OBJECTIVES

By the end of this unit you should:

- recognise what AfL looks like in the classroom
- know some of the assessment strategies that support learning
- begin to see how formative assessment fits alongside summative assessment
- be aware of the importance of involving the learner in the assessment process.

The word assessment derives from the Latin 'assidere', which means to sit beside, which sets a quite different hue to the meaning of the word from the feelings often experienced in the examination hall. While assessment does encompass summative examinations and may include tests intermittently, by far the main way that teachers need to use assessment is as a day-to-day tool in their classroom for monitoring learning and taking decisions about what to teach next. This more regular form of assessment is often called *Assessment for Learning*. This term was coined to distinguish it from assessment *of* learning; the difference being that the former informs the learning process while the latter provides a measure at a fixed point in the process. AfL can also be described as formative if the evidence from the assessment process is used to drive the next stage of teaching and learning. There is a body of firm evidence that formative assessment can raise standards (Black and Wiliam, 1998) and so it is an area of your practice worthy of the time spent in developing it.

There are no simple recipes for developing formative practices and the many educational experiments that featured in the review of formative assessment, *Inside the Black Box*, showed a diversity of approaches (Black and Wiliam, 1998). However, there were some features that arose in most, if not all, of the studies and these provide a starting point. Formative assessment, like all other ways to generate effective learning, requires pupils to be actively involved and so classrooms where pupils are encouraged to speak and do, rather than receive information, are more fruitful sites for formative assessment to function. Where teachers stick religiously to a transmission mode of teaching, where they focus on the subject matter that they have to teach, assessment becomes bolted on at the end of a teaching sequence as a measure of how much knowledge has filtered through to the learner. In these circumstances it becomes increasingly difficult, if not impossible, to feed assessment evidence back into the teaching and learning process. A more effective approach is to embed the assessment into the teaching-learning cycle (Capel *et al.*, 2009: 272) so that the pace and emphasis of the work can be matched to the needs of the learners.

For assessment to function formatively, teachers need to make teaching programmes flexible and responsive. This involves collecting evidence of how well pupils have understood part of a topic and refining future lesson plans to remediate any problems that have arisen, or changing direction or pace if the class have mastered ideas quickly and so require more challenge in their learning. It also involves dealing with learning opportunities when they arise within a lesson. You might find, for example, that students struggle with a piece of learning because they have a particular misconception or that they misinterpret data because they are lacking in some process skills. To help them make sense of the particular piece of learning, you might insert an alternative activity into your lesson or move the interpretation of the ideas into another context and spend time helping your class develop their understanding of a specific part of the lesson, rather than heading for the outcomes you had initially planned.

As new teachers, it is perhaps best to adopt a formative approach that spans from lesson to lesson initially. If you use some assessment tool, such as a concept cartoon (Naylor and Keogh, 2000), in one lesson to gather evidence of understanding then you have the opportunity to change your next lesson in response to that evidence. If, however, you find out that year 7 pupils can do the work you had planned for them there would be little gained from them doing that experiment in the next lesson. For example, you might ask your students to devise an experiment to demonstrate the differences between metal and non-metal objects and as they do this you clearly pick up that they can classify a range of materials into metals and non-metals. On the other hand, if you find that pupils keep referring to dissolving as 'the solid disappearing', this needs to be addressed in the next lesson to find out if it is simply slackness of language or a firmly held misconception of those learners. So the assessments and evaluations completed in one lesson modify future learning experiences. In time, as your confidence in the classroom grows, you are able to accommodate formative assessment practices in a more proactive manner and deviate from your lesson plan as and when the learning needs demand such a course of action.

AfL increases teachers' understanding of their pupils and so helps teachers provide quality feedback to improve their learning. It also helps to develop classroom cultures where collaboration dominates competition and in which learning, rather than performance, is the goal. This is because pupils need to understand that the main emphasis of the work they do in classrooms is about improvement. One feature that appeared in several of the studies on formative assessment is the development of self-assessment strategies in the learners. One of the many tasks that you need to achieve through your teaching is helping pupils become self-regulating in their work so that eventually they become learners independent of the teacher. This is not an easy task, as experienced teachers will inform you, and needs a careful training programme for learners where they gradually come to hold a concept of quality about their work similar to the one that their teacher holds in her head. From the focused feedback that they get from their teachers, pupils can begin to grasp what quality means within their work and, acting on advice, can start to achieve it.

CLASSROOM ASSESSMENT

Assessment plays an important role in the teaching–learning cycle since it can both drive and modify the learning experience so that pupils' needs are catered for. It provides evidence for teachers about the way pupils understand and perform particular tasks; it also provides feedback to the learner on what they have achieved and how they might improve their work. Equipped with this evidence, teachers can plan the next stage of teaching more effectively and learners can begin to comprehend what they need to do to make progress. The role of the teacher is to create regular opportunities for assessment to occur. This can be achieved through a variety of sources including:

■ classroom dialogue
■ class and homework activities
■ tests.

Each of these factors is addressed in turn below. These sources need to produce a rich source of data for teachers to make informed judgements that can then be fed back to the learner so that the pupil comes to understand both the concept of quality and the role of the assessment process in their learning. The focus needs to be on improvement and so the dialogue, activities and tests need to focus on establishing where a learner is in their learning and provide the detail of what they need to do next.

Classroom dialogue

To do this effectively, teachers need to create rich classroom dialogue where the quality of their questions encourages learners to reveal what they know and understand. If a class were asked to give a definition of friction, probably few children would attempt to answer. Rephrasing the question to explore pupils' ideas about friction might be done by a more open approach to questioning. For friction, this might be done with a question like 'Some people talk about friction as being the opposite of slipperiness. What do you think?' This opens up the possibility of learners discussing what they think they know and understand about friction and allows them to compare and build their understanding by both articulating their own thoughts and modifying these ideas in the light of what they hear from others. It is from these classroom dialogues that teachers can extract the evidence they need to judge whether specific children do, or do not, have conceptual understanding. This is because the question explores what is in children's minds rather than 'right answerism', where the questions being set have a fixed answer in the teacher's head that children have to guess at.

To encourage such discussions producing a rich source of evidence, teachers often try to leave several seconds thinking time before they take an answer. The time between a teacher asking a question and taking an answer is called 'wait time' (Rowe, 1974) and, for many teachers in her study, this was shown to be less than one second. This is insufficient time for learners to think what they know and to put together an answer that they can articulate in class. Thinking time can be further enhanced, if it is a particularly challenging question, by asking learners to discuss their ideas with a partner or in groups because then their answers can be trialled, developed and modified before being offered in the public arena of the whole class. A further benefit from this approach is that there is pair or group responsibility for an answer which is less threatening for some learners. It also means that the classroom response is likely to be rich because the first ideas that the teacher selects can be added to, challenged or agreed with, by other pupils since the answers given can be compared with those that the pair or group discussed. So follow-up questions such as, 'What might we add to Suzie's answer?' or 'How did Yagnesh's answer fit with Sally's idea?' broaden the discussion to involve more pupils answering and so enrich the evidence. This allows the teacher to make a more informed judgement about which steps to take next with the learning. However, to develop this approach the teacher needs flexibility and an ability to think on his feet. Such a demand requires careful planning and security in his knowledge of the topic.

Task 6.1.1 **Observing and collecting questions**

Begin work on this by observing experienced teachers working with their classes. Note down the questions that seem to prompt and promote dialogue and reflect on how the teacher handles the answers. Good teachers often manage questioning effectively without realising the skilled way in which they do this. It may be useful to ask them afterwards what they were trying to achieve with specific questions and how such questions have worked with other classes. Sort, sift and collect useful questions on different topics as well as collecting generic ones that you can use to develop and support classroom discourse.

Rich data can also be collected from classwork, homework activities and from tests, as long as the teacher plans for and supports learners by providing a means through which pupil understanding can be shown. Checking whether keywords are known or matching terms with definitions is only the beginning of the data collection that a teacher needs to do and caution needs to be applied because knowing a complex scientific word does not necessarily mean that a pupil has conceptual understanding in that area. Most pupils remember that green plants contain chlorophyll but this does not indicate that they realise that photosynthesis is an energy transfer process that forms the main part of plant nutrition. Indeed, it could be that they know that chlorophyll is involved and may even be able to write out the correct equation but they mistakenly believe that photosynthesis is plant respiration. Many such misconceptions are well documented (Driver *et al.*, 1994) and part of the teacher's role is to create activities where misconceptions can be revealed and challenged. The ways in which learners work with such activities again provides a rich source of evidence for assessment purposes.

Task 6.1.2 **Developing your own questions**

Start developing some questions of your own. 'What' and 'When' questions usually get descriptive answers that require only recall. 'Why' and 'How' questions require more thought. Use these stems to think of questions that you might use in a specific science topic:

■ What is similar and what is different about . . . ?

■ Is it always true that . . . ?

■ How would you explain . . . ?

■ What is wrong with . . . ?

■ What does that tell you about . . . ?

Classwork and homework activities

Different tasks set different demands for the learner and busy teachers are best advised to plan for assessment in those activities where the cognitive demands are high. Asking pupils to provide a written explanation of what they think would happen if a chemical was released that destroyed chlorophyll reveals far more of a learner's conceptual understanding than an activity where they describe the starch test. Similarly, setting work where pupils draw and explain what happens at the particle level when mercury expands in a thermometer gives more insight to understanding than asking pupils to copy drawings of the particle model idea for solids, liquids and gases from a textbook.

Many classwork and homework tasks involve noting key words and descriptions, while some document the developing ideas in a particular topic and others record the method, data and conclusions of a particular practical activity that demonstrates a scientific idea. These are the building blocks that pupils need to construct their ideas and understanding of science. While it is important that a check is kept on these to ensure that a specific pupil has the building blocks in place, other types of classwork and homework provide better information about conceptual understanding and it is on these that teachers need to focus their assessments. Homework tasks, in particular, need careful planning to ensure that the product provides useful information about understanding.

Task 6.1.3 **Planning for quality feedback**

1 Look through a sequence of lessons that you have taught or the scheme of work for a topic and decide which activities will produce work that needs checking and which will need more careful thought when marking in order to give quality feedback.
2 Decide what features of the activity, or product from the activity, suggest that more time should be devoted to giving detailed feedback.

Tests

Tests are a quick and simple way of sampling learning and for both teacher and learner can be a good check that key words and descriptions are known. Tests can be an effective way of monitoring factual knowledge but, in most cases, are less useful in assessing conceptual understanding. Thought needs to be given to the timing and frequency of tests; if given too late in the learning sequence, there is no time for remediation and improvement, and if set too often, they detract from the time available for learning.

RECORDING ASSESSMENT DATA

It might seem strange to look at recording assessment evidence at this point but this has implications for the way you approach marking and feedback. Most schools have policies that explain the purposes of marking pupil work and some system for marking and recording that provides coherence. The focus of this policy may be on reporting to parents and governors and suggest a summative evaluation that recognises accountability issues, as well as providing communication about individual pupil achievement on a specific piece of work. Other schools may have the primary aim of marking as a means of negotiating learning goals or targets with the pupil and seek to communicate progress rather than attainment in reports to parents. Yet other schools may do parts of both approaches and may have different approaches for different age groups of pupils. In order to understand the approach that you need to take in recording assessment evidence, you need to be clear about the policies for assessment and marking that exist in your school and how these play out in reality.

Task 6.1.4 **Understanding your school's assessment policy**

1 Obtain a copy of your school's assessment/marking policy and any information that the science department produces on these issues.
2 Read the documents carefully and check with your mentor any ambiguities, such as what 'marked regularly' means.
3 Ask experienced teachers how they interpret the policies on a day-to-day basis and ask them to show you evidence of what they do in the pupils' work and in their mark books.

4   Ensure that you know:

   a   when and how to set and mark work for your classes
   b   how to store assessment evidence for your purposes and for the usual teacher of that class
   c   what the assessment evidence is used for.

Decisions need to be taken about what to record in relation to a task that the learner has tried to do. Depending on the focus of the activity, you may want to record the processes that the learner used in completing the work (did they analyse data, make predictions or translate information into a different form?) or record attributes of the product they produced (was it a graph, table, drawing or prose?). Some teachers choose to record first attempts at a difficult piece of work as well as information on the final product because this gives them an idea of how pupils are responding to advice and moving forward with their learning. Other teachers choose to record data on finished products, and so use their mark book as a summative record.

The system of recording is complex and new teachers generally need several attempts at refining the process into a workable form. Most teachers use a mark book to record such data using coded systems to enable them to fit a large amount of information on one page. This allows them to record quickly but also gather an overview of the way individual learners are progressing. Again, simple grades or marks can rarely provide sufficient information to provide the detail needed to generate an overview of achievement or progress. That is not to say that summative assessments should not be recorded as these provide indicators of overall progress. Tests or quizzes that are used in a formative fashion during the learning process rarely need recording but if the teacher does want to keep such information it is far better to record what the learner doesn't understand or cannot yet do rather than the number of answers that they have got correct. This information helps the teacher devise more appropriate revision at a later stage.

FEEDBACK

Feedback has an essential part to play in the formative process. It provides the learner with the advice they need to promote their future learning. Quality rather than quantity is the key feature when giving pupils feedback on both oral and written work. The effort that many teachers devote to marking written tasks may be misdirected. A numerical mark or grade does not tell pupils how to improve their work, so an opportunity to enhance their learning has been lost. This judgement is supported by a study that established that, whilst pupils' learning can be advanced by feedback through comments, the giving of marks or grades has a negative effect in that pupils ignore comments when marks or grades are also given (Butler, 1988). Teachers are often surprised by Butler's study and yet it is easy to explain if you watch the way in which pupils in class respond to the marks/grades and comments in their books. Marks/grades are looked at and perhaps compared with peers but comments often get ignored and frequently go unread. So essential advice about improvement is unheeded in favour of being told week after week that you are B+.

The key to effective feedback is providing sufficient acknowledgment of what has been achieved alongside advice on what next steps to take. Some teachers use a technique called 'two stars and a wish' to achieve this in a concise but informative way. So a piece of work is assessed by noting two features that demonstrate the strength of the work or perhaps relate to an area that a specific pupil is currently targeting and then adding one aspect that might improve the piece. Learners can then begin to recognise for themselves what they have done well and understand where they need to put their efforts next. It also helps if the comment can be personally directed and written to encourage thinking. Examples might look like:

- 'James, you have provided clear diagrams and recognised which chemicals are elements and which are compounds. Can you give a general explanation of the difference between elements and compounds?'
- 'You have identified the anomalous results and commented on the accuracy of your experiment. What can you say about the sample size?'

Teachers also need to demonstrate to their learners that improvement is the main purpose of assessment, and opportunities for pupils to follow up feedback comments should be planned as part of the overall learning process. A particularly valuable way of doing this is to devote some lesson time to redrafting one or two pieces of work, so that emphasis can be put on feedback for improvement within a supportive environment. This can change pupils' expectations about the purposes of classwork and homework as well as provide polished pieces of work that they can be proud of. Implementation of such practices can change the attitudes of both teachers and pupils to written work: the assessment of pupils' work will be seen less as a competitive and summative judgement and more as a distinctive step in the process of learning.

While feedback benefits all pupils, it is particularly important that low attainers receive appropriate feedback, since they usually have greater difficulty than other learners in understanding the concept of quality that the teacher requires. The problem for the teacher is two-fold. First, they need to select the specific improvements that are needed and then to find the language to explain how the learner might approach the remediation work. However, it is only the learner that can close the gap between their current level and the new level that the teacher sets and so co-operation and a willingness to try is required. For some low attainers, feedback has been a painful experience where their shortcomings have been revealed and they have retired hurt from the learning process. Such learners often exhibit a type of behaviour that Carol Dweck (1986) term 'learned helplessness', where their self-esteem has been damaged by the assessment process and they are unwilling to engage in meaningful learning work. Teachers need to handle such learners carefully and find strategies to engage them once again with the learning process. In such a situation, marks seem to aggravate the problem and so this provides another reason for teachers using qualitative rather than quantitative data in their feedback to pupils.

Some schools have policies that require teachers to enter an achievement and an effort grade as a form of feedback. Effort is a difficult aspect to judge, especially where homework is concerned, and so quantity and neatness seem to be the criteria for judging this rather than time or concentration. Nevertheless, improvement in any of these factors may be a sign of progress and is to be remarked upon. While it is important to instil in learners that effort is needed if they wish to improve their work, effort grades detract from the message, if ill-judged.

Task 6.1.5 **Providing constructive feedback**

Collect in a set of exercise books from a class that you teach.

1 Select three books; one from an average pupil, one from a high-attaining pupil and one from a low-attaining pupil.
2 Look through the work since the last time the books were marked. Decide which pieces of work need checking and which need more time to devise suitable feedback. This is likely to be one or two pieces at the most.
3 For the one or two pieces that require time spent on them, write down three objectives that you can see or had hoped the pupils would have achieved in this piece of work. Think also what you would hope this work to lead on to in the near future. These are the criteria for judging the work.
4 It may be helpful for you to produce what you would consider to be either an acceptable or a model example for the piece of work to help you recognise the quality required for the criteria to work in the context of the piece.
5 Think carefully about what you could write in each of the three student's books. A good tip is to use the idea of 'two stars and a wish'; two things you feel that they have done well and one feature that you had hoped would be there or could be there in the next step of their learning journey. Comments should encourage pupils to read them, act on them and, hopefully, think. It is important to try and avoid the use of 'but' in this type of feedback as it suggests shortcoming rather than an urge to improve. Examples might be:

- 'The Haber process is well described and you have included the equation. Which variables affect the production of ammonia?'
- 'Good examples of adaptation and features are clearly shown. Look again at the way you have described the process of adaptation and check it against the explanation in the textbook'.
- 'You have provided clear circuit diagrams and correct examples for bulb brightness. Can you explain this in words as well as diagramatically?'

Pupils can be helped to understand the detailed advice in feedback by involving them in whole-class activities where they become engaged in discussing the strengths and weaknesses in a specific example of a learner's work. This task models for them the self-assessment processes that they need to pay heed to as they create their own work. It helps them see the importance of focusing on the learning intentions and the success criteria as well as allowing them to focus on what needs to be done to improve a piece of work.

PEER AND SELF-ASSESSMENT

Pupils need to be active participants in the assessment process rather than victims of testing. This can only be achieved if they develop the skills of self-assessment, understand their learning goal and can assess what they need to do to reach it (Sadler, 1989). Self-assessment skills are not easy to develop but the first and probably most difficult task is to get pupils to think of their work in terms of a set of goals. In doing this they begin to develop an overview of that work so that it becomes possible for them to manage and control it for themselves and they become self-regulated learners.

The impact of the review by Sebba *et al.* (2008) on students of self- and peer-assessment highlighted the need to include learners in decisions about how and what is being studied and insights into how the work is being assessed. In this way, learners become more informed about the learning process and play a more equal role with the teacher in making learning decisions. This has important messages for pedagogy since it is the ecology of learning that is called into question here and many teachers will need to change their classroom environments significantly to treat learners as co-constructors of the learning process. The review highlights the need for change in schools, for teacher commitment to learner control and for a move from dependency to interdependency between teachers and their pupils.

Task 6.1.6 **Finding research evidence for an interdependent relationship between teachers and pupils**

Read the following review and suggest why and how teachers and schools need to focus on an interdependent relationship between teachers and pupils rather than a dependency model, as found in many schools at the present time: Sebba, J., Crick, R.D., Yu, G., Lawson, H., Harlen, W. and Durant, K. (2008) 'Systematic review of research evidence of the impact on students in secondary schools of self- and peer-assessment. Technical report.' In *Research Evidence in Education Library*. London: EPPI-Centre, Social Science Research Unit, Institute of Education, University of London (see *Useful websites*).

In practice, peer-assessment turns out to be an important complement to self-assessment and a means by which the necessary skills can be developed. Peer-assessment allows pupils to begin to judge their own work by recognising similar or different qualities in the work of their peers. It is also uniquely valuable because pupils may accept, from one another, criticisms of their work, which they would not take seriously if made by their teacher (Black *et al.*, 2002) and is in a language and form that pupils themselves would naturally use and comprehend. However, self-assessment only happens if teachers help their pupils, particularly the low-attainers, to develop the skill. This process can take time and practice.

One way to practise self- and peer-assessment skills is to hold regular debriefing sessions towards the end of a lesson. A range of self-evaluation questions can be given which are linked to the learning intentions and success criteria for that lesson and pupils can be asked to voice what they feel they have achieved. Such questions might also ask 'Which parts of the lesson did you find easy and which parts difficult?' and discussions arising from this not only inform the teacher of areas they may need to return to but also highlight for the pupils where they need to focus their attention for improvement.

One simple and effective idea is for pupils to self-assess completed pieces of work using 'traffic light' icons, labelling their work green, amber or red according to their confidence levels with specific pieces of work. These labels serve as a simple means of communication of pupils' self-assessments. Pupils may then be asked to justify their judgements in a peer-group, so linking peer- and self-assessment. This linkage can help in the development of the skills and the detachment needed for effective self-assessment.

Another approach is to ask pupils first to 'traffic light' a piece of work, and then to indicate by hands-up whether they put green, amber or red. The teacher can then reorganize the working groups so that the greens and ambers can pair up to deal with problems between them, whilst the red pupils can be helped by the teacher to deal with their deeper problems. For such peer-group work to succeed, many pupils need guidance about how to behave in groups, e.g. in listening to one another and taking turns, and how to judge quality, e.g. familiarising themselves with criteria. Techniques, such as the 'two stars and a wish' approach described in the feedback section can also be used in developing these behaviours, particularly as they can be used to explore how the criteria for quality can be achieved within different pupils' work. Again, peer-assessment through collaborative group work provides the vehicle through which self-assessment practices can develop.

Another approach which you could use as a supplement to one of the above ideas, or as an alternative way of developing self-assessment, is to spend time regularly asking pupils to reflect on their work. This might be done once a week for 15 minutes in class or as one of the homework tasks. Because pupils need help in recognising their learning, you might use summary cards like these:

Name: ………Hannah S……………..   Date: ……..Sept 30th…………

Two things I have learned in this lesson:

    Photosynthesis is the way plants make food from carbon dioxide and water.
    Plants make starch and you can test for this with iodine.

A question I have?

    How does the plant make starch from a gas and a liquid?

▪ **Figure 6.1.1** Summary card

Another variation might be asking them to judge where the easy and difficult parts come in pieces of work or topics so that they are keyed in where to focus their effort when it comes to revision.

Name: ………Hannah S……………..   Date: ……..Nov 22nd…………

Things I found easy in this topic so far:

    That forces are measured in Newtons.
    That gravity makes things have weight.
    Using the forcemeter.

Things I found difficult in this topic so far:

    Drawing the pictures of where forces are acting.
    Understanding the experiment with the light gates.

▪ **Figure 6.1.2** Analysis card

The next step in helping pupils recognise their learning is by asking them to compare work done recently with that done earlier in the topic or earlier in the year.

Name: ....Hannah S................   Date: ....Dec 8th............

I used to:

    ask the teacher how to do the axes on my graph.
    join plot to plot.

And now I can:

    decide on the right scale for each axis.
    know which variable goes on the horizontal and which on the vertical.
    spot anomolous results.
    draw the line of best fit.

■ **Figure 6.1.3** Recognising learning card

Once pupils have mastered these techniques then they are ready to negotiate targets for their learning, along with appropriate time-frames and methods of self-monitoring to ensure they keep check on working towards their goal. All of these activities take time and effort to establish as working practice in the classroom and so need to be planned for as part of the unit of work.

SUMMATIVE ASSESSMENT

There is no shortage of encouragement, and pressure, for teachers to improve their work, raise their standards, improve children's attainment in test scores, and so on. This advice has often not taken into consideration the complexities involved in supporting learners in improving their work. In reality, there are many challenges that teachers face when attempting to offer guidance to 30 or more children in a classroom and advice that presents the situation in a simplistic way can be very disheartening for teachers.

Clearly, one aspect of teacher's ongoing work is to assess pupil progress and so systems to support this are necessary. In 2008, following the discontinuation of national testing by Standard Assessment Tests (SATs), at Key Stage 3 in England, the Secretary of State appointed a group of five educationalists to review and make recommendations on assessment at Key Stages 1, 2 and 3. The group reported in May 2009 and the Secretary of State accepted all of its recommendations. The summative assessment replacement for the national tests from 2011 will be a sample of some 10,000 pupils who will take tests in English, mathematics and science. This equates to approximately one class per state secondary school across England. The results of this sample will be used to monitor national performance year by year and aligned, as far as possible, to the Third International Mathematics and Science Survey (TIMSS) tests (DCSFc, 2009: 32–5). Under this model, all schools would produce teacher-assessed National Curriculum levels for each of their pupils, supported by assessed evidence. Evidence from a sample of schools, selected after submission of teacher-assessed levels, would be externally verified and the data produced used for monitoring year on year. In contrast to the SATs, the results will not be used for school or local authority accountability.

Over the last few years, a new system for assessment in English, mathematics and science has been piloted in schools, Assessing Pupil Progress (APP). APP could play an important role in filling the void in the summative assessment regime that removal of national testing for all has left. APP was developed by QCA in partnership with the National Strategies team. Its original intention was to help teachers make sound judgements about pupil attainment in relation to national standards. What is essential is that APP fits alongside other approaches in classrooms that have proved to be beneficial to learning and teaching, the most obvious one being AfL.

The first thing to do is to reveal the function of APP – it is continuous summative assessment. It sums up the learning over the previous phase of learning and the intention of the new approach being introduced is to do this periodically. Systems like APP can be useful in that they can help teachers and learners in reviewing learning and then using that information in a formative way to inform the learning over the next phase. It is not the same as AfL, where assessment works alongside the learning, but it can be useful in providing a check and safety net, in case aspects of learning have not been achieved and consolidated during the learning period. It can also help teachers and learners map the progress of learning over the course of the year, recognise that opportunities for assessment need to be planned over the long term as well as during the current spate of learning. Data from the continuous summative assessment, that APP offers, could be used to communicate with parents and others about pupil learning, aspirations and expectations.

APP has other uses. Inexperienced teachers can be helped in gaining an overview of the subject and help in understanding developmental pathways for learning. This will help them gain a better understanding of pupil progress within their curricular area and can then feed into their teaching programme, as they will be alerted to planning opportunities into topics where specific assessment foci can be worked on. However, one aspect that teachers need to be careful about is the validity of the APP system for their subject area. Validity refers to the degree that the assessment scheme measures what we expect it to measure for a particular subject. Sometimes assessment systems are limited in validity because they tend to measure only those aspects of the subject that are easily measurable, such as use of appropriate units, and fail to, or insufficiently, measure other aspects, which prove more difficult or elusive, such as creativity or problem-solving capability.

While APP is to be welcomed as a timely replacement for KS3 national testing, teachers need to take care that this system fits around their current AfL approaches in the classroom. Any new system that inhibits or prevents the AfL approach continuing and strengthening should be avoided and APP needs to be put in its rightful place in the classroom assessment regime – to inform continuous summative assessment practices.

SUMMARY AND KEY POINTS

This unit has addressed the role of formative assessment in the science classroom and outlined ways of working that allow you to collect a rich source of assessment evidence about your pupils. Assessment prioritises classroom dialogue, written work and tests as sources of evidence of learning and understanding and suggests how each of these might be used to make judgements about the next steps in the teaching and learning.

Your school will undoubtedly have systems in place for monitoring and accountability and part of your development will be making sense of how the formative and summative assessment systems can work together. At this stage of your teaching career it is essential that you try out and practise a range of assessment strategies and that you regularly discuss the implications of these on both teaching and learning with your mentor and peers.

This unit also highlights the pupil's role in assessment and offers ways into helping pupils develop self-assessment skills through a peer-assessment approach. Remember that setting up such practices in pupils who have not been encouraged in such behaviours is difficult and will take time and effort to achieve. When, and how, to move forward in this aspect of your teaching requires discussion and negotiation with the teachers in your teaching practice school.

FURTHER READING

Black, P. and Wiliam, D. (1998) *Inside the Black Box: Raising Standards Through Classroom Assessment.* London: King's College, School of Education.

Black, P. J. and Harrison, C. (2001) 'Feedback in questioning and marking: the science teacher's role in formative assessment'. *School Science Review*, 82 (301), 55–61.

Black, P. J. and Harrison, C. (2001) 'Self- and peer-assessment and taking responsibility: the science pupil's role in formative assessment'. *School Science Review*, 83 (302), 43–9.

Black, P., Harrison C., Lee, C., Marshall, B. and Wiliam, D. (2002) *Working Inside the Black Box: Assessment for Learning in the Classroom.* London: King's College, Department of Education and Professional Studies.

Black, P., Harrison, C., Lee, C., Marshall, B. and Wiliam, D. (2003) *Assessment for Learning: Putting it into Practice.* Buckingham: Open University Press.

Department for Children, Schools and Families (2009) *The Report of the Expert Group on Assessment.* London: DCSF.

Gardner, J. (2006) *Assessment and Learning.* London: Sage.

Naylor, S. and Keogh, B. (2000) *Concept Cartoons in Science Education.* Sandbach: Millgate House Education Ltd.

USEFUL WEBSITES

Information about APP

http://curriculum.qcda.gov.uk/key-stages-3–and-4/assessment/Assessing-pupils-progress/What-is-APP/index (accessed 24 September 2009).

If you wish to read further into the Assessment literature then the following websites have key reviews and papers that will help you make a start:

1. **The Evidence for Policy and Practice Information and Co-ordinating Centre (EPPI)**
    http://eppi.ioe.ac.uk/cms/ (accessed 24 September 2009).
    Contains a number of reviews on assessment matters. For example:
    - Harlen, W. (2004) 'A systematic review of the evidence of reliability and validity of assessment by teachers used for summative purposes'
    - Harlen, W. (2004) 'A systematic review of the evidence of the impact on students, teachers and the curriculum of the process of using assessment by teachers for summative purposes'

- Harlen, W. and Deakin Crick, R. (2002) 'A systematic review of the impact of summative assessment and tests on students' motivation for learning'
- Harlen, W. and Deakin Crick, R. (2003) 'A systematic review of the impact on students and teachers of the use of ICT for assessment of creative and critical thinking skills'

2. **The Association for Achievement and Improvement through Assessment (AAIA)**
http://www.aaia.org.uk/ (accesed 24 September 2009).
Contains reports, resources, research pieces and advice on several aspects of assessment including dealing with performance data.

3. **The Assessment Reform Group**
http://www.assessment-reform-group.org/ (accessed 24 September 2009).
Contains information and ideas on the policy and implementation of assessment practices and includes several downloadable publications. For example:

- ARG (2004) 'Testing, learning and motivation'
- ARG (2007) 'The role of teachers in the assessment of learning'
- ARG (2009) 'Changing assessment practices'

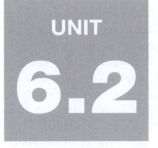

EXTERNAL ASSESSMENT AND EXAMINATIONS IN SCIENCE

UNIT 6.2

Jenny Frost

INTRODUCTION

Public examinations are part of *summative* assessment, and must be distinguished from the *formative* assessment-for-learning described in Unit 6.1. They lead to accreditation for nationally recognised qualifications and involve different tasks and tests to allow pupils to demonstrate the full range of skills, knowledge and understanding that they have gained.

Nationally recognised qualifications serve several purposes; they credit individuals' achievements, they contribute to selection procedures and are used for accountability for, say, judging schools' performances. As a result, they become 'high stakes' events both for individuals and schools; and teachers carry responsibility for ensuring that pupils do as well as is possible. Teachers need as good an understanding of schemes of assessment as of the content of a course; finding out about the assessment procedures and demands cannot be an afterthought. Teachers must know how assessment tasks are integrated into lessons and under what conditions, when written tests have to be done, what type of answers are expected, how to prepare pupils for the tasks and tests, what records have to be kept and what administration is necessary. For the teacher-assessed parts of the course, they need to understand marking criteria or mark schemes and how to participate in moderation procedures to ensure comparability of standards.

OBJECTIVES

By the end of this unit you should:

- be familiar with schemes of assessment in public examinations in science
- understand the place of teacher assessment in science qualifications and know about the ways in which teachers' own marking is moderated
- understand the implications of assessment arrangements.

WHAT SCIENCE EXAMINATIONS ARE AVAILABLE IN SCHOOLS?

You will already be familiar with the range of external examinations in science available generally, and in your school, from your study of the curriculum in Unit 2.3 of this book. Details of the awarding bodies are also given there. If you have not already done so, you should, together with this unit, read Unit 6.2 of Capel *et al.* (2009) *Learning to Teach in the Secondary School*, which gives background information about the development and structures of GCSE and GCE examinations and diplomas. It provides information on the use of external examination results for public accountability of schools, and describes what systems are in place to ensure that external assessments and examinations are both valid and reliable. It explains how comparability between the different awarding bodies is achieved.

Much of the advice given in this unit about how to prepare yourself and the pupils for GCSE and GCE, applies also to the schemes of summative assessment which are operating within your school at KS3. These will consist of a combination of, say, end-of-module tests and teacher assessment of practical and investigation skills. The development of the national scheme for Assessing Pupil Progress (APP) in science at KS3 was outlined in the previous unit, 6.1, by Christine Harrison.

UNDERSTANDING THE SCHEME OF ASSESSMENT IN A SPECIFICATION

Details of schemes of assessment for any course are contained in a range of publications from the awarding body, such as:

- the specification
- the teacher's guide
- exemplar material for internally assessed tasks and their assessment (often in the teacher's guide)
- specimen question papers and answers, or (better) a set of recent past papers
- a recent examiner's report, which gives information about how candidates tackled questions and where the main problems lay.

Your school may be able to lend you these; alternatively, download them from the awarding body websites (see *Useful websites* in Unit 2.3).

The specification contains most of the basic information about the scheme of assessment. In it you will find information about:

- units of assessment
- assessment objectives
- weighting of the objectives
- internal assessment
- mark schemes and criteria for marking internally assessed work
- help and support that teachers can give for internally assessed work
- moderation procedures
- administration.

Units of assessment

Do not confuse 'Units of assessment' with 'modules' of a course. The units of assessment tell you the nature of the assessment items, the time taken for each and the percentage of marks allocated to each. For GCSE sciences, awarding bodies vary as to how they break the assessment into units, but the overall pattern is approximately 75 per cent of the marks are awarded on written papers and 25 per cent awarded for tasks assessed by teachers (internal assessment). The exception to this is GCSE *Applied Science*, which has a higher proportion of marks for the internally assessed units.

For GCE sciences, there are three units of assessment for GCE AS level and another three for GCE A2, giving six units of assessment for the whole A-level. Twenty per cent of the marks are allocated to the internally assessed parts of the examination. (Again the *Applied Science* courses are an exception.)

Assessment objectives and weighting of objectives

The assessment objectives are derived from the aims of the course. Not all aims are assessable (aims about enjoyment of science, for instance). Assessment objectives for GCSE and GCE sciences are concerned with knowledge and understanding of science and of *How Science Works*; with the application of that knowledge and understanding, and with skills related to evidence and practical skills. All assessment objectives are subdivided into more specific sub-objectives.

Assessment objectives are not necessarily given the same weighting; the marks allocated to each objective may be different. Schemes of assessment give the weightings of the objectives and show how the testing of the objectives is distributed through the different units of assessment.

Internal and external assessment

Internal assessment refers to assessments where work is undertaken in class or homework time, where teachers support part of the work, and where teachers undertake the marking. 'Internal assessment', 'centre assessment' and 'teacher assessment' all mean the same thing (a 'centre' being a school or college offering the examination). The centre-assessed unit of assessment might well include more than one task. External assessment refers to elements of the examination set and marked by the awarding body, usually through written examination papers.

Internal assessments for GCSE, previously referred to as 'coursework' are now 'controlled assessments', in that the awarding body retains some control over the setting of the task, develops the criteria for marking, and stipulates the conditions under which the tasks should be carried out. For example, OCR currently has a task for the GCSE *21st Century Science* course that involves candidates having an article to read two or three weeks in advance. For the assessment, fresh copies of the article are provided and candidates answer a set of previously unseen questions about it. The awarding body chooses the article and sets the questions. The teacher supports the candidates in researching the topic, and marks the final script. In another task, candidates carry out data collection in a practical activity in normal lesson time, in preparation for questions about data interpretation and evaluation answered under examination conditions. Guidance on appropriate practical tasks is specified by the awarding body. Again teachers mark the scripts. In the related GCSE *Additional Science* course, the internal assessment consists of a research study, data interpretation and practical skills, each with varying degrees of control from the awarding body. (Look out for acronyms; AQA, for instance, uses ISAs (Investigations Skills Assignments) and PSAs (Practical Skills Assessments) for CAUs (Centre Assessed Units).)

Task 6.2.1 is a short exercise intended to extract the basic information about the schemes of assessment for courses in your school. For this you need to use only the specification. Later tasks (6.2.2 and 6.2.3) analyse the assessment in greater depth.

Task 6.2.1 **Understanding schemes of assessment for GCSE and GCE**

Use the specification only for the GCSE *science* course in your school.

1   Find:

   ■ the units of assessment, the time for each and the marks allocated to each unit
   ■ the tasks for the teacher-assessed component
   ■ the assessment objectives and the sub-objectives
   ■ the weighting of the assessment objectives and their distribution through the different units of assessment
   ■ the marks allocated for quality of written work or quality of communication.

2   Do the same for the GCSE *Additional Science* and GCSE *Additional Applied Science* and for a GCE A-level in your specialism.

3   Talk with your mentor about when the tasks and tests are done, and the opportunities which pupils have to retake units of assessment.

Keep notes in your professional portfolio, particularly of the features with which you are unfamiliar.

Marking criteria for internally assessed work

While specific mark schemes are suitable for some of the internally assessed tasks, other tasks require the use of criteria by which teachers can judge the level of attainment; this is particularly true for assessment of practical skills. Criteria may seem precise on first reading, but both judgement and experience play a large part in deciding reliably whether a candidate has reached a particular level or not. Criteria can be found in the schemes of assessment within the specifications and you will need to refer to them later, for Task 6.2.3.

Using question papers and controlled assessment tasks to interpret specifications

The specification is the 'rule book' for a public examination, and equally importantly, the question papers and the internally assessed tasks form the 'case law'. The question papers and internally assessed tasks show the depth of treatment expected in teaching the course, and the relative emphasis given to different parts of the content. You should therefore study them carefully at an early stage (see Tasks 6.2.2 and 6.2.3).

Task 6.2.2 **Analysing question papers**

This task involves answering and analysing examination papers. Using the same specifications that you used in Task 6.2.1, do the questions yourself and check against model answers. Then analyse the papers as follows:

1 Identify which assessment objectives are examined by the written papers.
2 Match the individual questions (or parts of questions) to the more detailed 'sub-objectives'. Identify the questions that test different aspects of *How Science Works.*
3 For GCSE identify the difference in demand between the foundation and higher tier papers.
4 For the GCE A-level papers find the questions that are synoptic (i.e. the questions which link different sections of the course) and those questions that are the 'stretch and challenge' questions, which distinguish the A* candidates from the A candidates.
5 Think what kind of guidance you would give to pupils taking these papers and make a list of your main suggestions.

Keep records of this task in your PDP. Discuss with other student teachers, your tutor or mentor any questions that you found difficult. Share your list of guidance suggestions with mentors; they may well be able to confirm your selection and add points from their experience.

Task 6.2.3 **Analysing the internally assessed components**

Using the same specifications that you used in Task 6.2.1, look at the guidance and examples for the internally assessed components. Decide how you would tackle the tasks yourself before answering the questions below:

■ Which assessment objectives are tested?
■ For GCSE, are the tasks the same for foundation and higher tier?
■ Do teachers and/or pupils have any choice? Is there guidance given about how to choose?
■ Can any of the work be done outside lesson time?
■ Can any work be done collectively (e.g. collecting data from a practical investigation)?
■ What is the nature of the final product? Answers to questions? A written report? A presentation? A set of laboratory skills? Other?
■ Are the tasks marked using criteria or a marking scheme?
■ Has the awarding body produced an explanation of the tasks and criteria specifically for pupils? If so, ask mentors how they use it.

> Write a brief summary of the key points related to the centre-assessed units of assessment and put this in your PDP. Talk with teachers about how they fit these assessments into the normal rhythm of their teaching, and which tasks present the greatest challenge to them and to the pupils.

Examination rules and professional judgement

It is the job of the department's teaching team to end up with *valid* and *reliable* marks for the internally assessed tasks to submit to awarding bodies. Do the pupils' marks reward success in skills in line with expectations of the syllabus and the mark scheme? If they do, they are valid. Is the standard of marking fair and consistent across different pieces of coursework from any one pupil, and across different teachers' marking? This is the test of reliability. Both issues are addressed by the awarding body's rules, and both are serious professional challenges.

VALIDITY AND 'AUTHENTICATION' OF COURSEWORK

As with tasks of any kind, what pupils achieve in their coursework depends on what they are asked to do, how it is introduced to them and the help and support available to them whilst doing it. Where there is choice (more likely in GCE than GCSE) this can be difficult for teachers and pupils, but guidance and exemplar material provided by the awarding body can be helpful.

The awarding bodies usually ask teachers to report the help given to pupils. 'Help' includes advice given to the class as a whole, for example through helpsheets, as well as to individuals. The teacher may be required to make a note on the pupils' scripts of help given to individuals. The awarding body gives strong guidance in the specification on help that can be given. In addition you should be learning from your schools about how to support pupils undertaking these assessments.

RELIABLE MARKING AND MODERATION OF INTERNALLY ASSESSED WORK

Moderation is the process through which marks for internally assessed work are brought in line with a common standard, thus making them reliable. 'Internal' moderation seeks to establish a common standard within the school. 'External' moderation makes the comparisons across schools and nationally.

Internal moderation may be carried out in various ways. In science, teachers generally aim to establish the correct standard of marking as early as possible. Usually, they look together at the awarding body's guidance and interpret it for their own circumstances; they may produce marking guidelines for particular internally assessed tasks, illustrating pupils' responses for different marks, and they will exchange scripts, mark them separately and then discuss them to resolve differences. The latter may be organised annually at a formal moderation meeting in the department. Even when teachers have become familiar with applying the awarding body's criteria, any marks reported to pupils or their parents are provisional since they will still be subject to external moderation. Feedback to pupils is valuable especially if there will be opportunities for them to improve their performance, but schools and departments may set their own rules about what feedback is allowed.

Task 6.2.4 **Internal moderation**

Compare your own judgements in marking an internally assessed task with another teacher's judgements. If possible, do this first with the teacher of a class you are working with and for a task you have seen them do.

Both you and the class teacher should mark the same scripts independently, without access to the other's marks. Mark at least six pupils' work, selected from the top, middle and lower ranges of achievement in the class. The first marker will need to annotate the script in line with the awarding body's guidance. Then compare the marks each of you has given; discuss the reasons for any differences and note how these are resolved.

You may be able to follow this up by attending a moderation meeting in your science department.

Science departments work out the marks for internally assessed tasks. A number of sample scripts are supplied to an external moderator appointed by the awarding body, selected from across the range of pupil achievement and from different classes and teachers. The moderator has the right to ask for additional scripts if necessary, so the department must keep all the pupils' scripts that contribute to their final marks until after the external moderation is completed. It is not uncommon for moderators to make adjustments to the school's marks. The adjustments are made to all pupils' marks from the school, even though based on a small sample. It is assumed that the sample is representative of the whole. External moderators write a short report on their decisions, a copy of which is returned to the school.

PREPARING PUPILS FOR THEIR PUBLIC EXAMINATIONS

Schools and science departments pay increasing attention to preparing pupils for examinations by:

- developing pupils' study skills for revision
- teaching 'examination techniques' for answering questions effectively
- providing specific resources to help revise course content
- actively supporting pupils during the revision process
- building up their confidence and motivation (most important of all).

Most schools make use of one or more of the published revision guides, some of which are exactly matched to each specification. There are usually also accompanying workbooks, though some schools channel pupils towards buying the workbook from a different publisher, since otherwise revision can amount to no more than an undemanding copying exercise from the page in the guide to the corresponding 'blanks' in the workbook.

However, only a minority of pupils are likely to find guides and workbooks helpful since they require a text-based learning style (and a good deal of persistence). There are lots of ways to revise, just as there are lots of ways to learn. Teachers need to introduce the different techniques to pupils using, for example, mind mapping, key fact summaries, problem-solving exercises, quizzes, paired testing as well as practice examination questions. Software packages for revision are also popular with many pupils. They include online revision, for example the well-established BBC Bitesize, and reasonably priced CD-based packages, some of which incorporate sophisticated tools for pupils to track their individual progress through the material.

EXAMINING NEW ELEMENTS OF THE SCIENCE CURRICULUM

While teachers need to keep the requirements of external examinations and assessments in mind and to prepare pupils for them, it is important not to be confined by them. Given, however, that *How Science Works* is a relatively new component of the science curriculum it is possible that, in the short term, it will become defined by the demands of the examinations. Task 6.2.5 asks you to identify the gap between the model of *How Science Works* in the specification and the way it is represented in the assessment tasks and examinations.

Task 6.2.5 Models of *How Science Works* in specifications and examinations

First read the following article, to see a theoretical approach to analysing the specifications: Baggott la Velle, L. and Erduran, S. (2007) 'Argument and developments in the science curriculum', *School Science Review*, 88 (324), 331–9.

Examine the models of *How Science Works* as denoted in the specifications of two GCSE science courses and analyse the extent to which this model is carried through to the assessment tasks and examination papers (i.e. you are examining the validity of the assessment and examinations tools).

An alternative M-level task relating to the influence of 'league tables' on the grouping within different subjects in schools is given in Task 6.2.6 in Capel *et al.* (2009: 346). This task is particularly pertinent to science, given that the percentage of pupils achieving the equivalent of Double Award Science at GCSE will be reported in the annual 'league tables' for schools.

SUMMARY AND KEY POINTS

Examination success is a highly visible and rewarding aspect of your teaching; good results are a source of professional satisfaction and pride. The annual set of results is one way in which individual teachers, subject departments and schools as a whole assess their performance, as well as an important basis on which they are judged, not least by their local communities. Understanding the nature of this summative assessment, so that you can prepare pupils adequately for it, is of paramount importance. You are strongly advised to try out the examination questions, to learn about the internal assessment tasks, to understand marking processes and to learn how to prepare pupils as soon as possible. Work with teachers on moderation procedures and learn what you can about the administration of the assessments and examinations.

FURTHER READING

Capel, S., Leask, M. and Turner, T. (2009) *Learning to Teach in the Secondary School*, 5th edition. London: Routledge.

■ Haydn, T. (2009) Unit 6.1 'Assessment, Pupil Motivation and Learning', 327–351.
■ Youens, B. (2009) Unit 6.2 'External Assessment and Examinations', 352–365.

Baggott la Velle, L. and Erduran, S. (2007) 'Argument and developments in the science curriculum', *School Science Review*, 88 (324), 331–9.

Lambert, D. and Lines, D. (2000) *Understanding Assessment: Purposes, Perceptions and Practice*. London and New York; RoutledgeFalmer.

This book provides a deeper guide into examination principles in the first half. The second half is devoted to formative assessment and is applicable to Unit 6.1.

RELEVANT WEBSITES

Specifications, exemplar examination material and mark schemes are available online from the awarding bodies AQA, Edexcel, OCR, CCEA, WJEC (see *Relevant websites* in Unit 3.3).

BBC bitesize science

http://www.bbc.co.uk/schools/gcsebitesize/science/ (accessed 24 September 2009).

JCQ (Joint Council for Qualifications)

Publishes annual examinations statistics.

http://www.jcgq.org.uk/national_results/index.cfm (accessed 24 September 2009).

OfQual: Office of the Qualifications and Examinations Regulator

http:: http://www.ofqual.gov.uk (accessed 13 August 2009).

National Qualifications Framework

http://www.ofqual.gov.uk/2368.aspx

Subject criteria for GCSE sciences

http://www.ofqual.gov.uk/743.aspx

Subject criteria for GCE A and AS level sciences

http://www.ofqual.gov.uk/471.aspx

QCDA (Qualifications and Development Agency)

http://www.qcda.gov.uk (accessed 10 August 2009).

Consultation on new GCSE science criteria for 2011

http://www.qcda.gov.uk/21855.aspx

QCA (June 2009) *Preparing students for 'stretch and challenge' in revised A2 assessments*. QCA 09 4299

http://www.qcda.gov.uk/23025.aspx

7 BEYOND QUALIFIED TEACHER STATUS

Jenny Frost and Ralph Levinson

INTRODUCTION

The initial teacher education course is the launch pad of your teaching career. This final chapter looks beyond attainment of Qualified Teacher Status (QTS) through the Newly Qualified Teacher (NQT) year towards your continuing professional development (CPD). Much of the advice you need is, however, contained in Chapter 8 of *Learning to Teach in the Secondary School* (Capel *et al.* 2009), so we focus here on issues that are particularly pertinent to science teachers.

OBJECTIVES

By the end of this chapter you should:

- be aware of the essential requirements when applying for your first teaching post
- be able to identify the preparation necessary for your induction year
- have learned what opportunities are available beyond your induction year.

GETTING YOUR FIRST POST

Although at the end of your initial teacher education course you have qualified as a teacher, you are still a beginner, so it is important that you find a post where you feel you are well supported and where you have opportunities to develop in the way you want. Unit 8.1 'Getting your first post' (Capel *et al.*, 2009: 425–42) gives clear, and detailed, guidance on what you need to think about and do when looking and applying for jobs. It explains how to prepare for the interview and for the lesson which you may well have to give. There is advice on the procedures for accepting a post if it is offered. Examples are given of letters of application, CVs, likely interview questions and a typical programme of an interview day.

When you are looking for vacancies, bear in mind that at the present time those specialising in physics are most in demand, followed only a little way behind by chemists. Advertisements for science posts, therefore, frequently indicate that a physical science teacher is preferred. Biology specialists should not, however, be put off from applying for such a post if, in all other respects, they have the attributes for the post and would like to work at the school. Remember that as an NQT, the main requirements are a good background in science, an enthusiasm for and competence in teaching science and being a good teamworker.

During your PGCE year your placement school might invite you to apply for a post. This should be taken as a reflection of the positive opinion the science department and the school has of your abilities but you should also stand back and think if this is the department and school you want. If this is your first placement school it is also the first school of which you have any knowledge. When applying for a job it helps if you have been able to compare different schools from the perspective of the teacher. If you are convinced it is the right job for you, then go ahead, but it does make sense to wait until you have experience of other schools before you apply for or accept a post.

There is a lot you can find out about schools from Ofsted reports, and the schools' own websites. When you apply for a job, further information is sent to you. If you are shortlisted, you have the opportunity to visit the school and we strongly advise trying to arrange this ahead of the interview day. You are more likely to see the department on a normal working day.

Examples of questions you may want to ask yourself are:

■ Is there a collegiate feel to the science department or do teachers tend to do their own thing? Are teachers friendly to you as well as each other? Do the technicians and the teachers have a good relationship? Do you feel welcome?

■ What facilities are available in the department? Are there sufficient technicians in each subject area?

■ Is there an 'atmosphere' in the school you feel comfortable with?

■ Are there contemporary posters on the walls? Is children's work displayed? Does it look fresh and interesting?

■ How will you be supported during your NQT year?

■ Will you have a dedicated laboratory or will you be moving round a lot?

■ Is there good IT support? Do the computers look as if they are used?

■ Is the science department isolated from the rest of the school?

Obviously, there is no one answer to these questions but you do need to give them careful thought.

Before your interview you are likely to be asked to prepare a lesson, to be given on the day. While you may be set something highly specific, e.g. a ten-minute episode on plant reproduction to Y9, be prepared also for a wide brief, e.g. a 30-minute lesson on *How Science Works* to Y7 where teachers would be looking for your ability to select from a range of possibilities. Try to prepare your own resources rather than ask the school for equipment. However, the lesson must be *yours*. On no account should you take in a video that takes up most of the teaching time.

If you are offered and accept a post, you should expect to visit the school again before the end of the summer term to collect schemes of work, a timetable and information about which classes you will be teaching. This will also give you an opportunity to talk with the teacher who will be your mentor for the induction year.

Unit 8.3 'Accountability, contractual and statutory responsibilities' (Capel *et al.*, 2009: 453–8) will help you to understand your responsibilities as a new teacher within the education system.

THINKING AHEAD TO THE NQT YEAR

The transition from initial teacher education to your first post can be smoothed if you think ahead to the demands of your new responsibilities and understand the support systems that are in place to help you achieve the 'core' standards for induction by the end of the year. Unit 8.2 'Developing further as teacher' in Capel *et al.* (2009: 443–52) provides relevant advice and information. One of its recommendations is to talk with NQTs in your placement schools, to identify the demands that have been made on them and the differences they have experienced between their initial teacher education year and their NQT year.

From your study of schools and science departments (see Unit 1.3 of this book) and your experiences in school, you may be formulating ideas about what career paths within science education you wish to take. Towards the end of the course you are likely to discuss future development formally with your tutor. (In England this is recorded on a Career Entry Development Profile (See *Useful websites*)). Planning your professional development is about using your strengths and developing those aspects of your teaching that would best underpin these strengths, and considering those areas in which you have not had much experience.

Career aspirations will also influence your preferred CPD. Two case studies illustrate this point.

> Tamsin had been offered a post at her first placement school where she had become fully involved in out-of-school activities. She saw her future in the pastoral role rather than as a science specialist. Science would be her main subject area but she aspired to be a head of year and eventually responsible for pastoral provision within a school. For one of her areas for development she included increasing her understanding of specialist pastoral responsibilities and requesting any CPD days to support these skills.

> Paul hoped to become a head of department. He saw a number of areas for development. Chemistry was his specialist subject and he felt he still needed to improve his understanding of physics. He therefore wanted to pay special attention to this during his NQT year, and continue the good work he had done in his PGCE year by taking a course for non-specialist teachers of physics. As a potential manager he also wanted to see how managers operated within the school and had identified this as another area of development.

BEYOND NQT

Your growth as a teacher continues throughout your career. The route you choose has to suit your own circumstances and make teaching a fulfilling and important part of your life. There are experienced science teachers who prefer to spend most of their time in the classroom rather than in management and others who see their future as a headteacher.

In the end, the happiest teachers are those who love what they do, have time to relax and enjoy themselves and are content with their responsibilities, regardless of salary.

Among the most effective ways of continuing your professional development are a variety of courses, notably:

■ Masters routes in academic institutions, which allow you to reflect on and interrogate your own teaching practice. Where you have gained Masters credits on your PGCE course, remember that you have only five years in which to 'cash them in'. (see Unit 1.1 for advice about Masters courses).

■ Doctoral courses available from HEIs. Studying for a doctorate is an enormous commitment and you should only consider starting once you have been teaching for at least three years and have completed your Masters degree. Doing a doctorate part-time, the usual route nowadays for practising teachers, will take five to seven years.

■ A wide range of CPD courses for science teachers provided by the network of science learning centres, which has been established across the country. You can register free online, outlining your specific areas of interest; information about relevant courses will then be sent to you (see *Useful websites*).

PROFESSIONAL ORGANISATIONS

Like other professions, teaching has its own professional body, the General Teaching Council (GTC) and you will be required to register (www.gtce.org.uk). We strongly recommend that you also join the Association for Science Education (ASE), a professional association for science teachers. In joining the ASE as a secondary teacher you receive the quarterly journal *School Science Review* which contains informed articles by teachers and educationalists on teaching and learning science, book reviews and practical tips.

The three organisations for the main subject areas in science, the Institute of Biology (IoB), the Royal Society of Chemistry (RSC) and the Institute of Physics (IoP) have their own educational sections and also run many stimulating activities and produce their own educational journals that contain invaluable contemporary information (see *Useful websites*). Education officers are also employed by some large industrial companies and organisations such as the Royal Society, the Association of the British Pharmaceutical Industry and the Engineering Council.

DOES A PGCE QUALIFY ME ONLY FOR TEACHING?

There are employment possibilities offered by the PGCE that go beyond the teaching profession. This comes with a strong rider: it is only after you have completed your induction year and a few years more of being an effective science teacher that they become a reality. Examples of careers linked to science education include:

■ local authority science adviser or science inspector
■ freelance consultant in, for example, running in-service courses
■ education officer or adviser for professional bodies or institutions
■ education officers and educators at science centres and science museums
■ writing science books and textbooks

- educational media including TV specialising in science education
- research in science education and teacher education.

It is generally committed and experienced teachers with a wide range of interests who wish for a change who are likely to be the best candidates for these posts.

SUMMARY AND KEY POINTS

This chapter has focused on the opportunities that face you as you progress from a pre-service teacher to an experienced professional, a route that opens out a wide range of possibilities. You need to be aware of the practice and accompanying documentation that supports a successful career as well as taking advantage of the courses that contribute to your progress as a successful science teacher.

FURTHER READING

Capel, S., Leask, M. and Turner, T. (2009) *Learning to Teach in the Secondary School*, 5th edition. London: Routledge.

- Taylor, A., Lawrence, J. and Capel, S. Unit 8.1 'Getting your first post', 425–42.
- Lawrence, J., Taylor, A. and Capel, S. Unit 8.2 'Developing further as a Teacher', 442–52.
- Leask, M. and Green, A. Unit 8.3 'Accountability, contractual and statutory duties', 453–58.

Bubb, S. (2009) *The Insider's Guide for New Teachers: Succeed in Training and Induction*, 2nd edition. London: Routledge.

Capel, S., Heilbronn, R., Leask, M. and Turner, T. (2004) *Starting to Teach in the Secondary School: A Companion for the NQT.* London: RoutledgeFalmer.

This covers issues faced by NQTs of all subjects and provides advice about settling into a new department and school, managing time and pressure and meeting the induction standards. It contains a theoretical dimension about teaching and learning and is supported by research evidence.

Parkinson, J. (2004) *Improving Secondary Science Teaching.* London: RoutledgeFalmer.

A book for experienced teachers but may provide stimulation and opportunities for reflection for NQTs who are progressing well.

Wallace, J. and Louden, W. (2002) *Dilemmas of Science Teaching: Perspectives on Problems of Practice.* London: RoutledgeFalmer.

A series of case studies addressing issues that face science teachers. The dilemmas raised are discussed by experienced practitioners providing a theoretical foundation for the discourse.

USEFUL WEBSITES

Association for Science Education (ASE)

http://www.ase.org.uk/ (accessed 18 September 2009).

National and Regional Science Learning Centres

http://www.sciencelearningcentres.org.uk/ (accessed 18 September 2009).

Institute of Physics

http://www.iop.org/ (accessed 18 September 2009).

Institute of Biology

http://www.iob.org/ (accessed 18 September 2009).

Royal Society of Chemistry

http://www.rsc.org/ (accessed 18 September 2009).

The Wellcome Trust

http://www.wellcome.ac.uk/ (accessed 18 September 2009).

Career Entry Development Profile

http://www.tda.gov.uk/teachers/induction/cedp.aspx (accessed 3 October 2009).

Core standards to be achieved by the end of the NQT year and what you can expect from induction

http://www.tda.gov.uk/teachers/induction.aspx (accessed 18 September 2009).

General Teaching Council

http://www.gtce.org.uk/ (accessed 18 September 2009).

REFERENCES

ACCAC *see* Qualification, Curriculum and Assessment Authority for Wales.

Adams, A. and Allday, J. (2000) *Advanced Physics*, Oxford: Oxford University Press.

Adey, P. and Shayer, M. (1994) *Really Raising Standards*, London: Routledge, pp. 98–107.

Adey, P. and Yates, C. (2001) *Thinking Science: The Materials of the CASE Project*, Walton-on-Thames: Nelson.

Alexander, R. J. (2009a) *Towards a New Primary Curriculum: A Report from the Cambridge Primary Review. Part 2: The Future*, Cambridge: University of Cambridge Faculty of Education http://www.primaryreview.org.uk/Publications/CambridgePrimaryReviewrep.html (accessed 24 June 2009).

Alexander, R. J. (2009b) *Children, Their World, Their Education. Final Report and Recommendations of the Cambridge Primary Review.* London: Routledge.

Alexander, R. J. and Flutter, J. (2009) *Towards a New Primary Curriculum: A Report from the Cambridge Primary Review. Part 1: Past and Present*, Cambridge: University of Cambridge Faculty of Education http://www.primaryreview.org.uk/Publications/CambridgePrimaryReviewrep.html (accessed 24 June 2009).

Amos, R. and Reiss, M. (2006) 'What contribution can residential field courses make to the education of 11–14 year olds?' *School Science Review*, 88 (322), 37–44.

Amos, S, and Boohan, R. (eds) (2002) *Aspects of Teaching Secondary Science: Perspectives on Practice*, London: RoutledgeFalmer for the Open University.

AQA (Assessment and Qualifications Alliance) online. Available at http://www.aqa.org.uk (accessed 25 August 2009).

Archard, D. (2000) *Sex Education*, Impact No 7. Philosophy of Education Society of Great Britain.

Arthus-Bertrand, Y. (2002) *The Earth from the Air Postcard Book*, London: Thames and Hudson.

Ashton, E. and Watson, B. (1998) 'Values education: a fresh look at procedural neutrality', *Educational Studies*, 24 (2), 183–93.

Asoka, H. and Squires, A. (1998) 'Progression and continuity', in Ratcliffe, M. *ASE Guide to Secondary Science Education*, Cheltenham: Stanley Thornes, pp. 175–82.

ASE (Association for Science Education) http://www.ase.org.uk/ (accessed 1 September 2009).

ASE Safeguards Committee (2006) *Safeguards in the School Laboratory*, Hatfield: Association for Science Education.

Attenborough, D. (1979) *Life on Earth: A Natural History*, Boston, MA: Little, Brown, and Company.

Attenborough, D. (1995) *The Private Life of Plants: A Natural History of Plant Behaviour*, London: BBC Books.

Baggott la Velle, L. and Erduran, S. (2007) 'Argument and developments in the science curriculum', *School Science Review,* 88 (324), 331–39.

Barton, R. (ed.) (2004) *Teaching Secondary Science with ICT*. Maidenhead: Open University Press.

REFERENCES ■ ■ ■ ■

Beauchamp, G. and Parkinson, J. (2005) 'Beyond the "wow" factor: developing interactivity with interactive whiteboards', *School Science Review*, 86 (316), 97–103.

Bebbington, A. (2006) 'Some prickly thoughts: does holly become more prickly when it's grazed?' *School Science Review*, 87 (320), 83–90.

Bennett, J. (2003) *Teaching and Learning Science. A Guide to Recent Research and its Applications*, London: Continuum.

Bishop, K. and Denley, P. (2007) *Learning Science Teaching: Developing a Professional Knowledge Base*, Maidenhead: Open University Press.

Black, P. (1987) 'Deciding to teach', *Steam*, London: ICI Science Teachers' Magazine No. 8.

Black, P. J. and Harrison, C. (2001a) 'Feedback in questioning and marking: the science teacher's role in formative assessment', *School Science Review*, 82 (301), 55–61, June.

Black, P. J. and Harrison, C. (2001b) 'Self- and peer-assessment and taking responsibility: the science pupil's role in formative assessment', *School Science Review*, 83 (302), 43–49, September.

Black, P., Harrison, C., Lee, C., Marshall, B. and Wiliam, D. (2002) *Working inside the Black Box: Assessment for Learning in the Classroom*, London: King's College, Department of Education and Professional Studies.

Black, P., Harrison, C., Lee, C., Marshall, B. and Wiliam, D. (2003) *Assessment for Learning: Putting It into Practice*, Buckingham: Open University Press.

Black, P. and Wiliam, D. (1998) *Inside the Black Box – Raising Standards through Classroom Assessment,* London: Kings College.

Boohan, R. (2008) 'Innovations in practical work from the Science Enhancement Programme', *School Science Review*, 89 (328), 85–95.

Borrows, P. (1999) 'Chemistry trails', *Education in Chemistry*, 6, 158–9.

Borrows, P. (2002) 'Risk assessment in science for secondary schools', in Amos, S. and Boohan, R. (eds) (2002) *Aspects of Teaching Secondary Science*, London: RoutledgeFalmer for the Open University.

Borrows, P. (2006) 'Health and safety in science education', Chapter 13 in Wood-Robinson, V. (ed.) *ASE Guide to Secondary Science Education*, Hatfield: The Association for Science Education.

Brain, M. (2001) *How Stuff Works*, New York: Hungry Minds.

Brain, M. (2003) *More How Stuff Works*, New York: Hungry Minds.

Brain, M. *How Stuff Works: Carbon Dating.* http://www.science.howstuffworks.com/carbon-14.htm (accessed 11 January 2010).

Braund, M. (2009) 'Progression and continuity in learning science at transfer from primary to secondary school', in *Perspectives on Education 2 (Primary/Secondary Transfer in Science).* Available online at: http://www.wellcome.ac.uk/perspectives

Braund, M. and Reiss, M. (2004) *Learning Science Outside the Classroom*, London: Routledge Falmer.

Braund, M. and Reiss, M. (2006) 'Towards a more authentic science curriculum: the contribution of out-of-school learning', *International Journal of Science Education*, 28 (12), 1373–88.

Brown, J. R. (1991) *Laboratory of the Mind: Thought Experiments in the Natural Sciences*, London: Routledge.

Burman, E. (2008) *Deconstructing Developmental Psychology* (2nd edn), Hove:Routledge.

Burton, D. (2009) 'Ways pupils learn', in Capel, S., Leask, M. and Turner, T. *Learning to Teach in the Secondary School: A Companion to School Experience*, 5th edn, London: RoutledgeFalmer, pp. 251–66.

Butler, R. (1988) 'Enhancing and undermining intrinsic motivation; the effects of task-involving and ego-involving evaluation on interest and performance', *British Journal of Educational Psychology*, 58, 1–14.

Calder, N. (1977) *The Key to the Universe: A Report on the New Physics*, London: BBC. Reprinted in Carey, J. (1995) *The Faber Book of Science,* London: Faber & Faber.

Capel, S., Leask, M. and Turner, T. (eds) (2009) *Learning to Teach in the Secondary School: A Companion to School Experience*, 5th edn, London: RoutledgeFalmer.

Carey, J. (1995) *The Faber Book of Science*, London: Faber & Faber.

CCEA (Council for the Curriculum, Examinations and Assessment) http://www.rewarding learning.org.uk/ (accessed 25 June 2009).

Chalmers, A. F. (1999) *What Is this Thing called Science?*, 3rd edn, Buckingham: Open University Press.

Chapman, J., Hamer, P. and Sears, J. (2000) 'Non-judgemental differentiation: teaching and learning styles for the future', in Sears, J. and Sorensen, P. (eds) *Issues in Science Teaching*, London: Routledge Falmer.

CLEAPSS (2004) *Hazcards*, Brunel University, London: Consortium of Local Education Authorities School Science Service (CLEAPSS).

Coffield, F., Moseley, D., Hall, E. and Ecclestone, K. (2004) *Should We Be Using Learning Styles? What Research Has to Say about Practice*, London: Learning Skills Research Centre.

Conoly, C. and Hills, P. (2008) *Collins Advanced Chemistry*, 3rd edn, London: Collins.

Crick, B. (2001) Citizenship and science; science and citizenship, *School Science Review*, 83 (302), 33–8.

Daintith, J. and Gjertson, D. (eds) (1999) *Oxford Dictionary of Scientists*, Oxford: Oxford University Press.

Dawkins, R. (1989) *The Selfish Gene*, Oxford: Oxford Paperbacks.

DCSF (Department for Children, Schools and Families) (2005) *Higher Standards, Better Schools for All: More Choice for Parents and Pupils*. Norwich: DfES/TSO.

DCSF (2008) *Review of Sex and Relationship Education (SRE) in Schools*, London: DCSF.

DCSF (2009a) *The National Strategies Framework for Teaching Science*, available online at: http://nationalstrategies.standards.dcsf.gov.uk/secondary (accessed 24 August 2009).

DCSF (2009b) *Every Child Matters*, http://www.dcsf.gov.uk/everychildmatters/

DCSF (2009c) *The Report of the Expert Group on Assessment*, London: DCSF.

De Silva, S. and De Meza, L. (2004) *More about Life: Sex and Relationship Education in Secondary School*, London: Forbes Publications Ltd.

Democritus, in Porter, R. and Ogilvie, M. (eds) *Dictionary of Scientific Biography*, 3rd edn, Volume 1, Oxford: Helicon, p. 290.

Dennison, P. E. and Dennison, G. E. (1989) *Brain Gym* (teacher's edition), Edu-Kinesthetics, http://www.braingym.com/ (accessed 11 January 2010).

Denny, M. and Chennell, F. (1986) 'Science practicals: what do pupils think?' *European Journal of Science Education*, 8 (3), 325–36.

DES/WO Department for Education and Science and Welsh Office (DES/WO) (1988) *National Curriculum Task Group on Assessment and Testing (TGAT Report)*, London: DES.

DES/WO (1989) *Discipline in Schools: Report of the Committee of Enquiry*, chaired by Lord Elton, London: HMSO.

DeWitt, J. and Osborne, J. (2007) 'Supporting teachers on science-focused school trips: towards an integrated framework of theory and practice', *International Journal of Science Education*, 29 (6), 685–710.

DfEE (1999b) *The National Curriculum for England Non-statutory Frameworks for Personal, Social and Health Education and Citizenship at Key Stages 1 and 2; Personal, Social and Health Education at Key Stages 3 and 4*, London: DfEE and QCA.

DfEE (2000) *Sex and Relationship Guidance*, London: DfEE.

DfEE/QCA (2000) 'Science – a scheme of work for KS3', available online at http://www.standards.dfes.gov.uk/schemes2/secondary_science/?view=get (accessed 14 December 2009).

DfES (Department for Education and Skills) (2001) *Key Stage 3 Literacy Strategy*. London: DfES.

DfES (2005) 'The learning outside the classroom manifesto', London: Department for Education and Skills. The website developed from the manifesto can be found at http://www.lotc.org.uk/

Diamond, J. (2006) *The Third Chimpanzee: The Evolution and Future of the Human Animal (P.S.)*,

New York: Harper Perennial.

Dickinson, C. and Wright, J. (1993) *Differentiation: A Practical Handbook of Classroom Strategies*, Coventry: NCET.

Dillon, J. (2000) 'Managing the science department', in Monk, M. and Osborne, J. (eds) *Good Practice in Science Teaching: What Research Has to Say*, Buckingham: Open University Press.

Dillon, J., Rickinson, M., Tearney, K., Morris, M., Choi, M.Y., Sanders, D. and Benefield, P. (2006) 'The value of outdoor learning: evidence from research in the UK and elsewhere'. *School Science Review*, 87 (320), 107–11.

Dixon, B. (1989) *The Science of Science*, London: Cassell.

Dixon, N. (2008) 'Can data logging improve the quality of interpretation and evaluation in chemistry lessons? *School Science Review*, 89 (329), 55–62.

DoH (Department of Health) (2001) *The National Strategy for Sexual Health and HIV*, London: Department of Health.

DoH (2004) *Choosing Health: Making Healthy Choices Easier*, London: Department of Health.

Donaldson, M. (1978) *Children's Minds*, Glasgow: Fontana.

Donnelly, J. (2001) 'Contested terrain or unified project? "The nature of science" in the National Curriculum for England and Wales', *International Journal of Science Education*, 23, 181–95.

Driver, R., Guesne, E. and Tinberghien, A. (1985) *Children's Ideas in Science*, Buckingham: Open University Press.

Driver, R., Leach, J., Millar, R. and Scott, P. (1996) *Young People's Images of Science*, Buckingham: Open University Press.

Driver, R., Squires, A., Rushworth, P. and Wood-Robinson, V. (1994) *Making Sense of Secondary Science*, London: Routledge.

Dweck, C. S. (1986) 'Motivational processes affect learning', *American Psychologist (Special Issue: Psychological Science and Education)*, 41 (10), 1040–48.

Earth Science Teachers Association (ESTA), Burlington House, Piccadilly, London WIV 0BN. http://www.esta-uk.net/ (accessed 11 January 2010).

Edexcel Awarding Body. http://www.edexcel.org.uk (accessed 12 February 2010).

Ellis, P., Ryan, R. and Macdonald, A. (2003) *Reading into Science: Physics*, Cheltenham: Nelson Thornes.

Erduran, S. (ed.) (2007) *School Science Review*, 88 (324), 29–90, Hatfield: Association for Science Education.

Erduran, S., Osborne, J. F. and Simon, S. (2004) 'Enhancing the quality of argument in school science', *Journal of Research in Science Teaching*, 41 (10), 994–1020.

Exploring science for teachers (resources for teachers including classroom activities). http://www.explorelearning.com/ (accessed 12 February 2004). See also ASE.

Falk, J. and Dierking, L. (2000) *Learning from Museums*, Walnut Creek, CA: AltaMira Press.

Farabee, M. J. (2002) *Biology Book*. http://www.emc.maricopa.edu/faculty/farabee/ BIOBK/BioBookTOC.html (accessed 23 July 2009).

Fearn, F. (2006) 'Data-loggers in ecological enquiry in school grounds and beyond', *School Science Review*, 87 (320), 69–73.

Feyerabend, P. (1975/1988) *Against Method*, rev. edn, London: Verso.

Feyerabend, P. (1993) *Against Method* (3rd edn), London: Verso.

Feynman, R. P. (2000) *The Pleasure of Finding Things Out*, London: Penguin Books.

Frost, R. (2002a) *Data Logging and Control*, London IT in Science.

Frost, R. (2002b) *Data logging in Practice*, London: IT in Science.

Galton, M. (2009) 'Moving to secondary school: initial encounters and their effects', in *Perspectives on Education 2 (Primary/Secondary Transfer in Science)*. Available online at: http://www.wellcome.ac.uk/perspectives (accessed 20 June 2009).

Gardner, J. (2006) *Assessment and Learning*, London: Sage.

Gardner, M. (1993) *Frames of Mind: The Theory of Multiple Intelligences*, London: Falmer.

Gayford, C. G. and Dillon, P. J. (1995) Policy and the practice of environmental education in England: a dilemma for teachers, *Environmental Education Research*, 1, 173–84.

General Teaching Council. http://www.gtce.org.uk (accessed 18 August 2009).

Ginnis, P. (2002) *The Teacher's Toolkit*, Carmarthan: Crown House Publishing.

Glackin, M. (2007) 'Using urban green space to teach science', *School Science Review*, 89 (327), 29–36.

Glauert, E. and Frost, J. (1997) 'Pedagogy in primary science'. Publication of the 3rd Summer Conference for Teacher Education in Primary Science. *Developing the Right Kind of Teacher*, Durham: School of Education, University of Durham, 94–103.

Goldacre, B. (2008) *Bad Science*, London: Fourth Estate.

Goldsworthy, A. and Feasey, R. (1997) *Making Sense of Primary Science Investigations* (2nd edn, rev. Ball), Hatfield: ASE.

Goldsworthy, A., Watson, R. and Wood-Robinson, V. (2000a) *Investigations: Getting to Grips with Graphs*, Hatfield: ASE.

Goldsworthy, A., Watson, R. and Wood-Robinson, V. (2000b) *Investigations: Developing Understanding in Scientific Enquiry*, Hatfield: ASE. (See also Watson.)

Goodwin, A. (2001) 'Wonder in science teaching and learning: an update', *School Science Review*, 83 (302), 69–73, Sept.

Gott, R. and Duggan, S. (2006) 'Investigations, scientific literacy and evidence', in Wood-Robinson, V., *Guide to Secondary Science Education*, Hatfield: Association for Science Education, 188–95.

Gott, R. and Duggan, S. (2007) 'A framework for practical work in science and scientific literacy through argumentation', *Research in Science and Technological Education*, 25 (3), 271–91.

Griffin, J. (2002) 'Look! no hands! Practical science experiences in museums', in Amos, S. and Boohan, R. (eds) *Teaching Science in Secondary Schools: A Reader*, London: Routledge/Falmer.

Hanley, P., Osborne, J. and Ratcliffe, M. (2008) 'Twenty first century science', *School Science Review*, 90 (330), 105–12.

Harrison, C., Simon, S. and Watson, R. (2000) 'Progression and differentiation', in Monk, M. and Osborne, J. (eds) *Good Practice in Science Teaching*, Buckingham: Open University Press.

Harrison, J. (1999) 'Reproduction and sex education', in Reiss, M. (ed.) *Teaching Secondary Biology* London: John Murray.

Harrison, J. (2000) *Sex Education in Secondary Schools*, Buckingham: Open University Press.

Health and Safety Executive. http://www.hse.gov.uk/schooltrips/ (accessed 30 June 2009).

HMSO (2002) Science and Technology – Third Report: online at http://www.parliament.the-stationery-office.co.uk/pa/cm200102/cmselect/cmsctech/508/508.pdf (accessed 24.8.09).

Hodgkin, D. (1988) 'Finding what's there', in Wolpert, L. and Richards, A. (eds) *A Passion for Science*, Oxford: Oxford University Press, pp. 69–79. Reprinted as 'Seeing the atoms in crystals', in Carey, J. (1995) *The Faber Book of Science*, London: Faber & Faber, pp. 467–74.

Hogan, K. (2002) Small groups' ecological reasoning while making an environmental management decision, *Journal of Research in Science Teaching*, 39 (4), 341–68.

Hollins, M. (2006) 'Science education 14–19', in Wood-Robinson, V. (ed.) *ASE Guide to Secondary Science Education*, Hatfield: Association for Science Education, pp. 56–62.

Hollins, M. (2007) *School Science Review 2007*, 89 (326), 25–91, Hatfield: Association for Science Education.

Houghton, J. T. (Chair) (2001) *Climate Change 2001: The Scientific Basis. Third Assessment Report of the Intergovernmental Panel on Climate Change*, Cambridge: Cambridge University Press.

House of Commons Science and Technology Committee (2002) *Science Education from 14–19*. London: HMSO.

Institute of Physics. http://www.iop.org (accessed 20 August 2009).

REFERENCES ▪ ▪ ▪ ▪

Intergovernment Panel on Climate Change (IPCC) (2007) *Fourth Assessment Report: The Physical Science Basis*, Cambridge: Cambridge University Press. Available online at http://www.ipcc.ch/pdf/assessment-report/ar4/wg1/ar4–wg1–frontmatter.pdf (accessed 25 June 2009).

International baccalaureate http://www.ibo.org (accessed 18 August 2009).

Jarman, R. (2000) 'Between the idea and the reality falls the shadow: provision for primary-secondary science curricular continuity', in Sears, J. and Sorensen, P. (eds) *Issues in Science Teaching*, London: RoutledgeFalmer.

Jarman, R. and McClune, B. (2007) *Developing Scientific Literacy Using News Media in the Classroom*, Maidenhead: McGraw-Hill/Open University Press.

Jerram, A. (2000) *Teaching Physics to KS4*. London: Hodder and Stoughton.

Johnson, K. (2006) *New Physics for You*, Cheltenham: Nelson Thornes Ltd.

Johnson, P. (2002) 'Progression in children's understanding of a "basic" particle theory: a longitudinal study', in Amos, S. and Boohan, R. (eds) (2002) *Teaching Science in Secondary Schools: A Reader*, London: RoutledgeFalmer for the Open University, pp. 236–49.

Jones, S. (1999) *Almost like a Whale: The Origin of Species Updated*, New York: Doubleday Publishing.

Joyce, B., Calhoun, E. and Hopkins, D. (2002) *Models of Learning – Tools for Teaching* Buckingham: Open University Press.

Kempa, R. (1992) 'Research in chemical education: its role and potential' in Atlay, M., Bennet, S., Dutch, S., Levinson, R., Taylor, P. and West, D. (eds) *Open Chemistry*, London: Hodder and Stoughton, pp. 45–67.

Kibble, D. (1998) 'Moral education dilemmas for the teacher', *Curriculum Journal*, 9 (1), 51–61.

Kind, V. and Kind, P. M. (2008) *Teaching Secondary: How Science Works*, London: Hodder Education.

King, C. (2000) 'The Earth's mantle is solid: teachers' misconceptions about the Earth and plate tectonics', in *School Science Review*, 82 (298) (September), 57–64.

Koufetta-Menicou, C. and Scaife, J. (2000) 'Teachers' questions – types and significance in science education', *School Science Review*, 81 (296) (March), 79–84.

Kuhn, T. S. (1970) *The Structure of Scientific Revolutions* (2nd edn), Chicago, IL: University of Chicago Press.

Lambert, D. and Lines, D. (2000) *Understanding Assessment: Purposes, Perceptions and Practice*, London and New York: RoutledgeFalmer.

Latour, B. and Woolgar, S. (1979) *Laboratory Life: The Social Construction of Scientific Facts*, London: Sage.

Lenton, G. and Stevens, B. (2000) 'Numeracy in science: understanding the misunderstandings', in Sear, J. and Sorensen, P. (eds) *Issues in Science Teaching*, London and New York, RoutledgeFalmer, pp. 80–88.

Levesley, M., Clarke, J., Johnson, P., Baggley, S., Gray, S., Pimbert, M., Coates, A., Brand, I., Shepperd, E. and Smith, S. C. (2008) *Exploring Science: How Science Works 7, 8 and 9 for KS3*, Harlow: Longman, Pearson Education.

Levi, P. (1995) 'The story of the carbon atom', in Carey, J. *The Faber Book of Science*, London: Faber & Faber, pp. 338–44.

Levinson, R. and Reiss, M. (2004) *School Science Review*, 86 (315).

Lock, R., Slingsby, D. and Tilling, S. (special edn eds) (2006) 'Outdoor science', *School Science Review*, 87 (320), 23–111.

Lubben, F. and Millar, R. (1996) 'Children's ideas about the reliability of experimental data', *International Journal of Science Education*, 18 (8), 955–68.

Lynch, D. and McKenna, M. (1990) 'Teaching controversial material: new issues for teachers'. *Social Education*, 54, 317–319.

McDuell, B. (ed.) (2000) *Teaching Secondary Chemistry*, London: John Murray for the Association for Science Education.

McKinney, D. and Michalovic, M. (2004) 'Teaching the stories of scientists and discoveries', in *The Science Teacher*, 71 (9), 46–51, November.

Marland, M. (1993) *The Craft of the Classroom: A Survival Guide to Classroom Management* (2nd edn), London: Heinemann. (See also 3rd edn, 2003, published by Oxford: Heinemann).

Matthews, B. (1996) 'Drawing scientists', *Gender and Education*, 8, 231–43.

Merton, R. K. (1973) *The Sociology of Science: Theoretical and Empirical Investigations*, Chicago, IL: University of Chicago Press.

Millar, R. (1998) 'Rhetoric and reality: what practical work is really for', in Wellington, J. *Practical Work in Science: Which Way Now?* London: Routledge, pp. 16–31.

Millar, R., Lubben, F., Gott, R. and Duggan, S. (1994) 'Investigating in the school science laboratory: conceptual and procedural knowledge and their influence on performance', *Research Papers in Education*, 9 (2), 207–48.

Millar, R. and Osborne, J. (eds) (1998) *Beyond 2000: Science Education for the Future: A Report with Ten Recommendations*, London: King's College London, School of Education.

Mitchell, R. (2006) 'Effective primary/secondary transfer', in Wood-Robinson, V. (ed.) *ASE Guide to Secondary Science Education*, Hatfield: The Association for Science Education.

Monk, M. and Dillon, J. (eds) (1995) *Learning to Teach Science: Activities for Student Teachers and Mentors*. London: Falmer.

Monk, M. and Osborne, J. F. (eds) (2000) *Good Practice in Science Teaching: What Research has to Say.* Buckingham: Open University Press.

Mortimer, E. F. and Scott, P. H. (2003) *Meaning Making in Secondary Science Classrooms*, Maidenhead: Open University Press.

Murphy, P. (1991) 'Gender differences in pupils' reactions to practical work', in Woolnough, B. E. (ed.) *Practical Science*, Milton Keynes: Open University Press.

Murphy, P. J. and Murphy, E. (2002a) 'Urban geological trails', *School Science Review*, 83 (305), 140–3, June.

Murphy, P. J. and Murphy, E. (2002b) 'A time line for geological time', *School Science Review*, 84 (306), 125–6, September.

Murray, C. (2007) 'Reflections on the UK National Curriculum', *School Science Review*, 88 (325), 119–23.

National Curriculum in England:

DfEE (Department for Education and Employment) and QCA (Qualifications and Curriculum Authority) (1999) *The National Curriculum in Science*, (for the KS1 and KS2 science curriculum). http://curriculum.qca.org.uk/key-stages-1-and-2/subjects/index.aspx (accessed 7 August 2009).

The National Curriculum in Science at KS3 and KS4. (England), http://curriculum.qca.org.uk/key-stages-3-and-4/subjects/index.aspx (accessed 7 August 2009).

National Curriculum for Wales:

http://wales.gov.uk/topics/educationandskills/curriculumassessment/arevisedcurriculum forwales/nationalcurriculum/sciencenc/?lang=en (accessed 10 August 2009).

National Curriculum for Northern Ireland:

The Statutory Curriculum at Key Stage 3: Supplementary Guidance.

http://www.nicurriculum.org.uk/key_stage_3/ (accessed 25 August 2009).

National Curriculum for Scotland:

http://www.ltscotland.org.uk/5to14/guidelines/ (accessed 26 August 2009).

Naylor, J. (2002) *Out of the Blue: A 24–hour Skywatcher's Guide*, Cambridge: Cambridge University Press.

Naylor, S. and Keogh, B. (2000) *Concept Cartoons in Science Education*, Sandbach: Millgate House Publishers.

Newton, P., Driver, R. and Osborne, J. (1999) 'The place of argumentation in pedagogy of school science'. *International Journal of Science Education*, 21 (5), 553–76.

Nicolson, P. and Holman, J. (2003) 'National Curriculum for science: looking back and looking forward', *School Science Review*, 85 (311), 21–7.

Nott, M. (ed.) (2001) *School Science Review*, 83 (302).

Nott, M. and Wellington, J. (1993) 'Your nature of science profile: an activity for science teachers', *School Science Review*, 75 (270), 109–12.

Nott, M. and Wellington, J. (1995) 'Critical incidents in the science classroom and the nature of science'. *School Science Review*, 76 (276), 41–46.

Nott, M. and Wellington, J. (1999) 'The state we're in: issues in Key Stage 3 and 4 science', *School Science Review*, 81 (294), 13–18.

Nuffield Curriculum Centre. *21st Century Science*, http://www.21stcenturyscience.org/home/ (accessed 11 February 2004).

OCR (Oxford, Cambridge and Royal Society of Arts) Awarding Body. http://www.ocr.org.uk (accessed 30 June 2009).

Ofsted (2002) *Good Teaching, Effective Departments*, London: Ofsted (HMI Report 337, January). http://www.ofsted.gov.uk/publications/ (accessed 12 February 2010).

Ofsted (2008) *Success in Science*. London: Ofsted.

Ogborn, J. (ed.) (2008) *Advancing Physics AS* and *Advancing Physics A2*, London: Institute of Physics.

Ogborn, J., Kouladis, V. and Papadotretrakis, E. (1996a) 'We measured the Earth by telephone', *School Science Review*, 77 (281) (June), 88–90.

Ogborn, J., Kress, K., Martins, I. and McGillicuddy, K. (1996b) *Explaining Science in the Classroom*, Buckingham: Open University Press.

O'Loughlin, M. (1992) 'Rethinking science education: beyond Piagetian constructivism toward a sociocultural model of teaching and learning', *Journal of Research in Science Teaching*, 29 (8), 791–820.

Open University Open Learning (2007) *Climate Change S 250_3*, Milton Keynes: Open University. http://openlearn.open.ac.uk/course/enrol.php?id=2805 (accessed 25 June 2009).

Osborne, J. (1998) 'Science education without a laboratory?' in Wellington, J. (ed.) *Practical work in Science: Which Way Now?* London: Routledge, pp. 156–73.

Osborne, J. (2008) 'Engaging young people with science: does science education need a new vision?' *School Science Review*, 89 (328), 67–74.

Osborne, J. F. and Collins, S. (2001). 'Pupils' views of the role and value of the science curriculum: a focus-group study', *International Journal of Science Education,* 23 (5), 441–68.

Osborne, J., Erduran, S. and Simon, S. (2004) *Ideas and Evidence and Arguments in Science* (IDEAS project) – an INSET pack with video. London: King's College. (This pack is available from King's, see Jonathan Osborne's website http://www.kcl.ac.uk/schools/sspp/education/staff/josborne.html

Osborne, R. and Freyberg, P. (1985) *Learning in Science*, Aukland: Heinemann.

Oulton, C., Day, V., Dillon, J. and Grace, M. (2004b) 'Controversial issues – teachers' attitudes and practices in the context of citizenship education', *Oxford Review of Education*, 30 (4), 489–508.

Oulton, C., Dillon, J. and Grace, M. (2004a) 'Reconceptualizing the teaching of controversial issues', *International Journal of Science Education*, 26 (4), 411–23.

Pappademos, J. (1984) 'An outline of Africa's role in the history of physics', in Van Sertima, I. *Blacks in Science: Ancient and Modern*. USA: Transaction Books based on articles in *Journal of African Civilisations*.

Parkinson, J. (2002) *Reflective Teaching of Science 11–18*, London: Continuum Books.

Parkinson, J. (2004) *Improving Secondary Science Teaching*, London: RoutledgeFalmer.

Peel, C. and Sample, S. (2006) 'Support staff in science departments', in Wood-Robinson, V. (ed.) *ASE Guide to Secondary Science Education*, Hatfield: Association for Science Education.

Popper, K. R. (1934/1972) *The Logic of Scientific Discovery*, London: Hutchinson.

Porter, R. and Ogilvie, M. (2000) *The Hutchinson Dictionary of Scientific Biography, Volumes I and II*, Oxford: Helicon.

Posner, G., Strike, K., Hewson, P. and Gerzog, W. (1982) 'Accommodation of a scientific conception: toward a theory of conceptual change', *Science Education*, 66 (2), 211–27.

QCA (Qualifications and Curriculum Authority) (1998) *Education for Citizenship and the Teaching of Democracy in Schools: Final Report*, London: QCA (The Crick Report).

QCA (2004) *Changes to the Key Stage 4 Curriculum: Guidance for Implementation from September 2004*, pp. 11–12. This document can be downloaded from http://www.qcda.gov.uk/7119.aspx (accessed 10 August 2009).

QCA (2005) PHSE Key Stage 4: sex and relationship education, Unit 12 Sexuality, QCA.

QCA (2007) *National Curriculum at Key Stages 3 and 4.* Available at http://curriculum.qcda.gov.uk/key-stages-3-and-4/index.aspx (accessed 15 December 2009).

QCA (2007) *Citizenship: Programme of Study for Key Stage 3 and Attainment Target*, London: QCA.

QCA (2007) *Programmes of Study, National Curriculum for Science at Key Stage 3 and Key Stage 4*, London: QCA.

QCA (2008) *The National Curriculum in Science at KS3 and KS4.* http://curriculum.qca.org.uk/key-stages-3-and-4/subjects/index.aspx (accessed 7 August 2009).

QCDA (2009) *A Framework of Personal Learning and Thinking Skills.* http://curriculum.qcda.gov.uk/key-stage-3-and-4/skills/plts/index.aspx (accessed 14 December 2009).

Qualification and Curriculum and Assessment Authority for Wales (ACCAC). http://www.accac.org.uk (accessed 15 June 2009).

Ramsden, E. N. (2001) *Key Science: Chemistry*, 3rd edn, Cheltenham: Stanley Thornes.

Ratcliffe, M. and Grace, M. (2003) *Science Education for Citizenship*, Maidenhead: Open University Press.

Reiss, M. J. (1993) *Science Education for a Pluralist Society*, Buckingham: Open University Press.

Reiss, M. (ed.) (1999) *Teaching Secondary Biology*, London: John Murray for the ASE.

Ridley, M. (1994) *The Red Queen: Sex and the Evolution of Human Nature*, New York: Macmillan Publishing Co.

Roberts, R. (2009) 'How Science Works' (HSW), *Education in Science*, 233, 30–1.

Rogers, L. and Finlayson, H. (2003) 'Does ICT in science really work in the classroom?' Part 1 'The individual teacher experience'. *School Science Review,* June 2003, 84 (309), 105–11.

Ronan, C. (1966) *The Ages of Science*, London: Harrap.

Rose, J. (2009) *Independent Review of the Primary Curriculum: Final report*, London: HMSO. http://www.dcsf.gov.uk/primarycurriculumreview/

Rowe, M. B. (1974) 'Wait time and rewards as instructional variables, their influence on language, logic and fate control', *Journal of Research in Science Teaching*, 11, 81–94.

Royal Society of Chemistry. http://www.rsc.org (accessed 20 June 2009).

Sadler, R. (1989) 'Formative assessment and the design of instructional systems', *Instructional Science*, 18, 119–44.

Salter's-Horner Advanced Physics (SHAP) 'The visit'. http://www.york.ac.uk/org/seg/salters/physics/course/index.html (accessed 2 October 2009).

Sanderson. P. (2006) 'Twenty-first century pollution detectives', *School Science Review*, 87 (320), 33–40.

Sang, D. (ed.) (2000) *Teaching Secondary Physics*, London: John Murray for ASE.

Sang, D. and Frost, R. (eds) (2005) *Teaching Secondary Science using ICT*, London: Hodder Murray.

Sang, D. and Wood-Robinson, V. (eds) (2002) *Teaching Secondary Scientific Enquiry*, London: John Murray.

Saunders, N. and Saunders, P. (2009) *AS Chemistry for AQA, Student Book*, Oxford: Oxford University Press.

Science for the 21st Century, http://www.21stcenturyscience.org/ (accessed 20 May 2009).

REFERENCES ▓ ■ ■ ■

Science learning centres. www.sciencelearningcentres.org.uk (accessed 1 October 2009).

Scottish Qualifications Authority (SQA). http://www.sqa.org.uk (accessed 13 June 2009).

Sears, J. and Sorensen, P. (eds) (2000) *Issues in Science Teaching*, London: RoutledgeFalmer.

Sebba, J., Crick, R. D., Yu, G., Lawson, H., Harlen, W. and Durant, K. (2008) 'Systematic review of research evidence of the impact on students in secondary schools of self and peer assessment. technical report', in *Research Evidence in Education Library*, London: EPPI-Centre, Social Science Research Unit, Institute of Education, University of London.

Sergeant, S. and Smith, S. (2007) *Earth and Space Book 2 in S104 Open University Course Exploring Science (Science Level 1)*, Milton Keynes: Open University.

Sex Education Forum (2005) *Sex and Relationships Education Framework*, London: Sex Education Forum.

Sex Education Forum (2008) *Young People's Charter on SRE*, London: National Children's Bureau. http://partner.ncb.org.uk/dotpdf/open_access_2/sef_ypcharter_a4.pdf

SHAP (Salters Horners Advanced Physics) (2003) *Exemplar Coursework: Visits*. Downloadable from: http://www.edexcel.com/quals/gce/gce-leg/physics/salters/Pages/default.aspx (accessed 15 December 2009).

Sharp, J. G., Bowker, R. and Byrne, J. (2008) 'VAK or VAK-uous? Towards the trivialisation of learning and the death of scholarship', *Research Papers in Education*, 23 (3), 293–314.

Shayer, M. and Gamble, R. (2001) *Bridging: From CASE to Core Science*. Hatfield: ASE.

Simon, S. (2000) 'Students' attitudes towards science', in Monk, M. and Osborne, J. (2000) *Good Practice in Science Teaching: What Research Has to Say*, Buckingham: Open University Press.

Simon, S. (2008) 'Using Toulmin's argument pattern in the evaluation of argumentation in school science', *International Journal of Research and Method in Education*, 31 (3), 277–89.

Simon, S., Erduran, S. and Osborne, J. (2006) 'Learning to teach argumentation: research and developments in the science classroom', *International Journal of Science Education*, 28(2), 235–60.

Simon, S. and Maloney, J. (2007) 'Activities for promoting small group discussion and argumentation', *School Science Review*, 88 (324), 49–57.

Smith, A. (1996) *Accelerated Learning in the Classroom*, Stafford: Network Educational Press.

Sobel, D. (1996) *Longitude: The True Story of a Lone Genius who Solved the Greatest Scientific Problem of His Time*, London: Fourth Estate.

Solomon, J. (2001) 'A response to Bernard Crick'. *School Science Review*, 83, 39–40.

SQA *see* Scottish Qualifications Authority.

Staples, R. and Heselden, R. (2001) 'Science teaching and literacy, part 1: Writing', *School Science Review*, 83 (303), 35–46.

Stradling, R. (1985) 'Controversial issues in the curriculum', *Bulletin of Environmental Education*. 170, 9–13.

Sutton, C. (1992) *Words, Science and Learning*, Buckingham: Open University Press.

Tan, K. and Koh, T. (2008) 'The use of Web 2.0 technologies in school science', *School Science Review*, 90 (330), 113–17.

TDA (Training and Development Agency for Schools) *Professional Standards for Qualified Teacher Status and Requirements for Initial Teacher Training (Revised 2008)*, London: Training and Development Agency for Schools. http://www.tda.gov.uk/partners/ittstandards.aspx

Turner, S. (2000) 'Health education is unavoidable', in Sears, J. and Sorensen, P., *Issues in Science Teaching*, London: RoutledgeFalmer.

Vygotsky, L. (1978) *Mind in Society*, Cambridge, MA: Harvard University Press.

Wallace, J. and Louden, W. (2002) *Dilemmas of Science Teaching: Perspectives on Problems of Practice,* London: RoutledgeFalmer.

Wardle, J. (ed.) (2009) *School Science Review*, 90 (332), 29–94, Hatfield: Association for Science Education.

Watkins, C., Carnell, E. and Lodge, C. (2007) *Effective Learning in Classrooms*, London: Paul Chapman.

Watson, R., Goldsworthy, A. and Wood-Robinson, V. (2000) *Investigations: Targeted Learning.* Hatfield: ASE.

Watson, R., Wood-Robinson, V. and Goldsworthy, A. (2000) *Investigations: Targeted Learning: Using Classroom Assessment for Learning*, Hatfield: ASE.

Watson, R., Wood-Robinson, V. and Goldsworthy, A. (1999) 'What is not fair with investigations?' *School Science Review*, 80 (292), 101–6.

Weaver, N. (2006) 'Physics outdoors: from the Doppler effect to F=ma', *School Science Review*, 87 (320), 65–8.

Wellcome Trust. Online http://www.wellcome.ac.uk.

Wellcome Trust (2009) *Perspectives on Education 2 (Primary-secondary Transfer in Science).* http://wellcome.ac.uk/perspectives

Wellington, J. (ed.) (1998) *Practical Work in School Science: Which Way Now?* London: Routledge.

Wellington, J. (2003) (special issue ed.) 'ICT in science education', *School Science Review*, 84 (309), 39–120.

Wellington, J. and Ireson, G. (2008) *Science Learning, Science Teaching*, London: Routledge.

Wellington, J. and Osborne, J. (2001) *Language and Literacy in Science Education*, Buckingham: The Open University.

Welsh Assembly Government (2008) *Key Stages 2–4 Science in the National Curriculum for Wales* http://wales.gov.uk/topics/educationandskills/curriculumassessment/arevisedcurriculum forwales/nationalcurriculum/sciencenc/?lang=en (accessed 10 August 2009).

White, J. (2005) 'Howard Gardner: the Myth of Multiple Intelligence'. *Viewpoint 16*, London: Institute of Education.

Wikid (ASE KS3 programme) http://www.upd8.org.uk/upd8-wikid.php

Wilson, E. (2000) *Teaching Chemistry to KS4*. London: Hodder and Stoughton.

Wilson, E. O. (1992) *The Diversity of Life*, New York: W. W. Norton and Co.

Wilson, J. T., in Porter, R. and Ogilvie, M. (eds) (2000) *Dictionary of Scientific Biography*, 3rd edn, Volume 2, Oxford: Helicon: 983–4.

Winterbottom, M. (2000) *Teaching Biology to KS4*. London: Hodder and Stoughton.

WJEC (Welsh Joint Examining Council) http://www.wjec.co.uk

Wood, D. (1998) *How Children Think and Learn: The Social Contexts of Cognitive Development*, Oxford: Blackwell.

Woolnough, B. and Allsop, T. (1985) *Practical Work in Science*, Cambridge: Cambridge University Press.

AUTHOR INDEX

SUBJECT INDEX